Grant Budgeting and Finance

Getting the Most Out of Your Grant Dollar

Grant Budgeting and Finance

Getting the Most Out of Your Grant Dollar

Frea E. Sladek
and
Eugene L. Stein

PLENUM PRESS • NEW YORK AND LONDON

Library of Congress Cataloging in Publication Data

Main entry under title:

Grant budgeting and finance.

Bibliography: p.
Includes index.
1. Fund raising. 2. Research grants. 3. Subsidies. I. Sladek, Frea E., 1939-
II. Stein, Eugene L., 1940-
HG177.G7 658.1'522 81-5887
ISBN 0-306-40607-1 AACR2

A Division of Plenum Publishing Corporation
233 Spring Street, New York, N.Y. 10013

Printed in the United States of America

To our families . . .

Frank, Kathy, Teri, Steve, Lori and Debbie Sladek

and

Enid, Craig, and Michael Stein

for all their love and encouragement
while we wrote this book on
"their time"

Preface

Do you work for an organization that depends on receiving grant funds for survival? Do you work for one that gives grants? Have you been in the grants business a long time? Or a relatively short time? Do you plan to work for a grant-giving or grant-receiving organization?

If you answered "Yes" to any of these questions, this book is written for you. It will save you money. You will share in professional secrets that, up until now, have not been in print. You will find out more about the roles that others play in the grant-spending process; thus you will have an advantage in dealing with others. You will receive tips for spending grant dollars effectively and will be alerted to obstacles that may prevent you from maximizing grant funds.

"Grants programs should be run more efficiently, cut out the organizational 'fat,' and develop better management techniques," a trustee of the Rosenberg Foundation was quoted as saying in the *Foundation News* recently. In this same issue, a leader of the Alcoholism Center for Women in Los Angeles told of trimming superfluous grant spending across the board. "We want to provide the same services," she stated. "We're cutting the fat." The topic of the article was California's Proposition 13 and its impact on nonprofit organizations that depend on grant funds for their survival.(1)

Not only are taxpayers revolting nationwide against paying ever-increasing taxes, but Congressmen are apparently listening. During Spring 1979, lawmakers passed only eight bills in the first three months—fewer than any Congress had passed in a comparable period in at least 40 years. Why? According to an item in *U.S. News and World Report*, "Message from the folks back home is getting through; don't burden us with new *schemes.* Just try to make existing programs work better, *cheaper.*"(2)

And when Congress interprets "cheaper," it does so conservatively. Despite cumulative inflation of 28% over the past three years,(3) it has not been uncommon to find federal grant programs receiving level or even decreased funding during this same period.

So how, specifically, *do* grant-receiving organizations "trim" and "cut" fat? How do they manage to survive level funding in the face of double-digit inflation? What if they have no fat to trim?

There are many "how-to-get" grants books on the market, and various granting agencies have published a bewildering amount of "how-you-*can't*-spend" grants regulations. Unfortunately, helpful "how-you-*can*-spend" advice is rare—in printed form, that is. Therefore, the purpose of this book is to provide both grant receivers and grant givers with information that will help them to spend grants cost-effectively. It aims to be responsive to the mutual goals of taxpayers, Congressmen, grant givers, and grant receivers—*to get the most out of the grant dollar.*

The specific objectives are fourfold. First, we would like to give to the "how-to-spend" grants audience the type of quality advice provided by Virginia White for the "how-to-get" grants audiences in her book *Grants: How to Find Out About Them and What to Do Next*. Second, we want to do so in a lively manner. Why should fiscal and budgetary matters be dull? *People* are involved in the spending process, and the interactions between these people are important in stretching grant dollars. Third, we plan to draw on the expertise of the pros—those grant planners and spenders at both grant-giving and grant-receiving organizations whose years of experience and volume of grant spending qualify them to speak with authority. By sharing the knowledge of experienced people in the field, we hope to spare newcomers years of seat-of-the-pants, hard-knocks learning. The more experienced grant spenders, we feel, may profit from the variety of experiences of their colleagues. The grants business being what it is, it is rare for even the most experienced of grant givers or receivers not to encounter new situations from time to time. Finally, we want to emphasize to all readers the cooperative nature of the grant-spending business—the fact that both grant-giving and grant-receiving agency personnel participate in the process and that only when they work as a team can grant dollars be maximized.

For that reason, we have consulted with professionals from both grant-giving and grant-receiving agencies, who contributed information enthusiastically. The persons who assisted represent billions of dollars of grant spending and hundreds of years of experience. They are from a variety of organizations: federal, state, and local government; private foundations; universities; hospitals; industries; and other nonprofit social-service agencies. They hold different positions in the grant-spending process; the representation includes project directors and grant administrators from grant-receiving organizations, and program officers, grant officers, and auditors from grant-giving organizations.

These professionals, and the many colleagues who have enriched our own grants knowledge over the years, have made major contributions to this book. Some completed a lengthy survey and/or coordinated the responses of others; some participated in interviews; some reviewed and commented on drafts of the book; all provided encouragement and valuable ideas. Recognizing that we can't name everyone, we'd like to take this opportunity to thank as many of our benefactors as possible.

Grantor friends who were especially helpful include Kenneth ("Mike") Foster, Bill Cole, Josephine Doherty, Elmer Havens, and Joanna Rom (all from the National Science Foundation); Fred Will and Janice Avery (Department of Education); Henry ("Hank") Brehm (Social Security Administration); Jacob Seidenberg and Joan Kelly (National Institutes of Health); Paul Nacon (Department of Health and Human Services, Region IX); and Katherine Lyall (formerly Department of Housing and Urban Development).

Grantee colleagues who gave us above-and-beyond assistance include: Raburn Howland (University of Michigan); Bob Lucas, Robert Griffin, and Edward Carnegie (California Polytechnic State University, San Luis Obispo); Rich Conkings (California State University, Los Angeles); Carl Baty, Bob McCabe, and Fred McFarlane (San Diego State University); Dan Oshiro (Harbor/UCLA Medical Center); Susan Hellweg and David Churchman (California State University, Dominguez Hills); and John O'Brian (University of Minnesota).

No expression of our gratitude to grants professionals is complete, however, without an acknowledgment of the contributions of the San Diego State University Foundation. During our years of employment there, we have been given the opportunity to learn a great deal. In addition, our colleagues Harry Albers, Bob Benshoff, Steve Bloom, and Verna Duarte have been particularly helpful, reviewing portions of the book and making valuable suggestions.

In conclusion, we want to recognize several persons who are not in the grants business. We especially thank Owenita Sanderlin (Frea's mother), who before helping us with this book knew little about grants, but practically everything about writing and editing. We are indebted to Frank Columbus of Plenum Publishing Corporation for his faith in our abilities and his encouragement as we wrote. The delightful cartoons were created by Bardy Wolff. And finally we thank Bob Nardelli, whose engineering of a workshop consultancy for Frea led directly to the idea for the book.

FREA SLADEK
EUGENE STEIN

San Diego, California

Contents

1

Stretching the Grant Dollar
The Players and the Process

"Scientists warn of funding lag," "FY 1980 budget figures for education/health down from last year–many programs eliminated," "Devastating cut for nurses," "Research libraries' collections hit hard by inflation," "Universities charged with widespread misuse of federal research funds," "Office of Education gets 'Golden Fleece' award," "Grant makers meet to form strategy in the wake of Proposition 13." The headlines are grim.[1-7]

Grant dollars, which purportedly flowed freely in the 1950s and 1960s, are now under attack from all sides. Pressures from cost-conscious taxpayers, vote-conscious Congressmen, Congressmen-conscious grant-giving agencies, and that general demon Inflation have combined to put the squeeze on available grant dollars as never before.

With radical tax-cutting initiatives in many states, spiralling inflation, decreasing funding levels by many grant givers, and increasing public demands for cost-effectiveness, grant spenders need help to stretch their grant dollars. Yet most available advice dwells on how to get the money in the first place, not on how to make the most of it afterward. Somehow, like "Monopoly" money, grant dollars seem a bit unreal and are therefore treated casually at times. The object is to pass "GO" and collect–not necessarily to make the best buys on the way around. And that is the bad news.

The good news is that *grant dollars can be stretched.* There are ways to make the best buys–and not to have to pass "GO" so often.

Fiscal matters can be approached creatively, as demonstrated by the story about the Vermont farmer who went to the bank to take out a loan. Asked how much, he said, "A dollar." The banker was surprised at how small the loan was but said that there would still have to be some collateral. The farmer offered a

$1,000 government bond, and the deal was made at 6%. The farmer paid his six cents, collected his dollar, left his bond, and departed. A year later, he renewed the loan, and again the next year. After several years, the banker couldn't resist asking the farmer why he was willing to hypothecate a $1,000 bond just to keep a one-dollar loan floating.

"I thought you'd get around to asking," said the farmer. "But if I gave you this bond for safekeeping, you'd charge me five dollars a year."

This farmer had a fresh perspective; by using his limited funds creatively, he made six cents do the work of five dollars. And so can you. Therefore, throughout this book, the emphasis is on the fresh perspective, the imaginative approach–the path to the Vermont bargain.

In the following chapters, the grant dollar is tracked from the day it is proposed until final audit. *Who is responsible for stretching the grant dollar? What happens to it in its short lifetime? How can it be stretched?* The term *grant* is used in its broadest sense to include any form of sponsorship, including grants, contracts, cooperative agreements, fellowships, and scholarships. (Definitions of these terms are contained in Appendix A.) Although most of the information provided in this book applies to all forms of sponsorship, when differences exist, they will be noted.

Who Is Responsible for Stretching the Grant Dollar?

In spending a grant, as in playing "Monopoly," there are several players who have control of the dollars at various times and in various ways. In "Monopoly," the players are awarded "grants" of play money at the beginning of the game. The objective is for one player to win all the money, thus forcing the others out of the game. This result generally occurs through a combination of strategy, a certain amount of risk taking, and some measure of luck. Each player plans strategy, or takes risks, depending on his or her assessment of what the opponents will be doing.

In grant spending, there are also elements of strategy, risk taking, and luck. For individual players to succeed, they must understand who the other players are as well as when and how each controls the money. Unlike in "Monopoly," however, where players must work against each other in order to win, success in the grant-spending game requires the cooperation and teamwork of all the players.

So, who are the players in the game of grant stretching? How and when does each control the money?

For every grant, there are four central players in the spending process. They come from both *grant-receiving* organizations (such as universities, hospitals, industries, nonprofit agencies, and, less frequently, profit agencies) and *grant-giving* organizations (such as federal, state, and local agencies; private foundations; and corporations). The *project director* and the *grant administrator* represent the grant-receiving organization; the *program officer* and the *grant officer* represent the grant-giving organization. These titles are common and will be used throughout this book; at some institutions, other titles may be used, as noted in the following brief descriptions of each of the players.

In addition to title differences, there is variety in the combinations of tasks assigned to the various players, depending on the kinds and sizes of organizations they work for. A grant administrator at one college, for example, may do no accounting or purchasing work at all, although his colleague at a nearby institution spends 50% of her time on these duties.

Players in the grant-spending game are depicted in Figure 1. Remember their faces; you will see them again.

Figure 1. The grant-spending team.

The Project Director

A key figure in the grant-spending process, the project director is primarily responsible for proposing the idea to be funded, requesting adequate resources (such as personnel and supplies), and successfully implementing the idea once it is funded—within the resource and time constraints set by the funding agency. The goal of the project director is to achieve technical program objectives, such as training 20 Venezuelan educators in planning school facilities or finding out why porpoises are being killed in tuna-fishing nets. Fiscal matters are of concern only as they relate to technical responsibilities. Usually the project director feels pressure to save money when funds are tight; otherwise, the pressure is to get the job done in the time allotted.

The project director should be thought of as the initiator; he or she is important in proposing the resources needed and in the timing of expenditures during the grant period. No spending is done until the project director requests it. The project director determines what is needed and when.

The project director frequently has responsibilities in addition to the grant project. He or she may be a faculty member at a university, with teaching, writing, and even administrative assignments. Doctors at hospitals commonly serve as project directors, retaining their responsibility to serve their patients, as well as carry out the grant activities. Even when project directors do not have other professional obligations, they may serve as project director for several grants. So there are competing demands on the time of many project directors, and rarely can their undivided attention be directed toward one grant.

On a research project (as contrasted with a training or service project), the person who directs the project is commonly referred to as the *principal investigator* or *PI.* Other titles used in place of project director are *project coordinator* and *program director.* No matter what title is used, the important functions of *initiating and implementing the technical plan* must be carried out by a player in the grant-spending game, and usually this player is called the *project director.*

The Grant Administrator

Most grant-giving agencies (grantors) prefer to award funds to organizations, rather than to individuals. Therefore, grants are usually given to an organization (grantee) for which the project director works, rather than to the project director directly. The grantee organization (such as a hospital or a nonprofit social-service agency) commonly assigns a grant administrator to assist the project director with budgeting and spending and to ensure that all grantor regulations are complied with. Thus, the grant administrator serves as a middleman[8] in the grant-spending process, with the dual responsibilities of (1) helping the project director to plan and to spend money and (2) ensuring that all grantor regulations are followed during the process.

To be a successful middleman, the grant administrator must interface between the project director and two environments. First, there is the *grantee institutional setting* in which the project is being conducted. Whether the grantee institution is a hospital, a college, a research institute, or a social service agency, there will be various policies and procedures to be followed, as well as obstacles to be encountered. A vital function of the grant administrator is to use these institutional "systems" creatively to help rather than hinder the project director.

The other environment is the *grantor institutional setting.* Again, the grant administrator serves as a buffer, interfacing between the project director and the grantor officials on all matters of grant administration.

The grant administrator first enters the game shortly after the project director has an idea for funding. At this point, the grant administrator prices the resources that the project director needs to complete the proposal budget and assists with submitting the proposal to a grant-giving agency. For example, if the project director has an idea to prevent porpoises from being killed in tuna nets, he or she asks the grant administrator to prepare a budget that will cover the costs of employing several divers for a specified time period, of buying specialized equipment to track the noises that porpoises make under water, and so forth. The project director knows what is needed to do the job; the grant administrator knows how much these resources will cost.

Subsequently, the grant administrator participates in negotiations concerning the amount and terms of the award; monitors spending during the grant period; and responds to audit questions after the project is completed. For example, the funding agency may not agree to award as much money as the project director asked for. The grant administrator, working with the project director, negotiates with representatives from the grant-giving agency, let's say the National Science Foundation. A goal of this negotiation is to ensure that the amount of money finally awarded will be enough to do the job as it is finally offered. Perhaps, at the proposal stage, the project director wanted to conduct two experiments, one on the East Coast and one on the West Coast. If the money is cut substantially, it would be practical to reduce the work scope to offer only one experiment.

Once the award is finalized, the grant administrator assists with and monitors the spending that the project director requests. For example, the project director may ask for a plane ticket to Tahiti. Is there enough money for this ticket in the grant budget? Is this type of expense allowed by the National Science Foundation? Must there be special approvals by the National Science Foundation before spending the money this way? Is the trip to Tahiti clearly necessary to achieve the objectives of the grant? Where can the ticket be obtained the most inexpensively, in plenty of time for the trip? These and similar questions must be answered by the grant administrator as each purchase request is received from the project director. In addition, the grant administrator must ensure that adequate documentation (air ticket receipts, travel claims, etc.) is kept on file at his or her organization, so that questions that the funding-agency auditors may ask later (sometimes years after the grant has been closed out) can be satisfactorily answered.

In a large grantee organization, the grant administrator is responsible for many projects. It is not unusual for one grant administrator to handle up to 100 awards at any one time, depending on the complexity and size of the projects involved. His or her expertise resides in knowledge of fiscal matters and knowledge of grantor agency regulations. Rarely does the grant administrator have in-depth programmatic experience. For example, he or she could not personally determine the research techniques for finding out how to prevent porpoises from being killed in tuna nets. Therefore, the grant administrator's responsibilities are primarily fiscal: to ensure that there is enough money for the project objectives to be accomplished and to ensure that the money is spent according to the sponsor's regulations. It is especially important that the grant administrator avoid overexpenditures on grants, since his or her organization (the grantee) must pay when this happens.

Grant administrators go by other names. A few are *contract administrator, grant–contract officer,* and *program development coordinator.* Sometimes the functions of helping the project director are split between a grant administrator who assists at the proposal–budget-negotiation stage and one who assists after the award is received. In smaller grantee organizations, the person who is the project director may also assume the grant administrator's role. No matter who plays the role, or what the title is, the functions of the grant administrator must be carried out in all grant spending: *to price the resources needed by the project director to complete the workscope; to monitor the spending of the award to ensure compliance with grantor regulations; and to respond to audit questions after the project is completed.*

The Program Officer

The first two players in the grant-spending game were from the grant-receiving organization. Now the location changes to the grant-giving organization. The third player to make a move in the grant-stretching game is the program officer from the grantor organization. The proposal that the project director has developed, assisted by the grant administrator, lands on the program officer's desk, along with competing proposals from many other prospective project directors. The program officer, with the help of a review panel, has the responsibility of selecting projects to be funded by the grantor agency that he or she represents.

For example, the program officer in the Biology Program of the National Science Foundation has an annual budget to spend on biology research. He or she has limited funds to award to (1) the most outstanding projects and (2) as many of these as possible. If the program officer, based on recommendations from other scientists, gives the tuna–porpoise project all the money requested, there will be fewer funds to spend on other worthy biology projects.

The program officer's expertise is similar to the project director's, being technical and scientific in nature. Thus, the program officer's main interest is in the merit of the scientific project or service–training project proposed. Fiscal matters are of concern secondarily—mainly because spending more money for one project makes the money unavailable for another. In making decisions about the technical merit of the proposal, the program officer often gets help from outside sources, such as peer review panels, field reviewers, and staff assistance within the grantor organization. Final authority over which proposals will be funded and how much they will receive, however, usually rests with the program officer.

The program officer plays the most critical but frequently the briefest part in the grant-stretching process. He or she generally has all the money available for particular kinds of projects (for example, career training, biological research) within one grant-giving agency at the beginning of the game (similar to the "bank" in a "Monopoly" game). Once the program officer, usually on the basis of review panel recommendations, has decided which project directors will receive the money, approximately how much they will receive, and what resources this money may be spent for, it is possible that the program officer will not become involved with fiscal matters again. However, the program officer does retain the authority to approve any changes in the way the money is spent from the way he or she approved its expenditure originally. Also, if more time or more money is needed to complete the project, the program officer's approval must be obtained. Although the program officer may be a quiet observer of the grant-stretching process, he or she is not to be forgotten after the award. The program officer has the responsibility of ensuring that the work is completed as proposed. If it isn't, all or some of the funds may be recovered by the grant-giving agency.

Program officers are normally responsible for many projects that are being conducted around the country. It is not unusual for one program officer to be responsible for as many as 10–50 projects at any one time, depending on the complexity and size of the projects.

Program officers go by various titles, a few of which are *program director, technical officer,* and *program manager.* In grants jargon, there is a very fine distinction between a "program" and a "project," and this distinction helps to explain why grant-giving agency officials are usually referred to as *program* officers, while grant-receiving people are more commonly *project* directors. A *program* is considered a relatively long-term activity (for example, the National Science Foundation has had a Biology Program for many years), while a *project* is usually shorter-lived, perhaps one to three years at the longest. For example, the experiments to find out why porpoises are being killed in tuna nets would be unlikely to last longer than several years, and therefore this activity would be known as a *project.*

No matter what title the program officer at the grant-giving agency goes by, the necessary functions of *selecting projects to be funded, deciding approximately how much money they will receive, and monitoring the technical progress of the project* must be assumed by a representative of the grant-giving organization, and that representative is usually known as the *program officer.* In a small grant-giving agency (for example, a local private foundation), the program officer may additionally assume the grant officer role.

The Grant Officer

The last player to become involved in the grant-stretching process is the grant officer at the grant-giving agency. Once the program officer has decided to award a certain amount of money to the project director at the grant-receiving organization, authority for this money to be awarded is given to the grant officer. The grant officer then participates in the grant-spending process, from the negotiation of the award until after the completion of the project.

Like the grantee grant administrator, the grantor grant officer monitors expenditures, ensuring that grantor regulations are being followed. Should there be a request for changes in spending from the way expenditures were proposed, it is the grant officer who must officially approve these changes. Sometimes the grant officer's approval must be obtained before money can be spent, even if an item is identified in the grant budget. For example, travel to foreign countries must usually be approved in advance by the grant officer. Similarly, if extra time or supplemental funds are needed to complete the project, the grant officer's approval is required. However, since it is technically the program officer's money that will be used for supplements, and since the program officer has responsibility for the timely completion of the project, the grant officer will not officially approve such requests unless the program officer concurs.

The grant officer's expertise is, like the grant administrator's, primarily fiscal and regulatory. He or she "protects" the expenditures and has responsibility for financial rather than programmatic or technical grant matters. Also comparable to the grant-receiving grant administrator, the grant officer serves as a middleman, with the dual responsibilities of (1) helping the program officer to spend money and then (2) ensuring that the grantee recipients of this money spend it according to grantor regulations.

Like the other players in the grant-stretching game, the grant officer has many responsibilities. He or she frequently handles as many as 100 different grants, located all over the country. Therefore, it is rare that undivided attention can be given to stretching grant dollars for one project. Titles given to the grant officer are varied (*grant–contract officer, contract officer, grant manager,* or even *grant administrator*), but these functions must be carried out by a player representing the grant-giving agency: *negotiating and monitoring the award expenditures on behalf of the grantor; officially approving any changes requested by the grantee; and in some cases, taking action on audit findings after the project has been completed.* As stated previously, the grant officer may also assume program officer's responsibilities in a small grant-giving organization.

The responsibilities of the four central players in the grant-stretching game are summarized in Figure 2. It is interesting to note, and important for successfully maximizing grant dollars, that there are counterpart relationships existing

GRANT RECEIVERS	GRANT GIVERS
PROJECT DIRECTOR	PROGRAM OFFICER
Create project idea	*Approve project idea as worthy of funding*
Identify resources needed	*Confirm resources needed*
Negotiate workscope & resources	*Negotiate workscope & resources*
Carry out project as awarded (within budget and time constraints)	*Monitor technical aspects of project and assist as needed*
Initiate spending requests	
Initiate & justify requests to change spending plans	*Agree with requests to change spending plans*
Initiate & justify requests to change dates of grant	*Agree with requests to change dates of grant*
Initiate & justify requests for supplemental funds	*Agree with requests for supplemental funds*
Report on technical achievements of project	*Review, approve (and disseminate as appropriate) technical achievements*
Respond to audit questions on technical (and sometimes fiscal) aspects of project	*Respond to audit questions on technical aspects of project*
GRANT ADMINISTRATOR	GRANT OFFICER
Price the resources needed	*Price the resources needed*
Negotiate price & terms of grant	*Negotiate price & terms of grant*
Implement spending requests from the Project Director, help save funds	*Help save funds, upon request of grantee*
Monitor grant spending to ensure compliance with grantor agency regulations	*Monitor grant spending to ensure compliance with grantor regulations*
Approve & forward requests for spending changes to Grant Officer	*Approve (upon agreement from Program Officer) grantee requests for spending changes*
Approve & forward requests to change dates of grant to Grant Officer	*Approve (upon agreement from Program Officer) grantee requests to change dates of grant*
Approve & forward requests for supplemental funds to Grant Officer	*Approve (upon agreement from Program Officer) grantee requests for supplemental funds*
Complete financial reports during and at conclusion of project	*Review and approve financial reports*
Ensure adequate cash flows during project	*Assist with cash flows to project as requested by Grants Administrator*
Respond to audit questions	*Take action upon audit reports*

Figure 2. Major responsibilities of the team.

between two sets of players. The project director at the grantee organization and the program officer at the grantor organization hold similar responsibilities–programmatic in nature. In contrast, the grant administrator at the grantee organization and the grant officer at the grantor organization share comparable duties–fiscal and regulatory, mainly. As you read this book, keep in mind the responsibilities and personal goals of the central players.

The Support Staff

Luckily, the central players can call on others for help. Among support staff for the players are (from the grantor) peer reviewers, accounting clerks, and auditors; (from the grantee) project administrative and clerical staff, purchasing clerks, personnel and payroll clerks, and accounting clerks.

On the giving end, peer reviewers assist the program officer in selecting and pricing the proposals to be funded. Accounting clerks ensure that invoices are received from and payments made to the grantee organizations, and that billings have been correctly calculated. Auditors check the grantee's spending records to determine compliance with the grantor agency's regulations.

On the receiving end, purchasing clerks help identify the best buys and obtain discounts; personnel and payroll clerks assist with salary payments; and accounting clerks ensure timely billing and cash receipt. Especially important, *project administrative and clerical staff* provide many kinds of support to the project director. They shop around for good buys, process paperwork, know and follow grantee and grantor regulations, frequently interface with the grant administrator on behalf of the project director, and generally serve to free a great deal of the project director's time so that he or she can carry on the technical work of the grant.

In large grantor and grantee organizations, there are many support personnel. In a very small agency (grant-giving or grant-receiving), there may be no supporting cast at all, so that the central players must take on all the duties associated with grant spending.

No matter what the size of the organization, there are central and supporting roles in the grant-stretching process. By cooperating, the players can help to make the most of the grant dollar. By delay or foot dragging, arbitrariness or misunderstanding functions, each can waste the grant dollar. Which role(s) do or will you play? Project director? Grant administrator? Program officer? Grant officer? Project administrative or clerical staff member? Peer reviewer? Grantee accounting clerk? Auditor? Purchasing clerk? Payroll clerk? Grantee accounting clerk? Or perhaps some combination of these roles?

As you read through this book, there will be special tips for you, as well as for others playing the game. Since, to play your role effectively, you must work with others on the spending team, it is useful to know what their goals, needs, and tips are as well.

What Happens to the Grant Dollar?

Now that you know something about the other players, the rest of this introductory chapter will provide a guide to the activities in the grant-stretching game. Each activity is discussed briefly, so that you may assess its importance to you.

A special mystique surrounds the grant dollar. Because of its frequently elusive nature, prospective project directors are often reluctant to go after it. They fear that it is just out of reach and don't want to try for it in vain. Especially if the attempt costs money. (Figure 3.)

In this book, all costs associated with grants will be examined, starting with the first decision ("Should you apply for the grant?") and ending with the audi-

Figure 3. Reaching for the elusive grant dollar.

tor's final blessing ("No questioned costs"). Throughout the grant cycle, from the project director's creative idea to the time the final dime is spent, there are ways to save money and stretch the grant dollar–for the good of the project director, the grant administrator, the program officer, the grant officer, and all the supporting cast.

What are these ways? And what happens to the grant dollar? The theoretical framework in Figure 4 tracks the grant dollar from its conception (the project director's idea) to the end of the cash-management stage, when all dollars are in, spent, approved, and accounted for. Chapters in this book are presented chronologically, to match the beginning-to-end stages depicted in the framework. The final three chapters of the book are intentionally not chronological. These three activities take place throughout the entire grant-maximizing process; they are perhaps most critical in the effort to stretch the dollar and so have been saved for the end of the book.

"How can I stretch the grant dollar before I even get the award?" you may ask.

Or, "What does gamesplaying have to do with how many rats I can buy?"

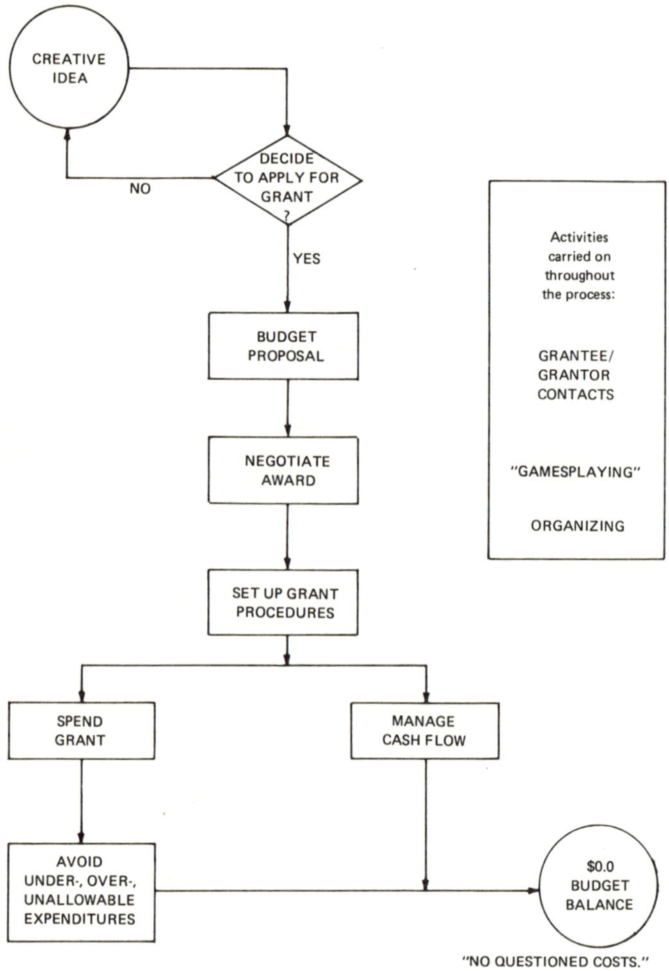

Figure 4. The grant-dollar stretching process: a theoretical framework.

Logical questions each, and to give you an idea of what is involved, a sampling of the kinds of information to be provided throughout the rest of this book follows, presented according to chapter titles.

The Proposal Decision: Should You Apply?

No matter which role you play, a decision to submit a proposal costs your organization money. Donated time, duplicating costs, and mailing and typing costs are not free. Usually, the prospective grantee organization absorbs the dollar costs; the project director frequently donates the creative proposal writing and planning effort.

The up-front dollar costs, which cannot be charged as a direct cost to a resulting grant award, are real costs, and therefore, the grantee organization must usually recover them later by charging higher administrative ("indirect") fees on grants—which, in turn, cost the grantor organization more and use funds that the project director would prefer to spend on scientific supplies and other direct costs. The project director's donated costs are opportunity costs in the sense that other valuable ideas, benefiting society, that the project director could have pursued have been preempted. So it is to everyone's advantage when proposal costs are limited to real funding opportunities and when indiscriminate shotgunning of proposals to many funding agencies is avoided.

How can proposal decisions be made cost-effective? If you are a project director or a grant administrator, how do you find out how much an application will cost—yes, *COST*—you? How do you know when a request for proposal (RFP) that the funding agency puts out is "wired" (i.e., someone else is slated to receive the award, no matter how superior a proposal you submit)? What cost sharing will be required if you receive the award? These are only a few of the questions that cost-conscious grantee personnel should explore before deciding to apply, that public relations-conscious grantors should consider, and that will be discussed in Chapter 2.

The Proposal Budget: Asking for the Right Amount

Persuasive language should not be limited to the technical proposal. Carefully planned and worded budget justifications help to influence proposal reviewers to approve larger awards than they normally would. One key to a good budget is flexibility. Experienced project directors and grant administrators know how to present costs so that later manipulation (without special approval by the grantor) is possible.

How do you convince the program officer and other proposal reviewers not to cut your budget? (Remember, you will probably not be there to discuss it with them at the time they are dividing up the available funds.) How do you retain maximum flexibility for postaward budget changes? How do you tie costs to specific program objectives? And what are the problems connected with doing this? Chapter 3 contains a wealth of detailed advice, much of which came from experienced project directors, grant administrators, program officers, and grant officers. Whether you prepare, review, negotiate, or approve proposal budgets, this information will be useful to you.

The Project Award: Negotiating the Best Deal

It is fairly common for project directors to request *X* amount of dollars to do a certain research or service project and to receive an offer of *X-minus* dollars to do the same amount of work. Frequently, the grantor sends the grantee a negotiation letter or arranges for a negotiation phone call or meeting. At this critical stage in the grant-stretching process, the grantee representatives have the opportunity to increase the amount of money planned for their individual project; the grantor representatives have the opportunity to decrease the amount of money for this same individual project so as to reserve more money to fund other worthwhile projects. Each "side" must defend its position.

What is your objective when you go into a grant negotiation? And what do you believe your "opponent's" objective is? How do you prepare for negotiation? How should you prepare? Can grantor agencies really come up with more money if the grantee presents a compelling case? Are grantees just out to get the maximum grant dollars, whether needed or not? What are the very different (and similar) needs of the grantor's and the grantee's representatives during the negotiations? How can these needs be used to your advantage, whichever agency you represent? A discussion of these and other questions about grant negotiations is contained in Chapter 4.

Grant Procedures: Putting Your Act Together

"Be prepared" is the key advice that a highly placed federal auditor gives grantees. "I worked for this company some years ago," he says, "a nonprofit company. There was a new federal regulation that allowed you to accrue vacation leave for an employee under certain conditions. You had to inform them of this benefit and had to pay them off if they left the grant project without using all their accumulated leave. One day, an IRS agent, well known for his disallowances on grants, came in and said to me, 'Let me see your policy on paying for vacation leave.' I remember very well I merely stood up, picked up a policy notebook on the shelf above my desk, and handed it to him. The man's whole nature changed. We went out to lunch and had a bite together, and it was over. No audit disallowances."

Whether for vacation leave, travel, or other grant costs, the key to efficient (and dollar-stretching) grant expenditures is to have formalized policies and procedures. "Be consistent" is more advice given by this same auditor. Having written policies and procedures in operation meets both the be-prepared and be-consistent advice.

What kinds of procedures should your organization follow? What are samples of successful ones? How can you benefit from others' efforts to improve on various policies and procedures? Where can you get advice or, for that matter, copies of written policies? Chapter 5 contains a great deal of specific advice for instituting policies and procedures to help stretch grant dollars.

Spending the Award: Getting More for Less

A consultant examined the purchasing practices at a relatively large university grants office. "Do you have practices that ensure that you get the best buy for your money?" he asked the purchasing clerk.

"Oh, yes," she responded and proceeded to show him impressively printed multipart purchase-order request forms, purchase-order forms, and catalogs from various sellers, offering large discounts. She even mentioned the office policy of requiring the project directors to get three bids on large purchases.

"Then, you won't mind if I examine a few of your equipment purchase records?" the consultant asked.

"Oh, no," the clerk answered, leading the consultant to the files.

The consultant randomly picked 10 equipment bills that had been paid. A couple of hours later, he reported to the director of the grants office.

"You are losing an opportunity to save a great deal of money on equipment purchases," he noted. "I telephoned the supplier of each of the equipment items listed on these ten billings and asked for an educational discount. The prices I was quoted totaled almost ten thousand dollars less than those that your office has already paid."

This really happened. Although the grants office had been getting competitive bids on large purchases, it had not instituted routine requests for all the discounts for which it was eligible. Could this happen at your organization?

Once the maximum grant award has been negotiated, and procedures to spend it have been set, how can the Vermont farmer's six-cent bargain be obtained? Chapter 6 contains detailed how-to advice on grant spending in all categories, including special discounts such as that described above. For example, would you like to know how to cut long-distance phone bills in half? Or, under special circumstances, how to cut them out completely? How to get equipment at one fourth the list price? How to get computer costs greatly reduced? How to "buy foreign" (cheaper) when your grant says "buy American" (more expensive)? How to minimize fringe benefit payments? Where the cheapest printing deals are? Ways to travel more and pay less? Most important, do you understand what the obstacles are to using these tips and how to overcome these hurdles?

Expenditures to Avoid: Over-, Under-, Unallowable

As of March 31, 1978, $8.6 billion was shown on the federal government's books as being obligated to grantees for projects whose official ending dates had long since passed.(9) Grantees had been unable to spend all this money before their projects terminated, and as a result, the funds would be deobligated as soon as the grantees' final fiscal reports were filed with the government. Why wasn't all this money spent? How could this have been avoided? What conditions lead to underexpending grants? Who is hurt by underexpenditures?

At the other extreme, grants are sometimes overexpended, resulting in a grant dollar stretch to the project director and the grantor agency initially, but later resulting in higher administrative (indirect) charges by the grantee organization, which bears the cost of the overexpenditure and must recover the loss in some manner. Who is responsible for overexpenditures? How can they be avoided?

Whether grant awards are over- or underexpended, unallowable expenditures can occur. And the more money a grantee organization receives, the greater a potential it has for unallowable costs to be identified by auditors. An eastern women's college was humming along rather quietly with a modest amount of grant business yearly. Nothing spectacular, and there was no special attention from auditors. Then an active grantsperson arrived on the scene. He successfully attracted over $40 million in grants for the college. Spectacular. The problem was, after the money was spent, auditors identified over $20 million as unallowable.

Unallowable expenditures are costly to all concerned. If they are intentional (dishonest), the parties involved can go to jail. Usually, unallowable expenditures are not intentional. They are a result of ignorance or inattention—and could have been avoided. No matter how innocent its cause, an unallowable expenditure that is identified by the auditor costs the grantee organization money. The grantor must be repaid. Ironically, the funds repaid could have been spent in an allowable manner.

"Know the rules" is the third piece of advice that the auditor quoted earlier gives to grantees. According to him, "The reason people have disallowances is that they are sloppy with their record keeping and don't know what the rules are." There is a special bonus to the grantee representatives for knowing the rules, he says, because "Sometimes the people in government don't know what they are doing, so it is important for the PI to know."

Of course, what appears to be "sloppy" record keeping to an autidor may be caused by her or his *interpreting* the documentation rules differently than the grantees.

In grants spending, as in "Monopoly," there are rules and interpretations of these rules. Know them, and you will enjoy an advantage—whichever game you are playing, whichever role you are playing.

Under-, over-, and unallowable expenditures all waste grant dollars, from the perspective of both grantee and grantor organizations. What are the simple ways they can be avoided? How can you easily learn the regulations that apply to your grants job (no matter which role you play) without having to learn all the regulations that apply to other grants? Chapter 7 has advice and encouragement. Despite the volume after volume of grant regulations that exist, finding the regulations that apply to your grant or grants is not really the needle-in-the-haystack operation it may appear to be at first glance.

Cash Management: Timing Your Dollars In and Out

Who cares about cash? So much of grant business is conducted on paper—the award letter, the special approval letters, the purchase-order requests, the purchase orders, the check requests, and so forth—that it is easy to forget that real money is being spent. If a grantee is spending its own money, in the expectation of collecting later, it is forgoing the interest earnings on this money. It is not uncommon for grantees to ignore the cash aspect of grants. According to one federal official, "Many grantees simply don't submit invoices for six to eight months at a time. I just don't understand how they can stay in business."

Once the grantees do receive the cash, however, the opposite situation may occur, and the government has a hard time getting the money back if the grantees do not use it. According to former Federal Budget Director James T. McIntyre, Jr., nearly $1 billion of unused federal funds was on deposit in idle accounts of universities, states, cities, and other grant recipients in the fall of 1978, and plans were being made to be stricter in claiming the money back.

"We don't want to be stingy with grantees," McIntyre said, "but we don't want to have hundreds of millions of dollars lying around while we're out borrowing money and paying interest on it."(10)

What are the cash management tips that your organization can use? Why do grantees fail to bill grantors regularly and frequently? When grantees do draw money in advance, why don't they return unused funds to the grantor? How can grantees receive funds before the project starts, or at regular intervals during the project? How can grantees and grantors work together to optimize the grant cash flow? Chapter 8 contains techniques for ensuring optimum cash flow to meet project needs.

Funding-Agency Contacts: Letting Them Help

Contacts between grantee and grantor representatives may and should take place throughout the entire grant-stretching process, from the proposal stage through the final audit.

How can the grantor help get the grantee inexpensive equipment, reduce computer costs, or help with telephone bills? How do the grantee and grantor representatives cooperate to avoid unallowable expenditures or to get supplemental funds (or to return unneeded funds in time for use elsewhere)? When is it appropriate for a prospective grantee to contact the grantor? When is it not appropriate? Are there typical lines of communication, and, if so, what are they? What are the "politics" of grantee–grantor contacts?

Chapter 9 provides insights into the communications process between grantor and grantee and shows how effective communications can result in stretching the grant dollar.

Gamesplaying: An Obstacle to Cost-Effective Grant Spending

Players in the grant-stretching game occasionally act as if they are playing "Monopoly"—that is, they are out to win, and the other players, instead of being a part of the team, are opponents.

Why don't grantor and grantee representatives work together better? For that matter, why don't members of the same organization (i.e., the project director and the grant administrator; the program officer and the grant officer) always head toward the same goal? How do the personal responsibilities and needs of each of the central players in the grant-spending process affect their actions? What are the needs of each, and how do these needs work for (or against) cost-effective grants spending? What are the problems? Are there solutions?

In Chapter 10, the gamesplaying that occurs between the central players in the grant-spending process will be examined. Suggestions for modifying the games, so that all players will be winners, are proposed.

Your Role: Organizing for the Grant $ S-T-R-E-T-C-H !

Knowing the questions and answers to stretching grant dollars will help your organization only if there is someone responsible for capitalizing on each opportunity to save. Whether you are the project director, the grant administrator, the program officer, the grant officer, or a member of the support staff or have some combination of these responsibilities, you cannot be expected to singlehandedly carry out all the grant-dollar-maximizing activities to be discussed in this book. Nor should you.

So the critical task is to assign the various responsibilities, thereby ensuring that someone is covering each of these grant-stretching activities. Who should be responsible for each one? At your organization, who *is* responsible? Do you have "gaps"—with a money drain because no one is overseeing a particular grant-dollar-stretching task? How can you identify the gaps? What organizing techniques can eliminate the money drains?

The final chapter summarizes the many tips to grant stretching presented throughout the book. It also provides a special checklist that your organization may use to ensure that it is capitalizing on all grant-stretching possibilities.

So, essentially, the board game of grants stretching has been described. The major players are identified. Many questions have been posed. As you read the following chapters, answers to these questions will be forthcoming. Depending on your own grants-spending role, the information will be worth *real* (not "play") money to you.

2

The Proposal Decision
Should You Apply?

Sometimes one pays most for the things one gets for nothing.
—Albert M. Einstein

The time to start thinking about getting the most out of your grant dollar is before the proposal is written. Though this statement may appear at first glance to be an anachronism, it is not. The most important decision an organization makes regarding any given proposal is whether to submit it or not.

In too many circumstances, universities, community agencies, and hospitals, as well as profit-making firms, apply for outside funding simply because the money is available. Little thought may be given to whether the award, if received, will enhance the functioning of the organization. In some instances, an award may actually be detrimental to an agency if, in its zeal to obtain as much grant and contract money as possible, it fails to foresee the effect of the award on facilities, personnel time, finances, and other resources. The outcome could be extremely costly. Indeed, an important component of effective grant administration is knowing when *not* to apply.

Before applying for a grant or contract, the potential grantee should ask some questions and establish some ground rules for itself. These ground rules will help the hospital, university, or community agency decide wisely whether to apply or not, and this decision will be based on facts instead of a general desire to obtain outside funding simply because it is available.

Why should ground rules be established? What questions should the prospective grantees ask themselves? There are several.

How Much Will the Application Cost You?

It costs money to apply for a grant, though many applicants don't take the time to consider that fact. The costs of staff time spent in meetings to discuss the proposal, travel, and long-distance phone calls to the funding agency during the preliminary phase can add up quickly. And that's before you've even begun writing the proposal. Once the proposal is being developed, weeks of staff time may be spent on it. Because of writing time—along with clerical support, duplicating, and mailing—costs can be higher than anticipated. Even a modest proposal can cost upwards of $1,062.* Though you may be successful and receive the grant, you cannot recover these up-front costs of preparing the proposal.

What Are Your Chances for Success in Receiving an Award?

Because it is expensive and time-consuming to prepare a proposal, you should make a realistic assessment of your chances of receiving an award before embarking on the proposal-writing adventure. Although no one can unequivocally state that you will or won't get an award, you can "test the water" in a variety of ways.

Talk to Funding-Agency Representatives

In a study reported in *Foundation News*, Sladek[2] found that the most important factor that distinguished successful university-based grant applicants from unsuccessful ones was contact with the funding agency. By a wide margin, faculty members who called or visited the potential sponsor(s) before applying were more successful in obtaining awards than faculty members who simply sent in a proposal without preliminary contact. This is not to say that preliminary contact will automatically assure the applicant of an award.

The significance of Sladek's finding rests on the assumption that program officers at the funding agencies are able to provide useful information that can help in the preparation of a good proposal. Clearly, a good proposal that has received the benefit of input from the funding agency is more likely to be funded than a proposal that has been submitted cold. Similarly, proposal ideas that do not fit in with the sponsor's interests and priorities can be filtered out *before* the proposal-writing activity begins.

In effect, when a program officer tells you over the phone that your project idea has only a slim chance of being funded, he is saving you $1,000 or more. You can then redirect your time, energy, and money toward finding a more receptive sponsor or toward writing a proposal that is more likely to be funded.

Use Proposal Prospectuses

Prospectuses are miniproposals, no more than two or three pages in length, which are submitted to funding agencies in order to determine if the sponsor is

*A study by the General Accounting Office in 1976 has estimated that a proposal of between 20 and 100 pages costs grant seekers approximately $1,062.[1]

interested in your idea or not. The prospectus will give the sponsor a concise look at your objectives, methodology, qualifications, and financial requirements. A prospectus is not a proposal; it is an inquiry to determine if your idea falls within the sponsor's funding interests.

Writing a prospectus will take you far less time than writing a proposal. Further, because a prospectus is not a formal reqest for funding, the sponsor often provides useful feedback. If your idea has weak points, program officers will usually point them out and, as a result, enable you to prepare a stronger proposal than you might otherwise have written.

In recent years, several federal funding agencies–including the Fund for the Improvement of Postsecondary Education, the National Institute of Law Enforcement and Criminal Justice, and the National Endowment for the Humanities–have begun requiring or recommending the submission of preproposals or concept papers prior to the development of formal proposals. These preliminary documents help to save the sponsor's as well as the applicant's time, and they are efficient tools for helping to assess the project's fundability.

After reviewing the preproposal, the grantor program officer will advise you that she or he is interested in your project and would like to see a full proposal or that your preproposal was not approved. Either way, you have not expended the great amount of time and money that a proposal requires. And, if you *are* asked to prepare a formal proposal, you now know that the sponsor is aware of your idea and has reviewed it somewhat favorably and that your chances for success are reasonably good.

It should be made clear at this point that despite the obvious advantages, some program officers will not review preliminary proposals. One argument states that the submission of a preliminary document gives one applicant an advantage over another, whose first contact with the sponsor is the formal proposal. Of course it does! That is the beauty of the preproposal, and the cost-conscious applicant will use such opportunities to his or her advantage. Formal proposals, once they are submitted, do not allow for follow-up telephone calls to the sponsor to ask for comments. Preproposals do, and if your preliminary efforts receive unfavorable feedback from the agency (or none at all), you still have a chance to improve your presentation when the formal proposal is written.

Talk to Your Competitors and Colleagues

When you are about to begin preparing a large, time-consuming proposal, speak to your colleagues in the field. They may also be your competitors and, therefore, sparing in their information, but there is always something to be learned. Perhaps your friend at a nearby institution has decided not to apply because one of the Ivy League universities, with a world-renowned investigator on its faculty, is going to submit a proposal. This is valuable information for you, especially if only one award will be made, as is sometimes the case.

For example, one prospective project director at an urban university was interested in applying for a major award from the Administration on Aging. He wanted to learn if he had a reasonably good chance of getting the grant for his institution's center on aging. Competition for the award would be intense, he knew, and only the best universities with the finest gerontology programs would apply.

The project director began phoning friends, colleagues, and possible competitors to ask if they would be applying for the award. Of special interest were the possible competitors in his own geographic region. The project director knew that if one or two other "superstar" universities were planning to apply, he had virtually no chance of winning the competition. If these other outstanding universities were not planning to seek the grant, he had a good chance.

The first few calls were to friends at other institutions who were not going to compete. Did they know if University X or University Y were going to apply? This plan of attack is called *beating around the bush.* Sometimes it works; your friends may have that single piece of information that you need.

In this case, beating around the bush failed. It became necessary to phone University X and University Y and ask the question directly: "Are you going to apply for the Administration on Aging award?" It should be noted that this important phone call was not made to the prospective project director himself at University X. It was made to a staff person, an acquaintance (i.e., a "safe" person), who was not reluctant to disclose the information.

It turned out that University X *did* intend to apply for the award. The key piece of information had been obtained from the competitor. Our project director now knew his chances of getting the grant were very slim, and he decided to spend his time on another proposal that had a better chance of being successful.

Talking to your colleagues can sometimes provide you with underground intelligence like this. Though it is not legal to do so, a request for proposals (RFP) may be "wired." That is, the likely winner of the contract is already known, even before the competition begins. The funding agency won't tell you that it already knows who the contractor or contractors will be, but a colleague at another institution may be willing to share this information. Most RFPs are not wired, but in the few instances where it is reasonably certain that a well-known corporation or hospital or university will receive the contract, you should consider carefully whether you want to spend your time, energy, and money on an endeavor that has only the slimmest chance of being successful.

What Cost Sharing Will Be Required If You Receive an Award?

It is important for your organization to ask itself if it should apply for an award because, as we have already seen, it costs money to prepare an application. But, ironically, it may cost your organization even *more* money if you are successful and receive the grant. Consequently, it is of paramount importance that you know, *before* you apply, the amount of cost sharing that your agency will have to provide.

By *cost sharing* we mean the contributions that grantees must make to help fund the total cost of some grant projects. These contributions are also known as *matching funds.*

Some funding agencies require the grantee's share of the project costs to be no less than 10%. Other agencies, depending on their own resources or rules, may require that the grantee provide up to 25%, $33\frac{1}{3}$%, or even 50% of the total cost of the project.

If you are planning a multiyear project, and cost sharing is involved, you will probably have to contribute larger and larger amounts with each year the project continues. For example, grantees who receive Department of Education funds for the Cooperative Education Program must be prepared for minimum sharing of 10%, 20%, 40%, and 60% during project years 2 through 5, respectively. The idea is, of course, that these grantees will be better prepared to continue the program after year 5, with no grantor funds necessary.

Whether you are applying for a single or a multiyear grant, a substantial amount of your organization's money may be involved. This commitment may be acceptable if the award you receive allows you to carry out a project that you planned to do with or without the award. If, however, you were embarking on the project primarily to obtain some grant money, you probably should not consider putting more of your own agency's funds into the project.

Some organizations that are not now heavily involved in sponsored programs would like to be. It is possible that these organizations will not find it too crippling to accept projects that involve a good deal of cost participation. Years ago, in the days when outside sponsorship of research and other programs was just getting started, every potential grantee was in that position. Cost sharing was universally acceptable. But as these sponsored programs grew to account for a significant portion of the grantee's budget, many grantees found that their cost participation was using funds that were desperately needed for the maintenance and necessary expansion of facilities and other programs.

If your agency has a modest amount of grants and contracts that pay less than their actual cost, it is certainly better to spend the sponsor's dollar in addition to your own 50 cents. But keep an eye out for the day when a million dollars from outside sources will require several hundred thousand dollars out of your own resources.(3)

That is precisely the situation that the public broadcasting station in one of America's largest cities found itself in recently. The station wisely chose not to apply for an award that it had a good chance of receiving. The grant was for several hundred thousand dollars, but the matching costs would have crippled the station—and would have left it unable to do the other things it wanted to do. Opting not to seek the grant was an example of good money management.

Less far-sighted was a college on the East Coast. Knowing that it would have a hard time meeting the required 50% match on an equipment grant, the institution chose to apply for the award anyway. The college's reasoning was that typical of many applicants, though the logic should not be viewed as a model of sound planning. It was felt that the grant, if it were awarded, would arrive in six to nine months. This was well into the next fiscal year, when the budget picture of the college was expected to be better. As it turned out, the award was received, the college's budget situation was worse, and the grant could not be fully utilized. The college was able to meet only half of its matching requirement and had to return money to the sponsor.

The moral of the story is this: if you know at the beginning of the fiscal year that you will be applying for grants that require matching funds, budget sufficient funds in advance to meet your anticipated needs. Don't sit back and hope that funds will materialize if and when you receive the grant. Usually, if you can't allocate funds for future matching requirements now, you should not apply for matching grants later.

In addition to the obvious cost sharing required on grants, there are often hidden costs and hazards as well. Good grant administrators try to uncover these hidden costs before proposals are submitted. Even under the best of circumstances, when no cost-sharing or matching funds are requested, the applicant institution will still realize no financial gain. In fact, an institution or agency can consider itself fortunate if it can break even on a sponsored contract or grant. At a meeting of grant and contract administrators recently, the director of sponsored research at a large university looked around, surveyed the 600 assembled conferees who were awaiting the arrival of a distinguished speaker, and with only half a smile said, "Look at all these people who came here to find new ways to lose money for their institutions."

Does the Project Fit with Your Organization's Mission?

Even though the application will cost you money, your chances of receiving the award are not high, and cost sharing will be required, you will probably want to apply for the award if the proposed project fits your agency's mission. On the other hand, if the project is tangential to your agency's long-range goals or represents a considerable disparity with them, you may decide not to apply, thereby saving your resources for other projects that will be more closely related to your business.

Obviously, in order to determine whether the project fits within your organization's mission, you must have a clear definition of what that mission is. In far too many cases in recent years, nonprofit agencies of all kinds have sought grant funds wherever they could be found and have spent little time considering how receipt of a grant would achieve their purposes. In effect, the search for funds became their *de facto* mission, rather than the delivery of health services, or community mental health, or education.

In many institutions of higher education, for example, there is continuous competition between research and instruction. Some universities are clearly research institutions, and some colleges have defined themselves to one and all as teaching institutions. But a great many haven't decided what they are or ought to be. They simply charge ahead and apply for whatever grant money is available. Their major purpose seems to be "to get grants."

Faculty members may be attracted to research because it provides opportunities for publication, which is the surest way to prestige and recognition in one's field. But the administration may be interested in seeking funds for new laboratory equipment for instruction, or money for a program for senior citizens or women. Is there a tug-of-war here or not? Should the university's mission be more clearly defined? Should your agency's mission be more clearly defined before you plunge into more grant seeking?

Before applying for a grant or a contract, consider what you expect your agency to be like one year, two years, five years down the road. Do you expect a change in purpose? Do you expect to be a larger agency? A smaller one? What kind of image do you want your organization to have? These are important questions, because receipt of a grant can help or hinder your agency's growth, affect its reputation, and influence the direction it takes in the future.

For example, a university that is planning to phase out its school of engineering should not apply for a multiyear engineering research-and-development contract. Receipt of such a contract would strengthen the engineering establishment at the university and serve to delay the planned phaseout. If, on the other hand, the school of engineering expects a new influx of students and foresees continued growth, a multiyear research contract could be an especially good idea.

Do You Have (or Can You Get) the Resources Necessary to Carry Out the Project?

Part of your assessment of whether to apply for a grant or not should involve a consideration of the special resources you have to offer. Do you have unusually talented people on your staff with expertise in the appropriate disciplines? Are your facilities unique or of special note? Is the geographic location of your agency an asset to performing the work required on the project? If you don't have the necessary staff or facilities available, how will you get them? These questions should be answered before the application is submitted.

A prospective project director at an eastern college believed that physicians in the surrounding suburban area could use trained medical assistants. Before preparing an application for a vocational training grant, the project director sent letters to the doctors within a 20-mile radius of the college to ask if their offices could be used as training sites for a few hours a week for the interning medical assistants. These doctors were also asked if they would hire the assistants after the training period was completed.

The doctors' responses were enthusiastic. Not only would they be willing to serve as trainers for a few hours, they would prefer to hire medical assistants instead of secretaries. For years, the doctors had been hiring secretarial students and doing the training themselves anyway. Now they would have better-trained personnel available, turnover might be lower, and the medical assistants would be more motivated, in general, than the secretarial students.

With these facts in hand, and with letters from the physicians as backup, a proposal was submitted. The project was funded and then renewed for a second year because the placement of program graduates was so successful.

This project director had done her homework. She had analyzed her resources, found where they were lacking, and taken steps to remedy the problem. She knew how to get the needed training sites and then went out and got them. She did not have to spend time finding these sites after the grant came in. When the award notice arrived, she was ready to begin the program.

Unless you can clearly show in your proposal that you will be able to provide the necessary resources, your proposal is not likely to be funded. You will be competing against agencies like yours that *have* the resources. If you can't make an extremely good case for yourself, you should save your time and money by not applying.

Who in Your Organization Decides Whether or Not You Should Apply?

It is true that not all of the sponsored projects that are available to an institution should be applied for; it is also possible that not all awards that are received should be accepted. If each proposal were evaluated objectively by a committee in your agency on the basis of relevance and its cost to you, it is probable that some proposals would not be submitted. Learning to say "no" is an important part of research administration. This is not to imply that research administrators should exercise veto power over proposals, but they should certainly share in making that kind of decision.[4]

The individual who decides whether your organization should apply for a particular grant may be the president or a dean or the director of sponsored research or the executive director. The person's title is not important. What is crucial is for the responsible individual to know about your agency's overall mission, finances, resources, and special competencies. If this is not the case or if no one is consciously making the decision, you may end up receiving grants that cost you money and perhaps run contrary to your agency's mission. Or you may simply be submitting a lot of applications that have little chance of being funded.

Looking at the multitude of questions and duties that attend your involvement in sponsored activities, it is clear that there are a number of factors you should consider before applying for any grant or contract. First, can you afford it if you should receive the award? This question should be asked whether there is cost sharing or not. Second, are your chances of success sufficiently high to justify the time, energy, and money that will be involved in preparing the application? Third, have you contacted the funding agency and others to learn as much as possible about the funding program? Fourth, is this the kind of program you would like to conduct in your organization with your own money, but simply don't have the money? Fifth, do you have the resources to carry out the project? Sixth, are these questions being seriously asked by a knowledgeable individual in your organization before the application is prepared?

If your answers are positive, you should apply with confidence.

3

The Proposal Budget
Asking for the Right Amount

To have enough is good luck, to have more than enough is harmful.
This is true of all things, but especially of money.

—Chuang-Tse

The budget is an effective management tool for both you and the granting agency. Contrary to what some may think, it is not merely a necessary appendage to a proposal. It is a live, working instrument that will be referred to again and again during the course of the project. Because the budget will be so important to you during the project, it must be given maximum thought at an early stage of proposal development so that problems that may arise later can be avoided. Not only is a well-planned budget an effective way to avoid potential problems, it is also an excellent device to help you get the most out of your grant dollar.

How Much Do You Need?

It is imperative, of course, to ask for enough money to conduct your project properly. Though this statement appears to be self-evident, many novices, inexperienced in budget preparation, short-change themselves by keeping their budgets unrealistically low in an effort to remain competitive. A "bare-bones" budget, or a budget that seriously underestimates costs, can lead to one of two undesirable situations.

First, your proposal may be rejected. The reviewers, who will be knowledgeable about the costs of your proposed project, will recognize that you have not carefully considered all the resources you will need. The reviewers will not know whether the underestimate was an oversight on your part or whether you really did not understand all of the ramifications of the work you were about to embark on.

For example, a research proposal was turned down by the National Science Foundation because the principal investigator had not included enough money for support staff. He planned to interview several hundred people by himself, with each interview lasting approximately two hours. The reviewers recognized that this was an impossible task and gave the proposal a poor rating. The investigator had been trying diligently to keep his budget down, but in so doing, he had weakened his methodology. He should have included in the budget sufficient funds to pay interviewers, and that is precisely what the National Science Foundation recommended when it suggested that the proposal be resubmitted at a later date.

Second, your proposal may be funded, but after the initial glow of excitement has passed, you may wish it hadn't been. Working on a project that is underfunded is extremely difficult, and when you are the one who is responsible (there are no bureaucrats to blame, since you developed the bare-bones budget yourself), it can be downright unpleasant. In the cold light of day, when you realize that you don't have enough money for staff or travel or supplies, you may wish you had been more generous with yourself at the budget preparation stage. If there is a moral here, it is this: plan your project carefully, think of all the things you will be doing and the costs involved in doing them, and include these costs in the budget. If you have insufficient funds in your budget, you lose—whether you are awarded the grant or not.

How Do You Know What They've Got?

Realizing that you must request sufficient funding for your proposal, you must next determine what the granting agency has to spend. It would be foolish to ask for $100,000 when the sponsor will be making awards only in the $50,000-$60,000 range. There will be times when you will have to work backward in the budget preparation stage. That is, you will have to find out how much money is available and then determine the scope of the project you can offer for that amount.

How do you find out what the granting agency has to spend? Sometimes, the sponsor's program guidelines clearly state the dollar range of the awards to be made. In some cases, the federal regulations that apply to the program will tell you, and in other instances, you may be able to get a list of the awards that were made by the program during the previous year.

There may also be a clue in the program guidelines or the request for proposal (RFP) suggesting that "three man-years of effort are anticipated"—rather than an indication of a dollar amount. If you recognize that a man-year is approximately equal to $55,000-$80,000* depending on the funding agency, you can easily get an idea of the size of the budget that the sponsor expects to fund.

Another method of determining the amount of money available is to call or visit a representative of the funding agency. If you do call or visit, it is a good idea to discuss other program matters as well. You will probably have many questions you'd like to ask. Take advantage of the opportunity to do so. The more information you have, budgetary and otherwise, the better off you are.

Never Pad a Budget

Just as it is a rule of thumb never to underestimate your project costs, it is equally important not to pad your budget with overestimates. According to Chuang-Tse, ". . . to have more than enough is harmful. This is true of all things, but especially true of money." It is harmful to ask for more money than you need (pad a budget) for two reasons.

First, your proposal may be rejected. The reviewers will recognize any inappropriate costs in your budget, as well as those that are appropriate. They will have an excellent idea of what your project costs should be. Therefore, you should make every effort to estimate these costs reasonably. Failure to do so may negatively affect the reviewers' confidence in your ability to manage the funds once you receive them.

Second, it is possible that your proposal will be funded at the padded level proposed. If this happens, you may not be able to spend all the money, even if you purchase luxury items and are not cost-conscious in your spending. If there are substantial funds left at the end of the project, it will appear to the grantors that you planned poorly. On a later occasion, when you really do need all the money you ask for, the grantors may not give it to you.

Therefore, every effort should be made to avoid padding. The costs shown in the budget should coincide with what you said you would do in your proposal narrative. Under no circumstances should there be items in the budget that do not clearly relate to your proposed project.

For example, don't surprise the reviewers by including 10% of your organization's executive director's time if he or she does not have specific responsibilities that are outlined in the proposal. Putting several thousand dollars into the budget for "miscellaneous" is a device that experienced grant seekers do not use. You should work costs out carefully and plan ahead sufficiently so that you can identify all your expenses without having to resort to a "miscellaneous" or "contingency" category in your budget. Also, travel to here, there, and everywhere—for no apparent reason—is obviously padding the budget. Travel is a legitimate item to be included in your proposal, but only if you can show how it relates specifically to the work you will be doing on the project.

*This amount is a current approximation. It will increase with inflation over the years.

Padding a budget takes remarkably little imagination. The test of a good budget-maker and proposal-writer is to request sufficient funds to conduct the project successfully while omitting items from the budget that are not called for in the work statement. It should always be kept in mind that the budget is a management tool that is being devised by you. If you are not scrupulous in preparing it, you will almost assuredly regret it during the life of the project and afterward—if the project gets funded. Furthermore, a poorly prepared budget will not help you to monitor your progress toward fulfilling the project's objectives, and its effectiveness as a management tool will thereby be seriously diminished.

When to Pad a Budget

After the above treatise on why the grant seeker should never pad a budget, a section on when to pad a budget must appear to be a contradiction. Padding should be done in two cases.

First, if you are undertaking a new project, you may not know exactly *how much* of a particular resource (i.e., computer time) will be needed. You will, however, usually be able to identify a high–low range. So it will be reasonable (because of uncertainty) to request funds in the middle-to-high range of your estimate.

Second, padding must be used to allow for reasonably expected price increases in cost items such as salary, equipment, travel, and supplies, at rates that can be defended. It normally takes as long as six to nine months after the date of submission for a proposal to be funded. At current rates of inflation, a cost item can increase in price during this time as much as 5–15% or more.

For your budget to retain its utility as a management tool, it must incorporate both known and unknown-but-predictable cost increases. If it does not, you may find it hard to work within the funding limitations after the award has been made. You may discover yourself trying to change, circumvent, adjust, or otherwise amend your original budget, and you will be spending extra time working on your budget when ideally it should be working for you.

What Do You Include in a Budget?

Knowing that you must ask for enough money, must relate your request to the grantor's ability to fund, and must avoid obvious padding, yet anticipate inflated costs and unexpected developments, now what specific elements should you include in a well-prepared grant budget?

There are four. All budgets include *direct costs.* Most budgets include *indirect costs.* Some budgets include *cost sharing* (also known as *matching funds*) and/or *program income.* Each of these budget components is discussed below. Methods to ensure adequate coverage of direct-cost items are also included.

Direct Costs

Direct costs are those costs that can be identified specifically with a particular sponsored project. For example, if you must hire several laboratory assistants to wash test tubes to be used in project experiments, their salaries will be direct costs to your grant. The categories of direct costs normally included in grant budgets are *salaries, fringe benefits, equipment, supplies, travel,* and *other direct costs.*

Salaries. The biggest dollar item in most budgets is the cost of personnel. Thus, it is in the salary category that the greatest care and planning should take place. Allow for any promotions, merit increases, and/or cost-of-living adjustments that you anticipate during the period of the grant. And don't forget to take into consideration the salary increases that may take place prior to the effective date of the grant. Remember that you are budgeting for a period almost two years into the future (six to nine months before the award is made and the full year the project will be conducted).

Using your agency's salary schedule as a base, try to anticipate all the promotions, cost-of-living increases, and merit raises that the personnel on your project can expect to receive during the next one-and-one-half to two years. If your institution functions under a multiyear labor agreement, the task of projecting salaries is made easy. You know precisely what each individual will be earning for several years and on which dates each person can expect a change in pay. On the other hand, if your organization's salary schedule does not project pay levels beyond a year, it is reasonable (even necessary) to incorporate into your budget a 6–7% inflation increase (more, if you have good reason to expect higher inflation).

Often, it may be difficult, if not impossible, to estimate exactly the amount of staff time and dollars you will need. In such cases, estimate a range of high-moderate-low time that will be needed. Then, prepare your budget toward the higher end of the spectrum. This is a more attractive solution than painting yourself into a corner in order to keep the budget down so that it will be competitive. Keep in mind that you want the grant—but not at any price.

Fringe Benefits. The direct-cost item that is most commonly overlooked by novice proposal budgeters is fringe benefits. Everyone knows that salaries must be budgeted in grant proposals to pay project workers for their services. But many people do not realize that every time a salary is paid, a fringe-benefits cost must be paid as well.

Fringe benefits include such items as social security, unemployment insurance, workers' compensation, sick leave, health insurance, life insurance, and retirement. Your organization, as an employer, is required by law to pay some of these benefits (for example, social security and workers' compensation). Other benefits may or may not be paid (health insurance, retirement), depending on your agency's policy.

For a variety of legal and practical reasons, fringe benefits do not afford much opportunity for padding. This budget category does, however, provide an opportunity to get more for your grant dollar if careful planning is done at an early stage of proposal development.

Usually, there are various categories of employees with different benefit rates. *Regular* (or *permanent*) and *temporary* are two common ways of classifying employees. The benefits that must be budgeted for temporary employees are generally less than those for regular employees. It is common to budget approximately 10% of salaries to cover the benefits of temporary workers. The fringe-benefit rates for regular employees may be 20–30% or more, depending on the generosity of the employer. And, as social security taxes increase, these rates are likely to climb even more. The lowest fringe-benefit rate applies to *student workers.* Because social security need not be deducted from student pay, benefits on student salaries may be only 6% or less.

Caution. Sometimes fringe benefits should *not* be included as a direct cost of your project. If fringe benefits are included in the calculation of your indirect-cost rate, they must not be budgeted as a direct cost. Occasionally, some elements of the benefits package (for example, vacation and workers' compensation) are calculated in the indirect-cost rate, while others (perhaps social security and health insurance) are not. It's important to find out which benefits (if any) should be charged as a direct cost to your grant and to budget accordingly.

Equipment. The federal "Cost Principles" define equipment as "an article of nonexpendable tangible personal property having a useful life of more than two years, and an acquisition cost of $500 or more per unit. However, consistent with institutional policy, lower limits may be established."[(1)]

If you are planning to purchase or lease equipment to conduct your project, get an up-to-date estimate of the costs from at least one and preferably two vendors. As scientific research equipment purchased during the late 1960s and early 1970s begins to wear out and become obsolete, more and more sophisticated equipment will be bought during the early 1980s. It is important to remember that the prices of such equipment have risen markedly in recent years, especially items manufactured in Japan and Germany.

In addition to inflation, the relative value of the dollar in relation to the yen and the German mark has caused even the most ambitiously padded budget to be inadequate. It has become common at many universities and hospitals around the country for principal investigators to downgrade their equipment purchases after realizing that they simply didn't have enough money in their budgets to pay for the materials that were originally proposed. Judicious padding of your budget to account for anticipated equipment-price increases during the coming year may save you much difficulty a year later.

Supplies. The *supplies* category can encompass a variety of items, large and small. Typically, items in this category are consumable; they will be used up during the grant period. Common categories of supplies are (1) *office* (pencils, paper, rubber bands, etc.); (2) *educational* (books, periodicals, tapes, records, etc.); (3) *research* (test tubes, rats, seedlings, chemicals, etc.); and (4) *expendable equipment* (any tangible personal property costing less than $500 *or* having a useful life of two years or less).

Although consumable supplies are usually not subject to the same grant price increases as equipment, be sure to include in your proposal budget sufficient funds for inflationary price hikes. In addition, be certain that you have not overlooked anything.

Travel. Travel costs include airfare to get project staff to where they need to be; per diem for room and board while they are on the road; ground transportation, such as taxis, buses, airport limousines, and rental cars; and business expenses, such as telephone calls, postage, and secretarial service, while you or your associates are away from the office.

Other travel costs may occur within your own city. It is common to reimburse grant project staff for using their own vehicles for project business. This is known as *local mileage,* and the rates are established by your own agency, or–in some cases–by the grantor agency.

Still other travel costs have to do with getting groups of people and their personal property moved. It may be necessary, for example, to charter a plane, bus, or boat; lease several station wagons or vans; or employ shipping and storage companies to move and store furniture.

Like equipment, transportation costs should be checked out carefully before they are included in your budget. Are you planning to give a paper at a conference in Chicago? Call a travel agent or airline and find out the air fare (coach) between your office and the Windy City. Include the cost of getting to the airport in your hometown and the expected cost of getting from the airport to your hotel in Chicago.

Are you flying in the summer or the winter? Airlines often adjust their fares up or down, depending on the season. Since deregulation of the airlines in early 1979, fares have fluctuated frequently, and they vary from one airline to another. Plan accordingly before completing your budget.

Does your organization have a standard travel policy that outlines in detail the amount of money to which a traveling staff member is entitled? Does that policy include per diem rates, acknowledging that certain cities are more expensive to stay in than others? And do allowed mileage charges for automobile travel anticipate the expected rise in gasoline prices?

There is a great deal of "guesstimating" that will be required of you even under the best of circumstances, but careful planning and checking–with a bit of a cushion for inflation–can give you a travel budget that will be adequate.

Other Direct Costs. The *other direct costs* category includes such items as communications (telephone and postage), duplicating, participant costs, consultants, space and equipment rental, publication costs, computer time, and other expenses that may be unique to your project. As with salaries, benefits, equipment, and travel, there are ways to ensure that you will be budgeting enough money.

For example, contact the consultants you plan to use and ask them about their fees. (You should advise them of their inclusion in your project under any circumstances.) Likewise, space rental must be considered when the project will be conducted away from your local organization. If you will be operating an office in the community, investigate the cost of renting space. The rates are usually quoted in cents (or dollars) per square foot. Also, desks, chairs, typewriters, file cabinets, and other furnishings may be needed for this off-site location. The funding agency may require that you provide sufficient justification for these expenses; the need for off-site space and furnishings may not be self-evident. Computer costs, communication, duplicating, and participant costs can usually be assessed relatively accurately, even a year in advance, if a moderate inflation increase is built into your calculations.

These, then, are the direct costs that are typically included in grant budgets: salaries, fringe benefits, equipment, supplies, travel, and other direct costs. In order to be sure that you are budgeting sufficient direct costs, it is important to:

1. Get up-to-date, realistic price estimates.
2. Allow for expected inflation between now and the time you expect to receive the award.
3. Be sure to look over your project carefully so that you don't forget any cost elements.

Indirect Costs

Asking for the right amount of money in a grant budget means asking for all the money you will need for the project. This money must cover indirect as well as direct costs. Indirect costs may be contrasted with direct costs in that indirect costs are *not easily identifiable with your particular project.* They are *real* costs, but the accounting work needed to identify them with each separately funded project would be horrendous, if it could be done at all.

Remember our saying that the salaries of lab assistants who washed test tubes for a grant project would be considered a *direct* cost? This salary was easily identifiable. Now imagine how hard it would be to trace the costs of heating the water used to wash those test tubes, particularly if the laboratory were being used by several other projects and by graduate students in connection with classwork. Although the costs of heating that water are real, it is almost impossible to allocate them equitably among the various users. Therefore, these costs are considered *indirect* costs.

Similarly, the heat and light bills for your agency, the costs of processing checks and doing accounting work, some portion of your purchasing agent's time, the costs of space and office furniture in your building, janitorial services, depreciation allowances–all these are indirect costs associated with your funded projects. If you do not request indirect costs as an integral part of your budget, clearly you are short-changing yourself.

It is important to understand that the kinds of costs that are used to calculate the indirect-cost rate are the same as direct costs in most cases. They include salaries, benefits, equipment, communications, and so forth. Usually a cost item is termed *indirect* instead of direct only when there are difficulties in allocating the cost among projects.

Your agency must decide which costs it is unwilling to account for on a project-by-project basis and include those in its indirect-cost base. Then, it is crucial that the persons preparing direct-cost budgets know what the components of the indirect-cost base are—and not double-charge the grantor agency. For example, if fringe benefits are included in the calculation of your indirect-cost rate, fringe benefits may not also be charged as a direct cost on projects.

"A problem we have," a federal auditor told the authors, "is that the people who prepare the indirect-cost rates and the ones who put project budgets together are often different people. There may be overlaps in charges."

Although the indirect costs cannot be identified with individual projects, you are entitled to recover these costs from funding agencies. If your agency has only one funded project—and that is your agency's only work—then all of the costs of running your organization are the indirect costs (also known as *overhead*) and should be charged to the sponsor.

It is more common, however, for agencies to be conducting a number of projects at the same time, and therefore, the indirect costs must be divided among their many projects. If you have federally funded projects, the federal government will negotiate an indirect cost rate with your organization. This rate will be updated periodically, so that it reflects current costs. Information about how to establish indirect-cost rates may be obtained from federal government publications.*

In general, the indirect-cost *rate* that is negotiated is expressed in terms of a percentage of one of the following *bases*:

1. Total direct costs (TDC)
2. Modified total direct costs (MTDC)
3. Salaries and wages (S&W)
4. Salaries and wages and benefits (S&W&B)

To calculate the indirect costs on a grant, apply your agency's officially negotiated rate to the appropriate base costs of your project. For example, assume that your organization's rate is 50% of salaries and wages, and you will be paying $10,000 in grant salaries. The indirect costs charged to your project will be $5,000 (50% rate × $10,000 base).

*Procedures for establishing indirect-cost rates for grants and contracts with DHEW are contained in publications OASC-1 (for colleges and universities); OASC-3 (for hospitals); OASC-5 (for nonprofit institutions); OASC-10 (for state and local governments); and Federal Procurement Regulations, Subpart 1-15.2 (for commercial organizations). These publications may be ordered from the Superintendent of Documents, U.S. Government Printing Office, Washington, DC 20402.

In the past, the most common base has been salaries and wages. Now, with the revised federal cost principles, educational institutions are being required to change to the modified total direct cost base. Other bases may be used only "where it can be demonstrated that they produce more equitable results."(2)

The modified total direct cost base, as defined by federal cost principles, consists of "salaries and wages, fringe benefits, materials and supplies, services, travel, and subgrants and subcontracts up to $25,000 each."(3) Therefore, when calculating the base for a particular grant budget, you must exclude equipment, student stipends, and any subgrant or subcontract costs above $25,000.

No matter which base your organization negotiates (S&W, S&W&B, MTDC, or TDC), you will collect approximately the same amount in total, spread over all your projects. However, for individual projects, the indirect costs will vary, depending on the base.

In addition to establishing an indirect-cost rate and base, it is necessary to decide on the *type* of rate you will use: (1) *provisional/final;* (2) *predetermined;* or (3) *fixed with carry-forward.* *

Most large colleges and universities and almost all state and local units of government are using the fixed rate with carry-forward. Small colleges and universities are using either the fixed rate with carry-forward or the predetermined rate. Most hospitals and nonprofit institutions use the provisional–final rate and, to a lesser extent, the fixed rate with carry-forward. The distinguishing difference between the rates lies not in how they are developed or the type of costs they represent, but rather in whether, and how, they are adjusted to ultimately reflect a grantee's actual cost.

An indirect-cost proposal is prepared in advance of the period in which it is going to be used. Thus, it is an estimate of both the direct and the indirect costs that an organization expects to incur during some future time period, usually the next fiscal year. Because it is an estimate, it will have to be adjusted at the end of that period if it is to reflect the grantee's actual cost. Federal agencies generally allow an organization six months after the end of its fiscal year to submit its adjusted proposal. The same proposal usually serves two purposes: to adjust the prior year's projected rate(s) to actual rates, and to establish the upcoming year's projected rate(s).

Once the grantee knows the actual cost, three alternatives are available:

1. The initial rate can be modified and adjustments made to the grants (and contracts) to which it was applied (i.e., a retroactive adjustment). This is a procedure that must be followed if a *provisional–final* rate is used.
2. The initial rate and the grants and contracts to which it was applied can remain undisturbed; adjustments can be made against the rate(s) for the

*The following discussion of indirect costs is adapted from *Federal Grants Management Handbook*, Grants Management Advisory Service, Washington, DC, September 1978, pp. 434:1–434:3, with the permission of the Grants Management Advisory Service.

forthcoming period. This is the procedure that is followed under the *fixed rate with carry-forward.*

3. The difference is ignored; no adjustment is made. That is what happens when a *predetermined* rate is used.

There are advantages and disadvantages to each type of rate. *Provisional/final* rates require retroactive adjustments, with the additional work and inconvenience that these entail. The more grants an organization has, the greater the work and inconvenience. Also, if the grantee's final (actual) rate is less than the provisional rate, it will owe the government a refund. On the other hand, if the final rate is higher than the provisional rate, the organization may not be able to recover from the government if the awarding agency fully expended its appropriated funds.

A *predetermined* rate is firm; it cannot be adjusted. Thus, before the government will agree to its use, it will be reasonably confident that the grantee's actual rate will be equal to or less than the predetermined rate. However, a grantee that is amenable to recovering lower indirect costs than it is entitled to may find the predetermined rate attractive because there is no after-the-fact adjustment, up or down, and it knows at all times how much indirect cost it will recover.

The *fixed rate with carry-forward* has all the attributes of the other two rate types and none of their disadvantages. An organization can adjust its estimated rate to the actual rate. It does not have to pay back retroactive adjustments as it would with a provisional–final rate, and it does not need to commit itself to an underrecovery of costs as it would with a predetermined rate. The one drawback is that it will not recover any monies due (as a result of its estimated rate's being less than its actual rate) until the new rate goes into effect—usually a year or more after the end of the grantee's last fiscal year. On the other hand, the same is true of the payback, should the estimated rate be greater than the actual rate. Because of the length of time it takes to effect the ultimate adjustment to reflect actual cost, fixed rates with carry-forward are used only with grantees that are relatively stable and have a long-term relationship with the federal government.

If a grantee meets the requirements for more than one of these rate types, the one that is used is a matter to be decided between itself and its granting agency. For larger grantees, the federal government is likely to prefer the fixed rate with carry-forward or a predetermined rate. For small grantees, the government is likely to prefer the provisional–final rate or a predetermined rate.

Many organizations have two indirect-cost rates. One is for projects that will be conducted on the premises; it is called the *on-site rate.* The other rate is used when the project will be conducted away from the main campus or building of the applicant, even though the applicant will maintain administrative responsibility for the project. This is called the *off-site rate* and is usually lower than the on-site indirect-cost rate, because the use of facilities, utilities, and maintenance are included in the on-site indirect-cost rate, and these items are not being provided by the grantee during the course of an off-site project. Consequently, the off-site rate can be lower.

It is also common for grantee agencies to have indirect-cost rates (both on- and off-site) for various kinds of grant activities and for different cost centers within their organizations. For example, many universities have negotiated separate indirect-cost rates for (1) research and (2) educational training projects. Within a university, there may be separate rates established for medical centers, agricultural stations, and other entities.

If your agency does not have a federally negotiated indirect-cost rate and happens to receive a federal grant, it is common for the government to allow you to claim 10% of the total direct costs of the project as indirect—but then to insist that you submit an indirect-cost proposal for negotiation within 90 days after receiving the award.

If your agency already has an established indirect-cost rate, there will be times when you use this rate in budgets—and other times when you won't. In general, you will use this rate when:

1. You are applying for federal funds and there are no specific federal program instructions against using it. (Sometimes, federally funded training programs limit indirect-cost recoveries to 8% of total direct costs, regardless of what your negotiated rate happens to be.)
2. You are applying to any other funding agency that does not restrict the payment of indirect costs. It is usually possible to tell by looking at the sponsor's guidelines whether indirect costs are allowable or not.

If you are applying for funds from a private foundation, it is possible that no indirect-cost recoveries will be allowed. Your agency will have to absorb these costs, and this should be recognized when you make the decision to apply or not. However, in an effort to get the most out of your grant dollar, you should try to identify some of the items you normally include in your indirect-cost rate—and charge the foundation for these items as *direct* costs.

For example, if office equipment and space are included in your indirect-cost rate (they usually are), then you could identify as direct costs the number of square feet of space needed for the project at the going rate per square foot per month for 12 months. You could also show that desks, chairs, and file cabinets will be needed. In this manner, you are reducing expenses to your agency, which is conducting the program without receiving indirect costs.

Another case arises when you apply to a state agency. Interestingly, some state agencies that are frequently conduits for federal monies refuse to pay the applicant its rightful federally negotiated indirect-cost rate. By taking this stance, the state is dispensing federal money without following federal rules. In other instances, where only state money is involved, the only consistency among state agencies is inconsistency!

For example, in California, the State Department of Health usually insists on paying no more than a specific percentage for indirect costs, while two other departments have different rates. In New York, within the State Education Department, indirect-cost payments vary from division to division, and in some programs, the state administrators refuse to pay the applicant any indirect costs at all.

In contrast, private corporations are generally willing to pay the negotiated rate—unless the funds are intended as a gift without any restrictions on their use.

Occasionally inexperienced (or even experienced) project directors believe that adding indirect charges to their budget may cause their proposals to be rejected. This rarely, if ever, happens. Grantor agency representatives understand the basis of indirect costs and expect to see these costs in the budget. In an article giving advice to grant seekers, Drs. Wendell McBurney and Doris Merritt wrote, "Inclusion [of indirect charges] is normally anticipated by the funding agency and in no way jeopardizes the project."[(4)] If a grantor were to object to indirect charges, she or he would discuss any objections during negotiations, rather than turn down a good proposal.

Therefore, indirect costs should be included at the fully negotiated federal rate in as many budgets as possible. If the sponsor restricts the indirect recoveries for some reason, then it is important to identify as many of the indirect costs as possible (space, office furniture, etc.) and place them in the direct-costs section of the budget. Ideally, your organization should have a policy for preparing budgets in which full indirect cost is not allowed, so that you can plan ahead to cover these costs and not be forced to react on a proposal-by-proposal basis.

Program Income

In addition to estimating the direct and indirect costs of your project, it may be necessary to forecast *program income* for your grant.

Will you be selling books, charging fees for counseling services, or making a product to be sold commercially? Rehabilitation clients, for example, have sharpened drills for local businesses as part of their job training. With grant funds, researchers have published bibliographies that have produced thousands of dollars in sales. Social workers have received grant money to provide meals to senior citizens and have charged modest amounts for these meals to some of their clients who could afford to pay. In these and similar ways, grant funds have been stretched.

If you will be collecting money as a result of your grant activities, a reasonable estimate of the income you expect to receive should be included in your project budget. Some grantor budget forms contain a line item for this estimate. Typically, you will add up all the costs of your project and subtract the revenue you expect to receive. The net cost will then be your request to the grantor.

In estimating program income, first estimate the demand for your service or product. If you or your colleagues have conducted a similar project before, examine its history. How many meals were served, books sold, and so forth? Are there any new trends to consider (for example, a higher population of senior citizens or a greater national interest in the topic of your book)? If you can not determine the demand based on past history and current published trends, talk to or survey some of your potential clients. As a result of these investigations, you will probably identify a high-low range of services or products that you can expect to sell.

Next, decide how much you will charge for your services or products. This is by far the easiest part of the projection. It may be based on agency regulations, past history, break-even costs, or what your clients can afford to pay. The high-low range of demand that you have identified may be affected by the price you decide on, so it is important to consider both factors as you make your decision.

As a final step, simply multiply your charges per product or service by the number of products or services you expect to sell. The critical rule to remember is this: be conservative. The amount of income that you project will be deducted from your grant, and you don't want to be caught short of funds by overestimating your income. Therefore, it is usually best to multiply the lower range of your demand estimate times the price you will be charging.

Cost Sharing

Some grantors will require you to contribute to the total costs of your project, or you may wish to volunteer resources. Therefore, a fourth element (in addition to direct costs, indirect costs, and program income) that may be found in budgets is *cost sharing* (also known as *matching funds*).

There are several categories of cost sharing, and it is important for the proposal budgeter to understand the distinctions among them.

Voluntary versus Mandatory Cost-Sharing. Many grantors do not require the grantee to pay any costs of the project. When there is no formal grantor requirement, any cost sharing you wish to contribute is considered voluntary. You may or may not calculate the value of the resources that you will be giving and show these costs in your budget.

If you do show the value of your contributions in the budget, you will be required to prove after the project that you did provide them. In fact, if auditors discover later that you did not contribute (or adequately document) the promised resources, your organization will have to pay money to the grantor.

If you do not calculate the value of your contributions and show it in the budget, you will not be accountable for it later. You can go ahead and contribute resources, but as long as you have not promised them in your proposal, you will not have to document these donations, nor can auditors question you about them later.

Voluntary cost-sharing that is identified and promised in your proposal is considered *formal* cost-sharing. If you voluntarily share costs without describing the contributions in your budget, this is considered *informal* cost-sharing.

Many grantee organizations establish policies that forbid formal voluntary cost-sharing. They do not want to incur the higher staff costs of documenting these contributions, nor do they want to assume any risk of audit disallowances.

On the other hand, some grantees believe that their proposals will be much more competitive if they do promise voluntary cost-sharing. They are willing to take on the extra costs and risks, in order to increase their chances of receiving project funds.

There is no research to help determine who is right. Each grantee must decide whether or not to formalize its voluntary cost-sharing, and sometimes this must be done on a project-by-project basis.

No such decision is necessary if the grantor requires the grantee to share costs. In this case, the cost sharing is *mandatory,* and you must calculate the value of your contributions and show them in the budget.

In-Kind versus Out-of-Pocket Cost Sharing. Whether you are providing voluntary or mandatory cost-sharing, your contributions will be classified as *in-kind* (*noncash*) or *out-of-pocket* (*cash*). Grantors who require cost sharing usually specify whether cash, noncash, or a combination will be acceptable.

Noncash contributions are universally preferred by grantees, as this is the least expensive way to share costs. Essentially, you are providing resources that your organization already has available. Some portion of your executive director's time and the use of your agency's van or computer equipment are examples of in-kind contributions. Also, if you are not allowed to collect your full negotiated indirect-cost rate on a grant, you are usually allowed to show the difference between that and what you actually collect as cost sharing.

Two words of caution. First, it is important to be sure that the in-kind contribution you promise is not already included in your indirect-cost rate. If, for example, all of your executive director's time has been used to calculate your rate, it cannot be used as cost sharing also. Second, none of the in-kind contributions can come from federal sources, if you are promising cost sharing for a federal grant.

In-kind contributions do not necessarily have to come from your organization, however. Can you get a local school or church to donate space? Will consultants give you free assistance? Can you get project resources from other sources? All of these items can be considered in-kind contributions. Your organization will not have to pay an extra cent; however, the project budget will show thousands of dollars of in-kind contributions.

In contrast, out-of-pocket (cash) contributions will require someone to spend extra money. Either your organization or some other nonfederal organizations or individuals will be putting out real money, once you receive the grant. For example, your agency may offer to hire and pay for a half-time secretary or buy a piece of equipment if you get the grant. Other agencies or individuals you have enlisted to help will send you a check to help support other project costs.

Identification of Cost Sharing. If you are the fortunate person who must identify cost sharing, you need only be (1) creative, (2) knowledgeable, and (3) reasonable.

First, you must be able to imagine all sorts of resources that will be used in the project. These resources must cost your agency nothing extra yet be worth a great deal of money.

Second, you must understand *why* these resources are worth money. You must be sure that they will not be paid for by federal funds. Nor can they be items that are included in the calculation of your indirect-cost rate. It won't help you if the resources were purchased before the starting date of your project, either; cost sharing must occur during your official project period.

Once you have creatively identified resources and have knowledgeably ensured that they are legitimate cost-sharing items, you must attach a reasonable value. Usually, this is the market value (i.e., what you would have to pay if these resources weren't being given to you).

Federal Management Circular 73-3, "Cost Sharing on Federal Research,"[(5)] provides a good summary of the conditions under which cost sharing is required, the *general* kinds of cost sharing that are acceptable, and the ways in which you can reasonably identify the value of contributions.

More *specific* ideas about potential cost-sharing sources are contained in the cost-sharing checklist in Figure 5. This list is by no means all-inclusive; however, it does provide a starting point to give you ideas to build on.

To sum up the discussion so far, when you plan a grant budget, (1) ask for enough money for the project you plan to do; (2) match your request to the grantor's ability to pay; (3) never pad a budget by asking for unjustified amounts; yet (4) be sure to inflate your costs reasonably and cover uncertainties. It's important not to forget any costs, and those that may be included in budgets are (1) direct costs; (2) indirect costs; (3) program income; and (4) matching funds. Knowing all this, how does one begin to develop a budget?

How Do You Develop a Budget?

Calculating the proposal budget and completing the required forms can be the most difficult part of preparing a grant application for some project directors. They may have less trouble writing a detailed proposal on molecular biology than preparing a three-page budget. Acknowledging this, most organizations that apply for external funding provide assistance to project directors who are about to submit proposals. Depending on the type of organization, there may be a grants office, a development office, a contracts office, or some similar location where a prospective applicant can get help.

One does not learn the intricacies of proposal budgeting overnight. It takes instruction, practice at the elbow of an experienced individual, and assistance from the office or person at your organization who is responsible for approving budgets. This latter point is especially important. Novice budget-makers may unknowingly "give away the store" by omitting a key element from the budget. A newcomer to the arena most commonly overlooks fringe benefits, indirect costs, and money for his or her own salary. When one is advised that one's own salary must be included in the budget, a question heard many times is "Why should I include my salary? I'm getting paid anyway by the university (hospital or other

COST SHARING CHECKLIST

Which of these resources will be contributed to your project? Place a check (or fill in a dollar amount, if you prefer) in the appropriate column(s) beside each cost item which will be donated. To qualify as in-kind cost sharing, these resources must be: 1) used to carry out your project; 2) priced reasonably at market value; 3) excluded from your indirect cost rate calculation; 4) contributed during the period of your grant; 5) documented during your grant period as to receipt and value; and 6) derived from non-federal sources if the cost sharing is required by a federal agency.

POTENTIAL CONTRIBUTORS	
YOUR ORGANIZATION	General management, your department, other departments
OTHER ORGANIZATIONS	Businesses, state or local governments, schools, hospitals
GROUPS	Volunteer groups, professional groups, charities, social groups
INDIVIDUALS	Project staff, consultants, volunteers, project participants or clients

CONTRIBUTIONS	*YOUR ORGANIZATION*	*OTHER ORGANIZATIONS*	*GROUPS*	*INDIVIDUALS*	*OTHER*
SALARIES					
Project Director					
Project Technical Staff					
Project Clerical Staff					
Interns					
Graduate Students					
Student Assistants					
Work Study Students					
CETA Employees					
Volunteers					
Other, ______					
______					
BENEFITS Fringe benefits on above salaries at appropriate rates					
EQUIPMENT					
Scientific					
Industrial					
Office					
Vehicles					
Computers					
Other, ______					
______					
Maintenance, repair, and insurance on above					

Figure 5. Cost-sharing checklist.

agency)." Unintentional errors of omission such as that must be caught before the proposal is submitted.

Fortunately, there are eight relatively simple steps that project directors and grant administrators (or other fiscal officers), *working together,* can take to develop grant budgets.

CONTRIBUTIONS	YOUR ORGANIZATION	OTHER ORGANIZATIONS	GROUPS	INDIVIDUALS	OTHER
SUPPLIES					
Books and Periodicals					
Tests, Tapes, Records					
Other educational supplies, ______					
Office supplies					
Chemicals, food, animals					
Seedlings, trees					
Other research supplies					
Other, ______					
TRAVEL					
Mileage, airfare, train, bus					
Room and board					
Shipping/freight					
Other, ______					
OTHER DIRECT COSTS					
Advertising and promotion					
Alteration and renovation					
Child care					
Consultants					
Insurance					
Meals					
Postage					
Printing, duplicating					
Publication costs					
Registration fees (for workshops, conferences)					
Services (word processing, animal facilities, etc.)					
Space/Buildings (office, classroom, laboratories, meeting rooms, storage)					
Space/Land (agricultural, recreational)					
Subject payments					
Telephone (installation, long distance charges)					
Tuition					
Utilities					
Other resources, unique to your project, ______					
INDIRECT COSTS					
Indirect foregone on grantor funded portion of project					
Indirect foregone on your contributions					

Figure 5. (Continued)

Step One: Read the Grantor Program Guidelines and Application Forms

Both the project director and the grant administrator should take the time to review agency guidelines and application forms carefully. It is important to find out what kinds of costs may be charged to the grant and what kinds may not.

For example, certain grantor programs allow payment for instructional salaries yet do not reimburse grant participants for tuition costs. In some cases, full indirect costs may be recovered, and in others, there may be a limitation on indirect recovery (such as 8% of total direct costs or less).

In addition, the guidelines will explain what cost sharing, if any, is required, and how to categorize certain costs. For example, some grantors require consultant travel costs to be itemized under the "consultant" category, while other grantors specify that these costs must be included in the "travel" or "other-direct-cost" category.

Larocque, in his book *Consumerism, Federal Grants, and You,* emphasizes the importance of reviewing guidelines:

> The administrative agency [grantor] usually provides standard budget forms for all projects. Instructions on how to present information on such items as personnel, facilities, travel, direct, and indirect costs, and cost sharing, if applicable, are also included. The instructions should be studied with care and followed meticulously.(6)

There is valuable information in the guidelines; reading them at the beginning of your budget development process can save you time later.

Step Two: Estimate Grantor Funds Available

Once you know the kinds of costs the grantor will allow, it is important to find out approximately how much money will be available for your project. Sometimes the guidelines specify a maximum grant amount; sometimes you will need to contact grantor representatives or look at a list of last year's awards to identify a reasonable amount of money to ask for.

Step Three: Identify Resources Needed to Accomplish Project Goals

It is usually the project director who has the major responsibility for deciding what resources (personnel, equipment, travel, and so forth) will be needed to carry out the project successfully. Therefore, in connection with accomplishing this step of the budget preparation, it is extremely helpful to draft a major portion or all of the proposal.

Although this is not mandatory, the very act of writing the proposal crystallizes one's thoughts about the items that will be needed to conduct the project. What looked like a two-person project before the proposal writing began may, when put into writing, appear to be an impossible task for only two people.

Other revelations arise as the proposal nears completion, and it is wise to hold off identifying necessary resources until then.

Step Four: Price the Resources and Provide for Flexibility

After necessary resources are identified, they must be priced. There is remarkable consistency in what various grantor agencies consider allowable direct costs and what resources project directors need to conduct their projects successfully. Consequently, any budget for virtually any grant or contract, whether it be for research or an educational program, has costs for resources that fall into some or all of the following categories:

Personnel: salaries and wages
Fringe benefits: at specified rates
Equipment: purchase and/or rental
Materials and supplies: expendables
Travel and per diem: foreign, domestic, local mileage
Publication costs: page charges, reprints, brochures
Consultants and honoraria
Computer services: computer time, keypunching
Stipends and participant costs
Communications: telephone, postage
Other direct costs: duplicating, space rental, payment to research subjects, participant costs
Indirect costs: at the federally negotiated rate or other rate identified by grantor

In pricing these resources, it is important to work with current information. Salaries, fringe-benefit rates, indirect-cost rates, and other components of a budget change periodically, and that is why it is so important for project directors to work with grant administrators. Grant administrators can provide the updated rates; they can determine what inflationary factor to allow for.

"When you estimate inflation," a federal auditor advised the authors, "don't use gross averages like the Consumer Price Index. Instead, call and get telephone quotes or base your projections on historical costs or trends for *each specific cost item.* Show us you have done your homework." In other words, grantors will look more kindly on a 20% increase in travel costs that can be justified based on documented telephone quotes than on a 10% inflationary factor that is applied indiscriminately to all your budget categories.

There are many ways, in addition to telephone quotes, for you to get price information. Salary schedules, benefits schedules, and indirect-cost agreements are available at your agency to back up your projections. Catalogs, price lists, and invoices for recent purchases can be used to substantiate your requests for supplies and equipment. Many grantors publish per diem and mileage rates to be charged to grant projects. Suppliers will provide written quotes, if you need to include these with your proposal. Armed with this type of information, you will be able to defend any attacks on your cost estimates by grantor negotiators.

As you estimate the costs of your project, a key objective should be to retain *flexibility* in your budget. Therefore, whenever you are uncertain as to the exact amount of several resources you will need, budget so that you will have minimum difficulty adjusting your expenditures later.

For example, suppose you are unsure whether you will need 10 or 15 hours of computer time. And you do not know whether you will be able to get a quantity discount on the microscope you want, because this discount depends on several of your colleagues' getting their grants at the same time as you do. Your program officer has advised you to keep your budget low, however, so you don't want to budget the entire 15 hours of computer time *and* the full price of the equipment. You are aware that the conditions of your grant will allow you to transfer funds out of other categories into the computer-costs category; however, no transfers may be made into the equipment category without prior approval of the grantor.

In this case, you can retain flexibility by budgeting the full price of the microscopes in the equipment category and only 10 hours of computer time in the computer category. If you end up needing more computer time, you can transfer savings from the equipment discount (if you get it) or savings from other categories into the computer category. You will have retained maximum flexibility, as you won't have to wait a month or so to get written approval from the grantor to transfer funds.

Keeping in mind how you can get prices for resources and the importance of flexibility, what items do you price first?

In most budgets, the largest single resource, in terms of dollars, is personnel. Personnel costs, therefore, should usually be estimated first and given special care during budget preparation. How much time will be required by key individuals? How many (or how few) people do you need to conduct a top-quality project? Can you operate the project with talented people, such as postdoctoral associates or graduate students, who traditionally earn less than full-time regular staff?

These are important questions to answer, because the number of people you include in your budget, the amount of time they spend, and their relative pay scales will determine how large your budget will be. If the funding agency has placed a ceiling on the amount of money that you can ask for, it would be wise to use qualified but lower-paid people than regular staff, if possible.

Salaries for personnel must be estimated carefully and accurately and with the cushion for inflation mentioned earlier. For example, suppose a project director, Dr. Bright, is earning $20,000 now. He will probably be earning more than that by the time the award is received. So if you assume that Dr. Bright's salary next year will be *the same* as it is this year, you will probably have insufficient funds in your budget. This is, however, a common error among inexperienced proposal writers.

Let us assume that you're applying for a grant in January and that if you receive it, you expect to begin the project in September. Let us also assume that Dr. Bright will receive a 7% cost-of-living salary increase and a 5% merit (step) increase on September 1. Your worksheet in this example would then read:

DR. BRIGHT

$20,000	×	1.07	×	1.05	=	$22,470
(Current salary)		(Cost-of-living increase)		(Merit increase)		(Anticipated salary at project start date)

If Dr. Bright's salary had been budgeted at $20,000 (i.e., the amount he is earning in January), the grant would not have been adequate to pay his salary in September. It would have been $2,470 too low. In addition, the grant would not have included the fringe benefits and indirect costs associated with the $2,470. In this case, the error of omission—that is, not accounting for inflation and a merit increase—could have cost your organization as much as $5,000!

Because personnel costs are typically subject to inflation and changes in salary rates, it is especially important to estimate them carefully. Most experienced grant budgeters prepare a personnel worksheet before preparing the formal budget documents. A sample worksheet is provided in Figure 6. This worksheet is for your proposal file and will be used after you receive the grant award; the worksheet is not submitted to the grantor with your proposal.

Once you have estimated personnel costs (salaries and benefits and, if appropriate, associated indirect costs), it is a relatively simple matter to price the rest of the resources you will need.

Step Five: Prepare the Management Budget

After gathering information in Steps One through Four of the budget development process, you are now ready to put it all together—to design your official grant budget. The hard work has been done, and the easy part comes next.

What should your budget look like? Remember that your budget will be a management tool that will be referred to again and again during the project. With this in mind, it is important to begin preparing it in a format that:

1. The funding agency can understand
2. You can work with after the award is received
3. Will help you and the sponsor monitor the progress of the project

The budget will show who will be conducting the project, how long it will take, and the resources that will be needed. All this information will also appear in the proposal itself, but the budget itemizes the costs.

Since your format must be one that the funding agency can understand, now is the time to refer back to the program guidelines and application form that

BUDGET WORKSHEET FOR SALARIES & BENEFITS

Dates	Budget Position & Occupant's Name	Salary Classification	Current Salary/Mo.	Increase for Inflation (7%)	Merit or Promotion	Budgeted Salary	Benefits Rate	Budgeted Benefits
12/20/79	Director Ben Bright	Soc. Worker Step 3	$1,500					
7/1/80				$1,605				
10/1/80- 11/30/80	. . . .	. . . .	. . . .	(2 mos. @ $1,605)	. . . .	$3,210		
12/1/80		Soc. Worker Step 4	$1,600	$1,712	$1,712			
12/1/80- 6/30/81	. . . .	. . . .	. . . .	. . . .	(7 mos. @ $1,712) . . .	11,984		
7/1/81			$1,712	$1,832				
7/1/81- 9/30/81	. . . .	. . . .	. . . .	(3 mos. @ $1,832)	. . . .	5,496		
						$20,690	20%	$4,138
12/20/79	Asst. Director Henry Hardworker	Jr. Soc. Worker Top Step (5)	$1,200					
7/1/80				$1,284				
10/1/80- 6/30/81	. . . .	. . . .	. . . .	(9 mos. @ $1,284)	. . . .	$11,556		
7/1/81			$1,284	$1,374				
7/1/81- 9/30/81	. . . .	. . . .	. . . .	(3 mos. @ $1,374)	. . . .	4,122		
						$15,678	10%	$1,568

PREPARED BY: *Bobby Budget*　　　　DATE: *12/20/79*

Figure 6. Sample personnel worksheet.

PART III - BUDGET INFORMATION

SECTION A - BUDGET SUMMARY

GRANT PROGRAM, FUNCTION OR ACTIVITY (a)	FEDERAL CATALOG NO. (b)	ESTIMATED UNOBLIGATED FUNDS		NEW OR REVISED BUDGET		
		FEDERAL (c)	NON-FEDERAL (d)	FEDERAL (e)	NON-FEDERAL (f)	TOTAL (g)
1.		$	$	$	$	$
2.						
3.						
4.						
5. *TOTALS*		$	$	$	$	$

SECTION B - BUDGET CATEGORIES

6. OBJECT CLASS CATEGORIES	GRANT PROGRAM, FUNCTION OR ACTIVITY				TOTAL
	(1)	(2)	(3)	(4)	(5)
a. PERSONNEL	$	$	$	$	$
b. FRINGE BENEFITS					
c. TRAVEL					
d. EQUIPMENT					
e. SUPPLIES					
f. CONTRACTUAL					
g. CONSTRUCTION					
h. OTHER					
i. TOTAL DIRECT CHARGES					
j. INDIRECT CHARGES					
k. *TOTALS*	$	$	$	$	$
7. PROGRAM INCOME	$	$	$	$	$

HEW-608T

Figure 7. Standard application budget form (HEW 608-T). This standardized application budget form is used to apply for billions of dollars of federal grants. Perhaps the most frequently used budget form, it is required by many Department of Education and Department of Health and Human Services programs. Notice that there is no room for budget details provided.

the granting agency has provided. In most cases, the form is more of a summary than a detailed management budget, but it will shed light on the kinds of costs that are allowable and how these costs should be presented. So, the first step in designing a budget is to look at the form you will be working with and then organize a creative and complete budget (with room for details) on separate sheets of paper. *Your detailed budget should follow the major categories in the form provided.*

For example, look at the budget application form used by many federal agencies (HEW 608-T) in Figure 7. Under "Section B–Budget Categories," notice that there is only one line for each major category. These categories are Personnel, Fringe Benefits, Travel, Equipment, Supplies, Contractual, Construction, Other, Total Direct Charges, Indirect Charges, Totals, and Program Income.

THE EXTRA SPECIAL MASSAGE PROJECT

PROPOSED BUDGET

October 1, 1980, to September 30, 1981

	Funding Requested from the Give Grants Agency	Do Good Institution Contribution
a. PERSONNEL		
1. Principal Investigator Ben Bright, Ph.D. 100% Time for 12 Months	$10,345	$10,345
2. Research Associate Henry Hardworker 100% Time for 12 Months	15,678	
3. Massage Technicians (4) To Be Named 100% Time for 6 Months	30,000	
4. Secretary Sallye Super 50% Time for 12 Months	6,000	
	$62,023	$10,345
b. FRINGE BENEFITS		
1. Regular Positions (a.1) $20,690 @ 20%	$ 2,069	$ 2,069
2. Temporary Positions (a.2,3,4) $51,678 @ 10%	5,168	
	$ 7,237	$ 2,069
c. TRAVEL		
1. Local Mileage 100 mi./wk. @ 17¢ mi. x 50 wks.	$ 850	
2. Airfares Los Angeles/Washington, D.C./Return 2 @ $500	1,000	
3. Per Diem 2 persons x 5 das. @ $50/da.	500	
	$ 2,350	
d. EQUIPMENT		
1. Model XYZ Bak-Massagers 4 @ $500	$ 2,000	
2. Model EXTR Reklnr Chairs 4 @ $200	800	
	$ 2,800	

Figure 8. Sample management budget.

	Funding Requested from the Give Grants Agency	Do Good Institution Contribution
e. SUPPLIES		
1. Utility Strength Lotions 10 gallons @ $30/ea.	$ 300	
2. Office Supplies	150	$ 150
	$ 450	$ 150
f. CONTRACTUAL	-0-	-0-
g. CONSTRUCTION	-0-	-0-
h. OTHER		
1. Subject Payments 400 @ $5	$ 2,000	
2. Communications (Telephone, Postage) 12 mos. @ $50	300	$ 300
3. Physical Fitness Consultant Jack Back, Ph.D. 4 days @ $100	400	
4. Child Care Costs 400 hrs. @ $2/hr.	800	
5. Computer Costs 2 hrs. @ $200	200	200
6. Publication Costs Professional Journal Page Charges 8 pages @ $70	560	
	$ 4,260	$ 500
i. TOTAL DIRECT CHARGES (a. - h.)	$79,120	$13,064
j. INDIRECT CHARGES		
1. Indirect Costs Requested 8% of $79,120 (Total Direct Charges)	6,330	
2. Indirect Costs Foregone 50% of $72,368 (Salaries & Wages) less Indirect Charges Requested		29,854
k. TOTALS	$85,450	$42,918

SUMMARY

Give Grants Agency Funds	$ 85,450	66.7%
Do Good Institution Contribution	42,918	33.3%
Total Project Costs	$128,368	100.0%

Figure 8. (Continued)

Therefore, whenever you are preparing a management budget that will be transferred to the HEW 608-T form, organize your detailed budget so that all costs are itemized under *these same major categories.*

A sample management budget, designed to complement this form, is contained in Figure 8. The Do Good Institution is asking the Give Grants Agency for $85,450 for a project to provide massage services to experimental and control groups of subjects. The project director, Dr. Bright, will try two distinctly different methods of massaging (one new, one traditional) and hopes to identify which method is most effective in relieving lower back pain. The salaries of the project director and the research associate have been calculated on the personnel worksheet (Figure 6).

There are several assumptions on which this budget is based. First, the funding agency will require a minimum $33\frac{1}{3}\%$ match. Therefore, the Do Good Institution is promising to contribute $42,918. The contributions are shown in the budget column entitled "Do Good Institution Contribution." For example, Dr. Bright will receive his full salary of $20,690. Half of it is being requested from the Give Grants Agency; the other half will be paid by Do Good. Therefore, $10,345 is shown in the budget under "Funding Requested from the Give Grants Agency"; $10,345 is shown as "Do Good Institution Contribution." Similarly, the costs of benefits on this salary are split between the two columns.

A second assumption is that the Give Grants Agency restricts indirect charges to no more than 8% of total direct costs. Since the Do Good Institution's negotiated federal indirect-cost rate is 50% of salaries and wages, the difference between its federal rate (50% S&W) and the amount it is permitted to collect (8% TDC) is offered as cost sharing.

If no cost sharing had been required, the budget would have looked the same, except there would have been no right-hand column entitled "Do Good Institution Contribution." And if there had been no restrictions on indirect cost recovery, the 50% S&W rate would have been used.

Notice how the major categories and even type styles (i.e., capital letters) in the sample management budget match those on the HEW 608-T form. Even the lettering (a-k) of major categories is the same. By organizing your detailed budget to match the agency's budget forms, you will be able to transfer the cost estimates more easily; grantor reviewers will appreciate your tailoring cost details to fit their categories.

The sample management budget contained in Figure 8 is designed specifically for the HEW 608-T form. *When other grantor forms are used, your management budget should be designed to match their major categories, type styles, and numbering or lettering.* If no form is provided by the sponsors, the needs of the project will determine the budget categories to use. You can be creative in designing your own management budget, without needing to match its components to standardized application forms. Or if you don't feel particularly creative, the model shown in Figure 8 is appropriate for almost any proposal. Also, there are a number of publications with information on budgeting techniques.[7-10]

No matter what management budget format you use, it can be a valuable tool six or eight or nine months into the future, when the award is made. It will not be necessary to spend time trying to remember what you had in mind when the budget was originally prepared.

Step Six: Transfer Management Budget Costs to Grantor Budget Forms

This step assumes that the grantor agency requires you to complete a budget form. Most grantors do. Samples of budget forms to expect when one applies to the U.S. Department of Education, the National Science Foundation, the National Institutes of Health or responds to an RFP from one of a variety of federal agencies are contained in Figures 9, 10, 11, and 12.

PART III - BUDGET INFORMATION

SECTION A - BUDGET SUMMARY

GRANT PROGRAM, FUNCTION OR ACTIVITY (a)	FEDERAL CATALOG NO. (b)	ESTIMATED UNOBLIGATED FUNDS		NEW OR REVISED BUDGET		
		FEDERAL (c)	NON-FEDERAL (d)	FEDERAL (e)	NON-FEDERAL (f)	TOTAL (g)
1. Health Research	13.XXX	$ NA	$ NA	$ 85,450	$ 42,918	$ 128,368
2.						
3.						
4.						
5. *TOTALS*		$	$	$ 85,450	$ 42,918	$ 128,368

SECTION B - BUDGET CATEGORIES

6. OBJECT CLASS CATEGORIES	GRANT PROGRAM, FUNCTION OR ACTIVITY				TOTAL
	(1)	(2)	(3)	(4)	(5)
a. PERSONNEL	$ 62,023	$	$	$	$ 62,023
b. FRINGE BENEFITS	7,237				7,237
c. TRAVEL	2,350				2,350
d. EQUIPMENT	2,800				2,800
e. SUPPLIES	450				450
f. CONTRACTUAL	-0-				-0-
g. CONSTRUCTION	-0-				-0-
h. OTHER	4,260				4,260
i. TOTAL DIRECT CHARGES	79,120				79,120
j. INDIRECT CHARGES	6,330				6,330
k. *TOTALS*	$ 85,450	$	$	$	$ 85,450
7. PROGRAM INCOME	$ -0-	$	$	$	$ -0-

HEW-608T

Figure 9. Sample U.S. Department of Education budget form (HEW 608-T). This budget form is commonly used by the U.S. Department of Education and Department of Health and Human Services programs. Notice that space is provided (Section A, Column f) to show grantee contributions. Cost estimates from the Extra Special Massage Project management budget (Figure 8) have been transferred to this form. Notice how easily this could be done because the major categories in the management budget match those in the HEW 608-T form exactly.

SUMMARY PROPOSAL BUDGET

FOR NSF USE ONLY						
ORGANIZATION Do Good Institution U.S.A.	PROPOSAL NO.			DURATION (MONTHS) Proposed	Granted	
PRINCIPAL INVESTIGATOR/PROJECT DIRECTOR Ben Bright, Ph.D.	AWARD NO.					
A. SENIOR PERSONNEL: PI/PD, Co-PI's, Faculty and Other Senior Associates (List each separately with title; A.6. show number in brackets)	NSF FUNDED PERSON-MOS. CAL.	ACAD	SUMR	FUNDS REQUESTED BY PROPOSER	FUNDS GRANTED BY NSF (IF DIFFERENT)	
1. Dr. Ben Bright, Principal Investigator	6			$ 10,345	$	
2. Dr. H. Hardworker, Research Associate	12			15,678		
3.						
4.						
5. ( ) OTHERS (LIST INDIVIDUALLY ON BUDGET EXPLANATION PAGE)						
6. (2) TOTAL SENIOR PERSONNEL (1-5)	18			26,023		
B. OTHER PERSONNEL (SHOW NUMBERS IN BRACKETS)						
1. ( ) POST DOCTORAL ASSOCIATES						
2. ( ) OTHER PROFESSIONALS (TECHNICIAN, PROGRAMMER, ETC.)						
3. ( ) GRADUATE STUDENTS						
4. ( ) UNDERGRADUATE STUDENTS						
5. (1) SECRETARIAL-CLERICAL				6,000		
6. (4) OTHER Massage Technicians				30,000		
TOTAL SALARIES AND WAGES (A+B)				62,023		
C. FRINGE BENEFITS (IF CHARGED AS DIRECT COSTS)				7,237		
TOTAL SALARIES, WAGES AND FRINGE BENEFITS (A+B+C)				69,260		
D. PERMANENT EQUIPMENT (LIST ITEM AND DOLLAR AMOUNT FOR EACH ITEM EXCEEDING $1,000; ITEMS OVER $10,000 REQUIRE CERTIFICATION) (4) Model XYZ Bak-Massagers @ $500 each (4) Model EXTR Reklnr Chairs @ $200 each						
TOTAL PERMANENT EQUIPMENT				2,800		
E. TRAVEL 1. DOMESTIC (INCL. CANADA AND U.S. POSSESSIONS)				2,350		
2. FOREIGN				-0-		
F. PARTICIPANT SUPPORT COSTS 1. STIPENDS $ 2. TRAVEL 3. SUBSISTENCE 4. OTHER				-0-		
TOTAL PARTICIPANT COSTS				-0-		
G. OTHER DIRECT COSTS						
1. MATERIALS AND SUPPLIES				450		
2. PUBLICATION COSTS/PAGE CHARGES				560		
3. CONSULTANT SERVICES				400		
4. COMPUTER (ADPE) SERVICES				200		
5. SUBCONTRACTS				-0-		
6. OTHER				3,100		
TOTAL OTHER DIRECT COSTS				4,710		
H. TOTAL DIRECT COSTS (A THROUGH G)				79,120		
I. INDIRECT COSTS (SPECIFY) 50% of on-site salaries and wages						
TOTAL INDIRECT COSTS				31,012		
J. TOTAL DIRECT AND INDIRECT COSTS (H + I)				110,132		
K. RESIDUAL FUNDS (IF FOR FURTHER SUPPORT OF CURRENT PROJECTS GPM 252 AND 253)				-0-		
L. AMOUNT OF THIS REQUEST (J) OR (J MINUS K)				$110,132	$	
PI/PD TYPED NAME & SIGNATURE*	DATE	FOR NSF USE ONLY				
		INDIRECT COST RATE VERIFICATION				
INST. REP. TYPED NAME & SIGNATURE*	DATE	Date Checked	Date of Rate Sheet	Initials - DGC	Program	

NSF FORM 1030 (8-80) SUPERSEDES ALL PREVIOUS EDITIONS

Figure 10. Sample National Science Foundation budget form (NSF 1030). This budget is used exclusively by the National Science Foundation, which awards approximately $1 billion per year. Cost estimates from the Extra Special Massage Project management budget (Figure 8) have been transferred to this form with two changes. No cost sharing is shown here, as cost sharing is not required. In addition, the full indirect-cost rate has been charged. Notice the poor "fit" between the management budget and this form. Costs could have been transferred more easily had the management budget been designed with categories "A. Senior Personnel" through "J. Total Direct and Indirect Costs."

PRINCIPAL INVESTIGATOR/PROGRAM DIRECTOR:

DETAILED BUDGET FOR FIRST 12 MONTH BUDGET PERIOD DIRECT COSTS ONLY	FROM 10/1/80	THROUGH 9/30/81
	DOLLAR AMOUNT REQUESTED *(Omit cents)*	

PERSONNEL *(Applicant organization only) (See instructions)*

NAME	TITLE OF POSITION	TIME/EFFORT %	TIME/EFFORT Hours per Week	SALARY	FRINGE BENEFITS	TOTALS
B. Bright, Ph.D.	Principal Investigator	50	20	$10,345	$2,069	$12,414
H. Hardworker	Research Associate	100	40	15,678	1,568	17,246
To be named	Massage Technician	50	20	7,500	750	8,250
" "	" "	50	20	7,500	750	8,250
" "	" "	50	20	7,500	750	8,250
" "	" "	50	20	7,500	750	8,250
" "	" "	50	20	6,000	600	6,600
	SUBTOTALS →			62,023	7,237	69,260

CONSULTANT COSTS *(See instructions)* Jack Back, Ph.D. (Physical Fitness), 4 days @ $100/day		400
EQUIPMENT *(Itemize)* Model XYZ Bak-Massagers, 4 @ $500 each Model EXTR Reklnr Chairs, 4 @ $200 each		2,800
SUPPLIES *(Itemize by category)* Utility Strength Lotions, 10 gallons @ $30 Office supplies ($150)		450
TRAVEL	DOMESTIC	2,350
	FOREIGN	
PATIENT CARE COSTS	INPATIENT	
	OUTPATIENT	
ALTERATIONS AND RENOVATIONS *(Itemize by category)*		
CONTRACTUAL OR THIRD PARTY COSTS *(See instructions)*		
OTHER EXPENSES *(Itemize by category)* Subject payments, 400 @ $5 Communications, 12 mos. @ $25 Child care costs, 400 hrs. @ $2 Computer costs, 1 hr. @ $200 Publication costs, 8 pages @ $70		3,860
TOTAL DIRECT COSTS *(Also enter on page 1, item 8)* →		$ 79,120

PHS-398
Rev. 10/79

Figure 11. Sample National Institutes of Health budget form (PHS 398). This form is used to apply for the billions of dollars awarded annually by the National Institutes of Health. Cost estimates from the Extra Special Massage Project management budget (Figure 8) have been transferred to this form. Notice how many recalculations had to be made for the management budget to "fit" this form. For example, benefits had to be calculated for each position separately.

CONTRACT PRICING PROPOSAL (RESEARCH AND DEVELOPMENT)		Office of Management and Budget Approval No. 29-RO184	
This form is for use when *(i)* submission of cost or pricing data (see FPR 1-3.807-3) is required and *(ii)* substitution for the Optional Form 59 is authorized by the contracting officer.		PAGE NO. 1	NO. OF PAGES 2
NAME OF OFFEROR: DO GOOD INSTITUTION	SUPPLIES AND/OR SERVICES TO BE FURNISHED: Research on massage methods to relieve lower back pain		
HOME OFFICE ADDRESS: U.S.A.			
DIVISION(S) AND LOCATION(S) WHERE WORK IS TO BE PERFORMED: Los Angeles, CA	TOTAL AMOUNT OF PROPOSAL: $ 110,132	GOV'T SOLICITATION NO. 80-001	

DETAIL DESCRIPTION OF COST ELEMENTS

			EST COST ($)	TOTAL EST COST[1]	REFERENCE[2]
1. DIRECT MATERIAL *(Itemize on Exhibit A)*					
a. PURCHASED PARTS					
b. SUBCONTRACTED ITEMS					
c. OTHER—*(1)* RAW MATERIAL					
(2) YOUR STANDARD COMMERCIAL ITEMS					
(3) INTERDIVISIONAL TRANSFERS *(At other than cost)*					
TOTAL DIRECT MATERIAL				-0-	
2. MATERIAL OVERHEAD[3] *(Rate %X$ base=)*					
3. DIRECT LABOR *(Specify)*	ESTIMATED HOURS	RATE/HOUR	EST COST ($)		
Principal Investigator	1,040	11.9365	12,414		
Research Associate	2,080	8.2913	17,246		
Massage Technicians	4,160	7.9327	33,000		
Secretary	1,040	6.3462	6,600		
TOTAL DIRECT LABOR				$69,260	(1)
4. LABOR OVERHEAD *(Specify Department or Cost Center)*[3]	O.H. RATE	X BASE =	EST COST ($)		
	50%	62,023	31,012		
TOTAL LABOR OVERHEAD				31,012	
5. SPECIAL TESTING *(Including field work at Government installations)*			EST COST ($)		
TOTAL SPECIAL TESTING					
6. SPECIAL EQUIPMENT *(If direct charge) (Itemize on Exhibit A)*				2,800	(2)
7. TRAVEL *(If direct charge) (Give details on attached Schedule)*			EST COST ($)		
a. TRANSPORTATION			1,850		
b. PER DIEM OR SUBSISTENCE			500		
TOTAL TRAVEL				2,350	(3)
8. CONSULTANTS *(Identify—purpose—rate)*			EST COST ($)		
Physical Fitness, 4 days @ $100			400		
TOTAL CONSULTANTS				400	
9. OTHER DIRECT COSTS *(Itemize on Exhibit A)*				4,310	(4)
10. *TOTAL DIRECT COST AND OVERHEAD*				110,132	
11. GENERAL AND ADMINISTRATIVE EXPENSE *(Rate % of cost element Nos.)*[3]					
12. ROYALTIES[4]					
13. *TOTAL ESTIMATED COST*				$110,132	
14. FEE OR PROFIT					
15. *TOTAL ESTIMATED COST AND FEE OR PROFIT*				$110,132	

OPTIONAL FORM 60

Figure 12. Sample contract budget form (Optional Form 60). This form is used to apply for many government contracts. Cost estimates from the Extra Special Massage Project management budget (Figure 8) have been transferred to this form, except that no cost sharing is shown above and full indirect costs are requested. Notice how poorly the management budget "fits" this form. In general, this form is appropriate for manufactured goods and not for services or research. It must be used, however, so it is important to have a management budget to serve as back up.

This proposal is submitted for use in connection with and in response to *(Describe RFP, etc.)*

80-001 Health Research

and reflects our best estimates as of this date, in accordance with the Instructions to Offerors and the Footnotes which follow.

TYPED NAME AND TITLE	SIGNATURE
Anne A. Administrator Executive Director	Anne A. Administrator

NAME OF FIRM	DATE OF SUBMISSION
DO GOOD INSTITUTION	3/1/80

EXHIBIT A—SUPPORTING SCHEDULE *(Specify. If more space is needed, use reverse)*

COST EL NO.	ITEM DESCRIPTION *(See footnote 5)*	EST COST *($)*
3.	(1) The labor rates include benefits of 20% on the	
	Principal Investigator's salary and 10% on the	
	remaining salaries.	
6.	(2) Model XYZ Bak-Massagers, 4 @ $500	$2,000
	Model EXTR Reklnr Chairs, 4 @ $200	800
7.	(3) Local mileage, 100 mi. wk. @ 17¢/mi. x 50 wks.	850
	Airfares (Los Angeles/Washington, D.C.), 2 @ $500	1,000
	Per diem, 5 days x 2 persons @ $50/day	500
9.	(4) Utility strength lotions, 10 gallons @ $30	300
	Office supplies	150
	Subject payments, 400 @ $5	2,000
	Communications, 12 mos. @ $25	300
	Child-care costs, 400 hrs. @ $2	800
	Computer costs, 1 hr. @ $200	200
	Publication costs (professional journal), 8 pages @ $70	560

I. HAS ANY EXECUTIVE AGENCY OF THE UNITED STATES GOVERNMENT PERFORMED ANY REVIEW OF YOUR ACCOUNTS OR RECORDS IN CONNECTION WITH ANY OTHER GOVERNMENT PRIME CONTRACT OR SUBCONTRACT WITHIN THE PAST TWELVE MONTHS?

☐ YES ☒ NO *(If yes, identify below.)*

NAME AND ADDRESS OF REVIEWING OFFICE AND INDIVIDUAL	TELEPHONE NUMBER/EXTENSION

II. WILL YOU REQUIRE THE USE OF ANY GOVERNMENT PROPERTY IN THE PERFORMANCE OF THIS PROPOSED CONTRACT?

☐ YES ☒ NO *(If yes, identify on reverse or separate page)*

III. DO YOU REQUIRE GOVERNMENT CONTRACT FINANCING TO PERFORM THIS PROPOSED CONTRACT?

☒ YES ☐ NO *(If yes, identify.)*: ☒ ADVANCE PAYMENTS ☐ PROGRESS PAYMENTS OR ☐ GUARANTEED LOANS

IV. DO YOU NOW HOLD ANY CONTRACT *(Or, do you have any independently financed (IR&D) projects)* FOR THE SAME OR SIMILAR WORK CALLED FOR BY THIS PROPOSED CONTRACT?

☐ YES ☒ NO *(If yes, identify.)*:

V. DOES THIS COST SUMMARY CONFORM WITH THE COST PRINCIPLES SET FORTH IN AGENCY REGULATIONS?

☒ YES ☐ NO *(If no, explain on reverse or separate page)*

OPTIONAL FORM 60

Figure 12. (Continued)

Each of these forms has been completed using the "Extra Special Massage Project" management budget developed in Step Five. You can see how easy it was to transfer the management budget information to form HEW 608-T, since the cost categories match exactly. In contrast, the massage project's budgeted costs had to be reorganized to fit into the NSF, NIH, and Optional 60 forms.

Because there was no cost sharing required on these last three forms, no information about the Do Good Institution's contributions is shown. Also, indirect charges are calculated at the negotiated rate of 50% salaries and wages, since the NSF, NIH, and agencies soliciting contracts normally allow full indirect recovery.

Step Seven: Prepare Specialized Budgets as Appropriate

Once you have completed your detailed management budget and transferred the cost estimates to grantor forms, it may be appropriate for you to prepare additional specialized budgets, such as (1) functional budgets; (2) optional budgets; or (3) calendar projections. Sometimes, the grantor requires these budgets as additional detail to support your management budget. In other cases, you may want to submit these extra budgets to strengthen your case during negotiation, as evidence (for the grantors) of how thoroughly you have planned, or merely to assist in project management after you receive the award.

Functional Budgets. One specialized method of presenting a budget, less commonly used but sometimes required, is the *functional budget.* That is, in addition to preparing the budget as shown on the previous pages, the applicant must show how much money in each category (e.g., personnel, travel, supplies) will be spent for each task outlined in the proposal.

Let us take as an example a project that proposes to (1) conduct a literature search; (2) design massage methods; (3) apply the methods to subjects; (4) collect data; (5) analyze the data; (6) evaluate the project; and (7) disseminate results. This project can be divided into seven discrete tasks. A funding agency may require the applicant, or the applicant may choose, to show the amount of personnel funds, travel funds, supply funds, etc., that will be expended in each of the tasks identified.

Preparing such a functional budget is not easy. Indeed, it requires a great deal of planning and thought about the use of resources. This last fact is perhaps the functional budget's greatest asset. In addition to helping the reviewer and the future program officer to understand the project more thoroughly, the functional budget forces the prospective project director to think very carefully about his or her time line, about the use of staff, and about which travel is really important and when.

Further, this exercise can save the project money and help to stretch the grant dollars when they arrive. The very act of preparing a budget, broken down by task, may shed light on when to hire certain people and when it is best to delay hiring. Personnel who may not be needed until the end of the project should not be hired at the beginning and carried for the duration. Although this seems simple enough to understand, many rushed proposal writers, straining to meet a deadline, may not think of it. The act of itemizing their resources, by task, causes the light to shine.

What does a functional budget look like? An example is shown in Figure 13. Its purpose is not to outline all the nuances of a functional budget; it is presented only to introduce the reader to the format of such a budget. The example is based on the Extra Special Massage Project discussed previously in this chapter.

This example of a hypothetical functional budget illustrates in a straightforward way the format to be used. It is also easy to see how such a budget can be an effective management tool for the project director as the project progresses. Note that this is not *the* budget for the project. When a functional budget is prepared, it is done in *addition* to a conventional budget of the type presented earlier.

Although there are many advantages to a functional budget, there is one disadvantage that must be considered. If you identify how much it will cost you for each project task, you face the danger that during negotiation the grantors will want to eliminate one or more tasks and cut your budget accordingly.

Take the Extra Special Massage Project, for example. Suppose the Give Grants Agency decided not to fund the dissemination task and decreased the budget by $7,116. What could happen to Secretary Super? Her salary would have to be reduced considerably during the last several months of the grant. Yet she would still be needed for other project tasks. Might she go looking for another job? You can see what havoc might occur in this case.

"Don't offer a functional budget," a federal program officer warned the authors, "unless your project lends itself to *separate tasks* that are carried out by *different employees*."

The functional budget is a valuable tool, but it must be used with care.

Optional Budgets. Another specialized budget is the *optional budget.* Actually when you prepare an optional budget you are offering the grantor a choice: (1) "Take my bare-bones budget as a minimum response to your program guidelines," or (2) "You can have these additional terrific services or products for X dollars more."

For example, suppose Dr. Bright had kept his budget low (using only 400 subjects) for competitive purposes. Yet he felt he could do a superior research project by working with 800 subjects. Also, there was the chance that the Give Grants Agency would have some end-of-the-year money available and thus be able to afford to make a larger grant. In this case, Dr. Bright could prepare an optional budget, pricing the costs for 800 subjects, as shown in Figure 14.

This sample optional-budget presentation assumes that no cost sharing is required and that full indirect-cost recovery will be allowed. Therefore, the *total* Option 1 budget request varies from the management budget in Figure 8.

Offering the grantors optional budgets can be an excellent strategy to (1) remain competitive with a low bid; (2) have a request for funding officially submitted in case the grantor has extra funds available; (3) respond to a vague RFP; or (4) be competitive when it is impossible to determine in advance how much money the grantors plan to award.

Holtz stressed the importance of the optional budget as a strategy to use in applying for government contracts: "It gives you the best of all worlds in some ways, giving the customer a low price, if that's what he wants, but keeping the door open to spend more if he chooses to."[11]

Calendar Projections. Yet another form that you may transfer your management budget costs into is a *calendar projection.* In this case, you itemize the costs as they will occur throughout the grant period. Usually, this is done

THE EXTRA SPECIAL MASSAGE PROJECT

FUNCTIONAL BUDGET

October 1, 1980, to September 30, 1981

	SEARCH LITERATURE	DESIGN MASSAGE METHODS	APPLY METHODS TO SUBJECTS	COLLECT DATA	ANALYZE DATA	EVALUATE PROJECT	DISSEMINATE RESULTS
PERSONNEL							
Principal Investigator	$1,034	$4,139			$2,069	$2,069	$1,034
Research Associate	784	1,567	$ 784	$7,839	2,353	1,567	784
Massage Technicians			30,000				
Secretary	600	600	600	1,200	600	1,200	1,200
	$2,418	$6,306	$31,384	$9,039	$5,022	$4,836	$3,018
FRINGE BENEFITS							
Regular @ 20%	206	829			414	414	206
Temporary @ 10%	138	218	3,138	904	295	277	198
TRAVEL							
Local Mileage			850				
Airfares							1,000
Per Diem							500
EQUIPMENT							
Massagers			2,000				
Chairs			800				
SUPPLIES							
Lotions			300				
Office	25			50		25	50
OTHER							
Subject Payments			2,000				
Communications	50	50	50	50		25	75
Consultant		200	100			100	
Child Care			800				
Computer					200		
Publication							560
TOTAL DIRECT CHARGES	$2,837	$7,603	$41,422	$10,043	$5,931	$5,677	$5,607
INDIRECT CHARGES On site @ 50% of Salaries	1,209	3,153	15,692	4,520	2,511	2,418	1,509
TOTALS	$4,046	$10,756	$57,114	$14,563	$8,442	$8,095	$7,116

Figure 13. Sample functional budget.

THE EXTRA SPECIAL MASSAGE PROJECT

OPTIONAL BUDGETS

October 1, 1980, to September 30, 1981

	OPTION 1 (400 Subjects)	OPTION 2 (800 Subjects)
PERSONNEL		
Principal Investigator	$10,345	$10,345
Research Associate	15,678	15,678
Massage Technicians	30,000	45,000
Secretary	6,000	9,000
	$62,023	$80,023
FRINGE BENEFITS		
Regular Positions (a.1) @ 20%	2,069	2,069
Temporary Positions (a.2,3,4) @ 10%	5,168	6,968
TRAVEL		
Local Mileage @ 17¢/mi.	850	1,700
Airfares (LA/WDC) @ $500	1,000	1,000
Per Diem @ $50/da.	500	500
EQUIPMENT		
Model XYZ Bak-Massagers @ $500	2,000	3,000
Model EXTR ReKlnr Chairs @ $200	800	1,200
SUPPLIES		
Utility Strength Lotions @ $30/gallon	300	600
Office Supplies	150	225
OTHER		
Subject Payments @ $5	2,000	4,000
Communications	300	450
Consultant @ $100/da.	400	400
Child Care Costs @ $2/hr.	800	1,600
Computer Costs @ $200/hr.	200	300
Publication Costs @ $70/journal page	560	560
TOTAL DIRECT CHARGES	$ 79,120	$104,595
INDIRECT CHARGES		
On site @ 50% of Salaries	31,012	40,012
TOTALS	$110,132	$144,607

Figure 14. **Sample optional budgets.**

on a month-by-month basis (as shown in Figure 15). Occasionally, costs may be projected on a weekly or other basis.

The advantages of calendar projections are that they can help you to plan more thoroughly for your project. You may find that certain personnel costs can be postponed until later in the grant period. You will also be able to plan for appropriate cash flow throughout the project. These projections are valuable in helping you to monitor fiscal performance during your project.

By June, have you spent as much money as you should have? If not, why not? If too much money has been spent, how can you reduce future spending so that your grant will not be overexpended? These and many similar questions are

THE EXTRA SPECIAL MASSAGE PROJECT CALENDAR PROJECTION OF COSTS
1980-81

	October	November	December	January	February
PERSONNEL					
Principal Investigator	$ 862	$ 862	$ 862	$ 862	$ 862
Research Associate	1,306	1,306	1,306	1,306	1,306
Massage Technicians				5,000	5,000
Secretary	500	500	500	500	500
Total Personnel	$2,668	$2,668	$2,668	$7,668	$7,668
FRINGE BENEFITS					
Regular Positions @ 20%	172	172	172	172	172
Temporary Positions @ 10%	181	181	181	681	681
TRAVEL					
Local Mileage				141	141
Airfares					
Per Diem					
EQUIPMENT					
Bak-Massagers			2,000		
ReKlnr Chairs			800		
SUPPLIES					
Lotions			300		
Office	50				50
OTHER					
Subject Payments				334	334
Communication	25	25	25	25	25
Consultant		200		100	
Child Care Costs				134	134
Computer Costs					
Publication Costs					
TOTAL DIRECT CHARGES	$3,096	$3,246	$6,146	$9,255	$9,205
INDIRECT CHARGES					
On site rate, 50% of Salaries	1,334	1,334	1,334	3,834	3,834
TOTALS	$4,430	$4,580	$7,480	$13,089	$13,039

Figure 15. Sample calendar projection of costs.

relatively easy to answer if you have a calendar projection of costs to work with. They are almost impossible to answer if you don't.

Sometimes, the funding agencies *require* calendar projections. In these cases, the projections must be submitted with your grant application. Usually, a calendar projection is not required. If you prepare one, it will not be necessary to submit it to the grantors. It should be retained in your proposal file, for use after you have received a grant award.

March	April	May	June	July	August	September
$ 862	$ 862	$ 862	$ 862	$ 862	$ 862	$ 863
1,306	1,307	1,307	1,307	1,307	1,307	1,307
5,000	5,000	5,000	5,000			
500	500	500	500	500	500	500
$7,668	$7,669	$7,669	$7,669	$2,669	$2,669	$2,670
172	172	173	173	173	173	173
681	681	681	680	180	180	180
142	142	142	142			
						1,000
						500
			50			
333	333	333	333			
25	25	25	25	25	25	25
					100	
133	133	133	133			
				200		
						560
$9,154	$9,155	$9,156	$9,205	$3,247	$3,147	$5,108
3,834	3,834	3,834	3,835	1,335	1,335	1,335
$12,988	$12,989	$12,990	$13,040	$4,582	$4,482	$6,443

Figure 15. (Continued)

Step Eight: Prepare a Budget Justification

In some circumstances, especially when the budget is long and complex, or the need for certain resources may not be clear to the reviewers, a separate budget-justification page or pages may be needed. This budget justification will explain any unusual items and document the need for large expenditures in certain categories, such as supplies, equipment, or travel. In most cases, the proposal and the itemized budget will be sufficient to explain all projected costs.

But where a budget justification is indicated, you will be doing both yourself and the proposal reviewer a favor if you prepare one.

A sample budget justification for the Extra Special Massage Project is contained in Figure 16. This justification relates to the management budget shown in Figure 8. Notice that the justification explains grantee cost-sharing, in addition to explaining the items that the grantor will be funding.

THE EXTRA SPECIAL MASSAGE PROJECT

BUDGET JUSTIFICATION

Salaries. Salaries are based on classifications and rates applicable to Do Good Institution employees. A 7% cost-of-living increase has been added, and provision has been made for 5% merit increases, according to Do Good Institution policy. (See attached salary schedule.) Note that 50% of the principal investigator's time will be charged to the grant; the remaining 50% will be paid for by Do Good Institution.

Fringe Benefits. The fringe benefits for "regular" positions are calculated as follows: social security (6%); vacation (3%); sick leave (2%); workers' compensation (2%); state disability insurance (2%); health insurance (2%); and retirement (3%). The benefits for "temporary" positions are social security (6%); workers' compensation (2%); and state disability insurance (2%). (See attached benefits schedule.)

Travel. Some subjects will be from low-income families; they will be reimbursed for using their personal car to travel to and from project headquarters. Payment will be at 17¢ per mile, according to Do Good Institution policy. In addition, the cost for the principal investigator and the research associate to travel to Washington, D.C., has been budgeted. They will present the results of their study at the 14th annual conference of Back Researchers on September 15, 1981. Airfare is based on telephone quotes, with a 10% inflation factor added. Per diem ($45) is based on Do Good Institution's out-of-state rate. (See attached travel policy.)

Equipment. Previous research has demonstrated the importance of massagers and recliner chairs to effectively reduce back pain. Four massagers and four recliner chairs will be used by subjects as an important component of the research design. Four of each will be needed because there will be four technicians applying massage treatments throughout six months of the project. The equipment prices budgeted are based on written bids (see attached quotations); no increase is anticipated.

Supplies. According to previous research, utility strength lotions have been an effective method of treating lower back pain; therefore, they will be used in the proposed research. The estimated price ($10 per gallon) is based on obtaining a 30% quantity discount by purchasing the lotions through Do Good Institution's Central Stores. The office supplies budgeted are inexpensive "start-up" items, such as calendars, staplers, and so forth. Do Good Institution will contribute all paper, stationery, and copying.

Subject Payments. In order to enlist the cooperation of subjects, a $5 payment will be offered. This modest amount will help compensate for the time subjects spend receiving treatments.

Figure 16. Sample budget justification. This budget justification explains the costs proposed in the management budget (Figure 8).

BUDGET JUSTIFICATION, Continued Page 2

Communications. Do Good Institution will pay for postage (estimated @ $150). The grant will be charged for long-distance telephone calls (estimated to be 50 calls averaging $3/each).

Consultant. Jack Back, Ph.D., has agreed to serve as a consultant to the project to assist in designing massage methods (2 days); training technicians to apply massage methods (1 day); and evaluating the project (1 day). His previously established rate is $100 per day.

Child-Care Costs. Some of the subjects must leave small children at home while they receive treatments. The money budgeted for child care ($800) is minimal; it will be used to reimburse subjects for baby-sitting expenses.

Computer Costs. Do Good Institution's Model 00C Computer will be used during the data-analysis phase of the project. It is estimated that two hours of computer time (@ $200 per hour) will be required. Do Good Institution will contribute one hour ($200) to the project; the remaining hour ($200) will be charged to the grant. (See attached computer-rate schedule.)

Publication Costs. As a method of disseminating project results to practitioners, the principal investigator will write an article to be published in Back-Track Journal. Page charges made to all authors are $70, so the cost to the grant for eight pages will be $560. (See attached page-charge notice.)

Indirect Charges. The federally negotiated predetermined indirect-cost rate for research projects conducted on site at Do Good Institution is 50% of salaries and wages. For the proposed project, total salaries are $72,368 (grantor-funded $62,023 plus grantee contribution $10,345). Therefore, the indirect entitlement is $36,184 (salaries of $72,368 @ 50%). Because indirect recovery is limited to 8% of total direct costs, $6,330 has been requested (total direct costs of $79,120 @ 8%) from Give Grants Agency. Indirect foregone, therefore, is $29,854 (entitlement of $36,184 less $6,330 requested). This is shown as a Do Good Institution contribution in the budget.

Figure 16. (Continued)

In summary, you can develop your project budget best by following these steps:

1. Read the grantor program guidelines and application forms.
2. Estimate the grantor funds available.
3. Identify the resources necessary to accomplish your project goals.
4. Price these resources and provide for flexibility between cost categories.
5. Prepare a detailed ("management tool") budget.
6. Transfer detailed budget costs to grantor budget forms.
7. Prepare specialized budgets (functional, optional, calendar) as appropriate.
8. Prepare budget justifications as appropriate.

Usually, project directors and grant administrators work together throughout the budget development process.

What Are the Characteristics of a Well-Prepared Grant Budget?

Experienced grants getters and givers were asked by the authors, "What are the characteristics of a well-prepared grant budget?"

Some answers given by project directors were:

"Item analysis."
"Realistic budget items."
"Cost items tied to technical objectives."
"Flexibility for later line-item rebudgeting without requiring prior agency approvals."

Grant administrators mentioned:

"Clarity (i.e., basis of calculation shown)."
"Negotiability."
"Accuracy–it must 'add up.' "
"Sufficient justification–the reviewer can't read your mind!"
"Futuristic–includes all anticipated cost increases and other situations that may occur between the submission date and the projected period of activity."
"Detailed–the more detailed, the better."
"Cost-consciousness."

On the grant-giving side, program officers looked for these characteristics:

"Total cost appropriate to value of the purpose of the grant."
"Cost elements (hours, rates, etc.) specified."
"Not overblown or padded–realistic."
"Presented in my agency's format."
"Reflects attention to detail."
"Clear categorization of cost (i.e., line items in the correct place)."

Grant officers responded:

"Justification of line-item costs."
"Reasonability of cost items."
"Identification of specific consultants, subcontracts, or other unusual items."
"Sufficient detail."

As demonstrated by their responses, experienced grants givers and getters agree on the characteristics of a well-prepared budget. Their answers confirm the importance of the budgeting philosophy and techniques discussed throughout this chapter.

Who in Your Agency Approves Grant Budgets?

Who should be responsible for approving budgets? Depending on the nature of your organization, it should be an individual who is knowledgeable about grant and contract budgets, who is experienced, and who has the ability to notice things that are unusual (e.g., the absence of indirect costs or fringe benefits, or extensive cost sharing). Such a person may hold the title of vice-president, contracts and grants administrator, grants officer, graduate dean, director of sponsored programs, executive director, department head, or other appellation. In no case, however, should a proposal be submitted in its final form without prior budget review in-house. This review could save your organization a great deal of money later on.

In summary, budgeting is a critical part of stretching your grant dollar. Allowing for inflation, asking for the right amount, making certain that needed items are included in the budget, and using the appropriate formats—all combine to make your finalized proposal budget an effective management tool. Prepare it wisely now and it will serve you well later—especially as you enter the negotiation stage.

4

The Project Award
Negotiating the Best Deal

"I've yet to see a prospective grantee turn money away!" skeptically commented a grant officer, upon being asked what he would do if a project director walked out on a grant negotiation because of budget cuts.

"What! The funding agency *increase* my award? You must be kidding!" incredulously exclaimed a project director who was asked under what circumstances her grant awards had been increased during past negotiations.

Contrary to the common experiences just expressed, prospective grantees should occasionally turn down grants. And funding agencies should sometimes increase awards. But do they? And, if so, under what negotiating conditions?

A great deal of mystique surrounds the grant negotiation process, particularly on the part of grantees. Unlike budgeting, over which the grantee's project director and the grant administrator have major control, the power in the negotiation game seems to reside with the grantor's program officer and the grant officer. After all, they have the final say on whether and how much money is awarded. And everyone knows that the award is usually less than what is requested. Grantees, more often than not, accept this passively.

"We seem to roll over quickly when they (grantors) want to reduce our budget," admitted a university research director, when queried about grant negotiation strategies.

Besides lacking control, grantees often have a hard time understanding the negotiation process. Preparing a budget is a relatively black-and-white matter compared with negotiating it. In budgeting, the project director knows what resources are needed, and the grant administrator knows how to price them. But in negotiating, how do you successfully estimate the seemingly gray area of feelings, needs, strategies, and other hidden agendas of the grantor representatives?

If grant officers offer less than you asked for, what arguments might influence them to restore the full amount? Why did they offer less to begin with? *People*, not numbers, are involved, and this complicates matters immensely.

Negotiations are occurring around you all the time. Different kinds of negotiations may be once-in-a-lifetime, yearly, or even daily occurrences. "Will you marry me?" or "Why don't you pick up your socks?" are sample topics that require give and take. Whether you are bargaining for a lifetime partner, the daily socks cleanup, or an annual grant renewal, basic negotiation ingredients are involved.

Yet, according to one expert on negotiation, "All too frequently we have had to learn to negotiate the same way we learned such things as sex—by trial and error . . . . Thus most of our knowledge . . . , unfortunately, has had to come from our limited personal experience."[(1)]

Negotiation at the time a grant is awarded is perhaps one of the most critical elements of the total grant-stretching process. If too much money is given, or the terms are too lax, grantor dollars will be wasted and other beneficial projects will not be funded. On the other hand, if too little money is awarded, or the terms are too harsh, the projects may fail, and, again, grant monies are not effectively spent. A fair grant negotiation provides the necessary base for a successful project—the ultimate goal of grantors and grantees.

Because grant negotiations are so important, the parties involved should be able to draw from more than their own personal grant negotiation experiences. In this chapter, some basic ingredients of negotiation are examined. Then, the personal observations of experienced grants givers and getters are presented.

Negotiation: The Basic Ingredients

There are at least five basic ingredients of any negotiation. These are people, preparation, individual and organizational needs, bargaining power, and strategies.

Individuals, either alone or supported by others, conduct negotiations. Each comes to the negotiation with a different set of knowledge, attitudes, and skills. Because *people* are involved, the psychology of negotiation* is extremely important. "Know thyself" is the first rule of negotiation. The second is "Know thy opponent." In following both, negotiators should work hard to identify their own and others' hidden assumptions.

In addition to understanding the psychology of people, successful negotiators should be prepared with every possible kind of information about the people with whom they are going to negotiate. They should also be knowledgeable about their own product and bargaining power. A minimum and maximum position should be agreed to and strategies developed, recognizing, of course, that circumstances may cause these strategies to change during the actual negotiation.†

*Nierenberg[(2)] provides an excellent discussion of the psychology of negotiation.

†Beckmann[(4)] offers practical advice on negotiating strategies.

In order to be fully prepared, it's important to understand what motivates people. Maslow, in his book *Motivation and Personality*, presented seven categories of *needs* as basic factors in human behavior[2]:

1. Physiological needs
2. Safety and security needs
3. Love and belonging needs
4. Esteem needs
5. Needs for self-actualization (inner motivation, to become what one is capable of becoming)
6. Needs to know and understand
7. Aesthetic needs

Each successive need occurs after a prior need has been at least partially satisfied. For example, a starving child whose friends are going to the movies will be more likely to spend his only dollar on a hamburger than on a ticket to *Star Wars*.

Nierenberg used Maslow's categories as a framework for studying needs in relation to negotiation. He believes that the more basic is the need the other party is trying to fill, the greater are your chances for success. Also, Nierenberg noted that *individual* needs may be transcended by *organizational* needs when people are negotiating on behalf of an organization. However, organizations cannot act by themselves, independently of people. Therefore, negotiators should recognize two active levels of needs: the organization's and the individual's.[3]

Besides recognizing needs, negotiators should examine the relative *bargaining power* of all parties. Beckmann[4] defined bargaining power as the relative strength or weakness of one party's total position, which affects the will or need to compromise in reaching agreement with the other party. In a procurement, these strengths and weaknesses result from tangible and intangible factors such as:

1. The number of qualified firms competing for a contract
2. The urgency of the seller's desire for a contract
3. The amount of time the buyer or seller has in which to seek an agreement
4. The accuracy of one party's assessment of the other's negotiating objectives, and the facts and estimates that support these objectives
5. The external pressures—regulatory, legal, political, public, and so forth—that one party can use to force agreement from the other
6. The accuracy of one party's evaluation of the other's bargaining position

It is only after knowledge about the negotiating parties and their needs and power have been estimated that *strategies* can be plotted. Nierenberg[5] offered general negotiating strategies based on needs. These strategies are ordered according to the amount of positive control that one party may have over the other party:

1. Negotiator works for the opposer's needs.
2. Negotiator lets the opposer work for his needs.

3. Negotiator works for the opposer's and his own needs.
4. Negotiator works against his needs.
5. Negotiator works against the opposer's needs.
6. Negotiator works against the opposer's and his own needs.

It is easier, for example, to work for the opposer (Method 1), than to let the opposer work for you (Method 2). Therefore, a team with comparatively little bargaining power would probably rely on working for their opposer's needs in a creative way that would enable them to meet their own needs.

People, *preparation*, *needs*, *power*, and *strategies*—all are important ingredients in the negotiation process, and all are discussed in the literature on negotiation in general. How do these ingredients mix in *grant* negotiations?*

Observations of Experienced Grants Getters and Givers

According to negotiation theory, negotiators should examine their own and their opposer's hidden assumptions before and during negotiation. What are the hidden assumptions that may be present in a *grant* negotiation?

"Grantors always reduce budgets" and "Grantees never turn down awards, no matter how badly budgets are cut" were two assumptions reported at the beginning of this chapter. Are they true? In all cases? Does everyone participating in a grant negotiation believe these statements, or do the experiences and resulting beliefs of the negotiating parties vary?

To answer these questions, representative and experienced project directors, grant administrators, program officers, and grant officers were interviewed and surveyed. The people who cooperated were from a variety of grantee and grantor organizations; they represented billions of dollars of grant spending annually and hundreds of years of experience collectively.

The information from their responses was used to develop the remainder of this chapter. As you read on, you will note that their perceptions are similar on some points and differ on others. Some variety is to be expected. *People*—the kinds of people you are or will be negotiating grants with from time to time—were answering questions, each based on her or his personal knowledge, attitudes, and skills.

Because you will be negotiating with individuals who may or may not be similar to the persons surveyed, the rest of this chapter *will not* provide a foolproof recipe for negotiation success under any circumstances. What it *will* do is examine the variety of ingredients that you can expect in grant negotiations. Because there are important differences between *grant* and *contract* negotiations, key features of contract negotiations will be identified as appropriate.†

*Grant negotiations are discussed by Willner and Hendricks,[6] Holtz,[7] and others.[8-9]
†Detailed procedures for negotiating federal contracts are contained in the *Code of Federal Regulations*.[10]

Questions to be answered in the remainder of this chapter, based on the perceptions of experienced grants givers and getters, are these: *Who participates in a grant negotiation? What are the topics? Why are awards increased or decreased? What are the methods of negotiation? How do grant negotiators prepare? What are their needs during negotiation? Who has the bargaining power? What strategies are useful in grant negotiations? What are the characteristics of an effective grant negotiator?*

Who Participates in a Grant Negotiation?

Usually the participants in a grant negotiation are the four central players in the grant-stretching process. The project director and the grant administrator make up the grantee team; the program officer and the grant officer represent the grantor.

There are variations, however. If the negotiation is very simple or if it is for a renewal project and the work scope of the proposal will not be affected, the grant administrator and the grant officer may handle the agreements alone. In these cases, it is not necessary for project directors or program officers to be involved. On the other hand, if negotiations are expected to be complex, involving an unusually large project, additional technical support may be called in by either or both sides. Lawyers may check for conflict of interest, accountants may review fee calculations, etc.

Under no circumstances do the program officer and the project director negotiate formally alone. The grant officer and the grant administrator must be present to legally bind their respective organizations to the agreement reached.

Informally, it's a different matter. The program officer and the project director fairly frequently "discuss" the prospective grant prior to negotiations. They may actually reach the agreement that is eventually formalized. A program officer and a project director, being interviewed together, claimed that "Ninety-nine percent of negotiations are carried out informally between the PI and the program officer."

A situation that both grantee and grantor personnel should avoid is the "triangle" negotiation. This occurs when the negotiation requires a change in the project work scope and only three parties are present:

Case One: Project director, grant administrator, grant officer (program officer missing)

Case Two: Grant administrator, grant officer, program officer (project director missing)

In either case, one of the two parties knowledgeable about and responsible for the work to be done is absent. Yet the project will be changed.

The first case occurs too often. It happens unintentionally because the program officer is too busy to be included in the negotiation or intentionally because it is tactically advantageous for her or him not to be there. Either way, the program officer instructs the grant officer how much money to award (maximum) and sometimes what budget items to cut. The program officer has reduced the proposal budget based on his or her understanding of the proposal. If the program officer had a complete knowledge of the project needs, there would be no problem. However, sometimes this is not so. Therefore, when the program officer is not present at the negotiation, the project director loses the opportunity to defend the items that have been cut and to explain the impact that the loss of funds will have on the project.

In California, for example, a project director proposed to provide technical assistance to Indian tribes in an area that included several states in the Southwest. He carefully identified the location of each tribe and estimated the transportation costs to travel to each location. Because of the distances involved and the frequency at which the technical assistance would be needed, the travel budget was quite large. During the negotiation, the program officer was missing. The grant officer informed the project director and the grant administrator that travel costs must be reduced by more than half.

"But I can't service my clients," protested the project director. The grant officer, relying on instructions given to him by the program officer, did not understand the impact of the travel cuts on the program. It became necessary to stop negotiations temporarily until the next day, when the program officer would be present. At that time, the matter was easily resolved. The project director presented a map showing the geographical locations of his clients. It turned out that the program officer, not knowing the Southwest well, had believed that several tribes were in southern rather than northern Arizona, and thus, the travel cuts were justified. *The grant officer, however, could not go higher than the maximum amount identified previously by the program officer.* Once the program officer was present and the need for the travel was established, the funds were reinstated.

A less-experienced project director, one eager to get the project funded at any cost, might not have been willing to insist on the program officer's presence. Yet, without the program officer, all opportunity to defend the reasonable minimum costs of doing the proposed project are lost. The grant officer is primarily responsible for legal compliance and organizational rules and regulations. The success of the work to be performed rests with the program officer. Therefore, grantees should always request the presence of the program officer when work-scope revisions (or cuts that will require work-scope reductions) are being negotiated.

In a Case One triangle negotiation, the grantee may suffer. In a Case Two triangle negotiation, the grantor is at a disadvantage. It is rare, but occasionally the project director is the party not present. Most project directors have one project only, and this project is important enough to bring them to the negotiation. However, if for some reason the project director is unavailable (out of the country on research, for example), a problem may occur if the grant administrator agrees to changes in the project's work scope that the project director, on return, cannot or will not carry out. This, in turn, causes unwanted complications for the funding agency, especially for the program officer.

The importance of negotiation to the grant-stretching process is evident from the number of parties who participate. Usually, all four central players (project director, grant administrator, program officer, and grant officer) should be involved.

What Are the Topics?

At the time a proposal is submitted, the project director describes what will be done, how, when, for how much, and under what special conditions. If the funding agency accepts everything as specified in the proposal and doesn't wish to add any requirements, then there are no topics to negotiate; there is no negotiation. The agency merely notifies the project director and the institution of their good fortune.

Usually, this does not happen. More often, the agency proposes to change the proposal in some way. Any requested change then becomes a topic for negotiation. The agency is giving a "Yes–but" blessing. It is saying, "Yes, we like your proposal, but no, we can't give you all that money," or "But we want to retain patent rights," or "But we don't want you to bother with Objective Nine," and so forth.

When negotiation is necessary, what topics are often included? The experienced grantspersons interviewed named the following topics as occurring frequently in their personal grant negotiation experiences:

- Total amount of award
- Effective date of award
- Work scope
- Line item amounts
- Special terms and conditions
- Indirect-cost rate
- Payment terms
- Qualifications of performers
- Degree of funding-agency participation

Each of these topics will be discussed briefly.

Total Amount of Award. This becomes a topic when the grantor proposes awarding less money than the grantee requested originally. This happens frequently. The "total amount" may also become a topic when the grantor asks the grantee to do more work than proposed. If the increased work scope will cost more money, the grantee should get additional funds.

Effective Date of Award. When will the project start? Funds may not be spent and project activities may not start until that date. The effective date may be very important because of the necessity of spending (to take advantage of discounts, to purchase equipment in advance so that it will be there when needed, or to cover the salaries of researchers and faculty so that there is continuity between grants). It may also be critical because of the timing of activities associated with the work scope.

For example, the project dates may have to coincide with the calendar or school year or even with Mother Nature's doings. At one large grantor agency, there was the time that grant officers were asked to hurry up an agriculture-related award because the sheep were in heat, so work had to start. The request got high priority, and the award subsequently was known as "the hot-sheep grant."

Work Scope. In return for money, the grantee promises to carry out certain activities, such as tutoring disadvantaged students or developing a special-education curriculum. These activities are known as the *work scope* (or *statement of work*, *work statement*, etc.). The work scope is negotiated when the grantors want to decrease, increase, or modify the activities proposed. For example, the grantors may ask the grantees to tutor 20 instead of 50 disadvantaged students. Or they may ask that the special-education curriculum emphasize the needs of teachers of gifted children. The work scope is most commonly negotiated, however, when the grantors want to give the grantees less money than the grantees wanted. In this case, many grantees accept less money and reduce the work scope accordingly.

Line Item Amounts. Sometimes, the grantors believe that certain items in the budget are unnecessary. For example, suppose the grantees have asked for $100,000, including $2,000 for travel to Hawaii and $1,000 for a self-correcting typewriter. If the grantors did not believe that the trip and the typewriter were essential to accomplish the purposes of the project, they would probably attempt to decrease the award to $97,000, specifically decreasing the travel and equipment items by $2,000 and $1,000, respectively.

Special Terms and Conditions. Either the grantors or the grantees may wish to negotiate favorable terms or conditions. These include patents, copyrights, privacy, security clearances, confidentiality of data, and many other topics.

Special terms and conditions are particularly important elements of *contract* negotiations. Sometimes, indeed, they are the only element. It is more common, in the experience of some grants professionals interviewed, for terms than for the amount of money to be negotiated.

"In responding to an RFP for a contract," a grant administrator advised, "carefully review the terms and conditions that the contracting agency plans to apply. If you object to any of them, say so in your proposal. Suggest appropriate clauses to replace inappropriate ones. Delete or modify others, providing a rationale for any changes you make. For example, many RFPs contain standard clauses that are applicable to businesses but not to educational institutions. By deleting these and proposing appropriate replacements, you may save yourself and the contracting officer hours of time and remove potential areas of disagreement."

Indirect-Cost Rate. If your agency does not have a federally approved indirect-cost rate, it will be necessary to negotiate one. (This will be done separately from your negotiation of an award with the grantors.) If your agency does have an approved rate, and if you are dealing with a federal grantor agency, the indirect-cost rate *should not be a topic of negotiation.* You are free, of course, to reduce the rate voluntarily, in order to make a grantee contribution, but there should be no pressure on you to do so. In fact, if the federal grantors try to get you to reduce the rate, you can usually enlist support from the federal employee at your federal audit agency who negotiated the indirect rate with your agency. On the other hand, if you are negotiating with a *nonfederal* grantor, the indirect-cost rate is frequently a topic of negotiation.

Payment Terms. How soon can you collect the funds once they are awarded? Will you receive an advance payment or progress payments? Are you eligible for payments through a letter-of-credit arrangement? Payment terms are fairly standard for federal grants, but there are frequently opportunities to negotiate these terms favorably during contract discussions or during negotiations with nonfederal agencies.

Qualifications of Performers. During the negotiation, grantors often review carefully the special skills and track records of key grantee personnel. By successfully convincing the grantors that proposed grantee staff will be star performers, grantees can enhance their overall negotiating position.

Degree of Funding Agency Participation. How much "say" will the grantors (especially the program officer) have in planning and carrying out project activities? Some program officers want a considerable amount of participation, while others prefer to have the grantors fully in charge, with minimal help from them. Whatever the case, the time to decide how much the grantors will be involved is during the negotiation state, so that there will be no unpleasant surprises once the project is under way.

How Should "Take-It-or-Leave-It" and "Best-and-Final" Offers Be Handled?

Topics frequently included in grants negotiations are the *total amount of the award*, *the effective dates of the award*, *work scope*, *line-item amounts*, *special terms and conditions*, *indirect-cost rate*, *payment terms*, *qualifications of performers*, and *degree of funding-agency participation.* On occasion, the grantor requests changes in a proposal, involving one or more of these topics, and *there is no negotiation involved.* Typically, this occurs in one of two ways: (1) a "take-it-or-leave-it" offer to the prospective grantee; or (2) a request for a "best-and-final offer" from the prospective contractor.

Take-It-or-Leave-It Offers. When a *grant* has been applied for, the funding agency may offer to award less money than the grantees asked for and may demand a revised budget. There is no opportunity for discussion, and prospective grantees have only one decision. Should they accept the award or not? This is known as a *take-it-or-leave-it offer*. (Figure 17.)

If the grantees proposed a padded budget initially, or if they are confident of finding other financial support for the project, or if they planned to do it anyway with their own funds, the choice will probably be "take it." On the other hand, if the project can't be reasonably done with the limited money offered, the decision should probably be "leave it." After all, why accept certain failure?

The delicate part of the take-it-or-leave-it offer is just this: identifying it as such. Grantor representatives never *say* "Take it or leave it" in so many words. Usually, the grantee receives a letter or a phone call saying, "You've been recommended for funding of X dollars; send a revised budget." The unknown factor is how firm the agency's stand is. If the project director appealed to the program officer, to the program officer's boss, or to the local Congressman, would more dollars be forthcoming?

Past experience, informal inquiries of other grantees being funded by the same agency, and informal inquiries of the program officer are ways to test the firmness of the offer. If other grantees have appealed and received additional

Figure 17. Grantors frequently offer grantees *far less* than they requested.

funds, or if the program officer is receptive to additional documentation of the need for funds, it is probably *not* a take-it-or-leave-it offer at all; it just appeared to be that from the wording and from the lack of an invitation to negotiate. In this case, initiate the negotiation yourself. However, if through your inquiries you find out that everyone is being treated similarly or that the program has historically funded at the level offered to you, then no attempts to negotiate should be initiated, as you may succeed only in antagonizing the people who are funding your project.

Best-and-Final Offers. The take-it-or-leave-it offer is associated with *grants*. Similarly, there is a nonnegotiating situation that is associated with *contracts*. In this case, the funding agency does not demand any specific changes in the original proposal. Instead, it gives the prospective fund recipient the *opportunity* to make a change or changes in any aspect of its original proposal. This is known as a *call for the best-and-final offer*. It is not a true negotiation because the proposer makes voluntary changes, without making agreements with funding-agency officials.

Normally, the funding agency asks for a best-and-final offer in competitive situations when it wants to get the very best deal (cost, terms, delivery, and so forth) possible. On receiving the request for a best-and-final offer, you have many decisions. Should you change any aspect of your original proposal? You don't have to. If you do make a change, what items should be covered?

Before making decisions, you should evaluate your bargaining position. Informal inquiries may be made to try to identify the competition. How badly does the funding agency want the proposed work to be done? Is there a time pressure on the funding agency? For example, must monies be committed before the end of the fiscal year, which is very close at hand? You should be aware that it is possible that you are the only bidder and that the funding agency is mainly trying to get the work done for a lower price.

Effective grantee negotiators understand the conditions surrounding the arbitrary take-it-or-leave-it offer and the voluntary best-and-final offer. They are prepared to make decisions unilaterally, without entering into discussions with funding-agency personnel.

Why Are Awards Decreased?

The most frequent grant negotiation topic is the total amount of the award. Since it is negotiated so often and since it is so important to stretching grant dollars, it is worth a closer look. Is the total always cut? If so, why?

The experienced project directors, grant administrators, program officers, and grant officers we contacted agree. The funds awarded are usually less than the funds requested. The reasons for budget cuts vary, with the most common reasons (in their experience) being:

1. Grantor's need to "spread" money among many good projects.
2. Correction of a "padded" budget.

3. Lower-quality purchases acceptable (a Chevy will do).
4. Elimination of unallowable items.
5. Elimination of unnecessary items.
6. Reduction in work scope.
7. Correction of budget errors, including incorrect indirect-cost rate.
8. Grantor's desire that grantee share costs.
9. Grantor's desire to demonstrate power.

Following is a brief description of each of the reasons that grant budgets may be reduced.

Grantor's Need to Spread Money. Respondents told us they have cut budgets (or their budgets have been cut) because of:

"A desire to spread the money around and fund as many projects as possible."
"Limited resources versus 'must-fund' projects."
"Insufficient funds."

Grantees have no control of the grantor's need to spread money, and yet insufficient grantor funds is one of the most common causes of budget cuts. The grantor's representatives, in contrast, do have a measure of control. Even with limited funds, they can do less spreading by funding fewer projects. Whether they are willing to do this or not depends heavily on the negotiating talents of the grantees.

Whenever the grantors reduce the budget in order to fund more projects, it's important for grantees to reduce their work scope so that it can be accomplished with the funds provided.

Correction of a Padded Budget. Some reasons given by all grants professionals except the project directors were:

"Part of the budget game; budget high for expected reductions."
"Proposed budget too high, unreasonable."
"Inflated costs for all or part of the work."
"Too much money for tasks."
"Excessive fee."

One grant administrator phrased this reason a bit differently, commenting that in his experience, some budgets had been cut because of the "*assumption* that we've padded, though we've only attempted to cover our expenses liberally."

Padded budgets are under the control of the grantees initially. They can be eliminated as a reason for budget reductions by not proposing them to begin with. The danger here is the possible assumption on the part of grantors that all budgets are padded. During negotiations, however, a reasonable (nonpadded) budget can be defended.

When preparing a renewal budget, grantees can intentionally or unintentionally pad through inaccurately estimating and reporting the amount of unspent funds from the prior year. (Renewal budgets are typically submitted three to six months before the end of the current grant period.) For example, a program officer, asked to report an incident in which a budget had been awarded at less than she originally planned to give, replied, "During the telephone negotiation, the project director stated that he had more than ten percent of last year's funds left over. Everything above ten percent had to be subtracted from the top as excess residual funds."

A Chevy Will Do. All parties except the project director recognized that sometimes budgets are reduced because some costs are for luxury items of a higher quality than is necessary to do the job. Some comments were:

"Lack of funding to afford a Cadillac when a Chevy will do."
"Satisfactory results obtainable at a lower scale of effort."

This cause for budget cuts is under the control of the grantee. Either a lower-quality item should be requested or the higher-quality one must be carefully justified in terms of programmatic need.

Unallowable Items. Reasons for budget reductions given by all except program officers were:

"Agency and federal rules prohibit specific items."
"International travel not allowable in some cases."
"Unallowable costs—salary over ceiling rate, advertising, fee on some grants."

Legislation and regulations implementing this legislation govern all federally funded programs. Other programs may be subject to the guidelines and policies of the sponsor agencies, such as private foundations. These regulations and guidelines are quite specific about allowable and unallowable costs. All parties to the negotiation should be familiar with the regulations governing the project under negotiation. Usually, printed documents are easily available from the sponsor agency.

Control when the budget is being cut because of unallowable costs belongs to that negotiating party whose knowledge of the regulations is most complete. For example, knowledgeable grant administrators will not propose unallowable costs. They will be prepared to defend any questioned costs through reasonable, persuasive interpretation of the regulations. Similarly, it is the grant officer's business to ensure that costs awarded are allowable according to the sponsor agency's regulations.

An example of how important it is to know the "regs" occurred several years ago. A large West Coast high school district had submitted a proposal for over a million dollars. The program officer and the grant officer believed that some of the tasks proposed were not authorized in the regulations. Therefore, they cut the funds offered to $800,000.

During the actual negotiations, on site in the school district, the district's grant administrator asked why the costs had been cut. He did not accept the grantors' belief that the tasks were unallowable. Instead, the grant administrator identified the passages in the regulations on which the questioned tasks had been based. As a result, according to the grant officer who reported this incident, an extra $250,000 was put back into the award.

The point is, don't always depend on everything the grantors say. Ask questions. Demand proof of their case. Better yet, be prepared to prove your case.

Elimination of Certain Cost Items as Unnecessary. All parties to the grant-stretching process agreed that awards were reduced to eliminate certain cost items, commenting:

"Reviewers point out 'frill' cost items."
"Program officer determines unnecessary costs."
"Grantor does not agree with proposal writer that certain costs are necessary."
"Insufficient justification of certain costs."

Control of this reason for award reduction is shared by all. The grantees have initial control through justifying the need for all items clearly, persuasively, in their proposals. The grantors have final control over accepting and understanding this need. During negotiation, the grantees may regain some control by bringing additional documentation and justification to the attention of the grantors.

For example, one program officer, when asked to describe an incident in which funds were reinstated during negotiation, said, "The project director called back after the original discussion with a well-developed need for the additional funds based on a careful analysis of the impact of the reductions on the research."

Desire to Reduce Work Scope. For a variety of reasons, the program officer (and the review panel) may not wish to fund the entire project as proposed:

"Part of the work scope duplicates previous or parallel work."
"Larger commitment of staff and resources than my agency intended."
"Review was critical of some aspects of the research."
"Disinterest in part of the work."

These were all explanations that program officers gave for reducing budgets. Grantee representatives did not cite this reason, nor did grant officers.

The reduction of work scope as a reason for cutting budgets is usually of interest only to the program officer. The grantees wanted to do the whole job or would not have proposed it; it is not the grant officer's responsibility to evaluate the merits of the work scope.

While the program officer has final control of this reason for award reduction, the grantee representatives, especially the project director, can influence the decision. By proving in the original proposal that the work does not duplicate existing or prior work, the project director can eliminate one possible objection. By carefully reviewing the program guidelines, the past history of funding patterns, and other printed materials, the project director and the grant administrator can estimate the level of effort desired and the appropriateness of the proposed project to the sponsor agency's mission. Most important, by talking directly with the program officer and with professionals in the field who may be reviewers, the project director can select the kinds of research or services that the grantor agency will *want* to fund.

Correction of Budget Errors, Including Incorrect Indirect-Cost Rate. Grant officers were the only respondents who identified correcting budget errors as a reason for award reductions. This is quite likely because it is their responsibility to check the budget calculations and confirm the indirect-cost rate prior to negotiations.

Errors are under the initial control of the grantees. Grant administrators should ensure that there are no errors and hence eliminate this reason as a factor for award reduction. The danger in not eliminating it is this. If grant officers discover a $2,000 overstated indirect rate or addition error, they will reduce the total award accordingly. However, if grant administrators discover errors before proposals are submitted, they can add the funds to a direct-cost line item where, for competitive reasons, the budget may have been low. This is particularly important when there is a predetermined ceiling on the amount that may be requested and the original budget is squeezed so as not to exceed this limit.

Grantor's Desire That Grantee Share Costs. Grantees claimed that grantors cut budgets in order to get grantees to share costs.

"They (grantors) seem to believe that an educational institution can do things at a reduced rate because of student labor, access to computers, and low faculty teaching loads," one project director said.

Interestingly, grantors did not recognize this as a reason for cutting budgets. However, it may or may not be a reason. If so, it is probably a function of the desire to spread limited grantor funds. As long as there are plenty of grantees who are willing to accept insufficient funds (necessitating cost sharing), the temptation is to give money to them rather than to institutions unwilling to do so.

Although the grantors have final control of budget reductions through required cost-sharing, grantees can influence grantor decisions. If you suspect that the grantors are trying to get you to share costs, you should be open about this with the grantors during negotiations.

Luckily, this situation is fairly easy to detect. For example, if the program officer cuts academic-year faculty salary out of a grant budget, yet the work scope calls for research to be done then, probably the program officer intends the university to absorb those costs. You should face the issue directly. If there are good reasons that the university can't share these costs, these reasons should be explained to the program officer.

Hidden assumptions may exist on the part of program officers, and grantees can clear these up. A common hidden assumption is that universities provide a great deal of time for faculty to do research. At some institutions, faculty teach only 3-6 course units per semester. At others, however, the load may be double that or more (12-15 course units plus committee assignments). If a program officer at the funding agency happens to have come from a "low-load" university, he or she may assume that all others enjoy research time and hence cut any budgets that require payment to release faculty from teaching loads.

Exactly this situation occurred three times within the past year at a large teaching university, reported one grant administrator. In every instance, at the beginning of the negotiation, funds for faculty time during the school year were eliminated. In every instance, these funds were reinstated after the program officer learned that the university did not and could not release the faculty members for research because of its primarily teaching mission.

Grantor's Desire to Demonstrate Power. "Demonstrate the authority of grantor; illustrate they're 'doing their job'" was a reason for award reduction given by a project director. Again, as with the idea that the grantors want to force the grantees to share costs, this may or may not be a reason. Grantors, for obvious reasons, did not cite it.

Final control lies with the grantors. However, during negotiation, any such arbitrary cuts can be attacked by the grantees, through reiterating the justification and the documentation of the original costs proposed.

In summary, the reasons for budget reductions are varied in content, in importance to the various negotiating parties, and in the amount of control over them possessed by the grantees and the grantors. Most important, yet uncontrollable by the grantee, is the grantor's need to spread money among many good proposals. Yet all the other reasons for reducing budgets are controllable, to a large extent, by the grantee. By eliminating as many of these reasons as possible, and through persuasive, skillful negotiation, you can ultimately affect the grantor's "spreading" need—at least to the extent that the grantor adequately funds your project and reserves the spreading for other, less successful grantee negotiators.

Why Are Awards Increased?

Happily for grantees, there are occasionally opportunities to *increase* awards from the amount originally proposed. Granted, these opportunities are rare, but they do exist. Despite widespread assumptions that this "never happens," even on the part of some experienced grantees (grantors know better!), it does.

Professional grantspersons were asked why awards had been increased (in their experience). Their reasons were:

1. Increased work scope
2. Increased indirect costs
3. Increased direct costs
4. Changes in regulations
5. Too modest a request initially
6. Correction of budget errors, including incorrect indirect-cost rate
7. Recommendations of review panel
8. New funding level at grantor agency

Following is a brief description of each of the reasons that grant budgets may be increased.

Increased Workscope. All negotiating parties agreed on the importance of an increased work scope. They commented that in their experience budgets were increased because:

"There was an increase in the outcome data requested and we built in increased cost."
"Special task associated with the project that grantor wants accomplished."
"Evaluation component needed by funding agency."
"Scale of effort or of duration insufficient to produce satisfactory level of confidence in results."
"Desire for additional dissemination efforts as part of the project."

In the specific examples just given, the control was apparently with the grantor. The program officer wanted the evaluation, dissemination, or increased effort and hence initiated a request during negotiation.

There is little that the grantee (especially the new grantee) can do to influence the grantor to add to work scope in this manner. However, any actions that the grantees can take to increase the program officer's confidence in their performance, reliability, and so forth will stand them in good stead. If program officers want additional tasks done and have the money, they are more likely to ask proven performers than to take chances on unknown quantities.

One program officer, commenting on why he distributes additional money for increased work scope to proven performers, said, "Hey, if I land these funds on Joe, I'm not going to be embarrassed by no final report or by a sloppy one with typos. More important, I know he'll do a good job for me."

Increased Indirect Costs. A second and common reason that awards are increased is a change in the grantee's negotiated indirect-cost rate during the period after the proposal is submitted and prior to the grant negotiation. Among our respondents, all parties except the project directors recognized this reason. Since project directors are concerned with receiving the direct costs of the project, this reason could easily be overlooked by them.

Many grantees, including grant administrators whose business it is to be interested, are not aware of the possibility of collecting increased indirect costs after the proposal has been submitted under a lower rate. Although grantors have final control over whether or not these increases are granted, it is the grant administrator's initial responsibility to request them. In some funding agencies (the National Institutes of Health, for example), such costs are routinely approved; in most other agencies, they are approved unless program monies for the funding period have been totally committed already.

Increased Direct Costs. Also because of a time lag between proposal submission and negotiation, the direct costs of a project may increase. Normally, such costs are inflated before proposal submission to allow for reasonably expected increases; however, an unusually long time-lag or inflationary increases that could not have been reasonably anticipated are justification for increasing awards so that the resources necessary to carry out the project will be available.

For example, in California, cost-of-living salary increases for state employees during fiscal year 1979 were vetoed by the governor. The legislature, in July of the following fiscal year, "made up" for the previous year by granting 15% salary increases, double what most grantees had been projecting. No one could have reasonably anticipated this year-later catch-up, particularly in light of the President's 7% average wage-price guidelines and the hard stance taken by the governor the previous year. As a result, some funding agencies that had enough funds increased awards to cover the mandated salary increases and thereby provide for the level of effort originally intended.

Again, the grantors have control of the final decision; however, the grantees must initiate the request to increase an award because of increased direct costs. The inflation that may occur in direct costs is usually more easily anticipated than an increase in indirect-cost rate. Therefore, it is far less common for grantors to increase awards to meet direct-cost changes than for indirect-cost changes.

Changes in Regulations. Some reasons given by grantor personnel for increasing awards were:

"Allowable cost ceiling for subsistence allowances in exchange grants went up."
"Change in regs to allow reimbursement of boat rental costs."
"Book allowance increased."

Although the grantee personnel may have read the regulations carefully at the time the proposal was submitted, there may be changes before the negotiation takes place. The grantor controls increases due to changing program regulations; however, the grantees can exert influence by making the initial request for an increase due to changing regulations.

Too Modest a Request Initially. Grant administrators and program officers noted that sometimes funds were increased because the initial budget was too low to do the job promised, saying:

"Necessary costs underestimated."
"Too modest a request initially (very rare)."
"Overlooked an item of cost."

One program officer, however, discounted this as a reason, commenting, "If a grant proposal looks too low, the reviewers would probably not recommend it for funding based on the 'lack of sophistication' of the investigator."

Obviously, it is chancy for the grantees to intentionally or unintentionally bid a project too low. If they do it intentionally (in order to be competitive, "win," and then ask for more money), they may be stuck with their unrealistic promises. If they do it unintentionally, they may be stuck also—or they may lose the award altogether because of lack of credibility. If an unrealistically low budget has been submitted, the grantees should be aware of this and try to correct the situation during the negotiation. The best defense is a project plan that is so outstanding that the grantor wants to fund it badly enough to overlook the poor original budget estimate and to fund the increased resources needed.

Correction of Budget Errors, Including Incorrect Indirect-Cost Rate. Grant officers listed budget errors as a reason for increasing awards; none of the other persons we contacted did. Apparently, in many cases, the grant officer is the one negotiating party who runs a tape on the proposal budget just prior to negotiation. The fact that grantors are willing to increase awards based on budget errors demonstrates their concern that adequate resources be provided to do the project. Normally, the grantee grant administrator should check the budget again prior to negotiation, to be aware of any possibilities of increased awards due to calculation errors, embarrassing as it may be to admit to them.

It's important to note that the errors are not always grantee errors. If the grantor agency tried to reduce the budget in some way, or to reallocate between line items, it's possible that a mistake was made then by the grant officer. It is definitely up to the grantee to catch that kind of error, since the grantor has finished the calculations, assumes they are correct, and has no reason to check them.

Recommendations of Review Panel. "The review panel may recommend additional personnel with special expertise, equipment or consultants," one program officer offered as a reason for increased awards. Control here does not lie with the grantees. Review panel members initiate the request, and program officers have final control over approving or disapproving.

New Funding Level at Grantor Agency. Project directors alone identified new funding levels as an opportunity for increased awards. It is possible that grantor representatives do not regard new money as "add-ons" to existing projects or proposed projects except as related to increasing work scope. In this case, the reason for the increased award would still be primarily the greater or new work scope involved. When asked about uses of new funds, a grant officer said that if additional funds become available at his agency, they would be used to fund more good projects. The good project could be added on to existing projects, or pending and approved proposals would be funded.

Control of new monies belongs to the grantor. It is not necessary for the grantor to advise the grantee of new money's existence. Grantees who wish to take advantage of new funding levels can best do so through maintaining excellent working relationships with program officers, keeping several "add-on" projects in mind and discussing them with program officers, and keeping in close communication. If the grantees' project is not fully funded (perhaps they have accepted a take-it-or-leave-it offer), a request for supplemental funds, documenting their need, should be on file at the agency.

In summary, the reasons for award increases are varied in content, in importance to the various negotiating parties, and in the amount of control grantees and grantors possess. Budget increases are relatively rare, compared with the commonplace budget cuts, yet opportunities for increases do exist through increased work scope, increased indirect-cost rates, increased direct-cost rates, changing program regulations, adjusting for too low an original request, corrections of calculation errors and indirect-cost rates, benefit from review panel recommendations, and new funding levels at the grantor agency.

While grantor representatives have final control over increasing budgets, the grantee representatives can and should exert considerable influence. Except for needs for increased work scope (usually generated by the grantor), the grantee should be alert to all other opportunities for increases and should initiate requests as they are appropriate and justifiable.

What Are the Methods of Negotiation?

Grants are negotiated in any one or a combination of the following ways: telephone, letter, meeting at grantor facility, meeting at grantee facility, telecopier, and telegram. There are some differences in the use of these methods between *grants* and *contracts,* and these differences will be specified as they occur.

Telephone. When a telephone negotiation is to be conducted, a grantor representative (usually the grant officer) calls a grantee representative (usually the grant administrator) to arrange a time for the negotiation to take place. Generally, the appointment is arranged within the following week or so. The length of the actual negotiation varies, but it is advisable to reserve one hour as a minimum; several hours may be needed for a negotiation if serious disagreements occur.

During the interim between the first call and the negotiation appointment, the grant administrator prepares for the negotiation, as does the project director. If conference speaker phones are available at the grantee facility, they are reserved for use during the negotiation, enabling as many parties as necessary to be present. The use of a conference phone is particularly advisable when the grantee negotiating team includes technical specialists other than the project director.

Grants professionals who were interviewed and surveyed reported that, in their collective experience, negotiations were conducted by telephone far more frequently than by any other means. The kinds of answers they gave when asked how often telephone negotiations were held were:

"Most common, it's fastest!"
"Almost always, usually routine."
"Most times—cheap, quick, convenient."

Based on their experiences, over three fourths of all *grant* negotiations and over one half of all *contract* negotiations are conducted by phone.

According to these same grants professionals, telephone negotiations are used in fairly routine situations, when serious differences of opinion are not anticipated. Typically, the telephone is used when negotiating extensions and renewals of existing grants, when the work scope of a project has been approved and only minor administrative matters are at issue, and/or when new projects are being considered but they involve relatively small amounts of funding.

Even if a project is nonroutine, it may become necessary to use the phone because of the pressures of time. If there is a grantor delay in announcing awards, the phone is the fastest. For example, if the grantor must commit funds before the end of the fiscal year or in time to enable the grantee to start the project as scheduled, the use of the telephone is advantageous. Even if there is not a fiscal-year or starting-date problem, the grantor may be too busy to use other methods of negotiation in nonroutine situations.

A telephone negotiation may or may not have the element of surprise. Sometimes the grant officer informs the grant administrator before the formal negotiation that certain changes will be required in the budget and the work scope. When this happens, the grantees can prepare more thoroughly ahead of time. Usually, however, this is not the case. The grantees do not know until the actual telephone negotiation just what concerns the grantors will express.

If the "surprise" is too great to be effectively handled during the telephone negotiation, the grantee should not hesitate to terminate the discussions temporarily. During a recess of a day or so, the grantees can gather additional information and support for their case. Some grantees hesitate to do this, for fear of exposing the fact that they weren't totally prepared for the negotiation or for fear of jeopardizing their grant. However, because the project is so important, and the terms of the negotiation will be in effect at least a year, it is important to present the strongest case possible, even if this requires a delay.

Letter. Grantors sometimes initiate negotiation by sending a letter to the grantees, advising them that their project has been approved at a specified level of funding, that such-and-such changes in the work scope will be needed, and/or that additional explanation of so-and-so tasks will be required. The letter is usually one to three pages long and indicates a deadline for sending a revised budget and the requested backup materials.

Letters are the second most frequently used method of *grant* negotiation, based on the experience of the grants professionals surveyed. Some grantors prefer them and use them almost exclusively because of the time that is saved, especially in high-volume programs. Instead of a program officer's and a grant officer's having to spend one to two hours on the telephone, the program officer can insert key conditions in a boiler-plate letter in a very short time and doesn't have to spend minutes, hours, or emotional effort listening to the grantee's displeasure with requested changes.

Letters are almost never used as the sole means of negotiation in *contract* negotiations. However, they are used in combination with telephone calls or visits. For example, letters are sometimes used to relay requests for best-and-final offers.

The optimal conditions for letter negotiation are very similar to those for telephone negotiations. Routine matters such as extensions or renewals, changes of an administrative requirement, and minor changes of any nature can be successfully negotiated through an exchange of letters. In addition, a letter is advisable when a nonroutine matter is involved. In this case, either the grantees or the grantors may wish to establish their formal positions for the record. Finally, as noted previously, the letter is an effective means of saving staff time. The grantee should use a letter as a follow-up to any telephone negotiation in which a budget cut was agreed to and the grantee must reduce work scope as a result.

There are no surprises in a letter negotiation. The grantees have time to respond to all changes requested; they know exactly what the concerns of the grantors are (provided, of course, the letter is well written). The disadvantage of the letter, from the grantee's perspective, is exactly what makes the letter advantageous to the grantor. The grantees do not have the opportunity to "give and take" with the grantors. They can't obtain further information or clarify points that the grantor has raised. They can't estimate how important particular points are to the grantor through voice tones or questions as they could in a telephone negotiation. This is not a serious problem with a *contract* negotiation, where there will probably be a follow-up meeting. It is a problem in a *grant* negotiation, where the only other communication that the grantor wishes is a letter back.

Novice (and even some experienced) grantees are likely to interpret a negotiation letter as a take-it-or-leave-it offer. And it may very well be. If the grantees have serious objections to the grantor's terms stated in the negotiation letter, however, they should try informally to find out whether it is indeed a take-it-or-leave-it offer. As mentioned previously, a good informal information source is the project director's phone call to the program officer.

Telecopier–Telegram. Variations of the letter negotiation are negotiation by telegram (fast, a day or less) and telecopier (even faster, minutes or hours). Sending requested changes by telegram or telecopier provides a written record, and it also has the advantage of being much faster than regular mail. The use of a telecopier can be especially effective as the initial negotiation method for a complex project where many issues are at stake. Many government agencies have telecopier machines located on their premises; universities frequently have them in their libraries. The grantor's concerns can be thoroughly described in writing, and then as many pages as necessary can be sent to the grantee within minutes. When extensive written information must be provided by the grantor to the grantee as a first step in the negotiation and time is of the essence, the use of a telecopier can save valuable days.

Meeting at Funding Agency. A grant or contract negotiation may be conducted at the funding agency's facility. When this is to happen, the grantor's grant officer makes arrangements with the grantee's grant administrator several weeks in advance. Depending on the complexity of the project and the number of issues at stake, the negotiation sessions may last from one half day to a couple of days. The negotiation teams are frequently larger than they are during telephone or letter negotiations. Technical specialists such as accountants, lawyers, and auditors may be included on either or both the grantor's or the grantee's teams.

Grant negotiations at the funding agency are rare. Probably fewer than 5% of all grant negotiations are held at the grantor's facility. It is more common for *contracts* to be negotiated at the funding agency, with over 10% of contract negotiations being held there in the experience of the grants professionals interviewed.

There are certain occasions on which it is advisable to hold negotiations at the grantor's facility. These include new projects requiring significant amounts, large renewal projects when a series of issues need clarification and a new budget with proposed changes may be needed, any awards involving complex issues or a major controversy, and complicated arrangements that grantors and grantees must make together. In general, negotiations at the grantor's agency are held under nonroutine circumstances.

This method of negotiation offers advantages to both the grantors and the grantees. They can exchange information and best analyze each others' needs. Nonverbal as well as verbal communications take place. A rapport may be established that will help lead to the success of the project through cooperative efforts during the project period.

A disadvantage, to both the grantees and the grantors, is the time involved. This may be minor, in terms of the time that will be saved later because of the careful planning at the beginning of the project. The grantees have two additional disadvantages. First, there is the expense (travel, per diem) of coming to the negotiations. For a new project, the grantor does not pay for the travel. In the case of a renewal, it may be possible to charge the grantor for at least the project director's travel, if the project director uses the trip to take care of ongoing project matters. Second, the grantee's team may not have access to all the documentation and support staff they need. Therefore, grantees should plan especially carefully and bring calculators, secretaries, and the project files along according to expected need.

Site Visit. Negotiations are carried on least frequently by holding meetings at the grantee's facility. This method of negotiating is known as the *site visit.* It occurs probably less than 5% of the time on grants, less than 10% on contracts. The site-visit negotiation is like the funding-agency meeting in most ways. The main differences have to do with the circumstances under which site visits are conducted and the advantages and disadvantages to the grantees and the grantors.

Site visits are conducted by grantor representatives when they must collect additional information about the grantees that is fully available only on the grantee's premises. Sometimes the grantors want to inspect grantee facilities. They may also need to examine special equipment, meet with grantee clients, or audit grantee costs and procedures.

The site visit offers grantees special advantages. They can show off their capabilities (special equipment, modern facilities) and also demonstrate need (inadequate laboratories, construction funds badly needed, etc.). Typewritten words in a proposal saying that your university has a fabulous research facility strategically located next to Sea World on the Pacific Ocean does not impress grantors in the same manner as walking through the facility, smelling the sea air, and admiring the colorful fish and landscaped grounds. Asking for hospital beds with words (letter) or verbally (visit at agency) is not the same as showing grantors sick people, in overcrowded conditions, with sagging mattresses on dilapidated beds.

The grantors also benefit. They know and understand the project much better than they ever could if the project had been negotiated in their agency conference room. However, the grantors have the disadvantage of paying for the travel, spending more staff time (several days compared with perhaps half a day), and being less prepared with support staff, equipment, and documentation. Also, more commitment to the project is implied by their visit, so if difficulties arise during negotiation, the grantor's representatives may have less bargaining power (and therefore have to "give in" more) than they would have had the meeting been held at their agency.

Best Method? So those are the traditional ways that grants are negotiated: by telephone, letter, telegram–telecopier, meeting at the funding agency, and site visit. Grants professionals were asked, "Which method do you believe offers the best opportunity for the grantee to receive the most funds?" and "Why?" Their answers were varied, including site visit, agency visit, telephone, and "no difference." No one believed that letter negotiations were advantageous. In general, the consensus was that a face-to-face meeting is best.

Grantee representatives thought so.

"Site visit," claimed one grant administrator. "We can use our powers of negotiation and persuasion."

Another recognized that "Psychologically, we have the advantage when negotiations take place here. A site visit is useful for determining need."

Project directors also preferred meetings.

"I prefer a personal relationship. It gives me a sense of dealing with a 'real person.' I can develop trust, be more thorough," said one.

Others commented that "Any face-to-face discussion will help in clarifying a proposal," and "I like the ability to 'sell' the project merits and impact."

Grantor officials agreed.

Program officers recommended, "Face-to-face persuasion with the opportunity to counter unforeseen objections" and "Direct personal communication because it permits direct exchange and resolution of problems and concerns."

Similarly, a grant officer commented, "Question-and-answer sessions are best in a face-to-face situation. Evaluation is easier to do."

As desirable as face-to-face negotiation may be, the facts are that time and expense prohibit its use in most situations. Also, the grantor, rather than the grantee, selects the method of negotiation. It should be comforting, then, to grantees, to know that a few grantor representatives believed that there is little or no advantage of one negotiation method over another.

One program officer, on being asked which method was best for the grantee, said, "None of these. The only answer is to write an outstanding proposal that gets superb ratings, and let the budget be appropriate for the project to be done."

Several grant officers remarked:

"Makes no difference."
"Insignificant."
"None. A well-prepared proposal with a carefully documented budget is what matters."

It is possible that, in some situations, at least, there is no difference. If so, there is probably no negotiation involved.

How Do Grant Negotiators Prepare?

No matter what method is to be used, preparation for the negotiation is of utmost importance. It is especially important for the grantees, who are essentially on the "defensive" and it's time to huddle now. They must be prepared to justify and document to the hilt. Everything in the original project plan is at stake. The grantees may or may not know what the grantor's game plan is.

Fortunately for the grantees, they are now in control. Although they couldn't select the type of method to be used, the amount of preparation they undertake is up to them. It is limited only by the amount of time that has been provided by the grantor between the notification and the negotiation meeting or the response deadline. If this time is not adequate, the grantees can request an extension or postpone the meeting. It's important to remember—and novice grantees may not be aware—that both parties to a negotiation can practice the art of delay.

What kind of preparations do grantees and grantors make for negotiations? Grants professionals were asked how they typically prepare. Their methods varied, depending on their roles.

According to their responses, there are certain preparations that all parties to the negotiation normally make. Everyone reads (or skims) the proposal, talks with the other member(s) of the teams, and estimates how much money will be left from last year if a renewal project is involved.

Grantee team members make some special preparations that grantors do not undertake. Project directors and grant administrators reported that they prepared optional budgets; developed strategies to reduce work scopes; obtained further justification for costs and tasks so that proposed cuts could be attacked; tried to find out what the sponsor had been negotiating with others; and agreed on minimum funds and conditions below which they would not agree to do the project.

Similarly, grantor team members made special preparations. Program officers and grant officers reported that they read reviewer comments on the proposal; checked on the track record of the grantee; and agreed to a maximum above which they would not fund the project.

There are some preparations, however, that individuals on each team apparently assume. The project director, for example, takes on the tasks of gathering informal information about the program officer who will be negotiating, what the grantor's concerns about technical work scope may be, and how much money the grantor may be willing to give. The project director does this through direct questions to program officers (if a relationship has been established already), through questioning colleagues who may have served on the proposal review panel or who may know someone who did, and through talking to competitors who applied for the same kind of program grant or even the same contract.

While the project director is collecting unprinted kinds of information, the grant administrator reviews the program regulations, RFP, and other printed materials that may support the grantee's case. The grant administrator may also check with colleagues at competitor institutions.

For example, at one institution, the grantees were offered $500,000 ($150,000 less than they needed to do the job as proposed). They did not accept this amount in the initial telephone negotiation but terminated the call until they could gather additional information. Subsequently, the grant administrator learned that a neighboring institution had negotiated to do exactly the same kind of work, but with fewer clients, for $750,000. When negotiations were resumed, the grantees brought this fact to the attention of the grantors. They backed this information up with documentation of the greater number of clients their program was serving. The result? Additional funds for the grantees.

On the grantor's side of the fence, the program officer looks at the track record of the project director, checks on other support that the project director has, recommends elimination of specific costs and tasks (if necessary), and identifies a recommended level of funding based on an analysis of reviewer recommendations. If a project is being renewed, the program officer also checks the progress of the current project and reviews the previous costs against previous estimates.

The grant officer then checks the calculations in the proposed budget and recalculates and reviews all proposed costs, to ensure that they are allowable within the agency and program regulations.

The similarities and differences in the kinds of preparation undertaken by the negotiating teams and the individuals on these teams demonstrate the responsibilities and interests of each party. In preparing for negotiation, it is important to be aware of what the others are (or should be) doing. If they have not adequately prepared, you will enjoy an advantage. If they have, you will have anticipated—and will therefore be better prepared to deal with—their concerns.

The amount of time that negotiating parties spend in preparation varies greatly, depending on their role in the process and the complexity and size of the project. The project director normally has the most time available to prepare. It is usually a once-a-year event for him or her; the outcome of the negotiation has the greatest impact on the project director's life. Loss of the grant could mean loss of the opportunity to do research next year; reduction of the award could mean laying off staff who have now become close friends or "nickel-and-diming" research supplies.

In contrast, the others involved (grant administrator, program officer, and grant officer) have many more grants to negotiate during the year. Also, the personal importance of the negotiation is not as great, since their daily working and living conditions will not be significantly affected by loss or reduction of funding for the project. However, because the grant administrator identifies closely with the project director personally and because of organizational goals that will best be achieved with a successful negotiation, the grant administrator makes the time necessary to prepare with the project director. For organizational reasons, the program officer and the grant officer spend the necessary time preparing.

Since preparation time is often inadequate and since no one is as intimately familiar with the proposal as the project director, the project director should not assume that all parties in the negotiation have read and fully understand the proposal. She or he should be prepared to listen carefully during the negotiation. Then, if there appear to be misunderstandings, she or he should eliminate them, explaining the project in terms that the grant officer and the grant administrator will understand, since their expertise is ordinarily administrative rather than technical.

There are many ways to prepare for negotiation. Effective grants negotiators will use all of them and will understand how others have or have not prepared also. A checklist of methods of preparing for grant negotiations is contained in Figure 18.

What Are Grant Negotiators' Needs?

During the actual negotiations, what individual needs does each party have? Are these needs relatively basic on Maslow's list (i.e., keep my job, bring home the bacon) or of a higher order (i.e., need to know and understand the proposal). What organizational needs are involved? Are individual needs subordinate to or do they take precedence over organizational needs?

After discussions with grants professionals, a list of their needs during negotiations was developed as follows:

1. Enhance own organization's reputation.
2. Get terms as requested (or wanted).
3. Get budget items awarded as requested (or wanted).
4. Get (or give) the total award amount according to your wishes.
5. Accept (or have the grantee accept) the award.
6. Have the grantees (or grantors) like you.
7. Avoid grantee's going to congressional representative(s).
8. Avoid grantee's having to go to higher authority in grantor agency.
9. Avoid grantor's having to go to higher authority in grantor agency.
10. Get the negotiation over with quickly.

Each need will be described briefly, and its importance to each member of the negotiating team will be discussed.

NEGOTIATION PREPARATION CHECKLIST

TYPE OF PREPARATION	PERSON RESPONSIBLE				
	PROJECT DIRECTOR	GRANT ADMINISTRATOR	PROGRAM OFFICER	GRANT OFFICER	OTHER
READ THE PROPOSAL					
TALK WITH TEAM MEMBERS					
IF RENEWAL PROJECT, ESTIMATE REMAINING FUNDS					
PREPARE OPTIONAL BUDGETS					
DEVELOP STRATEGY FOR REDUCING WORKSCOPE					
OBTAIN ADDITIONAL JUSTIFICATION FOR COSTS AND TASKS					
ATTEMPT TO DETERMINE WHAT GRANTOR HAS BEEN NEGOTIATING WITH OTHERS					
AGREE ON MINIMUM FUNDS AND TERMS ACCEPTABLE					
READ REVIEWER COMMENTS ON PROPOSAL					
CHECK GRANTEE INSTITUTION'S TRACK RECORD					
AGREE TO MAXIMUM FUNDS TO BE GRANTED					
GATHER INFORMAL INFORMATION ABOUT THE GRANTORS					
GATHER AND REVIEW GRANTOR REGULATIONS, RFP, OTHER MATERIALS					
CHECK PROJECT DIRECTOR TRACK RECORD AND OTHER SOURCES OF SUPPORT					
RECOMMEND ELIMINATION OF SPECIFIC COSTS AND TASKS					
RECOMMEND A LEVEL OF FUNDING					
IF A RENEWAL, CHECK PROGRESS OF CURRENT PROJECT AND COMPARE CURRENT COSTS WITH PREVIOUS ESTIMATES					
CHECK BUDGET CALCULATIONS AND INDIRECT COST RATE					
REVIEW PROPOSED COSTS FOR ALLOWABILITY WITHIN REGULATIONS					

Figure 18. Negotiation preparation checklist.

Organization's Reputation. "Getting (or giving) sufficient funds for the project to be done well so as to enhance your organization's reputation" was claimed as an important need by the project directors, grant administrators, and program officers contacted. Curiously, this need was rated low by grant officers, and one of them stated frankly, "That's the program officer's job." In terms of Maslow's needs, the need to enhance the reputation of one's organization is one of the higher-order ones.

Favorable Terms. "Having the other party(ies) agree to your terms (effective date, financing, etc.)" was very important to everyone but the program officers. They apparently consider this the grant officer's "job" and thus have little personal need involved. Whatever terms are agreed to must be lived with by the project director and the grant administrator. For example, if the grantor will not allow the grantee institution to patent a grant-funded discovery, dollars may be lost.

Budget Items. It was fairly important to project directors, grant administrators, and grant officers that budget items be agreed to as each proposed. For example, if the original budget contained $5,000 for travel, the grantee wanted the funds used in that manner rather than shifted to some other item, such as salaries. The program officers, in contrast, generally had a relatively low need to control the way funds were spent within the total amount awarded.

Total Amount of Award. All parties involved had a relatively high need for the opposers to agree to the total amount of money they requested (or offered) for the project. One program officer said that her most important need was to "Have the grantee accept the level of funding offered because this is the amount of money I have with which to fund the project, and the decision has been made that it is worth doing but not above that level."

Grantee's Acceptance of the Award. Among the professionals contacted, only the grant officers had a relatively low need for the prospective grantee to accept the award. This was a very basic need for project directors, as their salaries, their daily work schedules, and the opportunity to perform interesting scientific studies or to conduct challenging service programs were at stake. Similarly, the grant administrators had high values for accepting the award. Although their personal salaries were not dependent on the receipt of any one award, the failure of many negotiations could cause them to lose their jobs. Finally, because of the program officer's job responsibility for the work to be conducted successfully, the program officers had strong personal interest in having the awards accepted. Although there might be other projects in the wings, waiting to be funded, the program officers had already invested time and interest in the project and hence would have more to lose than the grant officers, who had probably heard of the project only shortly before negotiations were started.

Interestingly, there is a shift in need for the grantee to accept the award when a *contract*, as opposed to a *grant*, is being negotiated. One grant officer said that he would "push much harder for acceptance" during a contract negotiation because the "people vying for the contract bucks are not as 'hungry' as the grants people." Program officers recognized their greater need for a contract to be accepted also.

Have the Opposer Like You. This need was no need at all for the grant officers contacted, and it was low among the program officers' needs. Apparently, grantors are not dependent on the grantees' liking them for any basic physiological or security needs. In contrast, the project directors and the grant administrators rated being liked at about the middle of their needs. This ranking may reflect their dependence on the grantors' goodwill to receive continued funding, a basic personal and organizational need.

Avoid Grantee's Going to Congressmen. It is possible, during negotiations, for grantees to enlist the support of external advocates, such as their local

Congressmen. When asked how important it was to avoid getting into a situation where grantees go to their Congressmen, all parties contacted claimed that this was a relatively low need.

One grant officer said, "Sometimes, when you really get hassled, and the grantee says he's going to his Congressman, you really get negative. You try not to, but with all the negotiations we're in, and trying to do a good job, it's hard not to react negatively."

Another said, "So let him go. Unless the Congressman is extremely powerful or on the appropriations committee for my agency, it's not going to make any difference. If anyone tells you anything different than that, he's full of baloney."

Apparently, grantees don't need to avoid the effort of enlisting congressional help, but in most cases, such help will have no effect on the grantors' jobs or on their basic safety and security needs.

Avoid Grantee's Going to Higher Authority in Grantor Agency. It is also possible, during negotiations, for the grantee to appeal to the program officer's or the grant officer's boss, claiming unfair treatment or requesting special consideration. Although grantee representatives have a very low need to avoid doing this, the grantor representatives really don't mind if they do. Apparently, grantor representatives feel safe in their negotiation judgments and count on their superiors to back them up.

Avoid Grantor's Going to Higher Authority in Grantor Agency. If there are insufficient funds or if there are agency policies that must be "bent," it may be necessary for the program officer or the grant officer to go to his or her boss, to receive authorization to agree to the grantee's requests for more money or policy deviations or interpretations. None of the parties to the negotiation felt much need to avoid this.

Get the Negotiation over with Quickly. "Expedite timely processing" was the major need of one grant officer.

A program officer agreed, saying, "My primary need is to reach a quick agreement. There are thirty to forty other negotiations to be held in a short time span, and processing takes six to eight weeks once official revision is received."

As might be expected, grantors who have many projects to negotiate and are not intimately involved with any one project apparently have a higher need to save time. This is especially critical as the end of the fiscal year approaches and grantor funds must be committed or lost. Grantee representatives, in contrast, seem to have a low need to save time.

The above were the reactions of grants professionals to a list of predetermined needs. When these persons were asked to "Describe your most important need," some of their comments were as follows.

Project directors said:

"Obtain funds in an orderly manner to do research."

"The opportunity to perform and participate in interesting work."

"Receive adequate funding and not sacrifice the project's integrity."
"Understand what is being requested and why."

Grant administrators offered:

"Balance objectives of university and project director with the dollar and rule limits of the sponsor agency."
"Negotiate sufficient money to enable the investigator to do the proposed work."
"Assure adequate support for the research and full overhead."
"Protect university from financial risk."

Program officers volunteered:

"Serve the public interest, as I am able to perceive it."
"Ensure a good scientific study."
"Get the best possible work performance."

Grant officers commented:

"A good bargain without jeopardizing the project."
"Ensure the services will be performed according to regulations."
"Provide sufficient funding to do the proposed project well."

The needs expressed above were *individual* needs, yet they clearly reflect the needs of both the grantee and the grantor *organizations*. When respondents were asked to identify any additional needs that their organizations had, they generally agreed that in grants negotiation, organization and individual needs were similar.

"I have no 'personal' needs," stated a grant officer, "other than my organization's."

A project director said, "The individual working for an organization does it for the organization and not personal reputation."

A grant administrator agreed, claiming his primary need was organizational: "To maintain and enhance the reputation of the university as a responsible and professional research-educational service institution."

This duality of individual and organizational needs was summed up by a program officer, who said, "In a sense, there are never agency needs, except as translated by an individual. Mine relate to programmatic concerns; the grant officer's relate to administrative concerns. The 'directive' from higher up is general: get good-quality, relevant research done, in an administratively sound way. The agency will balk if the research seems unrelated to policy or program goals or has administrative 'wrinkles,' or if there is a 'political' problem—whether it is a small or a large program."

Despite the consensus that individual and organizational needs coincide, there are times when the individual needs may be so basic that they may take precedence. It is not uncommon, for example, for project directors who are relying on a grant for their weekly take-home pay to try to influence their organizations to accept a grant even when unfavorable and costly terms are involved.

This can cause a problem because the project director is, in effect, working on the grantor's team.

Also, the esteem and ego needs of the negotiating parties may arise. Are grants negotiators competitive, striving to "win" for an ego boost? Or is their main concern cooperation, even if they do not get everything they originally wanted?

When asked, "If you complete a grant negotiation and the opposers agree to exactly what you wanted, do you feel that you've 'won'?", two thirds of the grants negotiators queried said "no."

"It's not an adversary relationship," explained one grant administrator.

A program officer commented, "'Winning' and 'losing' don't fit the concept of the fair negotiation of an assistance relationship."

In a *contract* negotiation, as compared with a grant negotiation, there was a slightly less cooperative tendency, with about half (instead of two thirds) claiming that they don't feel as if they "won," even though they received everything requested.

What these responses mean, in negotiating grants and contracts, is that *one third to one half of the negotiators probably do have a competitive spirit*, with ego and esteem needs that must be considered. Therefore, if grants are to be negotiated successfully, some of the needs of all parties must be met, in order that everyone may be a winner to some extent.

A cooperative goal that all parties to grants negotiations should pursue creatively, and one that maximizes the individual and organizational interests of all parties, was stated by a program officer: "To negotiate the agreement that best serves the need of the program, the government, and the public interest, recognizing that a harsh or adverse agreement for the grantee (or contractor) does not serve the public interest as well as a fair one."

In the same spirit, a grant administrator indicated the cooperative stance that grantees should take, saying, "If negotiations have been fair and complete, less *is* best."

Who Has the Bargaining Power?

Beckmann, in describing bargaining power in a procurement, gave six very specific factors that influenced the relative bargaining power of the buyer and the seller. Since a grant negotiation is, in fact, a procurement of research or services or development, it is useful to reexamine Beckmann's factors in terms of Maslow's hierarchy of needs and the needs of grants negotiators as just discussed. The grantees are considered the "sellers"; the grantors are the "buyers."

Number of Qualified Competitors. In a grants competition, there are typically many qualified competitors applying for a limited number of funds. It is not unusual for a grantor to fund only 20-30% of all the proposals it receives. Should a grantee refuse to accept funding, there are many other qualified competitors waiting in line. Therefore, the grantor almost always enjoys all the bargaining power. Only if the prospective grantee can produce a proposal clearly superior to those of the competitors and/or of strong personal interest to the program officer will he enjoy equal bargaining power with the grantor.

Urgency of Grantee's Desire for an Award. If the project director depends on grant funds for salary, and if the proposal being negotiated has been sent to only one grantor, the grantee's desire for an award will be very urgent. The award is needed to fill the lowest-order physiological needs (food and shelter), and hence, again, all the bargaining power rests with the grantor. Even if the project director has other sources of salary support, the award may be necessary to fill safety and security needs (research track record needed for promotion) or self-esteem needs. Occasionally, the project director has many projects and therefore no urgent desire for one particular award. In this case, there is no difference in bargaining power between the parties, as each team may be equally willing to walk away from the negotiation.

The grantor, of course, does have an urgent desire to award funds to someone. However, the grantor usually has many applicants willing to fill his or her need, while the grantee usually has only one source.

Amount of Time Available to Reach Agreement. When one party has less time available to negotiate than the other, that party has less bargaining power. In a grants negotiation, typically the grantee (who is willing to spend as much time as necessary to reach agreement to his or her terms) has the bargaining power. The grantee (or contractor) is in an especially good bargaining position near the end of the fiscal year, when the grantor's funds must be committed or lost and there is no time for the grantor to locate others to do the project.

The Accuracy of One Party's Assessment of the Other's Negotiation Objectives. Here is where thorough preparation and outstanding negotiation skills provide one party or the other with the advantage. In a grant negotiation, the bargaining power that comes with accurately assessing the opposer's needs is not predetermined. Either the grantees or the grantors may take the advantage, or they may each control equal amounts of bargaining power.

The External Pressures–Regulatory, Legal, Political, and/or Public–That One Party Can Use to Force Agreement from Another. When one party can bring external pressures to bear on the other, that party has the advantage in bargaining power. Ways that grantees typically obtain this power are (1) becoming more knowledgeable about the grantor and the relevant regulations than the grantor is; (2) enlisting legal help to appeal unfavorable decisions; (3) obtaining the help of politically powerful Congressmen and their aides; and (4) campaigning for client support.

In order for external pressures to bring bargaining power to the grantee, however, they must be strong enough to cause the grantors to take them seriously. For example, one program officer commented that Congressmen can help only if they have "political clout."

If there is any bargaining power in a negotiation due to external pressures, it will probably belong to the grantee. In most grant negotiations, external pressures are not used. While they could bring about a "victory" in the negotiation of concern, chances are that long-term relationships with the grantor could be damaged, and most grantees are unwilling to take that risk.

The Accuracy of One Party's Evaluation of the Other's Bargaining Position. Here again, thorough preparation and outstanding negotiation skills provide one party or the other with the advantage. Either party may gain the most bargaining power, or they may share equal amounts.

Based on the six factors discussed above, it appears that in a *grant* negotiation, grantors usually have the most bargaining power. In particular, the number of qualified competitors and the urgency of the grantees' desires to be funded contribute to the uneven distribution of power. While grantees can benefit by bringing time and external pressures to bear, these two factors must be used with caution and are not usually sufficient to outweigh the others.

In a *contracts* negotiation, the bargaining power is usually more evenly distributed. The potential contractors may even have more power than the funding agency, particularly if they are the only or the best-qualified candidate.

The effective grant or contract negotiator understands the factors that contribute to bargaining power, arranges to take advantage of as much power as possible, and estimates the bargaining position of the opposer accurately.

What Strategies Are Useful to Grantees in a Grant Negotiation?

Given the relatively unfavorable bargaining position that grantees usually have, what negotiation strategies should they employ to achieve their bargaining objectives? Nierenberg identified six general strategies that are effectively used by bargaining parties. Restated to apply to grants negotiations, the strategies are:

1. Grantees work for grantors' needs.
2. Grantees let grantors work for grantees' needs.
3. Grantees work for grantors' and their own needs.
4. Grantees work against their own needs.
5. Grantees work against grantors' needs.
6. Grantees work against grantors' and their own needs.

These strategies are listed from most controllable and desirable to least controllable and desirable. Grantees, because of their less favorable bargaining position (and hence less control), are sometimes limited to creatively using the first strategy in order to achieve their objectives. Depending on the amount of bargaining power (and therefore control) that grantees believe they have, some mixture of these strategies should be used. Examples of each follow.

Grantees Work for Grantors' Needs. Grantor program officers are responsible for successfully carrying out their program mission. For example, a program officer may be charged with using the agency's money to provide vocational training to all blind people in a certain region. If insufficient funds are awarded to a project, and the blind people who expect to be served efficiently are not, the program officer's job performance may be discredited. Also, the program officer may be inconvenienced by many telephone calls, visits, and letters from unhappy blind people and their advocates. Therefore, one strategy that a grantee may take is to explain that sufficient funds are necessary to do a job that the funding agency will be proud of.

Grantees may work for grantor needs for apprciation and recognition as well. During the negotiation, grantees can show appreciation for the difficult job the program officer and the grant officer have to do (processing many awards, heavy work loads, etc.). This need is just above basic physiology and security needs on Maslow's scale.

Another grantor need is the need to know and understand. Although this need is less basic than the others, filling it is especially important because of the organizational goals of all parties. The grantor's need to know and understand can be filled by grantees in such ways as providing additional justification for either the tasks or the cost items proposed, using visual presentations to demonstrate a point, or notifying the grantor of a mathematical error in the recommended budget.

Several illustrations come to mind. In one instance, a grantee was providing technical assistance to school districts that were not in compliance with current federal legislation. The project had been going on for three years and was funded at the same level each year. The work was being done at the specific request of the government. Then, in the fourth year, the project director discovered that the work load would be almost double that of previous years. Accordingly, his budget request was higher (not double, because of economies of scale, but considerably higher). When negotiations commenced, the grantors informed him that the project was recommended for the same level of funding as in prior years. Well prepared, the project director produced hundreds of written requests from school districts for the services that the grantor expected them to receive.

"Which of these requests for technical assistance do you want me to turn down or postpone?" he asked the program officer. On reviewing the additional documentation and justification submitted by the project director, the program officer granted all the funds requested. She—and her organization—needed to know and understand the impact of their recommendations on the project.

In another case, the grantors' need to know and understand was used effectively by informing the grantors of calculation errors in the recommended budget.

A grants administrator reported gaining $27,000 in just this manner. The grantors had recommended a lower level of funding than the project director had proposed. The grantors, after saying that they would provide certain resources and eliminate others, offered a new reduced total award amount that had been incorrectly calculated. The grant administrator pointed this out, and the funds lost because of an addition error were reinstated. This negotiation was especially significant because in the following two years, there was no negotiation for the project at all. Funds were simply provided at exactly the same rate as they had been the preceding year, and so the grantee received two more

$27,000 increments that it would not have enjoyed without catching the calculation error in the first year.

In each of the instances just described, logic and persuasion were used to obtain sufficient funding to do the project as proposed. By working for grantor needs, the grantees filled theirs as well.

Grantees Let Grantors Work for Grantees' Needs. More desirable, of course—but less controllable—grantees may allow the grantors to fill their needs. Grantees can ask the program officers or grant officers to provide additional funds, to help resolve legal issues or problems with terms and conditions, or they may set an earlier (or later) starting date for the project. Since both parties have a stake in the overall success of the project, grantors are sometimes willing to fill some or all of these requests. In addition, if funds are cut, work scope is revised, or harsh terms are imposed, the grantee should ask the grantor why, thereby allowing the grantor to fulfill the grantee's need to know and understand. If the grantor's logic or persuasion is poor, or the unfavorable decision was based on erroneous information, the grantee then has the opportunity to refute it. Asking questions is a common way of getting the grantor to work for grantee needs. Unfortunately, it is frequently forgotten. Because grantees may be so busy providing information to grantors, they may overlook the possibilities inherent in listening.

Grantees Work for Grantors' and Their Own Needs. One way that grantees can work for their own and grantors' needs is to point out that other grantees with similar programs have received more funds to do less or the same work. The grantor needs to be perceived as treating grantees equitably (self-esteem), and the grantee needs to receive fair treatment (also self-esteem).

Grantees Work against Their Own Needs. There are several ways that grantees may successfully work against their own needs. Usually, they do this by making minor concessions in order to fill other more important needs.

For example, grantees could agree to drop or postpone part of the work scope that they wanted to cover but that the grantors weren't especially interested in and decreased the funding accordingly. An even more effective device occurs when a project director works against his or her own most basic need—and forgoes some part of his or her salary. This should absolutely convince the grantors that there is certainly no place else to cut the budget, since the project director's salary is usually regarded as sacred, for excellent reasons, and is usually the last item to go in any budget.

A creative way in which the project director can work against his or her own most basic need is illustrated in the following incident. A project director proposed a three-year project to prepare and publish an extensive scientific bibliography. The cooperation of colleagues in many Latin American countries was enlisted. Elaborate preparations were made for the printing so that all would be in order once the funding was officially awarded.

Several months before the expected starting date, a hitch occurred. Because of a change in program officers at the funding agency, the proposed budget was cut heavily. During the negotiation, it appeared that all the preparations were in vain, and the project director actually started to talk about withdrawing his proposal.

Fortunately, a possible solution occurred to him. If he agreed to exclude his summer salary from the budget in the third year, could the grantors help him to find an "administrative" way to replace it? Since the bibliography was to be sold, if sufficient sales were made, could some of the receipts be used to pay his third summer's salary? He recognized the risk that sales might not be high enough but was willing to take it. The grantors were impressed at the novel offer and found an administrative solution allowing him to do just that.

The project director had worked against his basic physiological need (guaranteed salary) in order to save the project.

Grantees Work against Grantors' Needs. Grantees may work against the grantors' needs in several ways. They may withdraw temporarily from the negotiation, postpone meetings, engage in long drawn-out discussions over "straw" issues, or generally practice the art of delay so as to work against the grantors' needs to save time and expedite the negotiation. This strategy assumes, of course, that grantees have plenty of time.

Another way that grantees can work against the opposers' need is to reduce the work scope in the way that is least acceptable to the grantors and most acceptable to them. For example, a project director may have proposed to tutor and provide special services to 50 disadvantaged students for one year for $100,000. If the grantor tells the project director, "You can have only $75,000," the project director could respond by retaining all of his high-cost administrative staff and cutting stipends and subsistence allowances so that only 25 students could participate in the program. Thus, 50 students for $100,000 or 25 for $75,000 would be the grantor's choice, in this case. Not a very cost-effective solution from the grantor's point of view, but "livable" and perhaps necessary for the grantee.

Still another possibility is for the grantee to appeal (or threaten to appeal) to the program officer's and/or the grant officer's boss, in hopes of obtaining a more favorable agreement. In this way, the grantee works against the grantor's needs for job security and esteem, by indicating that the grantor has failed and "couldn't handle" the negotiation.

A final way that grantees can work against grantor needs is to bring pressures from outside the grantor agency to bear, possibly jeopardizing the grantor's job security and self-esteem, and his or her recognition needs. Pressures can be exerted by enlisting political, legal, or public advocates such as Congressmen, lawyers, or client groups who benefit from grant activities.

In one unique negotiation, a large hospitial used a combination of these methods in order to achieve its goals. After the hospital staff had submitted what they believed was an extremely competitive best-and-final offer, the contract that they were bidding on was let to another contractor. Suspecting foul play on the part of the winning competitors, the hospital staff took several immediate actions. They notified influential Congressmen of the problem and hired a lawyer to investigate their options. Based on legal advice, the hospital appealed the award of the contract, claiming conflict of interest on the part of the successful bidder. While the lawyer and the Congressmen were effective in getting the original contract terminated and a new competition reopened, the hospital worked quickly to enlist the help of client groups. Hundreds of cables and letters of support were gathered; persons signing them praised the past services provided by the hospital and requested that these services be continued. Three months later, when the contract was readvertised, the hospital included these letters as backup to its proposal. Subsequently, the hospital was awarded the contested contract.

This is an extreme case. Because of special circumstances, the grantee's bargaining power was enhanced. The hospital knew and capitalized on this. Unless a grantee has considerable bargaining power and will not suffer from later negative reactions on the part of the grantor, this strategy should be avoided.

In fact, the strategy of working against any grantor's needs should be used only with great care and judgment. It is essential that grantees who use it understand both their own and their opposers' power bases and the effect that such use may have on future relationships.

Grantees Work against Grantors' and Their Own Needs. This is the least desirable strategy and is generally used only as a last resort. Grantees can reduce work scope so severely that the project will be a failure and thus discredit both the grantees and the grantors. Grantees can also terminate, or threaten to terminate, the negotiations. Grantees who use this strategy in hopes of ultimately obtaining concessions from grantors should be aware that such concessions will probably be forthcoming only if the grantor is in a desperate situation and must count on the grantee to do the project. Rarely is this the case.

What Are the Characteristics of an Effective Grant Negotiator?

No matter what strategies are developed, the final success or failure of a grant negotiation rests with the persons responsible for its outcome. Their knowledge, attitudes, and skills are a major factor throughout the process. As one of the negotiators in the grants process, what are the characteristics you should have to be effective? Experienced grants professionals were asked to "Think about the most successful grant negotiator that you know. How would you describe him/her?"

Responses given by project directors included, "Always prepared, quick thinking, articulate, knowledgeable of project, professional, responsible, open, warm, humane, organized, fair (no personal attacks), firm, confident."

Grant administrators added more requirements: "Persuasive, politically savvy, not locked in concrete (willing to give as well as take), persistent, honest and straightforward, analytical, practical, aggressive without being overbearing, glib, cordial, excellent memory, loving details, objective, detached (able to see picture from several sides and accept each as equally valid)."

Program officers were able to contribute still more: "Mature, understanding, perceptive, responsive, patient, able to communicate effectively."

And finally, grant officers said, "Stubborn but fair, not easily rattled, skeptical, keeps things on a friendly but not personal basis, keeps a step ahead of the other guy, lucid, concise, clear, and reasonable."

When these same grantspersons were asked, "What advice would you give to a prospective grantee, to help him/her negotiate most effectively?" they recommended the following:

First, in preparing for negotiation, you should "Know thyself":

- Know your proposal cold.
- Be able to convey the significance of the project.
- Have a detailed justification for why task items are needed.
- Be well prepared to state how the program will be managed to achieve its objectives.
- Have a detailed justification and backup documentation for cost items.
- Have a bottom line and don't be willing to accept the award underfunded.

In addition, you should "Know thy opponent":

- Identify the sponsor's motivation and goals.
- Know the grantor's rules and regulations, and don't assume that the grantor is as familiar with them as you are.

During the negotiation, besides exhibiting as many of the desirable characteristics of the effective negotiator as possible:

- Don't play power games or make threats.
- Don't lose your temper.
- Don't attack the person—only the process.
- Keep your personal ego out of the negotiation.
- Don't have an all-or-nothing approach; do put yourself in the grantor's shoes.

Above all, be willing to compromise so that "everybody wins" and the agreement finally attained maximizes the interests of both the grantors and the grantees.

5

Grant Procedures Putting Your Act Together

Another title for this chapter could read, "We Got a Grant—What Do We Do Now?" Virtually all large grant getters, including universities, hospitals, research institutes, and others know the answer. Smaller agencies, community groups, and colleges getting an award from a new (for them) federal source may not. It can be an awesome matter to be the recipient of tens of thousands of dollars, which have, it seems, an equal number of strings attached, and not to know how to spend the money properly.

Fortunately, the answer to "What do we do now?" is clear. If you have not already done so,

1. Identify one office and person(s) in your agency to be responsible for administering grants.
2. Develop in-house policies and procedures for administering grants. These will be unique to your agency.
3. Develop plans to comply with the grantor policies and procedures that are applicable to your grants.

Even if your organization already has policies and procedures, they must be evaluated and revised from time to time, to make them as effective and current as possible.

Why are policies and procedures important? What ones (at a minimum) should your organization have? And how can you develop and improve on them with minimum effort?

Why Are Grant Policies and Procedures Important?

There is a powerful grantor support player in the grant-stretching game, a player everyone is aware of. She or he has not begun playing yet—and won't—

until the game is almost over. Yet, like Pepe, Adela's lover in Federico García Lorca's *La Casa de Bernarda Alba,* this person is there as a major protagonist, influencing the action, guiding it, and keeping everyone on his or her toes without even making an appearance. All decisions and changes are made with this player in mind. Though absent, his or her presence is felt throughout the game.

This player is the auditor. He or she is an important reason for a grantee agency to establish written policies and procedures for the administration of grant funds. When it doesn't, it may end up with disallowed costs.

For example, an eastern college, newly involved in the grants game, was awarded money to purchase six keypunch machines for one of the vocationally oriented curricula. After some careful shopping and with an educational discount, the project director was able to purchase seven machines for the price he expected to pay for six. The business manager was delighted. No one, unfortunately, discussed this bargain with the grantors.

A year later, after the proper reports had been filed, the auditor disallowed the price of one keypunch machine. The grant was for only six machines, he correctly insisted, and any money that was left over should have been returned to the government.

If this eastern college had established procedures for monitoring grant expenditures to make sure that costs were allowable, this problem would not have occurred. Instead, the college lost money.

In addition to avoiding disallowances by establishing policies and procedures, a grantee agency will announce to prospective program officers and grant officers (as well as the auditors) that it has done its homework; it knows what has to be done to manage a grant or contract prudently and how to establish a financial management system with adequate control and documentation procedures. The financial management system, which is available for audit, announces that your organization is accountable for the outside funding it receives.

Although policies and procedures are needed to give grantee organizations credibility with grantors, an even more important reason for establishing them is that grantees *use* policies, procedures, and related forms to conduct their operations efficiently. As a result, project directors and grant administrators benefit greatly. They know what to do next after receiving grants; they are prepared.

How Do You Monitor the Technical and Fiscal Progress of Grant Projects?

When an award is received, it should be understood by everyone in the grantee agency that one office will administer the project and one person will be the project director. The opportunities for confusion, duplication, improper communication, and managerial inefficiency—not to mention malfeasance—are too great if it is not made clear beforehand which office is responsible for administering the award.

The office may be called the business office, the office of sponsored programs, the controller's office, the executive director's office, the grants office, etc., depending on the kind of organization you have. It will establish an account number against which costs can be charged, set up a file (preferably one with several sections so that correspondence, fiscal data, and award documents can be separated), and advise the project director of the procedures that must be followed during the grant period.

A system should also be established whereby the individual administering the award, as well as the project director, can tell at a glance the status of the budget on a line-by-line basis. Are supplies being expended too quickly? Is the personnel category going to have money left over at the end of the grant period? Why hasn't any equipment money been used? Is there a slight overexpenditure in travel?

At many grantee agencies, monitoring the budget may be all a grant administrator can do. In large universities or hospitals, for example, it is almost impossible to monitor the performance of sophisticated scientific research. The person who is doing the research (i.e., the project director) is the only one who really knows how well things are going.

Small agencies, such as community groups, may be in a different position. These groups may be better able to monitor the performance of the project because the work doesn't involve esoteric research in a private laboratory. On the other hand, small agencies are less likely to have a fully developed set of policies and fiscal controls. This is not to imply that these organizations are unable to administer grants effectively.

It means, though, that policies may be structured more by tradition and convenience. Because the awards that such agencies receive are likely to be just like the previous award, which was just like the one before that, policies sometimes have a tendency either to spring up by themselves as needed or, unfortunately, to be ignored when they are *most* needed. Both situations can cause the inexperienced agency to incur disallowances and can, possibly, lead to unflattering headlines in the news.

What Grant Policies Do You Need?

To be prepared to spend grant money, having a financial management system with tight controls and documentation procedures is critical. Without it, everything else fails. "You ought to have checks within your organization so that the obligation and the spending of money don't reside within the same individual," a federal auditor advised the authors.

In addition, experienced grant and contract administrators who know the rules of the game are invaluable. Agency experience is also useful, though lack of it doesn't exclude anyone from entering the arena. Knowing how to negotiate an award now and how to work with auditors later is also an asset.

Third, an organization that receives many grants should have a "suspense" system: a follow-up with project directors to find out whether progress reports have been filed on time. Failure to submit progress reports and/or final reports may prevent your agency from receiving future grants from the same sponsor.

It is also crucial that your agency comply with certain government regulations before you can receive an award. For example, when you apply for a grant or a contract, there will invariably be a question asking if your agency has filed an affirmative-action plan. You will also have to certify that your organization complies with the Civil Rights Act of 1964, Section 504 of the Rehabilitation Act of 1973 and, if you work at an institution of higher education, whether your school complies with Title IX of the Education Amendments of 1972.

These are just for starters, and it is helpful to the applicant if everything is taken care of *before* the proposal is sent out. Experienced grant-getting institutions will have no difficulty with these regulations; new players to the grants game will have some preparation to do.

The policies to which we have frequently referred, however, are something else. They are not the fiscal management system, the employment of experienced grant administrators, or the follow-up procedures with project directors. Nor are they compliance with federal regulations, strictly speaking, although many of these policies are influenced heavily by federal regulations.

Instead, they are the basic day-to-day guidelines that are of paramount importance to the smooth administration of grants and the prevention of future disallowances. These policies include but are not limited to:

Personnel and payroll	Consultants
Fringe benefits	Cost sharing
Purchasing	Patents and copyrights
Travel	Equipment inventory
	Indirect costs

Personnel and Payroll

Personnel policies are among the most important and frequently used of all. They include formal job descriptions, salary schedules, application forms, interview practices, vacation and sick leave regulations, affirmative-action procedures, time cards, and a host of special rules designed to put the right people on the right payroll lines. To ignore any of these may cost the applicant money and, worse, may violate a law.

A clearly written job description that outlines the qualifications and duties expected of the job applicant can save money. It helps the employer to hire someone at the appropriate level of education, experience, skills, and potential for improvement. The job description should include a specific salary range, so that the position may be advertised, thus preventing misunderstandings when salary is negotiated. This way, you will not be placed in the uncomfortable position of hiring someone who is more qualified than needed but—unfortunately—too expensive for your budget.

A job description that permits you to hire a less experienced and less expensive person can save your grant money. In addition, you will be able to show an auditor at some future date that the salary charged to the grant was not decided on arbitrarily. Since federal regulations require that grants be charged for a person's salary at the individual's actual base rate, the benefits of a job description that shows a concomitant salary range are obvious.

Large organizations receiving a substantial amount of federal assistance during the course of the year usually have detailed personnel policies. Some of these policies grew helter-skelter as the federal government began imposing more and more regulations on recipients of federal grants and contracts. Many of these experienced organizations may not have reviewed, updated, streamlined, or even understood their own personnel policies for the past decade. A thorough review—although it will take valuable time—could save the organization a good deal of money.

In such a review, consider such factors as: Can a job description be downgraded? Are full fringe benefits being paid for a part-time or temporary employee who is not required to be in the pension plan? Must employees paid from a grant receive pay for unused vacation time after the grant has expired? These are some questions that a new look into old personnel policies can answer.

Small community agencies receiving one or two grants or contracts per year may consider formal, detailed personnel policies a luxury they can't afford. Perhaps a personnel officer is out of the question, but someone should be assigned to perform a minimum of specified personnel duties. Failure to implement such a recommendation would be a false economy that could cost the agency more than it saves.

To illustrate, the authors sometimes are asked to help community groups prepare proposal budgets for submission to sponsor agencies. When we ask, "At what salary rate will you be paying this person?" the reply is often, "I don't really know. What do *you* think a reasonable salary would be?"

This question should have been answered by the community group itself *before* it came to university grant administrators for assistance. The fact that it was asked at all indicates that the agency had prepared no job description and had no salary schedule, no personnel officer, and perhaps no clear idea of the qualifications needed by an applicant for the job!

The community agency, pressed by its own budget woes and inexperience, was not prepared. It was so busy scurrying about for more money, writing more proposals, working on already-funded projects, and trying to maintain some administrative integrity that it had no time to catch up with the fundamentals it had neglected. It had entered the grants arena heavily without adequate preparation. There may have been an attitude of "Let's get the money; then we'll worry about personnel policies." But the result was that this agency probably paid more than necessary for its employees, since it hadn't thought out the job responsibilities. In six or eight months, the agency probably found itself in the red.

Grantees who *are* prepared have salary classifications and also personnel policies that include, but are not limited to, hiring procedures; employee benefits; hours of work; pay policies and procedures; attendance; general responsibilities of supervisors; employee relations; job training; promotions and transfers; safety; grievance and complaints; terminations and layoffs; and general rules concerning interviewing, advertising for positions, and preparation of job descriptions.

Fringe Benefits

Persons employed on grants and contracts are eligible to receive fringe benefits. Because some of the fringe benefits are mandated by federal, state, or local governments, grantees should have a policy that addresses the subject.

Some fringe benefits, as mentioned, are actually required by law and cannot be changed by the grantee. Other benefits, such as health and life insurance, can be offered to employees at the discretion of the employer (i.e., the grantee). Mandatory fringe benefits generally include but are not limited to:

- Workers' compensation insurance
- Unemployment insurance
- Social security (FICA)

Some states also require that disability or other similar insurance be provided. It is important to grantees that funds to cover the costs of these benefits be allowed for in proposal budgets.

Grantees should also establish a policy concerning the optional (i.e., nonmandatory) benefits that they will give their employees. For example, will a grantee provide health insurance, life insurance, dental insurance, and retirement funds for its workers? Will the grantee organization offer only some of these? And what about tuition remission, sports club membership, and other benefits? Clearly, this is not a decision that an organization can make on the spur of the moment. What about holiday and sick leave? On which holidays will employees have the day off? What about religious holidays? How much sick leave will employees be allowed, and will temporary or hourly employees be entitled to receive pay when they are ill? These are all matters that require a great deal of thought because they involve a great deal of money.

A policy regarding fringe benefits is clearly necessary to ensure that employees will be treated consistently and fairly. Auditors will check carefully to determine if fringe benefits that are charged to grants and contracts are consistent with regular grantee practices. It would be wrong, for example, to allow employees paid from a grant to receive more vacation time and sick leave than nongrant employees simply because the grant—not the grantee agency—is paying the former group's salary.

A good fringe-benefit policy would also establish a system to ensure that the accrual of vacation and sick leave time will be accurately kept for all employees who are entitled to this benefit. Permanent (or regular) employees should also be distinguished in such a policy from temporary employees who may not receive the full benefit package.

Fringe benefits are an allowable cost on grants and contracts and, consequently, should be included in all proposal budgets. Most grantees include fringe benefits as a *direct* cost when preparing a budget and make their calculations based on a specified, audited percentage of proposed salaries (see the example in Figure 8). Other organizations include their fringe-benefit costs within their *indirect*-cost rate. Naturally, these latter agencies will have a higher indirect-cost rate than if their fringe benefits were charged directly. In either case, it is important to determine how much fringe benefits *actually* cost your agency and to charge these costs to the grant or contract.

Employees of your organization who work with proposal budgets—whether they be project directors, grant administrators, vice-presidents, or others—should be kept up to date on current fringe-benefit rates and how much each item included in the rate costs. Some grantor agencies want to know what the fringe-benefit package is comprised of and how the rate was arrived at. It is advisable for your agency to prepare rate sheets for use by employees who will be preparing grant budgets. Grant administrators should keep project directors up to date, and project directors should communicate with their respective staffs about the fringe benefits available. Orientation meetings, printed material, and, above all, a clear policy all help to avoid confusion and future disallowances.

Purchasing

Purchasing of supplies, materials, and equipment on a grant-funded project can be a time-consuming endeavor. It can also be expensive, especially if some poor decisions are made by the purchaser. Indeed, purchasing is so important and allows so much opportunity for stretching your grant dollars that the subject will be discussed more fully in a later section. It should be noted here, however, that any agency that receives outside funding should have a purchasing policy that contains certain minimal requirements.

To begin with, bids should be sought from vendors. If the value of the article to be purchased is below a certain dollar amount (e.g., $500), telephone bids, properly documented, are sufficient. For articles costing more than your in-house minimum, written bids from at least three reputable vendors should be required. (Figure 19.) Such comparison shopping often pays dividends; the prices of certain items can vary markedly from one vendor to another.

It is also important to get bids because auditors will review your purchasing procedures. They will want to know if the project director bought all supplies from his or her brother-in-law who has a store down the street. If the brother-in-law had the lowest prices, that's all right. If not, or if no competitive bidding took place, the grantee agency may have some difficult questions to answer.

Figure 19. Project directors frequently complain (often with good reason) about paperwork.

In addition to requiring competitive bidding under specified circumstances, your purchasing policy should answer some of the following questions. Under what circumstances may a project director purchase items with her or his own money and then be reimbursed? Will there be a dollar limit to such reimbursements? What documentation must be submitted to collect reimbursements? Will quantity buying be encouraged? If so, how? Will prompt payments be made to ensure discounts? Will all special discounts to which your agency is entitled be routinely requested? How fast will purchase requests normally be processed? What paperwork will be used?

The answers to these, and similar, questions should be found in grantee purchasing policies. A sample policy is contained in Appendix B.

Travel

So many projects involve travel—either by auto or by air—that a comprehensive travel policy is a necessity for organizations that receive or intend to receive grants and contracts. The travel category in a project budget may involve a substantial amount of money, and there are opportunities for abuses here as well as opportunities to stretch the available dollars. In order to prevent misunderstandings by project directors and other travelers, a policy should be established that clearly states the kinds of expenses that are allowable and unallowable; the method of requesting reimbursement for travel expenses; the amount of money allowed for hotel, food, and mileage; and other related items.

What forms are needed? What is the per diem rate in a foreign city? How soon after returning home must a travel claim be filed? Will your agency give a travel advance? If so, how much? These are all questions that should be answered in a clearly written travel policy.

Such a document can outline the amount of money a traveler can expect to receive for an in-state trip that doesn't require an overnight stay, the allowance per mile for use of a private automobile, insurance provisions, meal allowances, use of vouchers, and a host of other factors that come into play when busy project directors travel around the country or overseas. The travel policy protects the project director and the grantee organization, and it shows the auditor that precautions have been taken against abuse. Such a foresighted and consistent policy will help prevent disallowances after a project is completed.

A sample travel policy is contained in Appendix C. Included with this policy are forms to be used in connection with it. Each grantee organization should, of course, tailor its travel policies and forms to fit its own needs (in line with grantor regulations). However, the sample incorporates the basic components of a travel policy and may be useful as a starting point for grantees who have not yet formalized their travel policies.

Consultants

Since many projects use consultants, particularly as evaluators, most large grantees have developed policies concerning their employment. Consultants are usually referred to as *independent contractors,* and a written policy should state the criteria used to define this term. A great deal of light can be shed on the subject by a reading of Internal Revenue Service Form SS-8 (revised May 1966). Some funding agencies also have their own guidelines to define consultants and to describe how and when they can be used.

As a minimum, consultants are employed for a relatively brief period of time and are not under the day-to-day supervision of the project director. They may be recognized experts in a particular field of endeavor and may be engaged to perform, independently, a specific job for a stated sum of money. The emphasis is on the completion of the task, and it may or may not be accomplished at the site of the project.

Often, institutions of higher education are not allowed to employ their own faculty members as consultants on projects, even though a particular faculty member may be highly qualified and the best possible choice. Colleges and universities may have rules against this, and/or the funding agency may not allow it. Grantors are by no means unanimous in their disapproval (or approval) of universities' hiring members of their own staff on funded projects. However, two points seem to weigh heavily against such a practice.

First, there is opportunity for abuse. Professor Smith hires his friend, Professor Jones, on one project at a rate of $100 per day for 10 days. Professor Jones is eminently qualified to consult on Professor Smith's grant, but both know that when Professor Jones gets his own grant, Professor Smith will be named as a consultant. Grants and contracts are not intended to be pork barrels, and grantee organizations should have policies to guard against this abuse. Some funding agencies do.

Second, implicit in the concept of the university is the intermingling of ideas and the sharing of information across the lines of the traditional academic disciplines. Some funding agencies recognize this and believe that consulting with one's colleagues on a university campus is to be expected as a normal part of a faculty member's job. Other sponsors feel that hiring the resident talent is an excellent idea and wholeheartedly support it.

On this matter, there is little consistency. However, there should be a definite policy that defines what can and cannot be done in the way of hiring consultants. Of course, if a colleague will be a consultant for free—because she or he cannot be paid or is willing to volunteer time—use her or him! It will help stretch your grant dollars.

Your agency's consultant policy will address other matters besides who is and is not permitted to be hired as a consultant. At a minimum, it should cover: How will the consultant be selected? What pay rate will he or she receive? Why? When will prior approvals from the grantor be needed (either for the appointment or for the pay rate, especially if it exceeds $100/day, or both)? How will the consultant's effort be documented? Will a final report be required?

Federal auditors reviewing consultant expenditures will ask these questions. You can be sure that the answers will be available if your agency has a consultant payment form that requires this information. A sample consultant form is contained in Appendix D.

Cost Sharing

Cost sharing has been discussed previously because it can be a decisive factor in whether to apply for a grant; also, it may be an important element of the proposal budget. If cost sharing is required, hard dollars may be promised before a proposal is submitted. Therefore, the grantee should establish policies for the use and distribution of available cost-sharing funds.

For example, some equipment grants provide only 50% of the cost of the items to be purchased. Sea Grant funds (Department of Commerce) will cover only two thirds of the cost of a project. Other examples in the fields of education, rehabilitation, and aging abound.

If your agency applies for a grant that requires cost sharing, where will these funds come from? Will an allocation for cost sharing be made at the beginning of the year? Will matching funds be sought helter-skelter on a grant-by-grant basis? Which department or division or school in your organization will be responsible for providing the funds? Will indirect-cost recoveries be used, or will some other pot of money be tapped?

These are the kinds of questions that a prospective grantee must ask itself before applying for grants that require cost sharing. Real money as well as in-kind contributions may be involved, and a haphazard decision can cost the applicant more money in the long run than the grant will bring in. Having a cost-sharing policy is part of being prepared. A policy that describes when costs should and should not be shared can be a real money saver.

The federal government gives grantees and contractors a great deal of help in preparing such a policy. Federal Management Circular 73-3 (FMC 73-3), *Cost Sharing on Federal Research,* describes the what, when, and why of cost sharing. All grantees, public and private, should incorporate this document's principles into an in-house policy statement. FMC 73-3 is applicable to all federal agencies' *research* grants, contracts, or other agreements with educational institutions, other nonprofit organizations, commercial and industrial organizations, and other recipients of federal funds.

The circular makes it clear that funding agencies will require grantees to share costs when the legislation mandates it, and they will encourage grantees to share costs even when the legislation does not mandate recipient cost participation. The rationale for this encouragement lies in the assumption that grant recipients will utilize their resources more efficiently, plan more soundly, and exercise more prudent fiscal policies if they participate in the costs of the project. As mentioned earlier, cost-sharing requirements may vary from one funding agency to another and even within funding agencies. But when the statutes do not require a specific amount of grantee costs participation, FMC 73-3 states that educational institutions and other not-for-profit or nonprofit organizations should share "at least 1 percent of total project cost."(1)

In many cases, cost sharing of less than 5% of the total project costs would be appropriate in view of these organizations'

> normally limited ability to recover the cost of such participation from non-federal sources. However, in some cases it may be appropriate for educational institutions to provide a higher degree of cost sharing, such as when the cost of the research consists primarily of the academic year salary of faculty members, or when the equipment acquired by the institution for the project will be of significant value to the institution in its educational activities.(2)

Cost participation by commercial or industrial organizations can vary widely, according to FMC 73-3. A reasonable range is between less than 1% of total project costs to more than 50%. Major determinants of the cost-sharing requirement here are what the level of national interest in the project is, whether a fee or profit will be involved, and whether the federal agency or the grant recipient retains title to inventions, patents, and technical information.

Some federal programs require that the budget that is submitted with the proposal identify the costs that will be borne by the grantee. The sponsor wants to see how much staff time or how much travel money, for example, will be provided by the recipient. The National Endowment for the Humanities, the National Endowment for the Arts, some National Science Foundation programs, and the Air Force Office of Scientific Research require this itemization.

Other agencies and programs do not require a budget breakdown of cost sharing. The National Science Foundation, for example, states that grantees must share in costs "at a rate not less than one percent of project costs." However, the NSF expects that grantees will share in the costs at a level that reflects their interest in the research, the potential benefits they may derive, and their ability to share costs. Institutions and organizations have a great deal of flexibility with regard to their approach to cost sharing under NSF-supported projects, and thus, they must assume and exercise responsibility in determining appropriate levels of cost sharing.[3]

The Department of Health, Education, and Welfare (now divided into the Department of Education and the Department of Health and Human Services) also had a policy that required cost sharing on all grants. Beginning with the 1966 Appropriation Act and continuing each year after that, DHEW's appropriation language contained a provision that prohibited the department from paying for the entire cost of a research project.

The DHEW encouraged the use of *institutional cost-sharing plans.* Even today, institutional plans:

- Provide a meaningful basis for showing the extent to which nonfederal funds contribute to the cost of research that is also supported by DHEW funds.
- Give maximum flexibility to grantees and contractors as to the method used to meet the established cost-sharing level.
- Simplify administration of the research project's application, review, negotiation, award, and reporting procedures for both the grantee and the awarding agency.

Responsibility for negotiating institutional cost-sharing agreements has been assigned to the Public Health Service. Grantees and contractors who need further information can write to:

> Chief, Cost and Audit Management Branch
> Office of Administrative Management
> Public Health Service
> Parklawn Building
> 5600 Fishers Lane
> Rockville, Maryland 20852

Prospective grantees should also obtain the latest copy of the extremely useful DHEW pamphlet entitled *A Guide to Institutional Cost Sharing Agreements for Research Grants and Contracts Supported by the Department of Health, Education and Welfare.* The *Guide* (DHEW Publication No. OS 75-50009) is issued by the Office of Administrative Management, Public Health Service.

Regardless of the amount of cost sharing required, federal agencies require recipients of research money to maintain records of all project costs claimed as being their contribution. These records should be kept in addition to records of costs that will be paid by the government, and they will be subject to audit. The sponsoring agency wants to make sure that your organization really did pay for the things it said it would pay for, and documentation is up to you.

In formulating your organization's in-house policy on cost sharing, you should be aware of at least the following:

1. Cost sharing can be in cash or in-kind. Both cash and in-kind donations can be made by the grantee and by nonfederal third parties.
2. Federal funds (except for revenue-sharing funds) cannot be used to share costs on a federal grant.
3. In-kind contributions can include services (e.g., consultant time), real property, and expendable and nonexpendable personal property.
4. Costs or contributions used as cost sharing or matching on other grants cannot be used as cost sharing on a new grant. However, when a contribution (a faculty member's time, for example) is related to two or more grants, it may be prorated among the grants involved.
5. Volunteer services are allowable. Rates of pay, which are needed to calculate the value of the cost sharing, should be consistent with rates paid for similar work in the grantee's organization or the local labor market.
6. Contributions of property, equipment, and land should be calculated at fair market value.
7. The cost-sharing contribution must be related to the efficient accomplishment of project objectives.

Keeping this information about federal requirements in mind, you should be able to develop a cost-sharing policy that will work for your agency. At a minimum, it should answer these questions: Will we enter into institutional cost-sharing agreements with grantors? Who will be responsible for identifying cash and noncash contributions? Who will approve cost-sharing offerings? Where will the cash cost-sharing come from? How much cash can we afford to contribute? How much noncash cost-sharing can we afford? Will we restrict cost sharing to only those programs and agencies that require it? Or will we put in voluntary cost-sharing in order to be more competitive? When will exceptions (i.e., "volunteering" if our normal policy is only to show required cost-sharing) be allowed? How will cost sharing be documented once we receive the awards?

A well-conceived cost-sharing policy answers all these questions. It can help you attract grants, help you enter into agreements you could not otherwise enter into, and provide clear documentation of project costs. A poorly conceived policy can cost your agency money while the grant is in progress or after the grant is over when some costs are disallowed.

Patents and Copyrights

Patent and copyright policies are useful for any organization that engages in research activity to a significant degree. As research proceeds, intellectual property may be developed, and along with it, a need to protect this property. Although a patent and copyright policy may not be an instrument that can help stretch available grant dollars, it *can* be of assistance in attracting and retaining income that may be realized from the production and distribution of intellectual property.

Basically, a good patent and copyright policy should take into consideration at least the following factors:

1. The United States Constitution provides for inventors and authors to have exclusive rights over their discoveries and writings for a limited time.
2. A patent and copyright policy should be written so as to encourage, not restrict, the creative energies of employees of the grantee. That is, there should be an incentive for the researcher or writer to pursue the work diligently, without fear that all of the royalties will be taken by the employer or the sponsor of the project.
3. The employer of the researcher–whether it be a university, a private firm, a hospital, or other grantee–is entitled to some portion of the royalties if there has been an investment of facilities, funds, or time by the employer. If a professor invents something while using university laboratory space and university-purchased supplies, for example, the university should be entitled to some specified percentage of the income generated by the invention, at least to equal a repayment of the investment made. If, on the other hand, the invention was developed on Sunday afternoons in the professor's garage, the university should not have a claim to royalty rights.
4. The sponsor–a government agency, for example–will also have a claim if an invention was developed on a grant or contract. The government's equity as a result of financing the research should generally be a nonexclusive, royalty-free license to use the invention for federal government purposes.
5. The public interest must be considered in preparing a patent and copyright policy, particularly at universities, Universities, by their nature, have a responsibility to serve the public interest.

For an excellent discussion of patent and copyright policies, particularly at universities, see Raymond J. Woodrow, *Management for Research in U.S. Universities.*[4]

The point to be made here is that inventions and copyrightable materials can be–and often are–produced on grants and contracts. While encouraging research, grantees should also have a policy to ensure that all parties (inventor or writer, employer, sponsor) will get a fair share of the royalties.

Equipment Inventory

An essential element of grants spending is keeping track of the equipment that has been purchased on grants and contracts. This means establishing an inventory system in which each item is tagged and logged. Large organizations often have sophisticated computerized systems for this. Some smaller organizations and even some with substantial amounts of grant monies have equipment inventory systems that can best be described as ineffective.

A workable inventory system for equipment—it does not have to be computerized—can help stretch your grant dollars by permitting you to know where the equipment you've purchased in the past is located, who in your organization is using it, and if, indeed, it is being used at all.

In recent years, the federal government has taken a hard line on this issue, particularly at colleges and universities. Before a major piece of equipment can be purchased (or even budgeted in some proposals), the institution must be inventoried to determine if such equipment has been bought in recent years and is available for use now. If so, no new equipment may be purchased. On the other hand, if the inventory shows that there is no such equipment, or that all available equipment is being used, then new equipment may be purchased.

If your agency has an efficient inventory system, there are benefits in addition to avoiding duplication and clearing the way for new equipment to be purchased. Unearthing a long-lost laser can be a real money saver for a project budget. It also prevents auditors from turning up embarrassing evidence of two similar pieces of equipment, bought in the same year, now gathering dust in a laboratory while a young researcher complains that he or she can't find the money to buy still another!

Federal regulations applicable to grant equipment management for universities, hospitals, and other nonprofit agencies are contained in Circular A-110, Section N, "Property Management Standards."[(5)] It will be useful to review these standards before establishing or updating an equipment inventory policy at your agency.

Indirect Costs

Perhaps no single topic in the grant-getting and grant-management field arouses more confusion—and tempers—than indirect costs. Misunderstandings are usually at the root of the problem, and no one involved is exempt—not project directors, chief executive officers, department heads, or grant administrators. A large-scale education program by grantees for their employees may be in order.

For example, employees should know that every agency receiving federal grants and contracts should have an established indirect-cost rate with the government. Usually, it is the Department of Health and Human Services* or the Department of Defense that works out the rate, using data supplied by the grantee agency. The agreement is usually for a period of a year or longer, because working out the details of an indirect-cost agreement is time-consuming, detailed, and difficult.

Employees should also understand that indirect costs must be included in grant budgets or the grantee will lose money. As noted in Chapter 3, indirect costs are real costs, just as salaries and travel and supplies are real costs. It is just that indirect costs are harder to see on a project-by-project basis.

In some cases, your agency may be willing to lose money by not recovering full indirect costs. In other cases, the grantors may not allow you to charge your negotiated indirect rate. It is not uncommon for project directors or even program officers to press for reduced indirect fees. For all these reasons, it is important that grantee institutions have formalized indirect-cost policies.

In developing or reviewing your agency's indirect-cost policy, it's important to address these issues: Will we use the fully audited indirect-cost rate whenever there are no restrictions against its use? If exceptions will be made, under what conditions? Should we routinely ask for less than full indirect costs, in order to show cost sharing and be more competitive? What will the auditors say if we charge less than our full rate? Would it be better to charge the full rate and then return some funds for project use? How many grants with restricted indirect-cost recovery (i.e., 8% or none) can we afford to receive? How will we recover the maximum possible for grants that pay low or no indirect-cost rates? For example, will we charge space and furniture as a direct cost? How will we educate our employees about the indirect-cost rate? Who will be responsible for negotiating the rate? Who will approve any deviations from it? Other questions may also be applicable to your institution.

Once you have answered these questions, and especially if you have done so in writing, it will be easier to avoid misunderstandings. Project directors, grant administrators, and auditors will appreciate the consistency inherent in such a policy.

Other Policies

Other policies and procedures may be necessary or appropriate at your organization, depending on your specific needs, situation, or type of business.

One large organization on the West Coast, for example, recently instituted a policy outlining the amount of risk it is willing to take before a grant or contract

*Formerly the Department of Health, Education, and Welfare (DHEW) established indirect cost rates. In May, 1980, DHEW was divided into the Department of Health and Human Services (DHHS) and the Department of Education. Although DHHS is currently assuming indirect cost rate responsibilities, it is anticipated that the Department of Education may become involved in this activity in the future.

is officially awarded. Many project directors know that they will be receiving their award soon, and a phone call to the sponsor will usually confirm this. But nothing is official yet, and no written notification of award has been received.

Can the project begin? Officially the answer is "no," but if the grantee organization is willing to take some risk and advance money on the basis of the unofficial information it has, then the project can begin.

Of course, if there is an unforeseen problem and the award is not made, the expectant grantee loses money. But the risks can be reduced if the organization knows whom it is dealing with.

How much risk is to be taken is the subject of a policy statement of a western organization. It identifies certain conditions under which expenditures may be authorized (i.e., receipt of partially executed award document, telephone confirmation of an award on a renewal project, etc.). It states who may approve certain levels of spending, with the highest level (over $25,000) reserved for the executive director. In addition, procedures for follow-up (to "hurry up" the award and to ensure that it will be received) are established.

All of the policies and procedures we have discussed so far have related to one topic (i.e., risk, indirect costs, patents, personnel). It is especially useful to incorporate all of these separate policies (or at least summaries of each) into a project director's handbook. This handbook should include all procedures to be used during the grant period. Such a publication is used effectively at many large grantee organizations and is extremely helpful in preventing costly mistakes before they occur.

How Can You Develop Grant Policies Effectively and with Minimum Effort?

If your agency does not have formalized policies for all the topics covered in this chapter (or if it has policies that need updating), the best source of help will probably be your colleagues and competitors.

What policies have they established? What problems have they encountered in implementing these policies? What features of their policies have worked out especially well? Will your colleagues or competitors give you copies of their policies, procedures, and forms?

Usually, they are glad to talk with you and will practically bombard you with printed materials, whether they know you personally or not! The authors have received sample policies, procedures, and special studies on many grant-related topics, from colleagues all over the country. Usually, the cooperation resulted from placing a simple phone call. In fact, we have never met many of the people who have helped us throughout our research administration careers.

The question, then, is usually not "*Will* they help?" but rather "How do you know *whom* to ask for help?"

If you live in a metropolitan area, there are probably at least a few other agencies with a grant volume and type of activity similar to yours. When this is the case, it is worth your time to pay a visit, to get to know people who have responsibilities like yours.

If you live in a small town, or if there are no similar agencies in your city, you will have to look further for help. Excellent sources of prospective contacts are professional organization directories. They contain the names, titles, organizational affiliations, addresses, and phone numbers of members.

For example, the Society of Research Administrators (SRA) has over 1,200 members (nationwide and even internationally) from universities, hospitals, and industry. Similarly, the National Council of University Research Administrators (NCURA) has members from colleges and universities of all sizes.

After you have reviewed policies from other organizations, however, remember that they must be tailored to fit the needs of *your* agency. It is especially important that these policies *help project directors to meet the objectives of their projects.* Therefore, it is a good idea for both grant administrators and project directors to work together to establish policies that will meet the requirements of federal legislation and prudent business practices, while efficiently working toward the project's goals.

Most institutions, for example, have ongoing human and animal subjects committees, comprised mainly of project directors (and perhaps a grant administrator or two). Similarly, project directors and grant administrators serve together on many institutional committees charged with developing patents, copyrights, affirmative action, or other policies.

The area where project directors are frequently left out (and should not be) is in developing, refining, and changing purchasing and personnel policies. These policies directly affect the day-to-day availability of the resources that project directors need to conduct their projects successfully. If included in the development of these policies, project directors could identify potential problems before they occur, as well as help to implement the policies once they are established.

No matter who develops them, policies and procedures that are designed to help your organization to be prepared may be diverse and complex or few and simple. The point that is stressed here is to have such policies and to have them fit your agency's needs.

Having your act together means not having to ask, "We got the grant—what do we do now?"

6

Spending the Award Getting More for Less

"We got the grant–what do we do now?" Why *spend*, of course. The groundwork has been laid. With an effective management tool (the budget), the optimally negotiated award, and policies and procedures in place, now comes the best part. *Using* the money that took a year or more of hard work, waiting, and uncertainty to get.

Just as a "Monopoly" player who passes "GO" collects the wherewithal to start purchasing properties, the successful project director (with the help of the grant administrator) earns the right and obligation to start buying up resources. These resources will be needed to accomplish the goals of the project.

Roget's Thesaurus gives several synonyms for *spend*: "use," "consume," "expend," and–perhaps significantly–"*waste*." "Waste" is not what this chapter is about. Quite the opposite, the emphasis is on how to *save* while spending grant money.

If the save-while-spending concept does not seem rational, just consider the large savings that you or your family may have made while indulging in 50%-off sales. The more you spent, as long as you really needed the item, the more you saved. Right?

And so it is with grant spending. By finding a good deal, by stretching grant dollars, more money is saved for other valuable resources. Grant dollars are real dollars. The responsibility for using them wisely should be regarded just as seriously as that of spending personal earnings.

Who shares this responsibility? To some degree, all four central players in the grant-stretching game. In addition, support players–such as project administrative and clerical staff, purchasing employees, and personnel-payroll clerks–often assist.

Normally, the heaviest responsibility rests with the project director, who must initiate all spending requests. However, once the project director or a project staff member has identified the resources needed, the grant administrator should provide valuable assistance in obtaining these resources for the least money. In doing this, the grant administrator frequently relies on the services of purchasing and personnel-payroll department staff.

As long as expenditures are made according to the grantor-approved budget, the program officer and the grant officer at the grantor agency need not be involved. However, if significant deviations from the budget are necessary, or if the grantors are needed to assist with some special spending problem, the program officer and the grant officer may be called on.

Grantees' purchasing and personnel-payroll operations vary greatly. Large hospitals, universities, and industries typically have established purchasing and personnel-payroll departments. The purchasing department staff usually:

- Maintain purchasing policies and procedures, routinely requesting discounts and taking advantage of prompt payment plans. (A sample policy is contained in Appendix B.)
- Assist by obtaining bids and maintaining price lists from various suppliers.
- Verify amounts charged and require adequate documentation and proof of delivery before authorizing payment.

Similarly, the grantees' personnel-payroll department staff provide a great deal of assistance. They may perform any or all of these services:

- Set market-price salaries for various job responsibilities.
- Recruit and advertise to fill grant positions.
- Maintain résumés of qualified candidates.
- Assist with the identification of low-cost employees (Work Study,* CETA†).

In contrast, at smaller hospitals and universities, and at some community social service agencies, there may be no official purchasing or personnel-payroll departments. Or perhaps there are departments, but minimal services are offered.

*The work-study program is a federally funded program to provide opportunities for students from low-income families to earn their way through college. Typically, the students earn minimum wages, with the program itself paying 80% of their salary and the student's employer (perhaps you) paying only 20%. Information about the availability of work-study students may usually be obtained at college or university financial-aids offices.

†*CETA* stands for the "Comprehensive Employment and Training Act." The program funded by this legislation provides free help in exchange for your training eligible workers. The Department of Labor (DOL), which administers the CETA program, designates "prime sponsors" throughout the country to solicit proposals for training activities and to award funds. If you are not already on it, you should get on the mailing list of the CETA prime sponsor in your area. A list of prime sponsors is published in the *Federal Register* periodically.

Under these circumstances, the project director and the grant administrator must put considerably more effort into spending activities.

Whether or not the grantee has support players in the form of purchasing and personnel-payroll staff, the opportunities for cooperation between several or many grantee projects vary. For example, at a large university, there may be a research center that administers many sponsored projects of a similar nature. This center has a unifying force—a director—who ensures that supplies for all projects are ordered together, thus guaranteeing a better price than would be obtained by ordering supplies for a single project. In a small community agency, which handles only one grant, there is not the same opportunity for cooperative buying, even if there is a purchasing department.

Although support staff and opportunities for cooperative purchasing differ considerably among grantees, there are still many techniques that any project director and grant administrator, no matter how large or small their projects, can use to stretch grant dollars. These techniques are presented in the rest of this chapter. They were gathered from experienced grantees and grantors nationwide. Topics to be discussed are *the purchasing decision (comparing alternatives); the purchase itself: paying less; saving by using grantee buying power; saving by using grantor buying power; specific examples of savings in budget items;* and *obstacles to savings and how to get around them.*

The Purchasing Decision: Comparing Alternatives

Should the "Monopoly" player buy Park Place—or Baltic Avenue? Should she or he put houses on Boardwalk—or use the money to pick up another property? Similarly, the project director has limited resources and must compare alternatives before spending money. For example, should she or he buy a top-of-the-line piece of equipment or settle for a lesser piece that will do the job adequately? The first step in saving grant dollars is to compare alternative resources and to select those that will do the job at the lowest cost.

There are two kinds of considerations: those that relate to the *tasks* to be done and those that relate to the *costs* to be incurred. For example, suppose a researcher must choose whether to collect data by mail survey or personal interviews. This is a task alternative. Once he or she decides to use personal interviews, now he or she has a cost alternative: whether to employ student help or professional interviewers.

Task-Related Alternatives

Research Design. "In policy research, a quick-response, lower-cost methodology of lesser confidence level that delivers results *when needed* may have a superior value in comparison with a highly rigorous study that arrives too late," advised a program officer who had been asked how to save grant dollars.

Several others agreed that the research design itself should be cost-effective. "Use the appropriate sample size," suggested one.

Another emphasized the importance of a "carefully stated hypothesis and research design."

The idea is to do the job necessary and not more.

Geographical Considerations. "Use a central locale for conferences," recommended a project director. "If you are going to put on a conference and reimburse participants for travel costs, then the conference should be strategically located so as to minimize air fares."

If your project will serve a large area, should you establish field offices (to save staff travel time)? If so, where should these offices be located? A San Diego-based project that served a large number of school districts in the Los Angeles area discovered that it was far less expensive to maintain an office in the LA area than to pay San Diego staff to commute to Los Angeles. In making the field office decision, the cost of travel time (salaries) should be considered as well as the cost of plane tickets, mileage, and per diem.

Scheduling of Activities. If the decision is not to maintain a field office, it becomes especially important to schedule activities so that the technical assistance provided to, let's say, various school districts in Sacramento is scheduled for the same week (or other discrete time period). In this way, travel costs can be reduced. Similarly, if a traveling consultant will be coming to your organization for several days during the project period, you may be able to schedule these days together, thus using only one air ticket. Likewise, if equipment must be rented, it should be scheduled for maximum use.

Staffing Creatively. "In doing research, use an appropriate mix of highly skilled, experienced, high-cost staff and lower-cost junior staff," recommended a program officer.

A project director suggested, "Use consultants when it is cheaper than hiring employees, and vice versa."

All sorts of opportunities exist for staffing a project creatively. Some specific examples are given later, but in general, the way to go about setting up alternative staffing patterns is this. Identify the *tasks* to be done in the project (for example, type survey letters, code and keypunch survey results, analyze data, and write final report). Then, to the extent practical, put lower-paid, routine, nonspecialized tasks into some position descriptions; put higher-paid, nonroutine, specialized tasks into other position descriptions. The idea is not to have the project director sharpening pencils and not to have the secretary writing the final report. Normally, grant employees are (and should be) paid according to their highest level of responsibility.

Cost-Related Alternatives

Don't Pay. Ideally, some items, services, and so forth may be donated or volunteered. If there is a possibility of getting something for nothing, by all means do so. One project director said that he saved money by not paying page charges to journals. He believed that many journals charge authors page charges (frequently as much as $80 per page) just because they know a grant, not an individual, will be paying the costs.

Grantee Contributions. Here is an alternative that has strong appeal to three of the central players. If, for example, a university grantee is willing to release a project director from teaching a class and agrees not to charge the grantors, the project director, the program officer, and the grant officer are pleased. The project director is thus given time to work on the project, and the grantors could have saved $15,000 or so during a nine-month period.

If grantor funds are limited, the project director may wish to ask his or her institution to do this. However, since the institution still must pay someone else to teach that class, there is a cost here that must be recovered later—perhaps through higher indirect-cost rates.

A program officer recognized both the desirability of and the problems inherent in asking grantees to contribute a project director's time. "If at all possible," she said, when asked how to stretch grant dollars, "it may be appropriate to have the university contribute toward the direct cost involved in faculty time on research projects during the normal academic year. However, the facility to do so varies among U.S. institutions."

Grantor Contributions. Occasionally, the grantor may be able to provide services or goods. For example, one grant administrator said that she had saved money by "getting the sponsor to provide some of the materials; for example, the Department of Forestry provided seedlings for a biomass project."

In his book *The New Corporate Philanthropy*, Frank Koch has listed ways that corporations can provide valuable support to nonprofit organizations, without making a cash contribution. Some items on the list are purchasing power; promotional materials and services; printing; bulk-mailing services; products for giveaways at fund-raising events; financial advice; executive, legal, and tax services; money loans; and use of company facilities.(1)

Loans. Another possibility for saving money is through borrowing instead of buying. Is there an X-ray diffractor on campus that is not being used? Could local library books be taken out instead of new books being purchased? In fact, some federal agencies are requiring that grantee institutions certify that similar equipment is not available before these agencies agree to fund new equipment in grants.*

Shared Use. Along these lines, even if equipment, books, and other materials are not free for the exclusive use of a project director, perhaps they could be shared. In this case, costs would be minimized, or perhaps there would be no costs. If equipment were not available at all, several project directors could

*The Office of Management and Budget Circular A-110, which contains standardized regulations for all recipients of federal grants, introduces a requirement to screen available equipment and to certify that any equipment requested in a grant proposal is not available at your institution for the project director's use.

contribute to its purchase. If equipment were available, it could be shared with no cost to anyone.

Used versus New. Considerable savings may be had by purchasing used rather than new items. School districts frequently hold auctions; dealers of expensive equipment often take trade-ins; and so forth. The rapid advances in technology in recent years have led to some equipment's becoming obsolete before wearing out. Yet, depending on project needs, obsolete equipment at a bargain price may do the job well enough and at a much lower cost.

Remodel versus New. "Cannibalize existing equipment," a project director volunteered as a way to save grant money. "It's possible that by purchasing a few parts, or by combining good parts from several out-of-commission machines, a remodeled piece of equipment may be obtained at minimal expense."

Make versus Buy. "Designing components and building them ourselves saved as much as half the cost per item (savings of $2,000 each) on transition boots," explained a project director.

"We were able to produce the equivalent of a Deu Point Hyglometer 880, costing close to $1,000 commercially, for about $300," another project director volunteered. "We found out about this through colleagues at another university."

If a grantee agency has or can hire skilled staff, the agency may benefit from custom-made items at a lower cost. At universities, an added bonus is that students can often help and thus gain experience while earning their way through college.

Lower versus Higher Quality. There may easily be savings by forgoing top-of-the-line equipment and supplies, first-class air fare, and other nonessentials. In fact, most grantors will not fund "luxury" items. As mentioned previously, one reason that budgets are reduced by grantors is that grantees have proposed "buying a Cadillac when a Chevv will do." Of course, it is not a savings to buy a low-quality item that breaks down or that entails additional staff labor. The key to stretching grant dollars is identifying the quality of purchase that is needed to do the job efficiently, and spending no more and no less.

Rent or Lease versus Buy. It is common practice for grantees to calculate the different costs associated with renting, leasing, or buying either equipment or space before selecting the method of purchase. Several factors enter into the decision. First, how long will the item be needed? The longer the time period, usually the more advisable it is to buy rather than to rent or lease it. Even if the project will need a piece of equipment a relatively short time, are there other grantee projects that could use it in the future? If so, it may be advisable for the grantee institution to purchase the equipment and rent it at the fair market rate to the grantor for the duration of the project. Finally, will the equipment or space become obsolete or need to be replaced soon? If so, renting or leasing may be less risky than purchasing.

Risk versus No Risk. Many projects involve elements of risk. For example, participants may need to be covered for health services. Perhaps there is a great deal of travel and thus a possibility of accidents. Or sophisticated equipment may be used, with a potential for expensive breakdowns. Naturally, the grantee wants to eliminate as much risk as possible and therefore must budget for costs such as maintenance agreements on equipment and health or accident insurance on people.

A program officer described the cooperative way her agency had saved a great deal of money by assuming some of the risk normally borne by grantees. Her agency had funded the purchase of computers at four grantee institutions: "Instead of funding separate computer maintenance contracts for each of the grantees, we guaranteed the grantees supplemental awards, *if* it became necessary to repair the computers. No supplements have been necessary to date, at a savings of about \$50,000 a year for four years. This \$200,000 will make several supplements possible for a real saving."

There are savings to be had by carrying risks, but in general, grantees should be extremely careful in doing this. Whenever possible, they should have backup from the sponsoring agency—or insist on funds for reasonable amounts of insurance to cover the risks.

Alternatives within and between Budget Items. An activity in all grants is communication. *Within* the budgeted funds provided for communications, what are the least expensive alternatives? Communication by letter, long-distance phone calls, cables, or inexpensive bulk mailing of printed matter? *Between* the funds provided for communications (one item) and travel (another item), could there be savings by, say, holding a teleconference rather than flying 20 people to another city for a traditional conference?

Similarly, *within* the travel category, is it cheaper to go by taxi, rental car, or bus—and under what circumstances? When should a grantee drive and when fly? *Between* the funds provided for travel (one item) and printing (another item), would there be savings by disseminating many copies of a report rather than traveling to a conference to give a speech?

All sorts of opportunities for saving grant dollars—without changing the objectives of the project—exist, simply by using the least-expensive cost alternatives within and between budget items.

New Technology versus Old Technology. "Shop around for the most appropriate equipment at the lowest cost," advised a program officer. "New items may appear after the proposal was submitted because of advances in technology."

New technology may reduce equipment costs; in addition, it may reduce expensive labor costs. Project directors and grant administrators should be aware of the possible savings that can result from new technologies. For example, it may be cost-effective for a large research center to purchase word-processing equipment, thereby enabling them to pay for fewer typists and related overhead costs.

To summarize what has been said so far, you can stretch grant dollars considerably, merely by *comparing* the many *task* and *cost alternatives* available. Like the Vermont farmer who spent his money on 6¢ interest payments instead of \$5 safety-deposit-box rental fees, you can pay less for necessary resources by creatively identifying and selecting among alternatives.

Ideally, selection of alternatives should be accomplished at the budget or negotiation stage of grant-dollar stretching. However, frequently the project director (and especially the *new* project director) cannot foresee all the options until the project is in operation. Therefore, throughout the period of the grant, project directors and grant administrators should work together to capitalize on opportunities to save funds.

If the alternatives selected vary significantly from the approved budget, it will probably be necessary to enlist the cooperation of the program officer and the grant officer.* Timely approvals of requests to transfer funds between budgeted items is the primary way that grantor representatives can help.

The Purchase Itself: Paying Less

Suppose the Vermont farmer had done some comparison shopping at several local banks. Could he have negotiated a lower interest rate? In addition to selecting the least expensive alternative, money may be saved by shopping wisely and obtaining the most favorable terms. Therefore, once you have chosen alternatives (or, in some cases, *as* you do this), old-fashioned dickering and creative buying practices can ensure the best deal possible.

Selecting the most cost-effective *alternative* is, in most cases, the project director's (or a valued project staff member's) responsibility. In contrast, the grant administrator (and support staff such as purchasing and personnel–payroll staff) should take main responsibility for the *purchase itself.* Ideally, the project director identifies the resources needed; the grant administrator then obtains them on the best terms.

There are a number of ways to do this. A few are *donations; trades; timing of purchases; bids for competitive prices and terms; discounts; negotiations; buying foreign; tax avoidance;* and *detection of overcharges.*

Donations

"For a demonstration project by the U.S. government, some companies gave products for the possible advertisement involved," stated a project director.

It is possible that some donations may be made to a grant project because the seller wants a tax break, a good public relations image, or future business. Since most grantee institutions are nonprofit organizations, companies or indi-

*Many grants and contracts allow expenditures to exceed most line items by 10–15%. Frequently, the equipment and travel items may not be exceeded at all without prior funding-agency approval. If in doubt, you should check the terms and conditions of your grant or contract.

viduals donating to them can claim a charitable deduction. Furthermore, since grantees are presumably engaging in worthwhile and even leadership activities, the public image of companies that donate to the grantees is enhanced. For companies that are more interested in their bottom line, donating may stimulate further business. Travel agencies, for example, will frequently give a free trip in order to take on future business.

One of the most valuable kinds of donations is free labor. Volunteers gain from the feeling of contributing to a worthwhile cause. In addition, they may gain specialized training that will help them compete for future jobs.

Trades

If goods or services can't be donated, perhaps a trade can be arranged. For example, when a rehabilitation center on the West Coast moved to new headquarters, their building was surrounded by fresh dirt and weeds. Students in the local community-college landscaping class traded their free labor for the opportunity to practice creatively on the center's grounds. All the center had to pay for was plants, at a considerable savings in labor. Often, grant projects offer valuable training opportunities and hence can find ways to pay little or nothing for labor, in exchange for training services.

Bids for Competitive Prices and Terms

It is usually possible to get the same piece of equipment or supply (even the same brand name) for widely different sums of money. Because sellers do offer competitive prices, grantees should ask several companies to quote prices (to bid) on large purchases. In fact, many grantor agencies require this. And auditors find out when this hasn't been done.

How large should the purchase be for bids to be obtained? Many grantees say $500. This is a convenient amount because the federal cost principles define equipment as "an article of nonexpendable tangible personal property having a useful life of more than two years, and an acquisition cost of $500 or more per unit."[(2)]

It takes time and effort to get bids. Therefore, unless substantial savings may be involved, it is usually neither advisable nor required to get bids for low-cost purchases. Should you bother? Estimate how much time it will take you to get bids for the item you want to buy. Calculate how much money that time is worth. Are you likely to save more than that amount of money by shopping around? (Consider the present purchase and *also* any possible future purchases of the item.) If you answer "Yes," get bids.

Discounts

Basically, there are four kinds of discounts that grantees may obtain: cash, quantity, trade, and those arising from special relationships with suppliers.

First, grantees may benefit from the *prompt payment* of invoices (cash discounts), frequently saving 2% of the bill if it is paid within 10 days.

Second, all sorts of possible savings occur because of *quantity* (bulk-buying or group-rate) discounts. Paper is a common example. One ream of paper may cost $5 or more if bought alone; when hundreds of cases are purchased, the price may drop to around $2 per ream or less. It is not even necessary to buy your yearly supply of paper at the same time in order to take advantage of quantity discounts. Many sellers offer cumulative discounts. In this case, grantees may order some specified amount of supplies over a specified period of time, as needed, at the quantity price.

Third, *trade* discounts are possible when grantees take advantage of lower prices because of their organizational status. Universities and school districts, for example, are eligible for "educational discounts" from many suppliers. Chemical companies and office equipment firms sometimes offer as much as 50% discounts to educational organizations, while office supplies may be offered at 10 to 15% off. Many purchasing departments routinely stamp or preprint "Educational Discount Requested" on their purchase order forms, since in order to receive these discounts you usually have to ask for them. These discounts are not limited to items commonly thought of as "educational," either. Hotels, for example, frequently offer room discounts to educators.

Finally, grantees may establish *special relationships* with suppliers and hence obtain price concessions. If a project director, for example, offers to give all the project business to a storage company, the prices quoted may be less than others would pay. Or the project may pay the same rates as others but receive extra services or favorable payment terms.

Timing of Purchases

"International flights can be much cheaper if booked ahead," noted a project director. "There are many opportunities to save on national travel as well. 'Supersaver' airfares are often hundreds of dollars less than economy fares—and the ride, seat, and meal are exactly the same as at the regular rate. All you have to do is reserve your flight well in advance and stay a certain number of days at your destination. A round-trip fare between the East and West Coasts, for example, is less than $300 at the 'supersaver' rate and more that $600 economy class."

Booking ahead is not the only way to save. Purchasing during the off season when there is low demand for goods and services is also economical. Hotel room rates in Kingston, Jamaica, for example, are much less during the hot summer months than during the winter and spring tourist season.

Similarly, the time of day may be important. Telephone calls placed between 11 P.M. and 8 A.M. every night are billed at a 65% discount rate, as are calls made between 8 A.M. and 11 P.M. Saturday and 8 A.M. and 5 P.M. Sunday. The 35% discount period is 5 P.M. to 11 P.M. Sunday through Friday and 8 A.M. to

11 P.M. on holidays. "Prime time"–at the full rate–is from 8 A.M. to 5 P.M. on Monday through Friday, the regular business hours for most grant projects.* By scheduling calls to coincide with discount time periods, grantees can save. Practically speaking, this means that West Coast grantees may come into the office a little early and call east. Easterners may stay a little late and call west.

No matter what season or time of day you are purchasing in, there are savings that accrue from your patience–from your being willing to wait. Computer costs are a good example. At one university, project directors who submit their computer jobs on a first in-first out basis pay 16¢ per CPU (Central Processing Unit). If they ask for special treatment, their job goes to the head of the line, and the costs are 64¢ per CPU. However, if they are willing to have their job remain at the end of the line until all priority work is completed, the cost per CPU is reduced to only 4¢. They may have to wait as long as a day to get their job back, instead of the hour or so it would take with top priority.

If grantees know or can find out when sales will occur, here is another opportunity for savings. In connection with sales, it may be advisable to do some advance buying. If the price of glassware, for instance, is expected to rise, it may be cost-effective to buy a year's supply ahead of time, during a sales period, rather than waiting for inflation to take its toll a year later.

Negotiations

Even if you get bids, obtain every available discount, and time your purchases to coincide with sales or off seasons, there may still be a possibility for more savings. This is especially true when you are making a large purchase or expect to do considerable future business with the seller. You can get additional savings by negotiating the purchase with the seller, rather than just accepting his or her bid.

If, for example, other sellers have offered you equally favorable terms and prices, you may want to point this out to the seller you hope to do business with (or to several sellers, for that matter). You may want to ask what further concessions (price or terms) are available–or to indicate under what circumstances you will do business with your preferred seller. Techniques discussed in Chapter 4 should be used. But remember, when you are buying, you are essentially taking on the role of the grantor, so your strategies, control, and so forth will change accordingly.

Buying Foreign

Although many grantor agencies require that you "Buy American," there may be substantial savings from buying foreign-made goods instead. If grantor

*Savings in effect June 28, 1979, according to the San Diego Suburban Telephone Directory. Rates may change if authorized by the Federal Communications Commission.

regulations require you to buy American-made goods, you will need written approval from your grant (or contract) officer to do otherwise. Normally, you can justify your request to buy foreign-made goods in one of several ways. One federal agency,* for example, exempts the following kinds of products from the "Buy American" regulation:

1. Those that are for use outside the United States.
2. Those that the government determines are not mined, produced, or manufactured in the United States in sufficient and reasonably available quantities and of a satisfactory quality.
3. Those for which the Secretary determines the domestic preference to be inconsistent with the public interest.
4. Those for which the Secretary determines the cost to the government to be unreasonable.

Usually, Number 1, 2, or 4 provides justification for buying foreign-made goods. However, if none of them applies, Number 3 allows a great deal of latitude.

Tax Avoidance

This way of saving money sounds illegal, but it isn't. In fact, it may be an unallowable cost if you *do* pay some taxes.

"Don't pay unnecessary state sales taxes," warned a grant administrator.

Another said, "We had to pay back the government over $300 because we paid state sales taxes on purchases for an Agency for International Development technical-assistance contract."

According to federal cost principles, if your institution is exempt from certain taxes, these taxes are unallowable on grant purchases. Or if the federal agency sponsoring your project is exempt from certain taxes (and makes the necessary exemption certificate available to you), these taxes are unallowable on grant purchases.(3)

A common type of tax exemption is from *state sales taxes*. Sometimes state agencies (such as universities or units of state government) are exempt from paying sales taxes within the state. Federal agencies sometimes obtain exemptions from paying state sales taxes on specific grant programs (Peace Corps or AID projects, for example) because title to supplies and property will be retained by the federal granting agency or because the purchases will be used outside the state and/or the country.

If you should be exempt from paying state sales taxes on certain grants, your

*The U.S. Department of Interior, U.S. Forest Service, applies the Buy American Act to all its research contracts, grants, and cooperative agreements except for those performed entirely outside the United States and its territories and possessions. It is common for most federal agencies to incorporate the act into contracts, and some agencies include it in grants as well. If you are in doubt as to whether this clause applies to your project, you should check with your grant (or contract) officer.

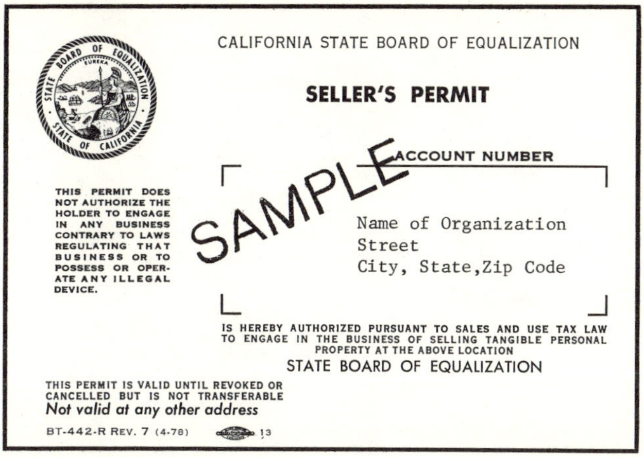

CALIFORNIA STATE BOARD OF EQUALIZATION

SELLER'S PERMIT

SAMPLE

ACCOUNT NUMBER

THIS PERMIT DOES NOT AUTHORIZE THE HOLDER TO ENGAGE IN ANY BUSINESS CONTRARY TO LAWS REGULATING THAT BUSINESS OR TO POSSESS OR OPERATE ANY ILLEGAL DEVICE.

Name of Organization
Street
City, State,Zip Code

IS HEREBY AUTHORIZED PURSUANT TO SALES AND USE TAX LAW TO ENGAGE IN THE BUSINESS OF SELLING TANGIBLE PERSONAL PROPERTY AT THE ABOVE LOCATION

STATE BOARD OF EQUALIZATION

THIS PERMIT IS VALID UNTIL REVOKED OR CANCELLED BUT IS NOT TRANSFERABLE

Not valid at any other address

BT-442-R REV. 7 (4-78) 13

Figure 20a. Example of a seller's permit. This is a sample of the kind of notice you will receive after applying to be exempt from paying state sales taxes on tax exempt projects. It should be displayed in your place of business, and the number on it should be used when you request tax exemptions from suppliers.

organization should apply for a "seller's permit."* This permit will enable you to "resell" your purchases to the federal agency which sponsors your grant project. This permit should be displayed on your business premises.

Suppliers, however, will not know about your organization's or the grantor agency's tax exemptions unless you tell them. Therefore, whenever you are purchasing for a tax-exempt project, the number of your seller's permit should be given to the supplier, and a tax exemption should be requested. Examples of a seller's permit and a request for tax exemption on purchase are contained in Figures 20a and 20b.

Even if you clearly state on your purchase order that sales taxes are not to be billed, sellers may overlook this and charge you anyway. It is the grantee's responsibility to check invoices carefully and to ensure that no unallowable sales taxes are paid. When they are, auditors usually find and disallow them.

Another type of tax that grantees may be exempt from paying is *import duty*. Normally, foreign goods imported to the United States are subject to import duty. However, if purchase of foreign goods has been approved by the granting agency, it may be possible to avoid paying duty. Typically, you can do this by completing a "Request for Duty-Free Entry of Scientific Instruments or Apparatus" form (ITA-338P), available from the U.S. Customs House in your area or from your customs house broker. Once the request is approved, a notice

*Seller's permits should be applied for through the organization in your state that is responsible for collecting state sales taxes. Usually, offices are located in key cities throughout the state. In California, the organization responsible for issuing seller's permits is the State Board of Equalization.

NAME OF ORGANIZATION
Number and Street
City, State Zip

SELLER'S PERMIT NO. SR FH 25 127177

I hereby certify that the tangible personal property which we have purchased from you is exempt from sales or use taxes because it is intended for resale to a United States Government agency.

N. Official
Name of Official
Title

Figure 20b. Request for tax exemption on purchases. This is an example of how to inform suppliers not to bill you for state sales taxes on tax-exempt-project purchases. This message may be printed on card stock and attached to purchase orders. In lieu of this (or in addition), the words "Tax-Exempt-Purchase–Seller's Permit No. ––" may be typed on purchase orders.

is published in the *Federal Register* (see Figure 21), and you will have saved grant dollars again.

Failure to request relief from import duty will not result in disallowances on your grant. However, it may result in unnecessary grant spending.

Many employers pay unnecessary social security taxes. There is no requirement to pay employer social security taxes or to withhold them from pay earned by employees while they are absent from work due to illness or disability. In the event your organization has been making such payments, it may file for a tax refund for up to four years' payments on its own and the affected employees' behalf.

Detection of Overcharges

Unallowable state sales taxes are not the only kinds of errors that may occur on invoices. There may be simple miscalculations of charges. These are easily detected when the figures are rechecked by the grantee before payment, but they can be expensive if they slip through. Or there may be complex mistakes, very costly and difficult to detect and prove.

For example, a large Agency for International Development project was ending several years ago. After completing a two-year educational-assistance mission in Jamaica, faculty members were returning to the United States with their families. Each family had been allowed to ship 2,500 pounds of household goods to Kingston at the beginning of the project. At its conclusion, they were allowed to ship the same weight back to their homes.

Fortunately, the shipping company employed by the project was slower with its service than with its billings. When the invoices arrived at project headquarters, showing four and five thousand pounds of goods per family being returned, the grant administrator recognized a problem. How would the faculty members feel about having to pay personally for an extra couple of thousand pounds of goods? (The contract funds covered only 2,500 pounds each.) More critical, were the charges valid? Why was everyone sending back so much more than they sent down?

After making a few telephone calls and discovering that, in general, the

NOTICES

[3510-25-M]

U. OF ILLINOIS AT CHICAGO CIRCLE

Decision on Application for Duty-Free Entry of Scientific Article

The following is a decision on an application for duty-free entry of a scientific article pursuant to Section 6(c) of the Educational, Scientific, and Cultural Materials Importation Act of 1966 (Pub. L. 89-651, 80 Stat. 897) and the regulations issued thereunder as amended (15 CFR 301).

A copy of the record pertaining to this decision is available for public review between 8:30 a.m. and 5:00 p.m. in Room 6886C of the Department of Commerce Building, at 14th and Constitution Avenue NW., Washington, D.C. 20230.

Docket Number: 79-00058. Applicant: University of Illinois at Chicago Circle, P.O. Box 4348, Chicago, Illinois 60680. Article: Laser Kit, Model H-103-2 and accessories. Manufacturer: Lumonics Research Ltd., Canada. Intended use of article: The article is intended to be used to study organic reactions initiated by infrared radiation. These reactions fall into three main categories: (i) Laser induced decomposition of molecules, (ii) Laser-induced isomerizations, and (iii) Biomolecular reactions such as the reaction of butadiene with vinyl chloride. The objective of this research is to discover if laser radiation can cause new chemical reactions or accelerate known reactions.

Comments: No comments have been received with respect to this application.

Decision: Application approved. No instrument or apparatus of equivalent scientific value to the foreign article, for such purposes as this article is intended to be used, is being manufactured in the United States. Reasons: The foreign article is capable of providing at least 8 joules per pulse. The National Bureau of Standards advises in its memorandum dated February 16, 1979 that (1) the capability of the foreign article described above is pertinent to the applicant's intended purpose and (2) it knows of no domestic instrument or apparatus of equivalent scientific value to the foreign article for the applicant's intended use.

The Department of Commerce knows of no other instrument or apparatus of equivalent scientific value to the foreign article, for such purposes as this article is intended to be used, which is being manufactured in the United States.

(Catalog of Federal Domestic Assistance Program No. 11.105, Importation of Duty-Free Educational and Scientific Materials.)

RICHARD M. SEPPA,
Director, Statutory Import Programs Staff.

[FR Doc. 79-7049 Filed 3-7-79; 8:45 am]

FEDERAL REGISTER, VOL. 44, NO. 47—THURSDAY, MARCH 8, 1979

Figure 21. Exemption of foreign-purchased item from import duty. This is an example of the notice that will be published in the *Federal Register* after you have applied for and obtained an exemption from paying import duties on foreign-made purchases. A copy of this notice should be kept with your purchase documents for audit review at a later date.

faculty members had unloaded goods in Jamaica (given away books, a piano, and sofas), the grant administrator made a decision. She would ask for a reweigh of one of the shipments on its arrival in the United States. (Several shipments had already arrived, and it was too late to reweigh them.)

As a result of the one reweigh, plus a comparison of shipping inventories of goods to Kingston at the beginning of the project and back from Kingston at the end, the grant administrator was able to negotiate a considerably reduced payment to the shipping company. No additional charges were levied on the families, and there was a net saving of over $10,000.

Grantees should check billings for possible calculation errors; in addition, they should be satisfied that the charges are reasonable.

So in making your actual purchases, you should capitalize on all opportunities to get reduced prices: donations, trades, bids, discounts, the timing of purchases, negotiations, and buying foreign goods. Once the lowest possible price has been obtained, you should ensure that the billings are accurate by checking for and correcting overcharges or miscalculations.

Throughout the process, it is important to keep in mind that frequently factors other than price must be considered. When can the goods be delivered? How reliable is the supplier? Will servicing be needed, and–if so–is it conveniently and reliably available? Will there be transportation costs? And you may be able to think of other considerations.

"Purchase from a reliable, responsible supplier, even if there is a somewhat higher first cost," advised a program officer, "if the purchase item is critical to the scheduled work and its delay would result in much higher offsetting costs."

In making the actual purchase decision, common sense must prevail. The optimum combination of favorable price and terms should always be sought.

Save by Using Grantee Buying Power

Whether you have a large or a small grant, savings may occur from piggybacking your purchases on the buying power of your institution. These savings are mainly from quantity buying or from receiving special prices because of organizational status. Typically, institutions can save through *quantity buying for all their grant projects and central administration*; *quantity buying through consortiums* (*or other memberships*); *and low-cost acquisition of surplus items.*

Quantity Institutional Buying

The more of a particular supply or equipment or travel item a hospital or university or other nonprofit agency buys, the lower the price is likely to be. If adequate planning is done, routine supplies that all projects and central administration are likely to use are purchased inexpensively by administration and charged back to grant projects at the low prices. Speaking in very small numbers, a bottle of Liquid Paper to correct typos can cost over a dollar if the project secretary picks it up at the local office-supply store. More, if you count his or her time and the transportation involved. Had the same Liquid Paper been purchased in quantity by the organization administering the grant, the cost could have been as low as 50 cents, and only a short walk to a central supply room would have been needed.

Quantity Consortium Buying

If the grantee organization has banded together with other organizations (for example, if it is part of a university and college system or belongs to a national professional group), even larger savings can be realized. The greater the combined buying power, the higher the potential savings.

Acquisition of Surplus Property

Many states provide access to state surplus equipment and supplies to state-funded agencies.* The idea is that what one state agency no longer needs may be useful to another. It's sort of a hand-me-down-between-organizational-relatives system. Usually, the state has several centrally located warehouses where potential buyers can pick over the merchandise. The cost is generally minimal. In California, the charge is 10% of the original cost to the state, and the grantee pays for or provides whatever transportation is necessary. The title to the property passes to the grantee on payment.

Similarly, the General Services Administration offers excess property to other federal agencies. If no federal agencies request this property, it becomes "surplus" and can be donated for authorized purposes such as education and public health. It can also be offered for sale to nonfederal organizations. Federal surplus property is usually not as useful as excess property. The good items have already been claimed as "excess" by one federal agency or another.

Save by Using Grantor Buying Power

Going just a step further in the quantity savings category, grantees can sometimes save substantial sums of money by capitalizing on *grantor* buying power. Under certain circumstances, the following options may be available to grantees: *federal excess property*; *National Technical Information Service* (*NTIS*); *data-processing-computer facilities*; *Federal Telecommunications System* (*FTS*); *General Service Administration* (*GSA*) *purchasing*; *and other in-kind contributions or discounts*.

*If you work for a state-funded agency, someone in your purchasing department or business office should be able to tell you where the surplus warehouses are located and whom to contact.

Federal Excess Property

If you have a federally funded grant (or contract), you may usually borrow federal excess personal property for grant-related purposes during the period of your grant. All sorts of property, from very specialized scientific equipment to office typewriters, are available from the government. Catalogs describing this equipment are published regularly. Look at Figure 22 to see a sample of a page from one of these catalogs.

If you want to get on the mailing list to receive excess property catalogs, the first step is to ask your grant officer for help. Once you receive catalogs and select property, you will need approval from your grant officer for the loan. The cost to your grant budget will normally be 25% of the original purchase price paid by the government plus transportation costs. Frequently, arrangements may be made for title to the property to pass to your organization after your project is completed. Again, this is done through your grant officer.

Reviewing the many excess property catalogs is a time-consuming process. Some institutions put a full-time person on this task. If your organization cannot afford this amount of time, you can ask the government to help you. Appendix E contains a list of the headquarters for the excess property program in each of the 10 federal regions. By contacting the chief in your area, you can find out where warehouses are located and ask area representatives to help you locate the specific items of property that you need for your project.

Various federal grantor agencies follow different procedures in administering the federal excess property program. Those used by the National Science Foundation are contained in Appendix F. No matter which federal agency is funding your grant, however, the first person you should contact for help in getting access to federal excess property is your grant officer.

National Technical Information Service (NTIS)

The National Technical Information Service is charged (under the Department of Commerce) with maintaining data and reports of technical information for distribution on a cost basis. Rather than spend grant money publishing and disseminating books or pamphlets about grant findings, it may be appropriate to give the information to NTIS and have them take over. Some of the results of the Research Applied to National Needs (RANN) programs at the National Science Foundation were disseminated in this manner, at a large savings to the project budgets.

Arrangements for using NTIS, as with many other government savings, must be made through your federal grant (or contract) officer.

Data-Processing/Computer Facilities

If your project involves a great deal of computer usage, and especially if it is funded by a contract, you may be able to save substantial funds through the use

TO PLACE A FREEZE FOR ITEMS ON THIS PAGE PHONE 415 556-2728

ITEM NO.	#GSA CONTROL, COND. CODE, QUANTITY, SRD	AGENCY REPORT NUMBER, DESCRIPTION, UNIT ACQUISITION COST *REPORTING ACTIVITY AND **PROPERTY LOCATION
95.	#042895(66) 0-3 1 ea 11/10/9	SE43009249L038, TID #FY17674619E NFSN 6625-89-476-800P TEST SET: Radio frequency. Mfr. Hewlett-Packard. Yr.'60. Mod. #DY-624C. (ID #532170). AC $ 2,255.00 * AFPRO/IR Hughes Acft. Co., Ph. 648-9730, P. O. Box 92463, Los Angeles, CA 90009 ** Hughes Aircraft Co., Centinela & Teale, Culver City, CA 90245
96.	#041707(36) 0-1 1 ea 11/11/9	790013, Item No. 1 NFSN 3610 TYPEWRITER,PHOTO, VGC, DISPLAY ENLARGE/REDUCED: Visual Graphics Corp. S/N 30 350. Mod. 3000. AC $ 4,338.00 * U.S. Environmental Protection Agency, EMSL LV., P. O. Box 15027, Las Vegas, NV 89114 ** U.S. EPA/EMSL LV, 3876 W. Patrick Lane, Bldg. 5, Las Vegas, NV 89118
97.	#041837(49) R-3 1 ea 11/11/9	DEPP23874, Item No. 2 NFSN 4910 DISTRIBUTION TANK: W/spray bar and engine. 800 gallon cap., dual wheels. S/N D15 5314. AC $13,461.11 * USDA, Forest Service, Region 5, 630 Sansome St., San Francisco, CA 94111 ** USDA, Forest Service, Sequoia Nat'l. Bill Butts Forest Warehouse, 480 N. Henrahan: 209/784 1500, Porterville, CA 93257
98.	#042942(91) N-2 888 gl 11/9/9	SZ31399229K016, NFSN 9150-00-223-4134 HYDRAULIC FLUID, PETROLEUM BASE: Service characteristics, antiwear, corrosion resistant, oxidation resistant. Red. Designed for synthetic rubber seal. Primary physical data, 500 centistokes at -40 deg F max.viscosity, 10 centistokes at 130 deg F min. viscosity, 200 deg F min. flash point by Cleveland open-cup test method, -75 deg F max pour point. Govt. Spec. Data, MIL-H-5606. Pkg. 1 gal. can. AC $ 3.04
99.	#043393(66) R-2 2 ea 11/16/9	SZ31399236K014 NFSN 6625-00-621-9038 RADIO INTERFERENCE MEASURING SET: Freq., 20 to 400 MC range, 6 bands, 6 channels, 20-33 MC, 32-54 MC, 53-89 MC, 88-146 MC, 145-241 MC, 240 to 400 MC. Porm 2 pct. freq. calibration accuracy. Indicator, meter type, voltmeter, DB meter, 1 to 100 microvolt and 0 to 40 DB ranges, porm 1 pct. accuracy. 50 OHMS input impedance. Oper. pwr. rqmts., AC, 110 to 125 V, 50 to 4000 cy., 1 ph., 210 to 250 V, 50 to 400 cy., 1 ph. O/a dim. of carrying case, 24-3/4" x 12-5/8" x 10-3/8" w/components and accessories. Mfr. JCENS. Type AN-URM-47A. For general purpose use. For making quantitative measurements on carrier radio freq. interference. AC $ 4,800.00
100.	#043331(61) N-2 72 ea 11/16/9	SZ31399236K008 NFSN 6115-00-249-6854 SWITCH TEMP SHUTDOWN: P/N 4271-0112. Mfr. Consolidated Diesel Electric. AC $ 93.48
101.	#043335(61) N-2 1 ea 11/16/9	SZ31399236K010 NFSN 6115-00-872-1775 GENERATOR, ALTERNATING CURRENT: Open protected inclosure, line to neutral low AC output connection and 446 V line to neutral high AC output connection. AC $ 5,291.47 * DPDO Pendleton, P. O. Box 1608, Oceanside, CA 92054 ** Location Same

Figure 22. A page from a federal excess property catalog. These are the kinds of property you may be able to borrow from the government. To do so, you must pay 25% of the original cost to the government plus transportation costs to your headquarters.

of government computer facilities. Many requests for proposals (RFPs) require that you demonstrate that your computer will cost less than government computers—or else you will be expected to use the government computers.

Arrangements for using government computer facilities must be made through your federal grant (or contract) officer.

Federal Telecommunications System (FTS)

Organizations that have a federal cost-reimbursable *contract* may request the use of federal telephone lines. This request should be initiated by the grant administrator for action by the sponsor's contract officer. There is no charge for the use of the lines. When a project requires a great many long-distance calls, the savings can amount to hundreds of dollars per month. Of course, the FTS line may be used only for the particular project for which approval was obtained—not for any other projects administered by the grantee organization.

General Services Administration (GSA) Purchasing

Again, when a federal cost-reimbursable *contract* is awarded, the grantee may request the privilege of buying from the General Services Administration. The quantity discounts involved here are substantial, as the GSA does all the buying for the government.

In the past, the GSA allowed many grant and contract recipients the privilege of buying. More recently, purchasing through the GSA has been restricted considerably, to the point where large national research centers are the main government-funded projects to benefit.

If your project will be buying equipment or supplies for which title will remain in the government's name, and if you have been funded through a contract, there is a possibility that you will be eligible to purchase through the GSA. You should explore these potential savings by initiating a request through the government contract officer.

Other In-Kind Contributions and Discounts

Sometimes a funding agency will provide some project supplies at no charge to the project. Typically, this is done because the sponsor can buy the same item for a large number of projects and therefore get a better price than a single project alone could get. For example, the Peace Corps has provided vaccines, syringes, air tickets (or charter flights), and orientation notebooks to many grantees who were training Peace Corps volunteers. Similarly, the Agency for International Development has encouraged its grantees to purchase books and educational materials for AID international participants from a central source that offers very low prices.

To sum up what we have said so far, there are many techniques for saving money on grants. By selecting the most economical task and cost alternatives; by comparison shopping once those alternatives are chosen; and by capitalizing on grantee and grantor total buying power, you can stretch your grant dollars considerably. A few specific examples of possible savings have already been given in the foregoing discussion of techniques. Now let's look at some more.

Advice and Examples of Savings from Experienced Grants Spenders

We asked project directors and grant administrators of all sorts of projects (medical, educational, social service, scientific, and others) to tell us how they had saved money on grants. Here are some of their answers, arranged alphabetically by cost category.

Advertising

"Get it donated."

"I used the campus telecommunications lab and student help."

"Interns in the educational technology program put together a terrific slide and tape show–no labor costs."

Air Conditioning

"We designed our own and installed it."

Alterations

"We employed a good student to redesign a project that was originally designed poorly by a private company."

"At CPSLO (California Polytechnic State University, San Luis Obispo) we often use students for alterations. A class in construction engineering is used for some work; they also get paid for work going beyond the valid instructional experience."

Books and Periodicals

"Of course, one tries to get the library to buy as many as possible!"

"Purchase subscriptions for longer periods of time."

"Buy used–request donations."

Child-Care Costs

"Use high school students or get volunteers."

"Group sitting at a central location saves money here."

"Let program participants do the child-sitting free."

Communications

"Limit them!"

"You don't need a phone on every person's desk."

"Californians have an advantage in telephoning as we can begin at 7:30 A.M.

and call east several times at a moderate rate. If I can't make a call at 7:59 to Washington, I'll try again about 9:30 (the middle of lunch there) so they'll call back."

"Don't return long-distance calls to parties you don't know; if they want to talk to you, they'll call again."

"I ask the program officer to call me back on the government line—saves on long-distance costs."

"Night letters are less expensive than day cables."

"Many grantees save money by using bulk-mailing permits. When mailing at least 200 pieces of printed matter, identical in size and weight, the postage is as low as 3.1¢ per piece, compared with 18¢ regular postage. There is a $30 one-time permit imprint fee, and following that a $40 annual fee. Information about bulk mailing may be obtained by telephoning the U.S. Postal Service ('Mailing Requirements' or 'Mailing Permits' section) in your city. In addition, you can learn a lot from the U.S. Postal Service Publication 13, 'Mailing Permits,' published by the Government Printing Office."

"Centralize the bulk-mail-permit function to qualify for lowest rates."

"Avoid regular use of expensive courier services—do some advance planning."

Computer Costs

"Use government facilities."

"Let your university provide computer time out of departmental budgets."

"Use low priorities instead of high priorities."

"Don't use more sophisticated equipment than necessary."

"Use central time-sharing."

Construction

"Employ students as opposed to contract labor. We have our own construction supervisor to act as an owner-builder on site at all times."

"Get bids—and references."

Consultants

"Try to get them free. Consultant fees may not generally be paid to an employee of the federal government, but federal employees are often willing to provide services."

"Maintain a listing of consultant services and fees."

"If you are purchasing equipment, request that consultant services be provided as part of the purchasing agreement."

"If several consultants have similar qualifications, hire the local (closer) one and save travel costs."

"Trade off with your colleagues; serve as a consultant on their grants in return for their doing the same for you."

Contracts

"Tie into existing materials and supplies contracts to save time."

"If another organization can do part of the job for less than yours (has a lower overhead rate, for example), subcontract to them."

Customs and Import Duties

"Avoid these by buying American goods; most contracts have a clause requiring this."

"If no equivalent-quality American goods are available and you must buy foreign, get an exemption from customs and import duties."

Duplication (Copying)

"For a large project (or several projects), lease a copier. This will save you personnel time (avoids running around), and the price per copy will be less."

"Avoid unnecessary copying."

"Figure your labor. It may be cheaper to send routine copying out to be done at 5¢ a page than to have your $4.50 an hour secretary standing an hour at the copier when you'll be charged 2–3¢ a page for her copies anyway."

"Be careful to have final reports offset-printed rather than xeroxed if the number of copies exceeds 30 or more."

"We're using dittos more and more because they're cheaper."

"Use the quality of machine necessary to do the job—that is, dittos are fine for mass, disposable handouts."

"You can save a lot of clerical labor by typing a form letter once, xeroxing it on your organization's letterhead, and then typing in the nonstandard information."

"Keep track of how much copying you are doing on your leased copier. If the amount increases substantially, it may be less expensive for you to lease a better-quality machine and pay a higher monthly rental but get your copies at a lower rate. For example, we pay less than a penny per copy (0.65¢) for each copy we make in excess of 50,000 on our large new copier. In contrast, the lowest rate we can get on a much smaller copier, no matter how many copies we make, is 1.4¢."

Equipment

"Banks in our area redecorate their offices often and are frequently willing to give away their 'old' office furniture. We just got three truckloads of executive desks, conference tables, chairs, and files—all in excellent condition and of much better quality than any we could have afforded. The bank made out because of the tax break."

"If the grant limits you to renting or leasing equipment, have your organization buy it and then rent it back to the grant until the initial purchase price is recovered."

"Federal excess and state surplus property are good sources of low-cost equipment, but you have to watch the catalogs and visit the warehouses regularly."

"We were running regular summer training programs for math students. They all needed calculators, which we rented at $15 per month. The salesman appreciated our business, and at the end of each summer, he'd give me several calculators. At the end of five years, we had enough to stop renting any."

Equipment Maintenance and Repairs

"Negotiate full preventative-maintenance service agreements with the purchase."

"Make sure that cost for maintenance is budgeted in advance and you'll save money. In the last few years, at least a few grantsfolks have got caught short here, and it hurt."

"We have a lot of fun reducing maintenance costs at our institute. Several years ago, when grant volume got up to well over $10 million, we had a lot of electronic calculators around—all with separate maintenance contracts at $110 per year each. On totaling the costs of all these contracts, we discovered that we were paying over $10,000 a year for calculator maintenance. Yet many of these calculators were never even being looked at. It was cheaper and more effective for us to hire our own maintenance man. We did, and he easily serviced all the calculators and other grant equipment, also. In other cases, we have simply decided to 'self-insure'—that is, we don't pay for any regularly scheduled maintenance but bear the cost of repairs or replacements as they occur."

Fringe Benefits

"Have competitive bidding on the components of the benefits package (i.e., health insurance)."

"Review the workers' compensation class codes to assure that the lowest rates are being applied to each position."

"At our university, the research foundation had traditionally gone in with the university in calculating the state unemployment rates. When we recently went in separately, we negotiated a much lower rate because our foundation employees had made many fewer claims than had the university employees."

"We routinely budget vacation benefits in grants so that if our grant employees are unable to take vacation during the project period, we can pay them for unused vacation days at the end of the grant. One way to save money is to require employees to use vacation days, so that no extra money will be needed to pay them off at the end of the grant."

"Hire consultants—then you won't have to pay any fringe benefits. Or hire students. Benefits on students are often as low as 5%, compared with 10-30% for other categories of employees."

"Hire faculty on overload or during the summer, with benefits of approximately 10% instead of the 30+% they normally receive during the academic year."

Insurance

"Use the student health insurance at the university for participants in training programs."

"Get competitive bids."

"Be explicit on the type of coverage you need, and get it only for the duration needed."

"Whenever possible, get insurance put on larger policies that your organization has already."

Land

"We've leased 320 acres of forest and pastureland for over nine years now—at no cost. The owners bought the land as an investment. They pay no taxes because our nonprofit research firm is using the land; meanwhile, the land is appreciating in value tremendously. We've been able to conduct longitudinal studies of plant growth under a variety of conditions."

Meals

"Most restaurants or caterers will charge you on a per plate basis, with a minimum guaranteed number of meals. It's usually a good idea to guarantee about 10% fewer meals than you actually expect to need because most places are prepared to serve up to 10% more meals than your guaranteed minimum. This way, you are covered for all your guests, but you don't end up paying for 'no shows.' Of course, the percentages may vary at different restaurants, so you should check on this ahead of time."

"We often have potlucks and family gatherings for our project participants—low cost, lots of fun."

"Our high school participants get a meal allowance. If they don't spend it all, they keep the difference. It's a good incentive for them to learn to save. We make sure, though, that their diet is balanced, by requiring that the evening meal be purchased at our low-cost student cafeteria."

News Releases

"Get them free. A local TV and radio station wanted to do stories on my project because they would be the first to cover it. Good advertisement—no costs incurred."

Overtime

"Plan better to avoid overtime."

"Hire temporary help instead of paying overtime."

"If possible, give compensating time off instead of overtime pay. Generally, my staff seem to like the opportunity to take a couple hours off midweek to get errands run."

"Limit overtime by position, and use compensating time off to be taken in slow periods."

Personnel

"Delay hiring."

"Use cheaper labor when possible–CETA, work-study, students, or interns."

"Don't hire overqualified personnel. For example, don't hire a senior clerical person when a junior one will do."

"Develop jobs so that more highly paid duties are concentrated in one position, lower duties in others."

"I always make sure that when a project director has enough projects going to justify hiring a clerical assistant (25% or more), this is done so as to relieve the project director (and the grants budgets) of the dollars involved in his or her doing paperwork."

"Establish job pools (clerical, dishwashing, etc.) between several projects, and share the costs according to use."

"Balance the work schedule to avoid peaks and valleys, thus avoiding staff down time for valleys and the necessity of hiring lower-quality temporaries for peaks."

"Pay students with tuition in lieu of salaries when grant regulations allow this. No additional overhead or benefits charges will then be applied."

"Enlist volunteers. Many experiments can be conducted with volunteers rather than paid human subjects."

"On our Peace Corps training programs, the participants themselves helped with a major portion of the routine clerical and child-care tasks–no charge to the project."

"Argue stipends as much as possible to get student aid out of the indirect-cost base."

"DON'T OVERPAY A POSITION JUST BECAUSE IT'S GRANT MONEY."

Publications Costs

"Be sure any charges for publication by journals are equitably applied to all papers regardless of the source of financial support."

"Sometimes journals charge for publication within six months. However, if you are willing to wait for a year, there may be no page charges. You should look into this when you submit your article."

Travel

"Don't believe the first fare quoted by a travel agency. Keep asking questions about budget, economy, supersaver, night flights, charters, etc., until they come up with something cheaper."

"Car rentals vary enormously, from agency to agency, depending on your particular needs. As long as the counters are next to each other, get three quotes."

"Use public transportation in most cities."

"Try to combine as many functions as possible into as few trips as possible."

"Choose the cheapest alternatives–taxis versus rented cars; actual expenses versus per diem; bus or train versus plane; private car versus other methods."

"Get group rates whenever possible. For example, the $50–$80 rooms at a Washington, DC, hotel were offered to conference attendees for $35 per night."

"If you have a large group traveling, a chartered bus or plane may be cheaper and more convenient than commercial bus rides or flights."

"Combine other project business with a conference trip. You may then take advantage of lower hotel rates for several days before or after the conference and avoid an additional plane fare altogether."

"When selecting the travel method, consider how much of your project staff time will be used. It may be less expensive in the long run to pay a higher-priced air fare (than bus fare) and to have your employee spending more time on the job at the destination."

Tuition and Student Costs

"Compare the costs of 'summer' and 'extension' course credits with those of 'regular' course credits. At my university, a state resident pays less than $10 for each regular course unit, but summer and extension units cost $40. In contrast, a nonresident actually saves by taking summer or extension units because nonresident charges for regular courses are much higher–over $60 per unit. Therefore, when we arrange programs for international students, we can save thousands of dollars by arranging as many of the credits as the university policy permits to be offered through extension and summer courses."

"Our extension and summer programs offer two budget options for grant-funded courses: (1) we can pay the instructor's salary and $10 per unit for each student; or (2) we can pay the regularly charged $40 per unit per student and not pay any instructional salary. When there is a large class, we save money by choosing the first option."

"Sometimes international students aren't interested in getting university 'credits,' as these students are learning technical skills and will not be completing the requirements for a college degree. In these cases, we provide certificates on the student's successful completion of classes, and the university does not charge any fees since no credits are involved."

Indirect Costs

Besides saving money in all the *direct*-cost categories we have just finished talking about, *indirect* costs may be reduced.

"Have an 'interest' in the way indirect costs are applied," advised a program officer, "if you want to cut total project costs."

We have already seen that there are two common indirect-cost bases: (1) salaries and wages (S & W) and (2) modified total direct costs (MTDC). The way to reduce the indirect charges on a grant project is to shift money out of the categories to which the indirect rate is applied.

For example, if your organization has an S & W base, indirect costs will be reduced if you hire consultants or subcontract for services instead of paying salaries and wages to personnel. A $100-per-day *consultant* will cost your grant just that: $100. A $100 *employee* will cost your grant the $100 *plus* fringe benefits (another $10–$30, probably) *plus* indirect costs (possibly $50 or so).

It is harder to save this way when your indirect base is MTDC because most budget categories are then subject to the indirect rate. However, some shifting is still possible. In the application of most MTDC rates, no indirect costs are applied to the following categories: equipment, stipends and other student support costs, and subcontracts or subgrants over $25,000.* One possibility is to establish a subcontract during the first year of your project. Although you will have indirect charges against the first $25,000, if you *add on* (rather than establishing a new subcontract) during succeeding years of your grant, there may be no indirect charges applied.

We have also seen that indirect rates are commonly based on either on-site or off-site costs. Usually, the off-site indirect rates are lower, but then the costs of project space and office equipment are charged as direct costs to the project. It may be possible to reduce the total project costs by conducting the project off-site, if the additional costs for facilities are less than the savings from using the lower off-site rate.

It is important to note that although indirect costs may be cut on a particular grant budget and therefore help one project director, the indirect costs borne by the grantee institution are real costs—they must be paid by all the grant budgets combined.

Obstacles to Saving and How to Get around Them

Grants spenders were asked what prevented them from using all the techniques for stretching grant dollars that they had recommended and that have just been described.

*It used to be common for grantees to have indirect-cost rates based on salaries and wages. As a result of Circular A-21 (p. 12374), all educational institutions are required to negotiate indirect-cost rates based on modified total direct costs.

You may recognize some of their reasons:

"Lack of time."
"Immediate need."
"Too much paperwork."
"Not enough information."
"Little or no incentives."

Project directors and grant administrators differed in assigning the blame for these obstacles. Project directors claimed savings were difficult because:

"The grant administrator can't process purchases quickly enough."
"Suppliers are slow with delivery."
"Foundation-university-government regulations get in the way."

Grant administrators reasoned somewhat differently, attributing the problems to:

"Alleged immediate need, individuality, and independence of each project director."

"Alleged quality need. Project director wants to pay top dollar when it is not necessary."

"Comparative shopping requires lead time. Awards are known to be delayed by the grantor; hence, time may be too short."

"Changes in grantor personnel, obscure or new regulations."

No matter who is responsible for them, the obstacles to stretching grant dollars can be overcome in many cases. Let's look at these obstacles again.

Lack of Time

Just as the student puts off an assigned term paper until a day or so before it is due, grants spenders sometimes put off initiating purchases until the last hours. Then the expenditure must be rushed and there is little opportunity for savings.

One way to avoid much of this haste is for the project director and the grant administrator to hold a "project spending meeting" near the beginning of each project. At this meeting–before there is a rush to buy supplies and equipment and hire personnel–the budget should be examined carefully. When will particular cost items be needed? What comparison shopping, actual purchases, and advertising for personnel should be started now? Remember, the budget is a management tool. It should be used this way at the beginning and throughout the project.

If the project director has never had a grant before, the grant administrator should use the project spending meeting to explain purchasing policies and paperwork so that the project director won't be learning new procedures under emergency purchase conditions. If project administrative or clerical staff will be helping with grant spending, it is important that they participate in this meeting.

Careful planning at the beginning of the project can save time for the project director and the grant administrator, as well as stretch grant dollars.

Immediate Need

Sometimes, of course, there are special reasons that supplies or other budget items can't be purchased at the beginning of the project. On a chemistry department project, for example, at a western college, formic acid (c-13 label) at about $500 per gram was needed. The problem was that this chemical is very unstable and "keeps" less than a day. Therefore, the researcher who was buying it had to purchase it for immediate use.

Even under these circumstances, it was not necessary for the project director and the grant administrator to spend more, just to hurry the purchase up. When they analyzed the budget at the beginning of the project, they knew that the formic acid (and other chemical supplies) would be needed at some point in the project. They shopped around to find the best discounts available for chemical supplies. After locating a supplier, the grant administrator sent an "open purchase order" to the supplier, arranging for the future purchase of chemical supplies on an as-needed basis. The project director could telephone in an order each time he needed a gram of formic acid. The only limit was the dollar amount of expenditures identified on the purchase order, which in this case was the dollar amount budgeted for chemical supplies in the grant budget.

An open purchase order is one that allows purchases as they are needed, with cumulative expenditures not to exceed a specified amount of money and with expenditures to be made during a specified period of time. It is a useful tool to make rush purchases less of an emergency, and to prevent unnecessarily high expenses for them.

Too Much Paperwork

"Inflation may occur by the time all the purchasing paperwork is taken care of," one project director grumbled.

True?

Typically, the project director initiates a purchase by filling out a "purchase-order request" form. The grant administrator must approve this request, checking to be sure that there are adequate funds remaining in the project budget and that the item to be purchased will be an allowable cost to the grant.

If the purchase will be a large one, more paper may start moving. Most organizations set some maximum amount, above which there must be bids from competing companies. Bids are sometimes obtained by phone, but more frequently a "request for quotation" form is sent to several suppliers. In turn, the suppliers send back their bids (on paper).

Once the best bid has been selected, another form, a "purchase order," is forwarded by the grantee organization to the supplier. At some point after the supplier completes all of its internal paperwork, the project director receives the goods ordered.

Samples of a "purchase-order request," a "request for quotation," and a "purchase order" are contained in Appendix B.

Depending on the size and type of organization you work for, the internal paperwork and review process for purchasing may be more or less (rarely) cum bersome.

What this all means is that the project spending meeting at the beginning of the project is critical. Not only does it allow proper time for comparison shopping and purchasing to begin, but it also enables the grant administrator to help the project director and her or his staff understand the paper requirements and to streamline them whenever possible.

Planning for open purchase orders can be especially useful in cutting down paperwork. For example, a project director who orders office supplies as needed, on a rush basis and from several different companies throughout the year, may have to fill out 20 or more purchase-order request forms. These forms, and all other resulting forms, separate billings, etc., will then have to be processed by the grant administrator and purchasing staff. An alternative is for the project director to prepare one purchase-order request at the beginning of the project, listing all the supplies (or kinds of supplies) needed. Some comparison shopping can be done, and then one open purchase order can be issued to the most competitively priced supplier.

There *is* a great deal of paperwork connected with spending grant dollars. But with good planning, much of it can be reduced or eliminated.

Not Enough Information

Project directors are *not* purchasing agents. They usually do not know where the best buys are. Even experienced project directors usually do not have time to keep up with changing prices. Nor should they. It's their business to do research, conduct training, and carry on project technical activities.

Yet project directors initiate the purchase requests. Often, they are familiar or feel comfortable with a particular supplier and therefore make all purchases through that supplier, even if prices are slightly higher.

Project directors, especially new ones, may not know about government surplus property, the FTS phone lines, educational discounts, and so forth. Grant administrators, rushing to fill last-minute-purchase requests, may not have had time to find out about all the possibilities for savings either.

But here is where the grant administrator *should* provide service to the project director. Lack of information *should not* be an obstacle to saving grant dollars. The kinds of information we have talked about in this chapter should be discussed with project directors at the beginning of their projects. In addition, grant administrators (and purchasing clerks) have access to a great deal of information about where the best deals are—simply because the grantee organization usually handles such a large volume of purchases. Updated price lists from various suppliers can be posted in the grantee's purchasing department. If the grant administrator knows that three project directors will be buying computer terminals, the grant administrator should send one request for quotation for three terminals, rather than three request-for-quotation forms for one terminal each.

A great deal of purchasing information is available within grantee organizations. It should be used.

Few or No Incentives

Too little information and time, too much paperwork—these are obstacles that can be eliminated or at least circumvented in most cases. A more serious hurdle to stretching grant dollars exists when there are few or no incentives to save.

"Once my proposal has been developed and a detailed budget has been awarded, saving money is not of paramount importance to me," admitted one project director, when asked for tips for stretching grant money.

In business, there are rewards for saving money. When expenditures are cut, revenues stay the same, and so profits are increased. The owners or directors of the business "look good."

In grants, the opposite may occur. Grants (and many contracts) are on a cost-reimbursable basis. If you spend the money, the funding agency will pay you back. If you don't spend it, you may be penalized in two ways.

First, it is common to fund renewal projects at the same level (or only slightly higher) than their *expenditure* (not award) level during the previous year. So, if you had a first-year $100,000 award and spent only $75,000, your second-year need would be figured at $75,000.

However (second penalty), since you have $25,000 left from the first-year award, the funding agency would allow you to carry over this money into the next year. Therefore, your official second-year award (new money, to be listed on your promotion papers, in news releases, and in the faculty-staff weekly paper) would be $50,000, half what you were awarded last year.

Neither the project director nor the grant administrator wants this to happen. The program officer and the grant officer frequently don't like it either, as their agency's next year's funding allocations frequently are tied to the prior year's expenditure levels as well. "Poor planning," it looks like.

One funding agency went so far as to invoke an extreme penalty for underspending grant money. A small college received money to buy instructional equipment from a state agency that was dispensing federal funds. Because of new technology and some extremely competitive bidding, the university was able to buy the equipment for almost $5,000 less than the funds awarded.

Two years later, the college applied for another instructional equipment grant from the same state agency. Although the college's proposal was rated by reviewers as one of the top technical proposals, the reviewers subtracted points from the total score because of the college's failure to spend all the monies it was previously awarded. The loss of points put the college just below the cutoff line for funding. Although the college's proposal was rated technically better than several other proposals that were funded, this proposal was rejected.

This, of course, was an extreme case. We have heard of no other like it. However, whether your grant is lost or simply reduced because of stretching grant dollars, there appears to be little incentive to save money when ample, or even excessive, funds have been awarded.

What can be done about this serious obstacle?

Probably nothing, *if* there really are excess funds in the budget.

Therefore, in the beginning, before the grant is awarded, the funding-agency representatives must take steps to ensure that funds are not excessive. In addition, they should try to institute rewards for stretching grant dollars.

A few rewards currently exist in connection with contract-funded projects. The fixed-price contract, for example, allows the contractor to keep all monies saved. The CPFF/AF (cost-plus fixed-fee–award fee) contract allows both the funding agency and the contracting agency to share in savings.*

Similar arrangements for recipients of cost-reimbursable grants to share in savings are rare. The Public Broadcasting Service offers a "cost reduction incentive" to some grant recipients, as follows:

> In order to promote efficient and effective utilization of available programming resources, producers of programs for PBS are entitled to a cost reduction incentive. This incentive provides that, if actual reimbursable costs (which does not include production fee) are less than budget, the producer should share in the savings. Accordingly, to the extent that cost savings are realized, 30% of the amounts saved are allowed as additional funding to the producer. The cost reduction incentive earned on any program will, however, be limited by a maximum allowable cost reduction saving of 15% of budgeted reimbursable costs. To the extent that actual reimbursable costs are less than 85% of budgeted reimbursable costs, the full difference between costs and 85% must be repaid to PBS.[4]

Despite the infrequency of rewards for saving grant monies, the fact is that stretching grant dollars is becoming a necessity. Because grant competition is becoming more and more fierce, because program officers (and review panels) are attempting to "spread the grant money" to more projects, there are not nearly as many amply funded projects as there used to be.

The project director quoted earlier as saying that saving money wasn't of "paramount importance" to him did not tell all. This man had directed an Upward Bound project for over nine years. In developing his very detailed budget, he had already used knowledge from his previous experience and done all the comparison shopping, pricing, and dealing necessary to present an extremely well-thought-out and competitive budget. The agency that he submitted his budget to knew this and would not have presumed to cut his budget or expect additional savings during the project. He had admirably planned to make the most of his grant dollars *before* receiving them. This contributed a great deal to the respect that this project director had earned from the grantors. It also enabled him to propose a lower budget than those of his competitors.

*In a CPFF/AF contract, a small fixed fee is established. Then, if the contractor saves the government money by doing the work for well below the original estimate, she or he will get a generous award fee. If the job has been done poorly, she or he will get a small, or possibly no, award fee.

In this chapter, we have presented many ways to save grant dollars as well as some obstacles to saving. In summary, what can you do to stretch grant dollars? To begin with, you can *learn* all the techniques for saving money, including the various methods of comparing cost and task alternatives; getting donations, trades, bids, discounts; timing purchases; negotiating; buying foreign; avoiding taxes; detecting overcharges; using grantee buying power; and using grantor buying power. You should be aware of what obstacles to expect: too little time; immediate needs; too much paperwork; not enough information; and few or no incentives. Then, in order to get around these obstacles, you can initiate good *planning* efforts. These include participating in a project spending meeting at the beginning of each grant, using open purchase orders to alleviate rush purchases and streamline paperwork, and collecting and disseminating the purchasing information available at your institution.

Grant dollars can be stretched. As our Upward Bound project director friend learned years ago, the two keys for getting more for less are simply these: *knowing the techniques and planning in advance.*

7

Expenditures to Avoid Over-, Under-, Unallowable

If you're going to do business with the government, there are going to be unreasonable demands on you.

—Anonymous Federal Auditor

In getting the most out of your grant dollar, there is more to be considered than just getting the best deal or getting more for less. It is even more important (1) not to spend money that may, in the future, be disallowed by the auditors and (2) not to spend money that you may not have. Also, although they are often overlooked as a problem, underexpenditures should be avoided. In an *indirect* way (pun intended), underexpenditures can cost your agency money just as surely as overexpenditures do.

How Do You Avoid Overexpenditures?

An overexpenditure occurs when you spend more money on a grant than you've been awarded. This does happen from time to time, but it is rarely intentional. In fact, it is the one unforeseen grant-related event that project directors and grant administrators fear most. Close communication between these two players can almost always prevent an overexpenditure.

Slipups, however, can occur, and it is these slipups that will result in a severe dollar stretch toward the end of the project or will actually cost your organization money. Higher administrative charges will inevitably be necessary if overexpenditures become common; the grantee will have to recover its losses somehow. Prevention is the answer.

How can overexpenditures be foreseen and prevented? Probably the most effective device for avoiding overexpenditures is a grant accounting system that includes *encumbrances*.

An Accounting System with Encumbrances: A MUST!

An encumbrance system gives the project director and the grant administrator information about project monies that have been *committed*, as well as information about monies that have already been spent.

Many grantees—large and small—do not yet have an encumbrance system because such a system is often difficult and costly to implement and requires daily updating of each project account. Unless there is enough money to be saved by an encumbrance system, a grantee agency probably will not initiate the use of one.

Therefore, most project accounting reports are prepared monthly (or twice monthly) and reflect only the expenditures that have actually been made. For example, assume that a purchase order has been sent to a vendor for a $3,000 piece of equipment. That $3,000 is committed, but because the bill has not yet been paid, the monthly accounting report will not reflect the transaction. The equipment category in the budget will appear as if nothing had happened.

In point of fact, something significant *has* happened, but because the accounting system has no way to record the $3,000 commitment, neither the project director nor the grant administrator has an accurate view of how much equipment money remains. Theoretically, the equipment category could have been overspent and no one will know it until a month or six weeks later, when the bill arrives.

Ideally, an encumbrance system reflects all transactions—salaries, travel, equipment, etc.—on a daily basis. A computer terminal can then be used to get an up-to-date picture—a "snapshot"—of the account as of four o'clock the previous day. But as was mentioned earlier, implementing such a system requires a good deal of time, work, planning, and money.

There are good software packages available from a number of private companies, but again, there must be a payoff for a grantee to make the investment. A university or research institute that receives $10 million or $20 million a year or more in grants or contracts can easily benefit from such a system; a $1-million-per-year community group or college cannot.

Some grantees, however, have adopted a monthly accounting report format that leaves a blank column on the printout so that the project director or the grant administrator can manually record (in pencil) all encumbrances. An example of this format is shown in Figure 23.

This system is not perfect, but it is better than no encumbrance system. Its fault lies in its reliance on the project director or the grant administrator to remember to record each commitment she or he makes. Further, expecting a

GENERAL ACCOUNTING SYSTEM
REPORT NO. 7

DO GOOD INSTITUTION
BUDGET REPORT

PERIOD ENDED 12/31/80 PAGE 1000
RUN DATE 12/31/80

ACCOUNT NO. 580-0012 PROJECT DIRECTOR B. BRIGHT

BUDGET CODE	DESCRIPTION	APPROVED BUDGET	SPENT TO DATE	SPENT THIS MONTH	UNSPENT BALANCE	ENCUMBERED FUNDS	UNENCUMBERED BALANCE
100	SALARIES	62,023	8,004	2,668	54,019		
101	PRINCIPAL INVESTIGATOR	10,345	2,586	862	7,759		
102	RESEARCH ASSOCIATE	15,678	3,918	1,306	11,760		
110	TECHNICIANS	30,000			30,000		
120	SECRETARY	6,000	1,500	500	4,500		
200	BENEFITS	7,237	1,059	353	6,178		
300	TRAVEL	2,350			2,350		
400	EQUIPMENT	2,800	800	800	2,000		
500	SUPPLIES	450	350	300	100		
800	OTHER OPERATING EXPENSES	4,260	275	25	3,985		
801	COMMUNICATIONS	300	75	25	225		
810	COMPUTER	200			200		
820	CONSULTANTS	400	200		200		
860	PUBLICATIONS	560			560		
870	SUBJECT PAYMENTS	2,000			2,000		
899	OTHER	800			800		
	TOTAL DIRECT COSTS	79,120	10,488	4,146	68,632		
900	INDIRECT COSTS	31,012	4,002	1,334	27,010		
	* TOTAL COSTS *	* 110,132 *	* 14,490 *	* 5,480 *	* 95,642 *		

PROJECT ADMINISTRATOR R. SHARP

PROJECT DATES 10/01/80 THROUGH 9/30/81

Figure 23. Sample budget report format with space to record encumbrances manually. This budget report format is designed to allow project directors and grant administrators to record encumbrances manually. Notice the column provided so that penciled entries may be made for purchase orders and other commitments.

project director to do daily bookkeeping chores instead of using his or her technical expertise is wasteful of grant dollars.

If your agency can afford it, having a computer terminal that is updated daily with encumbrances is preferable to keeping track of grant dollars manually or to having no method at all. The costs for such a system vary considerably, from a low of around $40,000 to well over $250,000. An example of a budget report from a computerized system that records encumbrances is contained in Figure 24.

Transfers between Line Items

It is important to look at overexpenditures in relation to budget categories (e.g., salaries, travel, supplies) within the grant, as well as the total amount of the grant. Most funding agencies will allow you to overspend in one category by a designated percentage (10% or 15% is common) if you underspend in another category.

In some cases, however, this practice is not allowed without special approval from the sponsor. Consequently, it is important to review the expenditures in the grant regularly by category and to be knowledgeable about the funding-agency regulations governing expenditures. If you discover that you need to spend more than you planned in salaries, for example, and less than you planned for travel, you may be able to adjust your budget by making *transfers between line items.*

There are two ways to make a transfer of money between line items. One way is by following the funding-agency regulations and transferring money that they allow to be transferred. Be sure to stay within the percentage allowances. Another way is to plan ahead and send a formal written request to the funding-agency representative justifying the need to make the transfer and asking for permission before you actually have to spend the money. Failure to use either of these two methods may result in a disallowance when the grant is audited.

In addition, you should be aware that auditors look for *late transfers* of funds between line items. Late transfers are those that are effected very close to the expiration date of a project.

In some instances, for example, a project director may realize that he or she has a substantial amount of salary money remaining in the budget and the grant is due to expire in two weeks. The project director realizes that all the remaining salary money can't possibly be spent within two weeks, but a badly needed piece of equipment can be purchased almost immediately. So, instead of returning the money to the federal treasury, the project director transfers money from the salary and fringe-benefits categories into the equipment category.

If the amount of money is not great, and if the agency regulations were followed, and if the percentage limitations were not exceeded, this is a legal transfer, although it can be questioned later on. If, however, there is some irregularity or if the transfer is effected after the project has officially ended, it is considered a late transfer and will be disallowed.

By carefully planning ahead, the project director might have predicted the surplus of money in the salary category; then there would have been time to request the funding agency's permission for the transfer.

This matter of transfers between line items is serious and should not be treated casually. It is an area for potential abuse, and whenever instances of alleged malfeasance in grant administration appear in the media, late transfers are frequently mentioned. The above example of a project director's transferring funds from the salary category to the equipment category may make the process sound a bit too easy.

The Public Health Service, in the "Addendum" to its *Grants Policy Statement*,(1) indicates the following:

> The prior approval authority established at the institutional level for purchase of an individual item of special-purpose equipment costing $1,000 or more involves not only *rebudgeting* actions, i.e., transfer of funds between budget categories, but also modification of activities as proposed in the approved budget. For example, the purchase of an individual item of special-purpose equipment costing $1,000 or more requires prior approval whether an actual transfer of funds between budget categories results or whether the cost of a specific item of equipment can be accommodated within the approved budget for equipment, but the purchase of *that* item of equipment was not foreseen or identified at the time of award.

Similarly, the National Science Foundation has outlined the instances in which approval of budget transfers must be obtained from either a program officer or a grants officer at NSF, or through the Organizational Prior Approval System (OPAS).(2)

The point here is that you should monitor the fiscal progress of your project carefully. If it appears that you will have savings in one budget category and come up short in another, write to the grantors. Ask for permission to transfer funds between categories, *before* it is necessary to do so. In this way, you will avoid questioned costs due to late transfers, disallowed costs because of transfers after the award is ended, or overexpenditures.

An example of a letter requesting permission to transfer funds between budget categories is contained in Figure 25. Notice that this letter explains why the approval is being sought.

"One thing you should tell your readers," a federal auditor advised the authors, when interviewed in connection with writing this book, "is that when you ask someone in government a question, try to decide what answer you want. Then provide good reasons so that the government employee can respond favorably."

Justification is an important ingredient of letters requesting permission to transfer funds.

GENERAL ACCOUNTING SYSTEM
REPORT NO. 7

DO GOOD INSTITUTION
BUDGET REPORT

PERIOD ENDED 12/31/80 PAGE 1000
RUN DATE 12/31/80

ACCOUNT NO. 580-0012 PROJECT DIRECTOR B. BRIGHT

BUDGET CODE	DESCRIPTION	APPROVED BUDGET	SPENT TO DATE	SPENT THIS MONTH	ENCUMBRANCES	UNENCUMBERED BALANCE	PER CENT COMMITTED
100	SALARIES	62,023	8,004	2,668	24,019	30,000	52
101	PRINCIPAL INVESTIGATOR	10,345	2,586	862	7,759		100
102	RESEARCH ASSOCIATE	15,678	3,918	1,306	11,760		100
110	TECHNICIANS	30,000				30,000	
120	SECRETARY	6,000	1,500	500	4,500		100
200	BENEFITS	7,237	1,059	353	3,178	3,000	59
300	TRAVEL	2,350				2,350	
400	EQUIPMENT	2,800	800	800	2,000		100
500	SUPPLIES	450	350	300		100	78
800	OTHER OPERATING EXPENSES	4,260	275	25		3,985	6
801	COMMUNICATIONS	300	75	25		225	25
810	COMPUTER	200				200	
820	CONSULTANTS	400	200			200	50
860	PUBLICATIONS	560				560	
870	SUBJECT PAYMENTS	2,000				2,000	
899	OTHER	800				800	
	TOTAL DIRECT COSTS	79,120	10,488	4,146	29,197	39,435	50
900	INDIRECT COSTS	31,012	4,002	1,334	12,010	15,000	52
	* TOTAL COSTS *	* 110,132 *	* 14,490 *	* 5,480 *	* 41,207 *	* 54,435 *	51

PROJECT ADMINISTRATOR R. SHARP

PROJECT DATES 10/01/80 THROUGH 9/30/81

Figure 24. (a) Sample budget report format with (b) computerized encumbrances. With this budget format, encumbrances are recorded by the computer automatically. Although only $14,490 has been *spent* to date, the project director and the grant administrator can tell at a glance that another $41,207 has been committed.

GENERAL ACCOUNTING SYSTEM DO GOOD INSTITUTION PERIOD ENDED 12/31/80 PAGE 1001
REPORT NO. 7 BUDGET REPORT RUN DATE 12/31/80

ACCOUNT NO. 580-0012 PROJECT DIRECTOR B. BRIGHT

* ENCUMBRANCES *

DATE	DESCRIPTION	ORIGINAL AMOUNT	CURRENT AMOUNT	NOTES
10/01/80	SALARY FOR BRIGHT THROUGH END OF PROJECT	10,345	7,759	
10/01/80	BENEFITS FOR BRIGHT	2,069	1,552	
10/01/80	INDIRECT COSTS ON BRIGHT SALARY	5,173	3,880	
10/01/80	SALARY FOR HARDWORKER THROUGH END OF PROJECT	15,678	11,760	
10/01/80	BENEFITS FOR HARDWORKER	1,568	1,176	
10/01/80	INDIRECT COSTS ON HARDWORKER SALARY	7,839	5,880	
10/01/80	SALARY FOR SUPER THROUGH END OF PROJECT	6,000	4,500	
10/01/80	BENEFITS FOR SUPER	600	450	
10/01/80	INDIRECT COSTS ON SUPER SALARY	3,000	2,250	
10/01/80	BAK MASSAGERS, INCORPORATED P.O. 234222	2,000	2,000	

Figure 24. (Continued)

DO GOOD INSTITUTION

March 1, 1981

Ms. May Approvit
Grant Officer
Give Grants Agency
Washington, D.C. 20500

RE: Grant No. GGA-81-000-0-01

Dear Ms. Approvit:

The Do Good Institution is requesting permission to transfer funds between budget categories on the above-referenced project.

We have been working on the project for approximately six months and are very pleased with the progress we are making. We have, however, noticed that at certain times of the day research subjects must wait up to thirty minutes to use one of the four Reklnr chairs which the project has purchased. We consider thirty minutes to be much too long to wait, and several subjects have informed us of their displeasure. In view of the fact that relaxation is a key variable in this project, and for some people a thirty-minute wait is not at all relaxing (indeed, may be anxiety-producing), we would like to purchase an additional EXTR Reklnr chair. This will reduce the waiting time for subjects.

In order to pay for the chair, we plan to spend $200 less on child care costs. It appears that fewer subjects than originally anticipated are claiming reimbursement for babysitting expenses. Therefore, we are able to reduce the "Other Direct Costs" category (which includes the "Child Care Costs" line item) without inconveniencing our research subjects. In fact, convenience will be greatly enhanced by the extra chair.

Budget Category	Original Budget	Change	Revised Budget
Equipment (Model EXTR Reklnr chair)	$2,800	+ $200	$3,000
Other Direct Costs (Child Care Costs)	$4,260	- $200	$4,060
Net Change		-0-	

We consider the purchase of the additional chair extremely important and hope that you will look upon this request favorably. Thank you.

Sincerely,

R. Sharp
Grant Administrator

cc: Dr. B. Bright
Principal Investigator

Figure 25. Sample letter requesting permission to transfer funds between budget categories.

Requests for Supplemental Funding

There may be times when, owing to unforeseen circumstances, you will have to ask the sponsor for more money in order to carry out your project and avoid overexpenditures. Of course, there must be good reason to do this because supplemental funding is not commonly awarded. Further, your request should be made before all the money in your grant is spent, not after you've discovered a budget overrun.

A request for supplemental support should be in the form of a letter to the sponsor, signed by the appropriate official from the grantee institution. The National Science Foundation requires that this letter be submitted at least two months prior to the need for the additional funds.

Although supplemental support is difficult to get, it can be obtained. Most agencies allocate their funds for a year. It is possible that when the fiscal year draws to a close, some grantees may discover that they will not be spending all their funds. Under these circumstances, the grantor agency may let you know this and you may be able to get supplemental money for your grant. The under-expenditures of other grantees will become the source of your supplement.

Since the grantors are more likely to let you know about end-of-year money if they know you will be needing it, it is important to tell them this—well in advance.

If you are asking for supplemental funds to expand the work scope you originally proposed, it is important to describe the extra work you plan to do and emphasize why this is important to the grantors and to the success of the project.

If you are asking for more money to finish what you formerly promised to do for less, explain why the original funds weren't sufficient. Tell what you tried to do to solve the problem. If possible, describe what your institution is willing to contribute to help make up the deficit. Point out the dire consequences of not receiving the supplemental funds. Persuade the grantors that the problem occurred through no fault of yours, that you and your institution have done and are doing everything you can to solve it, and that the small amount of money you are now asking the grantor to provide will save the project.

If they have the money, how can they refuse?

A sample of a letter requesting supplemental funding is contained in Figure 26.

In summary, by maintaining an encumbrance system, transferring between line items, obtaining supplemental funding, or some combination of these precautions, overexpenditures can be avoided.

In addition, it should be mentioned that in the effort to avoid overexpenditures, common sense is the best ally of all four key players in the game.

For example, the project director may know at the outset of the award that she or he will not have enough money for a full-time secretary, although such a person would be of great help. The project director, along with the grant administrator at his or her institution, can determine precisely how much secretarial time can be bought with the money available.

Is a secretary really needed during the first month or two of the project? Perhaps not. Would a part-time secretary, paid on an hourly basis, be sufficient for the first three or four months of the project? This is worth thinking about.

DO GOOD INSTITUTION

March 1, 1981

Ms. May Approvit
Grant Officer
Give Grants Agency
Washington, D.C. 20500

RE: Grant No. GGA-81-000-0-01

Dear Ms. Approvit:

The Do Good Institution is writing to request $4,400 in additional funds for the above-referenced project.

Recent research findings published in the latest issue of the National Journal of Relaxation have presented some exciting breakthroughs in the field. Specifically, an article published by Dr. Brett Rest of the Bedd Institute indicates that there is a minute quantity of *xyz* enzyme in the blood of relaxed subjects. This is a new development in relaxation research which we could not have foreseen when we began our project.

Dr. Rest's findings now put us in a unique position to carry the research a giant step further. We have our laboratory, our equipment, our staff, and our subjects already in place. We would like to expand our workscope to include a blood test on our research subjects who consent to it. We propose to draw a small sample of venous blood from each subject and analyze the sample for the presence of *xyz* enzyme. Although it is impossible at this time to predict what we will find, we do have the capacity to corroborate Dr. Rest's findings at minimal cost.

We have spoken with the Smith City Blood Bank, and it is willing to contract with the Do Good Institution to draw blood at the extremely low price of five dollars per subject. In addition, the Getwell Hospital has agreed to analyze the blood for six dollars per sample, well below the usual rate. Dr. L. Y. Downs of the Do Good Institution, a nationally-known hematologist, has offered to serve as an unpaid consultant on this additional portion of the project. He will devote at least five hours per week to this research.

We are all aware of the excellent opportunity we have at this time to expand the frontiers of biochemistry, sleep research, and other scientific disciplines at minimal expense. Unfortunately, we cannot perform the new work proposed without an additional $4,400, budgeted as follows:

Figure 26. Sample letter requesting supplemental funding.

Not hiring a full-time secretary in this instance, or hiring a secretary later in the project, can be a saving that will help prevent an overexpenditure. Delayed hiring in other positions can also help.

Making an effort to predict the cash outgo, month by month, can be effective when it is done at the beginning of the project. Don't wait until a substantial

Ms. May Approvit -2- March 1, 1981

Smith City Blood Bank:
Draw blood, 400 subjects @ $5 each $2,000

Getwell Hospital:
Analyze blood samples, 400 subjects @ $6 each 2,400

Total Supplemental Funds $4,400

The Do Good Institution will not request indirect costs nor will Dr. Downs request recompense.

This is an outstanding opportunity which we ought to pursue. We hope that the Give Grants Agency agrees and sees fit to award us the supplemental funding we request.

Thank you for your consideration.

Sincerely,

R. Sharp
Grant Administrator

cc: Dr. B. Bright
Principal Investigator

Figure 26. (Continued)

portion of the award has been spent. Predict expenditures early, and you can avoid overexpenditures later.

How Do You Avoid Underexpenditures, and Why Should You?

If you don't spend all the money you were awarded, you will have underexpended your grant. When underexpenditures occur, you and your agency will lose. How?

First, you will lose the opportunity to spend money for the direct costs of your project. In addition, your agency will lose the opportunity to collect the related indirect costs.

Indirect costs are calculated as a percentage of the money you spend (usually as a percentage of salaries and wages or a percentage of total direct costs). Therefore, your organization will collect less money for indirect costs as a result of your spending less on the project.

Since your agency may have been counting on receiving the full indirect-cost recovery on your project and may in fact have already budgeted that amount toward next year's operating expenses, your underexpenditure will inadvertently cut your own agency's budget. A grant-receiving organization cannot afford to underspend on too many projects.

This is not to say that money should be spent simply for the sake of spending. It is wise, however, to plan your budget carefully and to predict expenses early in the project. The same techniques that function to prevent overexpenditures can serve to prevent underexpenditures.

What are these techniques?

An Accounting System with Encumbrances: A MUST AGAIN!

As suggested previously, an effective encumbrance system is invaluable. It helps the project director and the grant administrator to determine how much money remains in each category, how much time is left to spend it, and the rate at which the money is being spent. If the rate of spending is unexpectedly low, you can find out why. You will know that you may have money left at the end of the project and act before then to avoid underexpenditures.

Expenditure Projections during the Grant Period

In addition to using an encumbrance system, it is important to make expenditure projections at key times during the grant period. Expenditures are projected by adding (1) all the monies *actually* spent to some specified date on the grant, plus (2) your best *estimate* of monies that will be spent from this specified date through the end of the project.

For example, suppose your one-year project is halfway completed. You can tell for certain how much money has been spent during the first six months by looking at your project budget report. Now, examine the spending categories: salaries, benefits, and so forth. How much more do you expect to spend in each?

In making the calculations, consider any expenses that may have been incurred but not paid during the first six months. For example, do your telephone bills arrive several months late? Has the subcontractor billed you yet for services performed last month? Be sure to include such costs in your projections.

You can usually determine when to make expenditure projections by reviewing monthly budget reports. After the first three or four months of the project, if the reports show that spending is being accomplished according to the original plan, it's unnecessary to do a projection. On the other hand, if spending is faster or slower than the level originally anticipated, you can find out why by making an expenditure projection.

If you discover that you will *not* be spending the entire amount, there are two things you can do: (1) request carryover funding, or (2) request a no-cost extension.

Requests for Carryover Funding

If your project will be continuing next year, you can send a written request to the funding agency explaining why you believe the total grant award will not be spent during the current grant period. You can then request that the money remaining be carried over into next year's continuation grant. There are often good reasons that grant funds cannot be spent during the prescribed period.

For example, the award letter may have arrived late—perhaps after the expected starting date of the project—and staff were hired late as a result. (You

DO GOOD INSTITUTION

July 1, 1981

Ms. May Approvit
Grant Officer
Give Grants Agency
Washington, D.C. 20500

RE: Grant No. GGA-81-000-0-01

Dear Ms. Approvit:

The Do Good Institution is requesting permission to carry over into the next funding period the amount of $2,090 on the above-referenced project.

Due to a prior commitment, Mr. Henry Hardworker, the project's Research Associate, was unable to become part of our staff until one month of the project had already passed. Consequently, during the first year of the project, Mr. Hardworker will be paid for only eleven months. We would like to carry over into the second year of the project the unused $2,090 which was budgeted for his salary and fringe benefits, as well as the indirect costs associated with his salary.

Salary:	Mr. Hardworker ($15,678/annum)	$1,306
Benefits:	10% of salary	131
Indirect Costs:	50% of salary	653
		$2,090

We will use the money during the second year of the project to increase the amount of time which the project's secretary, Sallye Super, now works. Ms. Super is presently employed only half time, but we expect that the volume of data which we are collecting will require her to spend more time typing papers and disseminating research findings.

Thank you for your consideration. We look forward to hearing from you.

Sincerely,

R. Sharp
Grant Administrator

cc: Dr. B. Bright
Principal Investigator

Figure 27. Sample letter requesting carryover funding.

could hire a research technician for only 10 months instead of a year, for instance, because of the late arrival of the award notice.)

Carryover funding, if permitted, will allow you to spend this year's unexpended money next year. A sample letter requesting carryover funding is contained in Figure 27.

Requests for No-Cost Extensions

If your grant will not be continuing next year, and there are some good reasons that you have been unable to spend all the money this year, you can write to the sponsor requesting a no-cost extension. A request for a no-cost extension is just what it sounds like. It is a letter to the funding agency explaining why you haven't been able to complete the project (i.e., spend all the money) during the time period of the grant award, and asking that the time period be extended for a specified number of months.

Naturally, the time extension will not be accompanied by additional funds. In its award letters for research projects, the National Science Foundation routinely includes a six-month extension period. As the NSF acknowledges that research is an exploration into the unknown and knows that results of scientific experiments cannot be rushed to coincide with the calendar, its automatic six-month extension is an enlightened approach to both science and grant management.

A sample letter requesting a no-cost extension is contained in Figure 28.

As with possible overexpenditures, it is important to keep in touch with the funding agency when you foresee unavoidable underexpenditures. Let the agency help you. Request a carryover of funds or a no-cost extension. Remember that an underexpenditure will cost your agency money, so make careful budget projections at appropriate intervals. If you have an encumbrance system, use it to help make these projections as well as to record committed funds.

How Do You Avoid Unallowable Expenditures?

In the argot of grant and contract administration, there is hardly a term that is more self-explanatory than *unallowable expenditures*. Briefly, it means that money on a project has been spent for a purpose that the sponsor does not permit. In most instances, unallowable expenditures are made unintentionally. Still, they are costly to all parties because the grantee will have to refund the money to the funding agency. If the expenditures were made intentionally, the responsible parties could be subject to prosecution.

It is these unallowable expenditures—or even a suspicion of them—that most often make the newspaper headlines or Jack Anderson's syndicated column.

DO GOOD INSTITUTION

July 1, 1981

Ms. May Approvit
Grant Officer
Give Grants Agency
Washington, D.C. 20500

RE: Grant No. GGA-81-000-0-01

Dear Ms. Approvit:

The Do Good Institution is requesting authorization for a no-cost extension of the above-referenced grant.

The research we have been doing has been going extremely well and that is why we are requesting the extension. We have collected more information than we originally thought we would. As a result, we have not yet completed an analysis of the data. In addition, the journal articles which we plan to publish will be delayed until we finish the analysis.

We are therefore requesting a six-month extension of the project at no additional cost to the Give Grants Agency. Our latest budget projection shows that the only funds which will remain unobligated when the project officially ends will be $200 for computer time and $560 for page charges. These are the funds we will need to analyze and publish the data. An extension of six months during which we can utilize the $760 will allow us to complete this very worthwhile project.

Thank you for your support of our project during the past year. We look forward to receiving your approval to extend our work for six months.

Sincerely,

R. Sharp
Grant Administrator

cc: Dr. B. Bright
Principal Investigator

Figure 28. Sample letter requesting a no-cost extension.

Interestingly, it is the most experienced grant managers, in the largest organizations, who are most vulnerable to charges of negligence or malfeasance.

Unfortunately, the more grant and contract money an agency receives, the more opportunity exists for mistakes or communication failures. It is probably no coincidence that Harvard University and the University of California were recently reported by the media as being charged with unallowable expenditures.

Smaller agencies are also subject to costly mistakes in their administration of grants and contracts. Often community groups do not have the experience and background to know all the rules and regulations of grant management.

A Knowledgeable Grant Administrator: Indispensable!

It is important for all groups, from the largest to the smallest, to enlist the services of someone who is knowledgeable and responsible in grant administration. This is not a job for a novice; the myriad of rules and regulations confound even the long-time professionals in the field. What good is a sizable award to your agency if, two years from now, you learn from the auditors that several thousand (or hundreds of thousands of) dollars in unallowable expenditures must be returned to the government? The grants that you are so pleased to receive now may cost your agency later. A capable grant administrator will prevent unallowable expenditures.

Updated Funding-Agency Regulations

Winston Churchill once said, "If you have ten thousand regulations, you destroy all respect for the law." Surely, the regulations governing grants number hundreds of thousands!

The CFR, ASPR, A-110, FMC 73-3, OASC-10, and on and on. It seems the supply of alphabetical-and-numerical-grant-rule soup is endless. The CFR (Code of Federal Regulations), for example, has shelves of volumes, all sporting small print. Since many of its regulations are constantly changing, it is updated yearly.

How do grant administrators and project directors maintain their respect for the law in the face of so many changing regulations? The key lies in understanding the basis of the regulations and then in learning and following only those regulations that apply to *their* grants.

The Basis of Federal Regulations. The basis of federal regulations is relatively simple. There are four steps:

1. The U.S. Congress makes a *law* that authorizes a particular federal agency to grant money for specified program purposes.
2. The federal agency publishes (in a document known as the *Federal Register*) *regulations* to implement the program that was authorized by Congress. (See Figure 29, which depicts these first two steps of legislation and regulations.)
3. The federal agency publishes a brochure or pamphlet (known as *program guidelines*) that simplifies and interprets the regulations and gives prospective applicants instructions for applying for funds. If these funds will be awarded as a *contract* (instead of a grant), the instructions for applying will be called an *RFP* (request for proposal) instead of *program guidelines*.
4. The federal agency prepares an *award document* describing and/or referencing the regulations that will apply to each grant or contract.

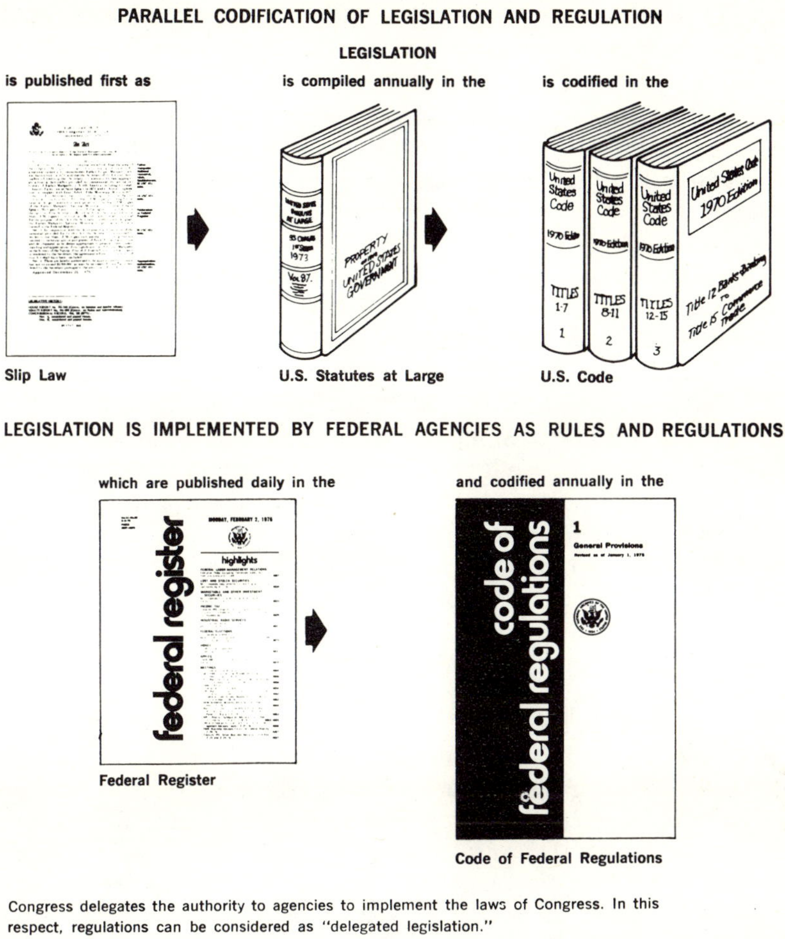

Figure 29. Basis of federal regulations. Reprinted from "The Federal Register: What It Is and How to Use It," Office of the Federal Register National Archives and Records Service, General Services Administration, January 1, 1977, p. 7.

For example, after it became apparent that it would be advantageous for the United States to convert to the metric system, Congress passed legislation (Public Law 93-380) that authorized the Office of Education to grant funds to support metric education programs around the country. This legislation was fairly general and left the details of implementation up to the Office of Education.

Subsequently, the Office of Education staff developed regulations for implementing the program; they published them in the *Federal Register* on September 8, 1975. As is commonly the case, what they published first were the "proposed" rules. A 30-day period was provided for interested parties (potential project directors especially) to comment and make suggestions for changes in these regulations. Then the "final" regulations were published on April 21,

1976. Since then, as changes occurred, notices of deadline dates, as well as revised regulations, have been published.

As Office of Education staff were preparing the notices to be published in the *Federal Register*, they were also getting program guidelines ready. These guidelines included instructions and forms for applying for the Metric Education Program funds, as well as interpretations of some of the regulations.

Finally, once the applications were received and the funding decisions were made, grant award documents were drawn up, incorporating rules and regulations developed in the first two steps and any special interpretations made in the third step.

So there are essentially four tiers of rules and regulations that apply to any grant you may receive. The first tier is the *law*, the second is the *regulations*, the third is the *program guidelines* (or RFP), and the fourth is the *grant award*. In the case of a *conflict* between any of these four (and this occasionally happens), the first tier takes precedence over the second, and so on down the line.

If you have a federal grant, then, there are four documents you should be familiar with: the *law* authorizing your programs; the final and any follow-up *regulations* published in the *Federal Register*; the *program guidelines* or *RFP,* which are available from the grantor; and your *grant award.*

Once you have these documents in hand, it is important to read them carefully. It is probable that the regulations and/or the program guidelines will refer to other documents. These other documents will contain additional rules that apply to your grant.

The reason that these other rules are not included in the text of either the regulations or the program guidelines is simple. The government, in its wisdom, is trying to cut down the paperwork. There are certain standardized rules that apply to many grants. Far easier, then, to reference them than to print them again each time a new grant program is introduced. These referenced rules are easily obtained from the grantor, if you do not already have them in your agency.

What is encouraging to remember is that you don't have to pore over all the fine print in the bewildering array of existing government regulations in order to spend your grant funds properly. You simply read through the four documents that apply specifically to your grant and then read through the standardized rules that are referenced in these documents.

Insofar as government regulations are concerned, you *can* find the needle in the haystack!

So that you may have a head start in your search, here is a list of the documents that any well-stocked grantee administrative library should have.

The Federal Register. If you are going to be applying for (or already have any) federal grant program funding, it is easy to see why your agency must have access to the *Federal Register*. This document, as mentioned previously, contains proposed, final, and revised rules and regulations for implementing all government-funded grant programs. Published daily, Mondays through Fridays, it is massive in size. Fortunately, the items you will need to read can usually be located by scanning the cover page "Highlights."

A subscription to the *Federal Register* costs $50 yearly; it may be ordered from:

Superintendent of Documents
U.S. Government Printing Office
Washington, DC 20402

The Code of Federal Regulations (CFR). The *Code of Federal Regulations* (commonly referred to as the CFR) is a yearly codification of all the regulations that are published in the *Federal Register*. The price for the set of well over 50 paperbacks is $450; single-copy prices vary. Unless your agency does a great deal of grant business, it will probably be unnecessary to invest in the complete set. It is advisable, however, to order copies of those volumes containing regulations applicable to your grants.

If you are unfamiliar with the *Federal Register* and the CFR, it will be useful to order "*The Federal Register: What It Is and How to Use It.*" This publication and the CFR are both available from the Government Printing Office.

Federal Management Circulars (FMCs). The following circulars contain certain basic standard requirements that relate to federal assistance programs. Note that some circulars apply to all grantees; others are prepared for certain categories of grantees, such as hospitals and educational institutions. Your organization should have copies of the circulars that apply to it specifically; you should also have the general circulars, which may be obtained from:

Publications Office, Room G-236
Office of Management and Budget
Executive Office of the President
Washington, D.C. 20503

FMC 73-1 "Federal Management Circulars and Notices," August 30, 1973. Notifies federal agencies of the FMC process and explains their responsibilities to this process.

FMC 73-2 "Audit of Federal Operations and Programs by Executive Branch Agencies," September 27, 1973. Gives standards for federal agencies when auditing their assistance programs. Explains need for cooperation and coordination among federal, state, and local auditors.

FMC 73-3 "Cost Sharing on Federal Research," December 4, 1973. Provides guidance to educational, nonprofit, and commercial organizations concerning cost sharing in research grants and contracts.

FMC 73-6 "Coordinating Indirect Cost Rates and Audit at Educational Institutions," December 19, 1973. Provides procedure for single determination of allowable indirect costs and single audits for educational institutions.

FMC 73-7 "Administration of College and University Research Grants," December 19, 1973. Establishes procedures for administering contracts and research grants at educational institutions. Project changes, expenditures, transfer of ownership of equipment, and advance payment are covered.

FMC 74-3 "Government-Wide Procedures for Processing Preaward Protests against Contract Award," August 29, 1974. Establishes guidelines for preaward procedures for prompt consideration of protests against award of contracts.

FMC 74-4 "Cost Principles Applicable to Grants and Contracts with State and Local Governments," July 18, 1974. Contains rules for determining both direct and indirect costs of grants and contracts. Allowable and unallowable costs are also explained.

Responsibility for the FMCs listed above has been transferred from the General Services Administration to the Office of Management and Budget. The plan is eventually to retitle them with OMB Circular A- numbers.

Office of Management and Budget (OMB) Circulars. The OMB circulars are similar to the Federal Management Circulars in that they impose basic standards on federal grant recipients. The circulars may be ordered from:

Publications Office, Room G-236
Office of Management and Budget
Executive Office of the President
Washington, DC 20503

OMB A-21 "Cost Principles for Educational Institutions," March 6, 1979. Contains principles for determining direct and indirect costs applicable to grants, contracts, and other agreements with educational institutions. Explains allowable and unallowable costs.

OMB A-102 "Uniform Administrative Requirements for Grants-in-Aid to State and Local Governments," August 24, 1977. Contains information on standard application forms, grant payments, matching funds, financial management systems, procurement standards, property management, bonding and insurance, program income, reporting requirements, program performance, budget revisions, closeout procedures, and record retention.

OMB A-110 "Grants and Agreements with Institutions of Higher Education, Hospitals, and Other Nonprofit Organizations," July 30, 1976. Sets uniform administrative standards similar to those listed in OMB A-102, which is applicable to units of government.

OMB A-122 "Cost Principles for Nonprofit Organizations," July 8, 1980. Contains principles for determining direct and indirect costs applicable to grants, contracts, and other agreements with nonprofit organizations. Explains allowable and unallowable costs.

Office of the Assistant Secretary, Comptroller (OASC) Publications. The OASC publications serve to impose basic standards applicable to *DHEW* grant recipients. The publications were prepared by the Office of the Assistant Secretary, Comptroller, within the former Department of Health, Education, and Welfare.* They may be ordered at a nominal price from:

Superintendent of Documents
U.S. Government Printing Office
Washington, DC 20402

OASC-1 "A Guide for Colleges and Universities," September 1974. Cost principles and procedures for establishing indirect cost and other rates for grants and contracts with the Department of Health, Education, and Welfare.

OASC-3 "A Guide for Hospitals," July 1974. Cost principles and procedures for establishing indirect-cost and other rates for grants and contracts with the Department of Health, Education, and Welfare.

OASC-5 "A Guide for Non-Profit Institutions," August 1974. Cost principles and procedures for establishing indirect-cost and other rates for grants and contracts with the Department of Health, Education, and Welfare.

OASC-10 "A Guide for State and Local Governments," December 1976. Cost principles and procedures for establishing indirect-cost and other rates for grants and contracts with the Department of Health, Education, and Welfare.

Grantor Agency Policy and Procedure Manuals. Many grantor agencies publish their own policy manuals, based—of course—on the federal regulations contained in the *Federal Register* and the FMC, OMB, and OASC circulars. These policy manuals are usually much easier reading than the other documents referenced. The typesetting is larger, the paper stock more attractive, and the writing more interesting, not obscured by "governmentese."

Policy manuals may be ordered (often at no cost) from the public information department of the grantor agency(ies) you do business with. The National Science Foundation *Grants Policy Manual* and the Public Health Service *Grants Policy Statement* and the "*Addendum*" are excellent resources if you have NSF or PHS grants.

Program Guidelines and RFPs. Granting (and contracting) agencies publish a separate document for each program they fund. This document is known as a *program guideline* when a *grant* is being given and as a *request for proposal* when a *contract* is being let. These documents may be ordered at no cost, directly from the sponsoring agency.

Recognizing Unallowable Costs

In addition to knowing and keeping updated on government regulations affecting your program(s), you can help avoid unallowable expenditures by recognizing them.

*In 1980 the Department of Health, Education, and Welfare was divided into the Education Department and the Department of Health and Human Services. Until new basic standards are approved for the separate departments, the OASC guides will be applicable.

Unallowable expenditures are those that are specifically prohibited by the regulations and/or guidelines that pertain to your particular award. In some cases, one funding agency will allow a certain type of expenditure, such as construction or remodeling, and another agency won't. It is important for both the project director and the grant administrator to become intimately acquainted with the rules governing the award. If you are uncertain as to whether a cost is allowable, you should contact your grant officer at the funding agency. You should not be afraid to ask questions; it could save your organization thousands of dollars.

Before calling the grant officer, it is best to become familiar with the four tests of allowability and the kinds of costs that are typically unallowable.

The Four Tests of Allowability. The federal government has identified four factors that affect the allowability of costs.[3] To be an allowable charge to a grant or contract, the cost must: (1) be reasonable; (2) be allocable; (3) be consistently treated; and (4) conform to any limitations or exclusions in the sponsored agreement. Any cost which can not pass all four tests is an unallowable cost.

What does the federal government mean by *reasonable*? The cost principles define the term as follows:

> A cost may be considered reasonable if the nature of the goods or services acquired or applied, and the amount involved therefore, reflect the action that a prudent person would have taken under the circumstances prevailing at the time the decision to incur the cost was made.[4]

Suppose, for example, a project director wanted to pay for a trip to Hawaii from grant funds. This would be a reasonable cost if he or she were going there to disseminate the results of his or her grant study at a meeting of scientists there. On the other hand, if the grant's work scope was to provide hot meals to senior citizens in a northeastern city, and there was no provision for disseminating information, the cost would clearly be unreasonable—and therefore unallowable.

The second factor is allocability. According to federal cost principles:

> A cost is allocable . . . if the goods or services involved are chargeable or assignable to such cost objective in accordance with the relative benefits received or other equitable relationship. Subject to the foregoing, a cost is allocable to a sponsored agreement if (1) it is incurred solely to advance the work under the sponsored agreement; (2) it benefits both the sponsored agreement and other work of the institution, in proportions that can be approximated through use of reasonable methods; or (3) it is necessary to the overall operation of the institution and, in light of the principles provided in the Circular, is deemed to be assignable in part to sponsored projects."[5]

Suppose a project director worked for a university and needed to do both university and grant business in Hawaii. In addition, she or he had relatives in Thailand and planned to return from Hawaii by way of Bangkok. As long as the part of the travel costs that related to grant business could be easily identified, it would be allocable and therefore an allowable cost.

In this case, the project director would probably ask the travel agency to put the price of a round-trip ticket to and from Hawaii on the bill as an information item. He or she would then charge the grant only that amount for air fare. The per diem charged to the grant would be for only those days in Hawaii spent doing grant business. If the project director mixed university and grant business, he or she would estimate the proportion of time on the grant and charge accordingly.

Consistent treatment is the third test of allowability. What this means is that the generally accepted accounting principles appropriate to the circumstances must be applied. For example, suppose the university pays a per diem rate of $50 to anyone doing university business in Hawaii. If the charge to the grant were $75 a day, $25 of the cost would be unallowable. The charges to various grants, as well as to your institution, must be consistently treated.

The final test of allowability is that the cost must conform to any limitations or exclusions set forth in the sponsored agreement as to types or amounts of cost items. For example, suppose the grant prohibited out-of-state travel and the university was not in Hawaii. The cost of the trip would be unallowable. Or suppose the maximum per diem allowed by the grant award were $35; any charges above that would be unallowable.

These four tests apply to the expenditure of all federal funds. It becomes easy to recognize unallowable costs when you remember that they are any costs that are:

1. Unreasonable
2. Unallocable
3. Inconsistently treated
4. Excluded or limited in the sponsored agreement

Keeping in mind the tests of allowability, it's useful to look at some costs.

Typical Allowable and Unallowable Costs. The Public Health Service (PHS), in its *Grants Policy Statement*,[6] clearly outlines examples of allowable and unallowable expenditures on its grant programs. Although the listing is applicable only to PHS grants, the newcomer to the grants arena would do well to use this comprehensive outline as background. It is necessary, however, for a grant administrator to know what is allowable and unallowable on each grant from every sponsor agency she or he is working with.

The Public Health Service list includes, among other items:

Advertising—allowable for recruiting of staff and for other purposes.

Alteration and renovation—allowable under some circumstances, but with a specific dollar limit.

Animals—allowable if money is used to purchase and care for experimental animals.

Communications—allowable when necessary to the project.

Construction—some construction costs are allowable; others are not. The PHS *Grants Policy Statement* is helpful on this matter.

Consultant services—allowable, but with certain conditions. Travel and per diem for consultants are also allowable costs. It is expected, however, that the grantee institution will have its own policy with respect to the use of consultants.

Contingency funds or reserves—generally not allowable.

Customs or import duties—allowable.

Depreciation or use charges—normally not allowable as a direct cost but may be included in the grantee's indirect-cost pool.

Dues—allowable if it can be shown that membership in a professional organization is necessary to accomplish the objectives of the project.

Entertainment—not allowable.

Equipment purchase—allowable. Each grantee should have its own policy for acquisition and control of equipment.

Equipment maintenance and rental—allowable when the equipment is used specifically for the project being funded.

Fringe benefits—allowable in proportion to the salaries charged on the grant. Some grantees include fringe benefits as a direct cost in the proposal budget; others have fringe benefits included in their indirect-cost pools.

Fund raising—not allowable. Also, it should be mentioned that a grantee cannot use federal grant funds to attract more federal money.

Insurance—allowable. Insurance is usually treated as an indirect cost. In certain situations, however, where special insurance is required because of risks peculiar to the project, the premium may be charged as a direct cost.

Leave—allowable for employees on the project and may be treated as a direct or an indirect cost. Time and effort reporting by the grantee must be meticulous.

Preaward costs—costs incurred prior to the beginning date of the budget period of a new grant are not allowable unless authorized in writing by a responsible official of the granting agency. However, a grantee may, at its own risk, incur obligations prior to the beginning date of a noncompeting continuation grant if these obligations are otherwise allowable.

Publication costs—costs of publishing works in journals is allowable under most conditions. The cost of publishing books, monographs, and pamphlets may be allowable with the sponsor's approval. The purchase of journals and reprints is also allowable.

Recruitment costs—allowable when an individual is recruited for employment by the grantee organization, if payment of recruitment costs is normally made in other cases. Moving costs and help-wanted advertising are allowable under this heading.

Registration fees (for symposia and conferences)—allowable if it can be shown that they are necessary to accomplish project objectives.

Rental or lease of facilities—allowable, but with some limitations.

Salaries and wages—allowable for people working on a grant project and when the rate of pay conforms to the established, consistently applied salary-and-wage policy of the grantee institution. The grantee must maintain time-and-effort records. This is the area where grant organizations must apply great energy to record-keeping, and it is the budget category that is most likely to be closely examined by auditors. It is also an area where many disallowances can occur.

Subgranting and subcontracting—allowable under certain conditions and with approval from the funding agency.

Subject costs—payments to research subjects are allowable.

Supplies—allowable for supplies directly required for the project.

Taxes—certain taxes, such as sales tax on equipment purchases, are allowable.

Travel—allowable, where travel will provide direct benefit to the project, including attendance at meetings. Less than first-class air travel must be used when available. If foreign travel is involved, U.S. flag carriers must be used when available. It is extremely helpful for the grantee institution to have its own formal travel policy. Per diem rates and allowable mileage charges are determined by the funding agency.

The above listing, lengthy as it is, is not exhaustive. Other less common types of expenditures can be made with grant funds. It is important for the grantee to know about allowable and unallowable costs before incurring them.

The Importance of Documentation

In your zest to avoid unallowable expenditures, even if you do everything we have mentioned so far (have a good grant administrator, follow updated grantor regulations, and spend money only on allowable cost items), you can still end up with the auditor disallowing costs.

How can this happen? Easily, if you fail to *document* the otherwise allowable expenditures that you have made (see Figure 30).

Documentation of all expenditures is crucial. The recent emphasis on accountability places almost as much importance on *showing how* your organization spent its grant and contract money as on *what* the money was used for. The subject of documentation is far too broad to cover thoroughly here, but the reader should note that accountability requires a grantee organization to (1) be *willing* to document virtually all expenditures and (2) have a strong grant-administration system in order to be *able* to document these transactions.

Although all grantee organizations appear to have this problem, in the past universities were under fire from the former HEW on the matter of documentation. Testimony delivered in late 1979 by Mr. Edward Stepnick and Mr. Henry Kirschenmann, both of HEW, centered on the unwillingness of many universities to document expenditures to a degree sufficient to assure that federal funds were used for the purposes for which they were provided. Both men stated that the problems of accountability at universities involved five major areas(7):

Figure 30. Project directors often complain about the "paper trail" required by grantors.

1. Salary-and-wage documentation
2. Improper and undocumented cost transfers
3. Undocumented consultant charges
4. Weak cash-management systems
5. Poor procedures for acquisition, control, and accountability for equipment and supplies

If expenditures are not properly documented, an auditor may regard them as questionable, or even unallowable, simply because she or he may not have enough information to decide otherwise in borderline cases.

A Word about Political Pressures

Even when you know all the rules and understand the importance of documentation, you may still find it difficult to avoid unallowable expenditures owing to political pressures within your organization.

At one time or another, there may be pressure from a high official—perhaps a dean or an executive director or an administrator—to borrow money from a grant, to use it for a purpose that is not normally allowed, or to bend the rules in some other way. In some cases, this high official may be the project director. This problem is rare, but it is serious in its implications.

It is difficult to reject the wishes of an otherwise honest individual whom you respect and like. Still, if you are a project director or a grant administrator who is faced with the dilemma either of refusing the wishes of a high official or of misspending project money, it is best to do the former but with a clear explanation as to why the action is being taken. Although circumstances vary, it is wise to point out the possibility of disallowances after an audit, of repayments to the sponsor, and of other serious consequences.

The grant administrator (or sometimes a project director) who is put on the spot should tactfully suggest that permission be obtained in writing from the funding agency. The response from the agency will give you feedback as to whether the action is permissible and will thus give all members of your organization clear direction. It will also give the high official or project director who made the request a cooling-off period. Knowing that there may be some legal complications may persuade him or her not to pursue the original suggestion.

In summary, there are many ways to protect against unallowable expenditures. These include having a knowledgeable grant administrator; reviewing updated funding-agency regulations and program guidelines; recognizing unallowable costs; documenting charges adequately; and resisting political pressures to spend unallowably.

Do You Hold Project Spending Meetings?

The wise grant administrator calls a meeting with the project director as soon as possible after notice of the award is received and before work on the project actually begins. This meeting is typically referred to as a *Project Spending*, *Kickoff*, or *Orientation meeting*. At a minimum, the following activities occur:

1. The project director and the grant administrator review the budget as awarded. If less money was given than requested, they make plans to deal with this discrepancy.
2. The project director identifies the expenditures that must be initiated immediately (i.e., specialized equipment; salary for the project director and other staff who are ready to work; any purchases that require a long lead time; items that may be much less expensive if ordered in bulk).
3. The grant administrator provides the project director with the forms (i.e., purchase-order requests, check requests, mileage claims) that will be necessary to initiate these expenditures. (If the project director is unfamiliar with these forms, the grant administrator explains them.)

4. The grant administrator gives the project director copies of any grantee institutional policies and procedures (travel, personnel, purchasing, and so forth) that will apply to the grant. (If the project director has not had a grant before, the grant administrator explains these policies and answers questions.)
5. If the project director is new, the grant administrator shows her or him how to read the grantee budget reports. Since the project director will be initiating all expenditures, it's important that she or he know how to use these reports, how often they will be provided, and what additional budget information the grant administrator can supply between budget reports.
6. If personnel are to be hired, the grant administrator explains hiring practices to the project director and gives him or her the necessary forms.
7. The grant administrator asks the project director what space, office or laboratory equipment, or other institutional resources (not included in the grant budget) will be needed, so that the grant administrator can assist the project director in obtaining them.
8. Once internal grantee institutional matters have been taken care of, the grant administrator makes sure that the project director has copies of the appropriate grantor documents, especially the rules and regulations (if it's a federal grant); the grantor program guidelines (or RFP); and the grant (or contract) award. The grant administrator explains the grantor regulations as necessary.
9. Throughout the discussions, the grant administrator listens carefully and asks questions so that she or he can understand better the technical objectives that the project director is trying to achieve.

Often, there are others in addition to the project director and the grant administrator present at the meeting. If the project director has an administrative assistant or a secretary who will be completing many of the forms and assisting with grant spending, it is important for that person (or those persons) to attend. If the grant administrator relies on the services of personnel, physical facilities, and/or purchasing staff, they, too, should be represented during the meeting if possible.

After the initial meeting, the project director (and/or his or her staff) and the grant administrator should get together periodically to review and plan for project spending.

In addition to helping the project director on an individual basis, the grant administrator should give in-house training to groups of project directors and their staff as necessary. For example, if the federal regulations governing a number of grants change, here is an opportunity for the grant administrator. He or she can arrange a workshop or seminar–coffee for those who will be affected by the change. It is useful to schedule this activity at a location and time convenient for the project directors.

Early and frequent meetings between the grant administrators and the project directors are valuable tools for establishing and maintaining cooperative relationships. Very often, problems in grant administration are really only communication problems; two of the four players, located at the same organization, simply don't talk to each other often enough. Each assumes that the other knows his or her job, and they start talking only if problems arise.

"Project spending meetings," at the beginning of and during the grant period, emphasize the importance of constant communication. Effective communications between project directors, grant administrators, and grantee support staff can help you to avoid costly over-, under-, and unallowable expenditures.

8

Cash Management

Timing Your Dollars In and Out

Just as the previous chapter focused on ways to avoid poor use of grant funds, this chapter will emphasize the importance of making good use of all of your organization's financial resources. Efficient cash management—whatever the source of the cash may be—can add to the income of your agency. Cash is an asset that, when properly managed, can earn even more money for a grantee. Failure to "time" your grant and contract income with necessary project-related expenditures will cost your organization money. Indeed, one might say that not making full and effective use of available cash by investing it properly, even on a short-term basis, is as wasteful as leaving lights on in an empty room or not turning off the hot water after the dishes have been washed.[(1)]

This chapter concentrates on the total picture that your grant budget presents and on how to manage cash flow. It is an area that many grantee agencies, particularly small ones, overlook. The idea is to get the grant or contract funds, as well as other monies, into your organization's bank account as soon as possible. Using your own money to finance a project while waiting for the sponsor to send you a check costs you money. You lose interest on the amount you lay out, and if you actually have to borrow money to cover "start-up" costs, then it is clear that you are beginning the project with a financial loss. Usually, you should not have to spend your organization's money for grant purposes. There are several things you can do to avoid it and to ensure the best possible cash position for your agency.

Receipt of grant funds is the first step in the grantee organization's cash flow. The whole process of managing these funds is most important in those instances where a check is not received at exactly the time, or in the amounts, needed to cover expenditures. In fact, in educational institutions, school districts, and hospitals, the flow of grant funds is more uneven than the inflow of cash in private enterprises.[2] This is the very situation that presents a greater opportunity for substantial short-term investing of temporarily idle cash in colleges and universities.

A grantee organization's cash manager should be constantly aware of three guiding principles:

1. Collecting grant funds as quickly as possible from sponsor agencies
2. Disbursing payments for purchases as slowly as possible, but on a regular schedule and in time to meet due dates
3. Maximizing resources by investing idle cash as quickly and efficiently as possible, using short-term investment instruments

It is clear that if the first two items above are performed effectively, there will be more cash available for investment purposes.

How Fast Can You Collect the Grant Funds?

It is to your organization's advantage to receive grant (and contract) money as quickly as possible in order to avoid disbursing your own money until the government check arrives. To this end, the federal government has devised a number of mechanisms that minimize the amount of time between the transfer of funds to the grantee and the grantee's disbursements on the project. One such mechanism is the letter of credit.

Letter of Credit

If you have a continuing relationship with a funding agency, you may apply for a letter of credit. This will allow you to draw the funds you need for the project periodically. Its great advantage is that your organization can draw the money in advance, before it becomes necessary to start spending. What is a letter of credit? Briefly stated, it is an "instrument certified by an authorized official which authorizes a [grant] recipient to draw funds needed for immediate disbursement in accordance with Treasury Circular No. 1075."[3] Letters of credit can be used to pay grantees when all of the following conditions exist[4]:

1. There is or will be a continuing relationship between the grantee and the funding agency for at least a year, and the total amount of advances to be received from the grantor is $120,000 or more per year.
2. The grantee has maintained, or demonstrated the willingness and ability to maintain, procedures that minimize the time elapsing between the transfer of funds from the Treasury and their disbursement by the grantee.
3. The grantee's financial management system meets certain standards for fund control and accountability.

Standard Form 1194 6 Treasury FRM 1000 Fiscal Service Bureau of Accounts	**AUTHORIZED SIGNATURE CARD FOR PAYMENT VOUCHERS ON LETTER OF CREDIT**	Letter of Credit Number (1) Federal Reserve Bank (2)

Letter of Credit Issued in Favor of *(Recipient)*	Issued by *(Federal Agency)*
(3)	(4)
SIGNATURES OF INDIVIDUALS AUTHORIZED (5) ☐ ONLY ONE SIGNATURE REQUIRED ON PAYMENT VOUCHERS or TO DRAW ON THE CITED LETTER OF CREDIT (6) ☐ ANY TWO SIGNATURES REQUIRED TO SIGN OR COUNTERSIGN	
Typed Name and Signature (7)	Typed Name and Signature (7)
Typed Name and Signature (7)	Typed Name and Signature (7)
I CERTIFY THAT THE SIGNATURES ABOVE ARE OF THE INDIVIDUALS AUTHORIZED TO DRAW PAYMENT VOUCHERS FOR THE CITED LETTER OF CREDIT. (8) DATE AND SIGNATURE OF AUTHORIZING OFFICIAL *(Recipient)*	APPROVED: (9) DATE AND SIGNATURE OF AGENCY CERTIFYING OFFICER

Figure 31a. Authorized Signature Card for Payment Vouchers on Letter of Credit.

INSTRUCTIONS FOR SF 1194

BLOCK NO.	EXPLANATION

1. For the initial opening of an NSF Letter of Credit, this block will be completed by the NSF. For subsequent signature changes, insert the 8 digit number shown in the "Letter of Credit Number" block on the Letter of Credit, TFS 7577 (SF 1193A).
2. Delete the words "Federal Reserve Bank" and enter the name of the Treasury Regional Disbursing Office or Center serving the recipient's state. The names and addresses of the Treasury Regional Disbursing Offices and Centers and the states they serve are listed in Exhibit 4-5.
3. Enter the name and address of the recipient. If additional space is required, use the reverse side of the form.
4. Enter "National Science Foundation, 1800 G Street, NW, Washington, D. C. 20550."
5. Check if only one signature is required on Requests for Payment, SF 183.
6. Check if any two signatures are required on Requests for Payment, SF 183.
7. Enter the typed names and signatures of the officials who are authorized to sign Requests for Payment, SF 183.
8. Enter the date, typed name, title, and signature of the official who is authorized to certify the authenticity of the signatures in block 7. The official signing on this line must not be the same official signing in block 7. Authenticated documentation, including specimen signatures, must be attached to establish the authority and delegation of this authority to the official signing in this block.
9. Leave blank—to be completed by the NSF.

Figure 31b

If you are eligible to receive a letter of credit, the funding agency will notify you. The National Science Foundation, for example, will send you two forms: The Authorized Signature Card for Payment Vouchers on Letter of Credit and Designation of Depositary for Direct Deposit of Grant and/or Contract Funds (see Figures 31 and 32). These forms are to be completed by your organization and returned to NSF, which forwards one copy of the form (SF 1194) to the designated Treasury Regional Disbursing Office or Center. The National Science Foundation then prepares a letter of credit (see Figure 33) and sends your organization and the Treasury Regional Disbursing Office or Center a copy. You will also be furnished with a supply of Request for Payment on Letter of Credit and Status of Funds Report (see Figure 34).

Following the effective date of the letter of credit, your organization can complete the request-for-payment form and submit it to the Treasury Regional Disbursing Office or Center in order to receive funds to meet immediate cash needs. The Treasury Regional Disbursing Office or Center then mails a treasury check directly to your designated depository or directly to your organization.

Each time funds are needed to meet current expenses, you will have to submit a request for payment. The grantors (in this example, NSF) expect grantees to exercise sound financial judgment and planning to ensure that the requirements for maintaining minimum cash balances are met. In preparing the request-for-payment form, careful consideration of such key factors as payroll dates, payments to subgrantees or contractors, and major fixed costs will be required in order to determine when funds will be needed. Careful consideration of the mail time required for the transmission of the form to the Treasury Regional Disbursing Office or Center and for transmission of the treasury check to you or your bank will be necessary. For example, if $20,000 will be needed on the 15th of the month in order to meet payroll expenses, to pay bills on hand, and to provide funds to subgrantees to meet their current disbursement needs, and normal mail time from the date the request for payment is submitted to the date the treasury check is received by you is seven days, then these funds should be requested by the 8th of the month.

Once the letter-of-credit system has been in operation a short time, you will have determined the disbursing pattern and will have calculated mail time so that withdrawals will be timed as close as is administratively feasible to actual cash disbursements. Controls should be maintained on a current basis so that cash balances do not exceed your immediate disbursement needs.

Advance Payments

Another way to receive money from a federal sponsor is through advance payments by treasury check. This method of payment can be used when the grantee does not have a continuing relationship with the grantor and/or the amount of money needed is less than $120,000 per year. The grantee is still required to maintain procedures that minimize the amount of time elapsing be-

NATIONAL SCIENCE FOUNDATION	DESIGNATION OF DEPOSITARY FOR DIRECT DEPOSIT OF GRANT AND/OR CONTRACT FUNDS
SECTION I (TO BE COMPLETED BY RECIPIENT ORGANIZATION) PLEASE TYPE OR PRINT	
1. NATIONAL SCIENCE FOUNDATION LETTER OF CREDIT NO.	
THE	2. NAME OF BANK OR LOCAL GOVERNMENT TREASURY
	STREET ADDRESS
	CITY, STATE, ZIP CODE
has been designated as the depository for all funds to be received directly from the U.S. Treasury Department resulting from grants and/or contracts executed with the National Science Foundation for deposit to:	
3. ACCOUNT NAME AND/OR NUMBER	
4. NAME OF RECIPIENT ORGANIZATION	5. ADDRESS (including zip code)
6. TYPED NAME OF EXECUTIVE OFFICER	7. SIGNATURE OF EXECUTIVE OFFICER
8. TYPED TITLE OF EXECUTIVE OFFICER	9. DATE

NSF Form 931 (2-75) NOTE: REVERSE SIDE TO BE COMPLETED BY DEPOSITARY

(reverse side)

SECTION II (TO BE COMPLETED BY THE DEPOSITARY) PLEASE TYPE OR PRINT	
THE ACCOUNT IDENTIFIED IN SECTION I HAS BEEN ESTABLISHED WITH THIS BANK (OR TREASURY AS APPLICABLE). ALL NECESSARY DOCUMENTATION, INCLUDING A POWER OF ATTORNEY WHERE NECESSARY, WHICH WILL LEGALLY ENABLE THIS DEPOSITARY TO RECEIVE U.S. GOVERNMENT CHECKS DIRECTLY FROM THE U.S. TREASURY DEPARTMENT FOR DEPOSIT TO:	
10. ACCOUNT NAME AND/OR NUMBER	
WITHOUT THE PAYEE'S ENDORSEMENT HAVE BEEN RECEIVED AND ARE IN THIS DEPOSITARY'S CUSTODY	
11. DEPOSITS INSURED BY	
12. NAME OF BANK OR TREASURY	13. STREET ADDRESS (INCLUDING ZIP CODE) WHERE CHECKS SHOULD BE MAILED
THE DEPOSITARY HEREBY AGREES TO IMMEDIATELY NOTIFY THE RECIPIENT ORGANIZATION WHEN A DEPOSIT IS MADE IN THE ABOVE ACCOUNT.	
14. TYPED NAME OF AUTHORIZED BANK OFFICER	15. SIGNATURE OF AUTHORIZED BANK OR TREASURY OFFICER
16. TYPED TITLE OF AUTHORIZED BANK OFFICER	17. DATE

Figure 32a. Designation of Depositary for Direct Deposit of Grant and/or Contract Funds.

tween receipt of the Treasury funds and their disbursement. Accountability, of course, will also be required for advance payments.

If advances are not prescheduled, the grantee must submit its request for payment on a monthly basis. Less frequent requests are not permitted by the federal government because they would result in advances covering excessive periods of time.

If you will be applying for funding on Optional Form 60 (Figure 12), there is a box to check to indicate that you will be requiring advance payments. In addition to checking this box, you should make arrangements for advance payments with the grant or contract officer at the beginning of the project.

INSTRUCTIONS FOR NSF FORM 931

BLOCK NO.	EXPLANATION
1.	For the initial opening of an NSF Letter of Credit, this block will be completed by the NSF. For subsequent designations, insert the 8 digit number shown in the "Letter of Credit Number" block on the Letter of Credit, TFS 7577 (SF 1193A).
2.	Enter the name, address, and zip code of the depositary designated to receive Treasury checks.
3.	Enter the bank account name and/or number.
4.	Enter the name of the recipient.
5.	Enter the recipients's address (street, city, state, zip code).
6.	Enter typed name of executive officer.
7.	Enter signature of executive officer
8.	Enter executive officer's title.
9.	Enter date signed by executive officer.
10.	Enter the recipient's bank account name and/or number.
11.	Not required.
12.	Enter the name of the recipient's bank.
13.	Enter complete address of the recipient's bank where Treasury checks are to be mailed.
14.	Enter typed name of authorized bank officer.
15.	Enter bank officer's signature.
16.	Enter bank officer's title.
17.	Enter the date signed by the bank officer.

Figure 32b

Progress Payments

If your organization, for one reason or another, does not qualify for either a letter of credit or advance payments, you may have to settle for progress payments. Progress payments are, in effect, reimbursements. You spend some money and then are reimbursed periodically. This method of payment is also used when the major portion of the program funds is obtained through private market financing or federal loans, and when the federal grant assistance constitutes a major portion of the program funding.

If your organization will be receiving progress payments, it is important that you initiate:

1. Timely computation of indirect charges (overhead) so that you can be reimbursed for as many of your costs as possible.
2. Timely billings to the funding agency, so that you can be reimbursed as quickly and as often as possible.

ISSUING AGENCY	LETTER OF CREDIT Auth: Treasury Department Circular No. 1075, Revised	LETTER-OF-CREDIT NUMBER AMENDMENT NUMBER
AGENCY STATION SYMBOL	(FOR AGENCY USE)	EFFECTIVE DATE
TO: Treasury Disbursing Center or Regional Office	Address:	

In accordance with the authorization of the Fiscal Assistant Secretary, Department of the Treasury, there is hereby authorized for the account and responsibility of the issuing agency a letter of credit:

IN FAVOR OF:		TREASURY CHECKS TO BE MADE PAYABLE TO:	
AMOUNT AUTHORIZED $	TIME DESIGNATION ☐ EACH FISCAL YEAR ☐ WITHOUT TIME LIMIT	PRIOR AUTHORIZATION $	THIS CHANGE Increase $ Decrease $

Time Designation: Each Fiscal Year

☐ The unpaid balance of this letter of credit is revoked at the end of each fiscal year and the full amount authorized is reestablished at the beginning of each fiscal year unless you are advised in writing that this letter has been revoked.*

OR

☐ The unpaid balance of this letter of credit is carried forward at the end of each fiscal year and will remain available during the following fiscal year and, in addition, the full amount authorized is reestablished at the beginning of each fiscal year unless you are advised in writing that this letter has been revoked.*

Time Designation: Without Time Limit

☐ The unpaid balance of this letter of credit will remain available until you are advised in writing that this letter has been revoked.*

The amount of this letter of credit is hereby certified to be drawn against, upon presentation to you of Standard Form 183, Request for Payment on Letter of Credit and Status of Funds Report, by the official(s) of the recipient organization whose signature(s) appear(s) on the Standard Form 1194, Authorized Signature Card for Payment Vouchers on Letter of Credit, attached hereto or previously or subsequently furnished you.

The amount of each Request for Payment paid by the Department of the Treasury to the recipient organization at a designated commercial bank shall constitute payment to the recipient organization by the United States.

I certify to the Department of the Treasury that the payments authorized herein are correct and proper for payment from the appropriations or funds legally committed and available for the purpose, when paid in accordance with the terms and conditions cited above.

*This letter of credit is irrevocable to the extent the recipient organization has obligated funds in good faith thereunder in executing the authorized Federal program in accordance with the grant, contract, or other agreement.

DATE CERTIFIED ______________ ______________

AUTHORIZED CERTIFYING OFFICER

____

TYPED NAME AND TITLE

STANDARD FORM 1193A

Figure 33a. Letter of Credit.

The federal government says that requests for reimbursement may be submitted monthly, but if the grantee is properly authorized, more frequent billings are permitted. The government does attempt to pay grant recipients promptly, which usually means within 30 days after receipt of the request for reimbursement.

Sample forms for reimbursements (or advances) and for reporting on the fiscal status of projects are contained in Figures 35 and 36.

EXPLANATION OF TFS 7577 (SF 1193A)

BLOCK NO.

1. The NSF mailing address will appear in this block.
2. This is an 8 digit number assigned by the NSF to the Letter of Credit.
3. Changes to the Letter of Credit are made by amendments. Amendment numbers begin with "1" and continue in numerical sequence for each Letter of Credit. The amendment number is not required on the related Request for Payment or signature card changes.
4. This is an NSF identification code assigned by the Treasury.
5. This block will be left blank.
6. This is the date on which the recipient may begin to draw against the Letter of Credit. Normally, this date will be fixed to coincide with the date the Letter of Credit will be received by the Treasury Disbursing Office or Center, with consideration given to mail time.
7. This block will show the Treasury Regional Disbursing Office or Center to which Requests for Payment are sent by the recipient. The names and addresses of the Treasury Regional Disbursing Offices and Centers and the states they serve are included in Exhibit 4-5. The Treasury Disbursing Office or Center name shown in this block and the address shown in block 8 will take precedence over the name and address shown in Exhibit 4-5.
8. This address, along with the name of the Treasury Disbursing Office or Center (in block 7), must be used as the mailing address for Requests for Payment.
9. The name and address of the recipient will be shown in this block. Normally, this is the name used in the award letter.
10. The recipient's name and address as shown in block 9 will be entered here as payee unless checks are to be mailed to a different location; i.e., the recipient's bank designated on NSF Form 931, or address other than the address shown in block 9.
11. This amount is cumulative of all amendments issued during the fiscal year, and represents the amount of cash authorized to be drawn for the current fiscal year.
12. The availability period for all NSF Letters of Credit is "Each Fiscal Year."
13. A Letter of Credit amendment will reflect the "Amount Authorized," block 11, of the prior Letter of Credit or amendment in this block.
14. Increases to the "Amount Authorized," block 11, will be reported here.
15. Decreases to the "Amount Authorized," block 11, will be reported here.
16. This block will be designated for all NSF Letters of Credit.
17. Not applicable to NSF Letters of Credit.
18. Not applicable to NSF Letters of Credit.
19. Date certified by the NSF.
20. This space will be used to identify changes other than changes in the "Amount Authorized" when amending a Letter of Credit.
21. Signature of the NSF certifying officer.
22. Name and title of the NSF certifying officer.

Figure 33b

REQUEST FOR PAYMENT ON LETTER OF CREDIT AND STATUS OF FUNDS REPORT

SECTION I—REQUEST FOR PAYMENT

AGENCY STATION SYMBOL	LETTER-OF-CREDIT NUMBER	DOCUMENT NUMBER	AMOUNT REQUESTED $

NAME AND ADDRESS OF U.S. AGENCY	NAME AND ADDRESS OF DRAWER	PAID BY *(Treasury Use Only)*
NAME AND ADDRESS OF TREASURY DISBURSING OFFICE	MAKE TREASURY CHECK PAYABLE TO:	
		VOUCHER APPROVED *(Treasury Use Only)*
		CHECK NUMBER *(Treasury Use Only)*

SECTION II—STATUS OF FEDERAL FUNDS *(Must Be Completed By Drawer)*

ITEMS	ESTI-MATED NO. OF DAYS SUPPLY	AMOUNT
1. FEDERAL FUNDS ON HAND *(Beginning of Federal Fiscal Year)*		$
2. ADD: ADVANCES RECEIVED, FISCAL YEAR TO DATE		
3. ADD: COLLECTIONS, REFUNDS, AND/OR MISCELLANEOUS RECEIPTS		
4. Subtotal		
5. LESS: ACTUAL DISBURSEMENTS, FISCAL YEAR TO DATE		
6. FEDERAL FUNDS ON HAND AT TIME OF THIS REQUEST		
7. ADD: AMOUNT OF THIS REQUEST FOR PAYMENT		
8. ADD: UNPAID REQUESTS FOR PAYMENT PREVIOUSLY SUBMITTED		
9. TOTAL →		$
10. OUTSTANDING ADVANCES TO SUB-GRANTEES—NUMBER TOTAL $		*Treasury Use Only*

SECTION IIA—REMARKS *(Drawers Use)*

SECTION III—CLASSIFICATION OF THE AMOUNT OF THIS REQUEST *(Must Be Completed By Drawer)*

PROGRAM, GRANT NO. OR OTHER IDENTIFYING NO.	AMOUNT	PROGRAM, GRANT NO. OR OTHER IDENTIFYING NO.	AMOUNT
	$		$

TOTAL *(Must Agree with Amount of this Request for Payment)* $

SECTION IV—CERTIFICATION *(Must Be Completed By Drawer)*

I certify that this Request for Payment has been drawn in accordance with the terms and conditions of the Letter of Credit cited and that the amount for which drawn is proper for payment to the drawer or for credit to the account of the drawer at the drawer's bank. I also certify that the data reported above is correct and that the amount of the Request for Payment is not in excess of current needs.

DATE	SIGNATURE	TITLE
DATE	COUNTERSIGNATURE	TITLE

Standard Form 183

Figure 34a. Request for Payment on Letter of Credit and Status of Funds Report.

INSTRUCTIONS FOR SF-183

NOTICE TO DRAWER

Drawdowns to the letter of credit shall be made only in amounts necessary to meet current disbursement needs. Such drawdowns shall not ordinarily be made more frequently than daily, or be in amounts less than $5,000 and in no case more than $5,000,000 unless so stated on the letter of credit.

Complete money amounts (including the cents figure) must be used in all three sections.

SECTION I—REQUEST FOR PAYMENT

Blocks 1, 2, 3, 4, 5, 6—Information to be shown in these blocks shall be the same as shown on the related Letter of Credit, SF-1193A.

Block 7—Enter in this block the next consecutive document number.

Note: The document number shall commence with "001" at the beginning of each fiscal year and shall progress in consecutive order. Alphabetical designations shall not be used as part of the document number. Amendments to the Letter of Credit shall not interrupt the progression of the numbers assigned to the Request for Payment by the drawer. A rejected Request for Payment shall be treated as a completed document: the corrected Request for Payment shall be numbered with the next sequential document number.

Block 8—Enter the total dollar amount requested to be paid.

SECTION II—STATUS OF FEDERAL FUNDS

Other Federal agency requirements for this Section may differ from NSF specifications listed below, particularly with respect to lines 3 and 5. NSF requirements for these lines should conform (and give the same results) as the cash computation included in the OMB Circular A-110, Federal Cash Transactions Report.

LINE NO.

1. Enter the total amount of NSF cash on hand at the beginning of the current Federal Fiscal Year (October 1). This amount includes all NSF funds on deposit with commercial bank or maintained as imprest funds and received but undeposited Treasury checks.
2. Enter the total of advances received from the beginning of the Federal Fiscal Year (October 1) to the date of this request.
3. Enter the NSF share of project income which has been designated for credit to award costs.

   NSF requirements for this line may differ from other Federal agencies with respect to the following items:

   a. Refunds of previous project disbursements should be netted in line 5 of this Section and not reported on this line.
   b. Interest income on advance payments (if any) is not to be reported on this form.
   c. Project income (proceeds from the sale of goods and/or services, royalties, etc.) is to be reported on this line only to the extent that the income has been designated for credit to award costs.
4. Enter the sum of lines 1, 2, and 3.
5. Enter the total of NSF cash disbursements, fiscal year to date, including disbursements of cash received as project income. Refunds of previous project disbursements should be netted in the amount reported on this line.

Figure 34b

6. Line 4 minus line 5. Also report, in the stub provided, the estimated number of working days until the amount reported will be disbursed. Insert zero number of days for negative (deficit) balances. This estimate includes the day on which this request for payment is prepared but does not include the day on which the funds will be disbursed. For example, if the request for payment is prepared on a Tuesday and the recipient expects to disburse the NSF funds on hand on the same day he is preparing the request for payment, this represents a zero days supply of NSF funds.
7. Enter the same amount as entered in the "Amount Requested" block of Section I. In the stub provided, enter the estimated number of working days until the amount requested will be disbursed; count the number of days beginning with the anticipated receipt date of the funds being requested. This estimate includes the expected day of receipt, but does not include the day of disbursement. For example, if the recipient expects to receive the NSF funds requested on a Friday and disburse these funds on Monday of the following week, this represents one day supply of NSF funds, assuming Saturday and Sunday are not workdays.
8. Enter the total amount of Request(s) for Payment previously submitted to the Treasury Disbursing Office or Center for which payment has not yet been received.
9. Enter the sum of amounts reported on lines 6, 7, and 8.
10. Enter the total number and amount of outstanding advances to subgrantees or subcontractors. Enter NA if nonapplicable.

SECTION IIA—REMARKS (DRAWER'S USE)

Enter any comments to NSF relative to this request or any coding, references, etc. for internal use.

SECTION III—CLASSIFICATION OF THE AMOUNT OF THIS REQUEST

In the absence of special instructions from NSF, enter "NSF Awards" in the description column and the amount requested on the same line and on the "Total" line in the "Amount" Column. The total of this Section must be the same as the "Amount Requested" under Section I and the "Amount of This Request for Payment" under Section II.

SECTION IV—CERTIFICATION

Only the designated officer(s) whose signature(s) appear on the Authorized Signature Card for Payment Vouchers on Letter of Credit, Standard Form 1194, shall sign on the line(s) provided. The date and title(s) of the designated official(s) shall be entered on the appropriate lines.

Figure 34b (Continued).

3. Systematized follow-up on late payments, so that you will recognize when payments are late and will be able to take appropriate action to remedy the situation.

Your agency should devise a "trigger" mechanism that alerts you when payments are late. If you should overlook late reimbursements and must disburse your own money as a result, you are losing income. Great effort should be devoted to catching late payments before they become *very* late.

How Advantageously Can You Pay Out the Grant Funds?

In this context, *advantageously* can be loosely translated as meaning "slowly." We are not suggesting that you pay your bills late; we are only raising the point that a well-managed disbursement system will both save your agency money and maintain your good credit rating. Your credit rating will not improve if you pay your bills a week or two early. Pay bills on time to avoid any late charges, but don't do your suppliers any favors by sending them your money before it is due. The longer you keep your money in your own possession, the more interest it can earn for you. We will return to this point shortly.

It is important to remember in the administration of grants and contracts that the money you are expecting from a grantor doesn't always arrive precisely when you need it and in the amounts you require. It will help you to live with any slow payments from funding agencies if you have arranged for *credit from suppliers* and *favorable payment terms.*

Credit from Suppliers

Even when you have advance payments set up with the funding agency, there may be times when something in the "system" delays the payment. So, your ability to charge purchases, with billings on a monthly or similar basis, may help you to avoid using your own agency's cash at times. Neighborhood suppliers, anxious to obtain your business, may extend favorable credit terms and may be willing to wait a week or two more than usual for payment. The use of credit cards (restricted to a minimum number of responsible users, of course) can also save your organization money.

As an illustration, let us assume that you know that several funded projects will be using $100 of office supplies in a month. Your central supply room could charge the purchases with a credit card and wait for the bill.

Let us also assume, using the same example, that you know that all purchases made after the 20th day of the month do not normally appear on that month's invoice. The purchases you make after June 20, for example, will appear on the bill you normally receive on *July 31.* The bill you receive on July 31 will be due on or about August 25. Consequently, you have had the use of the office supplies for more than two months (from June 20 to August 25) and have not had to pay a cent.

If you can time your purchases to occur after the 20th of each month you will have, in effect, borrowed money for two months from the issuer of the credit card with no interest payments or finance charge. In the meantime, the check you were expecting from the government will probably have arrived, and you can then pay the bill on August 25 with grant funds instead of your agency's money.

Although this is only a small illustration, major grantees receiving millions of dollars a year can save substantially by "playing the float." If your agency must

REQUEST FOR ADVANCE OR REIMBURSEMENT

(See instructions on back)

Approved by Office of Management and Budget, No. 80–RO183

PAGE OF PAGES

1. TYPE OF PAYMENT REQUESTED — a. "X" one, or both boxes: ☐ ADVANCE ☐ REIMBURSEMENT; b. "X" the applicable box: ☐ FINAL ☐ PARTIAL

2. BASIS OF REQUEST: ☐ CASH ☐ ACCRUAL

3. FEDERAL SPONSORING AGENCY AND ORGANIZATIONAL ELEMENT TO WHICH THIS REPORT IS SUBMITTED

4. FEDERAL GRANT OR OTHER IDENTIFYING NUMBER ASSIGNED BY FEDERAL AGENCY

5. PARTIAL PAYMENT REQUEST NUMBER FOR THIS REQUEST

6. EMPLOYER IDENTIFICATION NUMBER

7. RECIPIENT'S ACCOUNT NUMBER OR IDENTIFYING NUMBER

8. PERIOD COVERED BY THIS REQUEST — FROM *(month, day, year)* — TO *(month, day, year)*

9. RECIPIENT ORGANIZATION

Name :

Number and Street :

City, State and ZIP Code :

10. PAYEE *(Where check is to be sent is different than item 9)*

Name :

Number and Street :

City, State and ZIP Code :

11. COMPUTATION OF AMOUNT OF REIMBURSEMENTS/ADVANCES REQUESTED

PROGRAMS/FUNCTIONS/ACTIVITIES ▶		(a)	(b)	(c)	TOTAL
a. Total program outlays to date *(As of date)*		$	$	$	$
b. *Less:* Cumulative program income					
c. Net program outlays *(Line a minus line b)*					
d. Estimated net cash outlays for advance period					
e. Total *(Sum of lines c & d)*					
f. Non-Federal share of amount on line e					
g. Federal share of amount on line e					
h. Federal payments previously requested					
i. Federal share now requested *(Line g minus line h)*					
j. Advances required by month, when requested by Federal grantor agency for use in making prescheduled advances	1st month				
	2nd month				
	3rd month				

12. ALTERNATE COMPUTATION FOR ADVANCES ONLY

a. Estimated Federal cash outlays that will be made during period covered by the advance	$
b. *Less:* Estimated balance of Federal cash on hand as of beginning of advance period	
c. Amount requested *(Line a minus line b)*	$

13. CERTIFICATION

I certify that to the best of my knowledge and belief the data above are correct and that all outlays were made in accordance with the grant conditions or other agreement and that payment is due and has not been previously requested.

SIGNATURE OF AUTHORIZED CERTIFYING OFFICIAL — DATE REQUEST SUBMITTED

TYPED OR PRINTED NAME AND TITLE

TELEPHONE — *Area Code* — *Number* — *Extension*

This space for agency use

STANDARD FORM 270 (7–76)

Figure 35a. Request for Advance or Reimbursement.

INSTRUCTIONS

Please type or print legibly. Items 1, 3, 5, 9, 10, 11e, 11f, 11g, 11i, and 13 are self-explanatory; specific instructions for other items are as follows:

ITEM	ENTRY
2	Indicate whether the report is prepared on cash or accrued expenditure basis. In determining the amount of funds required for the advance period, 11d or 12a should be estimated on a cash basis.
4	Enter the Federal grant number or other identifying number assigned by the Federal sponsoring agency. If the advance or reimbursement is for more than one grant or other agreement, insert N/A; then show the aggregate amounts in either section 11 or 12. When section 11 is used to request advance and/or reimbursement on more than one grant, the recipient shall list on a separate sheet each grant or agreement number, the Federal share of net program outlays to date made against each grant or agreement and, for advance payment, the allocation of advances by grant or agreement for up to a thirty day period. When section 12 is used to request advance payments on more than one grant or agreement, the recipient shall list on a separate sheet each grant or agreement number and the allocation of requested advances by grant or agreement for up to a thirty day period.
6	Enter the employer identification number assigned by the U.S. Internal Revenue Service, or the FICE (institution) code if requested by the Federal agency.
7	This space is reserved for an account number or other identifying number that may be assigned by the recipient.
8	Enter the month, day, and year for the beginning and ending of the period covered in this request. If the request is for an advance or for both an advance and reimbursement, show the period that the advance will cover. If the request is for reimbursement, show the period for which the reimbursement is requested.

Note: The recipient who is authorized to be paid on an advance basis has the option of completing either item 11 or 12. See item 4 above for instructions relating to the use of either 11 or 12 for requesting advance payment on more than one grant or agreement.

ITEM	ENTRY
11	The purpose of the vertical columns (a), (b), and (c), is to provide space for separate cost breakdowns when a project has been planned and budgeted by program, function, or activity. If additional columns are needed, use as many additional forms as needed and indicate page number in space provided in upper right; however, the summary totals of all programs, functions, or activities should be shown in the "total" column on the first page.
11a	Enter in "as of date", the month, day, and year of the ending of the accounting period to which this amount applies. Enter program outlays to date (net of refunds, rebates, and discounts), in the appropriate columns. For requests prepared on a cash basis, outlays are the sum of actual cash disbursements for goods and services, the amount of indirect expenses charged, the value of in-kind contributions applied, and the amount of cash advances and payments made to subcontractors and subrecipients. For requests prepared on an accrued expenditure basis, outlays are the sum of the actual cash disbursements, the amount of indirect expenses incurred, and the net increase (or decrease) in the amounts owed by the recipient for goods and other property received and for services performed by employees, contracts, subgrantees and other payees.

Figure 35b

11b Enter the cumulative cash income received to date, if requests are prepared on a cash basis. For requests prepared on an accrued expenditure basis, enter the cumulative income earned to date. Under either basis, enter only the amount applicable to program income that was required to be used for the project or program by the terms of the grant or other agreement.

11c Recipients who use section 11 to request advance payments on an individual grant, shall show the Federal share of net outlays to date in the space provided below for agency use.

11d Only when making requests for advance payments, enter the total estimated amount of cash outlays that will be made during the period covered by the advance.

11j When a recipient is specifically authorized to request advance payments on an individual grant or agreement for more than thirty day period, the recipient shall complete this section of the report so that advance payments may be prescheduled over a three month period.

12 When a recipient is authorized to be paid on an advance basis this section may be completed to request advance payments for up to a thirty day period on one or more grants or agreements. If the payment request covers more than one grant or agreement, the recipient shall list on a separate sheet each grant or agreement number and the allocation of requested advances by grant or agreement for up to a thirty day period. When only section 12 is used to request advance payment, the recipient must submit quarterly either a Financial Status Report for each grant or agreement or the Federal Cash Transactions Report. (Recipients should note that the Federal Cash Transactions Report shall be submitted at least quarterly when monthly advances to a recipient exceed $10,000.) Further advance payments will not be made until either the Financial Status Report(s) or the Federal Cash Transactions Report is received by the Endowment's Grants Office.

13 Complete the certification before submitting this request.

Figure 35b (Continued).

advance $100,000 per year to keep its grants and contracts in operation, it is losing the interest it could have collected on that $100,000. At 10%, this amounts to $10,000 per year, not an insignificant sum. Whenever possible, it is best to use the funding agency's money, not your own, and this normally means that you will not rush to make your payments.

Favorable Payment Terms

There is, however, one circumstance where good cash management dictates that you *do* pay your bills almost immediately. This circumstance, discussed briefly in Chapter 6, arises when discounts are offered by suppliers if you pay within 10 days or within a specified time limit.

Taking advantage of cash discounts, when they are available, is a prime rule of good cash management. If a cash discount of "$\frac{1}{2}$% in 10 days" is offered but payment is made instead in "net 30 days," you have lost the discount. It is true that your agency has retained the cash for an additional 20 days, but that cash must be invested at 9% merely to equal the lost discount. Under most conditions, an investment yield high enough to offset even the lowest of forfeited cash discounts is not possible. Taking all cash discounts offered is probably the most productive way of using institutional cash.[5]

One of the least productive ways of using institutional cash is to have a system whereby bills are paid whenever they are approved for payment rather than on a prescribed schedule. At best, this method of cash management is not a system at all. Many smaller institutions are unable to hire a professional cash manager, and so they do not establish periodic payment dates for net invoices. They simply pay the bills on a haphazard basis. A single supplier, as a result, may be sent three or four or five separate checks per month instead of the one or two that would be sent under an organized payment system. If one figures that it costs between \$3 and \$5 (including labor) to process a check, it is clear that the institution that does not plan its payments is costing itself a substantial amount of money.

According to Lordan,[6] indiscriminate bill paying is an unnecessary drain on cash resources and is costly. Paying a \$10,000 bill that is due in 60 days within, for example, 15 days, would cost the payer \$75, even if the money earned only 6% ($\$10{,}000 \times .06 \times \frac{45}{360}$). If the money were to be invested at 10% for an additional 45 days, the real loss to the indiscriminate bill payer can be calculated as being far greater than \$75. And if the grantee (i.e., the payer in this case) is a large institution, the losses could well be thousands of dollars per year.

These losses bother few people because they are invisible. They are not disbursements, and there is nothing unusual or questionable. Perhaps they can be viewed as forfeited earnings rather than losses, but they still affect the institution that paid the bills. Eventually, the higher costs for this poor cash management will be reflected in a higher indirect-cost rate. The alternative is to establish efficient payment schedules.

Some institutions (fewer than in the past) still allow idle cash to build up in checking accounts (demand accounts) so that funds are available for disbursements. There is no management problem when an agency follows this procedure, but neither is the idle cash earning any money for the agency. The idle cash, which should be viewed as a commodity, is not being productive at all. When disbursements checks are prepared, there is no problem about there being sufficient funds to cover them. The money is already in the bank. Indeed, it has been there too long!

An alternative to this unproductive system is "time-of-release" funding of the demand bank account.[7] Under this system, cash is kept invested until disbursement checks are mailed. At that time, cash is shifted from interest-bearing investments or savings accounts to the checking (demand) account to cover the checks being mailed. Depending on the nature of the investment, cash can be shifted automatically by your bank according to your instructions, through the use of drafts, the sale of securities, or the sale of other investments.

FINANCIAL STATUS REPORT

(Follow instructions on the back)

1. FEDERAL AGENCY AND ORGANIZATIONAL ELEMENT TO WHICH REPORT IS SUBMITTED

2. FEDERAL GRANT OR OTHER IDENTIFYING NUMBER

OMB Approved No. 80–RO180

PAGE OF PAGES

3. RECIPIENT ORGANIZATION *(Name and complete address, including ZIP code)*

4. EMPLOYER IDENTIFICATION NUMBER

5. RECIPIENT ACCOUNT NUMBER OR IDENTIFYING NUMBER

6. FINAL REPORT ☐ YES ☐ NO

7. BASIS ☐ CASH ☐ ACCRUAL

8. PROJECT/GRANT PERIOD *(See instructions)*
FROM *(Month, day, year)* TO *(Month, day, year)*

9. PERIOD COVERED BY THIS REPORT
FROM *(Month, day, year)* TO *(Month, day, year)*

10. STATUS OF FUNDS

PROGRAMS/FUNCTIONS/ACTIVITIES ►	*(a)*	*(b)*	*(c)*	*(d)*	*(e)*	*(f)*	TOTAL *(g)*
a. Net outlays previously reported	$	$	$	$	$	$	$
b. Total outlays this report period							
c. *Less:* Program income credits							
d. Net outlays this report period *(Line b minus line c)*							
e. Net outlays to date *(Line a plus line d)*							
f. *Less:* Non-Federal share of outlays							
g. Total Federal share of outlays *(Line e minus line f)*							
h. Total unliquidated obligations							
i. *Less:* Non-Federal share of unliquidated obligations shown on line h							
j. Federal share of unliquidated obligations							
k. Total Federal share of outlays and unliquidated obligations							
l. Total cumulative amount of Federal funds authorized							
m. Unobligated balance of Federal funds							

11. INDIRECT EXPENSE
a. TYPE OF RATE *(Place "X" in appropriate box)* ☐ PROVISIONAL ☐ PREDETERMINED ☐ FINAL ☐ FIXED
b. RATE c. BASE d. TOTAL AMOUNT e. FEDERAL SHARE

12. REMARKS: *Attach any explanations deemed necessary or information required by Federal sponsoring agency in compliance with governing legislation.*

13. CERTIFICATION
I certify to the best of my knowledge and belief that this report is correct and complete and that all outlays and unliquidated obligations are for the purposes set forth in the award documents.

SIGNATURE OF AUTHORIZED CERTIFYING OFFICIAL

DATE REPORT SUBMITTED

TYPED OR PRINTED NAME AND TITLE

TELEPHONE *(Area code, number and extension)*

STANDARD FORM 269

Figure 36a. Financial Status Report.

INSTRUCTIONS

Please type or print legibly. Items 1, 2, 3, 6, 7, 9, 10d, 10e, 10g, 10i, 10l, 11a, and 12 are self-explanatory, specific instructions for other items are as follows:

ITEM	ENTRY
4	Enter the employer identification number assigned by the U.S. Internal Revenue Service or FICE (institution) code, if required by the Federal sponsoring agency.
5	This space is reserved for an account number or other identifying numbers that may be assigned by the recipient.
8	Enter the month, day, and year of the beginning and ending of this project period. For formula grants that are not awarded on a project basis, show the grant period.
10	The purpose of vertical columns (a) through (f) is to provide financial data for each program, function, and activity in the budget as approved by the Federal sponsoring agency. If additional columns are needed, use as many additional forms as needed and indicate page number in space provided in upper right; however, the totals of all programs, functions or activities should be shown in (g) of the first page. For agreements pertaining to several Catalog of Federal Domestic Assistance programs that do not require a further functional or activity classification breakdown, enter under columns (a) through (f) the title of the program. For grants or other assistance agreements containing multiple programs where one or more programs require a further breakdown by function or activity, use a separate form for each program showing the applicable functions or activities in the separate columns. For grants or other assistance agreements containing several functions or activities which are funded from several programs, prepare a separate form for each activity or function when requested by the Federal sponsoring agency.
10a	Enter the net outlay. This amount should be the same as the amount reported in Line 10e of the last report. If there has been an adjustment to the amount shown previously, please attach explanation. Show zero if this is the initial report.
10b	Enter the total gross program outlays (less rebates, refunds, and other discounts) for this report period, including disbursements of cash realized as program income. For reports that are prepared on a cash basis, outlays are the sum of actual cash disbursements for goods and services, the amount of indirect expense charged, the value of in-kind contributions applied, and the amount of cash advances and payments made to contractors and subgrantees. For reports prepared on an accrued expenditure basis, outlays are the sum of actual cash disbursements, the amount of indirect expense incurred, the value of in-kind contributions applied, and the net increase (or decrease) in the amounts owed by the recipient for goods and other property received and for services performed by employees, contractors, subgrantees, and other payees.
10c	Enter the amount of all program income realized in this period that is required by the terms and conditions of the Federal award to be deducted from total project costs. For reports prepared on a cash basis, enter the amount of cash income received during the reporting period. For reports prepared on an accrual

Figure 36b

basis, enter the amount of income earned since the beginning of the reporting period. When the terms or conditions allow program income to be added to the total award, explain in remarks, the source, amount and disposition of the income.

10f Enter amount pertaining to the non-Federal share of program outlays included in the amount on line e.

10h Enter total amount of unliquidated obligations for this project or program, including unliquidated obligations to subgrantees and contractors. Unliquidated obligations are:

Cash basis—obligations incurred but not paid;

Accrued expenditure basis—obligations incurred but for which an outlay has not been recorded.

Do not include any amounts that have been included on lines a through g. On the final report, line h should have a zero balance.

10j Enter the Federal share of unliquidated obligations shown on line h. The amount shown on this line should be the difference between the amounts on lines h and i.

10k Enter the sum of the amounts shown on lines g and j. If the report is final the report should not contain any unliquidated obligations.

10m Enter the unobligated balance of Federal funds. This amount should be the difference between lines k and l.

11b Enter rate in effect during the reporting period.

11c Enter amount of the base to which the rate was applied.

11d Enter total amount of indirect cost charged during the report period.

11e Enter amount of the Federal share charged during the report period.

If more than one rate was applied during the project period, include a separate schedule showing bases against which the indirect cost rates were applied, the respective indirect rates the month, day, and year the indirect rates were in effect, amounts of indirect expense charged to the project, and the Federal share of indirect expense charged to the project to date.

Figure 36b (Continued).

This system requires some management, but it also produces some investment income. If the amount of income is sufficient, which might be the case at a large grantee institution, it may be advantageous to hire a full- or part-time employee as a cash manager.

How Efficiently Can You Invest Idle Cash?

In addition to collecting cash quickly and paying it out as advantageously as possible, a third guiding principle of money management is to invest idle cash efficiently, using short-term investment instruments.

In order to do this, first you must determine how much cash will be available for investments. This is done by making cash forecasts.

Cash Forecasting

The basic tools of cash management are cash forecasts. These forecasts, which can be designed to project either cash flows or financing requirements, tell an organization how much money will be needed to run its operations for certain future periods. Cash forecasts can be either short-term or long-term. Short-term forecasts are usually highly detailed, while long-term forecasts are more likely to reflect only rough estimates.[8] Short-term projections are those that cover a period of one year or less; forecasts that extend beyond this are considered long-term.

A common forecasting mechanism used for the short term—perhaps a week to several months—is called the *receipts-and-disbursements method.* The main idea behind this method is to pinpoint as closely as possible the organization's inflows and outflows of cash. Such a forecast, to be effective, must include all receipts and disbursements that significantly influence the organization's day-to-day cash position.

The greatest problem with this type of forecast is estimating receipts—not only their amounts but also the time they will arrive. Experienced guesses are often wrong, and even a phone call to the funding agency may not provide accurate information. The federal bureaucracy often (and easily) turns a two-week wait for a check into a month or more.

Disbursements, on the other hand, are usually easier to estimate. Your organization has the advantage of knowing its own costs. Furthermore, it has some control over them if flexibility in using cash is required.[9]

Short-Term Investments

Once you have estimated the excess of receipts over disbursements, you will know how much surplus cash is available for short-term investments. Although the subject of short-term investments is too broad to discuss comprehensively in this book, still, it is useful to note here that there are many money-market instruments used by profit and nonprofit corporations. These instruments have varying yields, maturities, price stability, and marketability.

In a survey of 120 companies conducted by the Conference Board, Inc., favored money-market instruments included (in rank order)[10]:

- U.S. Treasury bills
- Negotiable time certificates of deposit
- Finance company commercial paper
- U.S. Treasury notes and bonds

- Repurchase agreements
- Industrial-service company commercial paper

Other instruments were used, but these, which combine liquidity, short maturities, and reasonable yields, are generally favored.

Short-term investments are the topic of many good books and articles. The reader is referred to the following in particular for an extensive discussion of the subject:

Fisher, David I. *Cash Management.* New York: The Conference Board, Inc., Report No. 580, 1973.

Handbook of Securities of the United States Government and Federal Agencies. New York: The First Boston Corporation, 1970.

Money Market Instruments. Cleveland: Federal Reserve Bank of Cleveland, 1970.

Money Market Investments: The Risk and the Return. New York: Morgan Guaranty Trust Company of New York, 1970.

Monhollon, Jimmie R. (ed.). *Instruments of the Money Market.* Richmond, Va: Federal Reserve Bank of Richmond, 1968.

What Are the Obstacles to Effective Cash Management?

Even with the best of intentions, perfect cash management is difficult or impossible to achieve, especially in the grant and contract business. The vagaries of government payment schedules, the needs of the project directors, and the budget period of the project do not always mesh.

For example, how the project money is spent—and when—is up to the project director. However, she or he may be a brilliant chemist or biologist or psychologist but may never have taken a business course. She or he knows that a grant has been awarded and that the money must be spent yet may not know whether her or his institution has received the necessary funds. The award letter has arrived and that means "go" to the researcher. Although this situation may be inconvenient for the money manager, this is the way it has to be. Cash flow is not the project director's problem. It is the money manager's.

To compound the problem, the cash needs of the project director are often greatest just at the time that funds for the project are at their scarcest, that is, at the beginning. Payment from the sponsor may not have arrived, yet the researcher needs an expensive piece of equipment now. The equipment will be of little use if it is purchased during the middle or toward the end of the project. The research requires that it be used continuously.

If you are the money manager, what do you do? You have no choice but to follow through with standard purchasing procedures to obtain the equipment.

You will have to get bids, open them properly, and send out a purchase order. After the equipment arrives, you may have some time thereafter to pay for it. If all goes well, funds from the sponsor agency will have arrived.

If the money has not arrived, all your planning and forecasting will go by the boards for the moment. You will have to pay the bill, borrowing from the bank, if necessary, to do it. Or you can transfer funds from an investment account at one bank to a demand account at another.

It is wise to effect this transfer at the latest possible moment. If you transfer $100,000 into a demand accound one day too soon, for example, you will lose $16 in interest even if the $100,000 was earning only 6%. If this is done repeatedly on a number of projects, your agency will lose thousands of dollars a year. Careful cash management can save your organization a great deal of money.

Does Your Organization Have a Cash Management Policy for Grants?

It is advantageous for agencies in the business of administering grants and contracts to have a cash management policy and personnel responsible for implementing the policy. This policy should incorporate the guiding principles of cash management discussed in this chapter: collecting grant funds quickly, disbursing payments advantageously (usually slowly, but retaining good credit ratings), and investing idle cash efficiently.

Some smaller community agencies, colleges, and hospitals may not be accustomed to such "business world" procedures. Larger universities, profit-making organizations, and research institutes are generally familiar with the need for effective cash management. All organizations, however, whether large or small, will benefit from establishing a cash management policy.

Who in Your Organization Is Responsible for Cash Management?

The size of an organization has a major bearing on who is responsible for cash management. At a small college, for example, conscious and planned cash management may be a luxury to be taken care of when the business manager or financial vice president "has time." All too often, that means never. When a cash management policy *is* followed, it is usually accomplished in small agencies by a person who also has other duties. It may be an accountant or even an experienced clerk, but certainly it is not done by a full-time professional.

Large universities, hospitals, and research institutes may have a full-time professional working on cash management. His or her skill in timing expenditures in and out can easily pay the position's salary for the year, assuming that the volume is sufficient and that the manager is aggressive in pursuing all avenues open to him or her.

The individual who is responsible for cash management should be known to all concerned and should have specific authority. Indeed, Jones and Howard[11] state:

> For maximum effectiveness, the authority and responsibility for the cash management program must be clearly assigned. Because communication among people in many departments is a prime ingredient in an investment system, the responsible officer must have authority to cross organizational lines and to establish proper procedures for channeling information from the many sources that must feed into the system.

Procedures and changes that may be needed to facilitate cash control should be under the authority of the individual responsible for cash management.

Whether the individual responsible for cash management is called the vice-president for business affairs, the controller, or the accounts payable–receivable clerk, he or she must work closely with others. For example, the entire business staff plays a role. All incoming checks should be brought to the cash manager's attention. Checks left undeposited for a day or two actually cost your agency money. Similarly, the accounts payable staff should take advantage of all discounts and avoid prepaying invoices.

An example of what can happen when no one is responsible for cash management occurred at a medium-sized western university that recently changed its grant accounting system to make it compatible with a new computer it had acquired. During the transition from a largely manual operation to a computer operation, there were additional paperwork burdens placed on the staff. Finally, when the computer system was complete and working, there appeared to be a failure in the communication network between the accounts payable staff and the data-processing staff. The number of checks written per week suddenly quadrupled. Until the problem was ironed out through an established schedule for paying invoices, it is safe to say that cash management was temporarily nonexistent and an untold amount of money was not earning interest.

In summary, it is important that someone in the grantee organization be given overall responsibility for cash management. This person should develop and implement policies to follow the three guiding principles of cash management: *collecting grant funds quickly; disbursing them slowly* (but in time to maintain good credit ratings and obtain discounts); and *investing surplus grant funds on a short-term basis.*

9

Funding-Agency Contacts
Letting Them Help

"In the final analysis I would like to remind you that research is not only a paper business, it is a people business too."[1]

–R. Woodrow

In a national address to university grant administrators, Ray Woodrow of Princeton emphasized the importance of personal contact:

> Most of you have or will have gotten to know those grants and contracts officers with whom negotiations on projects are generally consummated. I have found that visits however brief to *program* officers can pay real dividends in, if nothing else, conveying the impression that you have a real interest in the research to be done and not only how much overhead it will pay.[2]

Henry Brehm, Chief of Research Grants and Contracts at the Social Security Administration, echoed this theme from the grantor perspective, stating succinctly, "Nothing replaces becoming known to persons in the granting agencies."*

Why is it so critical to know the grantors? Louis Urgo, in his book *Models for Money: Obtaining Government and Foundation Grants and Assistance*, offers an explanation: "As you know, people love to tell other people what they know. Being human, most civil servants are willing–even anxious–to impart their expertise to the public."[3]

In the authors' personal experience–and in the experience of the many grants professionals we have interviewed–grantors have provided a great deal of

*Interview with Sladek.

assistance, and they generally enjoy it. Getting to know them, making the right contacts, can make the difference between a successful and a so-so project or even having a project at all.

What are some of the ways you can let grantors help?

Let Them Help You Decide Whether or Not to Apply

"That's GARBAGE!" A Department of Energy program officer shoved a draft prospectus back across the desk to a stunned grant administrator.

Literally, it *was* garbage. The project idea had been to do a solid-waste-management demonstration project. Because the dumps in their home county were being filled so quickly and landfill areas were being used up, the project proposers had devised a resource recovery operation. They had proved on a pilot project scale that over one half of the trash that was deposited in a certain section of a southwestern dump could be recovered and reused.

No high technology was involved; instead, workers manually picked and sorted through deliveries at a central location near the landfill entrance. Reusable items were marketed locally. In the one-year pilot project, the break-even point between workers' salaries and product sales had been achieved. Now the questions were: Could this sort of operation be feasible commercially? On a larger scale, might there be profits? In addition to the environmental benefits, what energy savings would accrue?

Unfortunately, the program officer who had been asked to review the draft prospectus was not being literal. When she referred to it as "garbage," she was not displaying her understanding of the project's central component.

Actually, she thought the *idea* "stunk"! She wanted no part of it.

Despite her reverse enthusiasm, the program officer ended up being helpful. When the grant administrator inquired why she had reacted so strongly against the project, it turned out that this program officer had a history of supporting high-technology resource-recovery programs. A low-technology operation such as this had no appeal. The idea of people having to pick and sort through garbage was distasteful to her. Once she recognized her personal bias, she spent over an hour with the grant administrator, providing names and phone numbers of other federal representatives who might be interested in supporting the program (even some within her own agency). She told him how to contact the one other person in the country who was doing a somewhat similar project and gave advance information that saved the project from duplicating the efforts of others.

Preliminary Idea Review

It is unlikely that any program officer will call your idea garbage. Most of them, however, will let you know if it has little chance of being funded by their agency. And they will encourage you to apply if your idea does have good prospects.

In fact, grantors usually *want* you to contact them before you ask them for money. When we asked grantors what problems they had experienced in their contacts with project directors, one program officer said, "Submission of proposals that do not meet the objectives of my program. There was no previous inquiry by the applicant!"

"Both the major Foundations and the Government encourage informal preliminary inquiries to save time from the practical standpoint not only for the granting officials, but for the applicant," advises Urgo.[4]

There are two ways of saving time by not submitting an unlikely-to-be-funded proposal. First, there are all the hours that you would have spent *writing* the proposal. Perhaps more important are the months (frequently six to nine) of *waiting* before you are notified that the proposal will not be funded—time that delays your project.

A hopeful project director for an educational radio and television station found this out, to her dismay. Dr. Grate knew exactly what needed to be done and how to do it. She didn't discuss her idea with any grantors. After writing a proposal to provide radio reading services to the blind, she sent it off to the Office of Education and confidently waited for the review period to be over so that her project would be funded and she could get her show on the air.

At the end of nine months, her proposal was rejected. Was it a poorly developed project?

Not at all. The concept simply was not a priority at the Office of Education program she had submitted the proposal to. Had Dr. Grate spend 10 minutes on the phone with the program officer, she could have found this out before she ever wrote the proposal.

As it was, there was a one-year-later happy ending. Dr. Grate made some contacts and discovered a program officer who was extremely interested in the project (from another program within the Office of Education, as it turned out). Without a word of the proposal's having to be rewritten, it was funded. But 12 months of reading to the blind had been lost in the meantime.

Grate's experience confirms what Herman Holtz, in his book *Government Contracts: Proposalmanship and Winning Strategies*, tells grantees:

> An unsolicited proposal coming "out of the blue" with no advance discussion is extremely unlikely to be successful. Successful unsolicited proposals are usually the result of a personal discussion of ideas with individuals in the agency and some advance expression of interest by the agency.[5]

Usually, it is best to make contacts for your preliminary idea review in two steps: first, by sending a written prospectus and, second, by following up with a meeting or phone call.

A prospectus is a written document that describes briefly what you want to do, why, when, how, who will do it, and for how much. Usually the prospectus is no more than five pages, and it is frequently shorter.

Some sponsoring agencies require a preliminary written statement of your idea. The Fund for the Improvement of Postsecondary Education (FIPSE), for example, has so many applicants for funds that its staff would never be able to process all the applications if they had to read formal proposals. Therefore, FIPSE has two application deadlines. Early in the year, there is a call for preliminary proposals, not to exceed five pages. Then, those applicants whose *ideas* are of interest to FIPSE staff are invited to submit a longer formal proposal.

It is advisable to provide a prospectus even if there is no grantor requirement to do so. If you give program officers a chance to read about your idea before you talk to them, they will be better prepared to discuss it with you.

Once program officers have your prospectus in hand, you should meet with them (first choice) or call them (next best). Although you can use this meeting or phone call to get many kinds of information, the most important question to answer is this: Do *they* want to do what *you* want to do? (Do your interests match?)

If the answer is "yes," you can proceed to apply, tailoring your proposal to best fit *their* needs, which you found out by talking to them.

If the answer is "no," you will have saved proposal-writing time and months of waiting around. You can put your energies to work for more promising results elsewhere.

Either way, the contact will have helped you.

Interpretations

Sometimes no preliminary idea review is necessary. So far, we have been talking about *unsolicited* proposals—where you have the idea and must find out if it is of interest to grantors.

Many times, however, it is the grantor agency that decides what is to be done and *solicits* organizations to do it. They describe what they want done in a document entitled a *request for proposal* (RFP). Even though the grantor may have prepared a 40- or 50-page RFP specifying the tasks to be done, you may need to contact the grantor for interpretations of these specifications.

Grantors recognize how important it is for prospective grantees to understand what they are being asked to do. Grantors also recognize the limitations of relying on printed words. Therefore, they often conduct a public meeting for prospective grantees, before the proposal deadline, to explain the solicited project in detail and to respond to questions. This meeting is called a *preproposal conference*.

If you plan to apply for a project, and such a conference is being held, you should attend. If you cannot be there personally, you should try to find someone to represent you. Many organizations can call on representatives in Washington offices to do this. Participants in the Office of Federal Programs* (American

*Additional information about the Office of Federal Programs may be obtained by writing to: Office of Federal Programs, American Association of State Colleges and Universities, One Dupont Circle, N.W., Suite 700, Washington, D.C. 20036, or by calling 202-293-7070.

Association of State Colleges and Universities), for example, can arrange to have OFP personnel attend preproposal conferences that are held in Washington.

The information that can be collected at a preproposal conference can help you decide whether or not to apply. First, you will find out who the competitors are. Next, you can probably tell from their questions how well they understand the project and even how they may be planning to do the work. Not only will you get a sense of the competition, but your understanding of agency concerns and the personal characteristics of agency representatives will be increased.[6]

If a preproposal conference is not being held, and you do not understand some part of the RFP, by all means contact the funding agency. The cover letter to most RFPs usually gives the phone number of the contract officer. Sometimes the phone number of the program officer is provided as well.

Many grantees hesitate to call or visit, either for fear they will ask a dumb question or because contacts this way may be regarded as unfair to the competition.

Actually, when the RFP is vague or incomplete (and this is frequently so), you should try to get as much help as possible from the grantors. You probably won't be asking a dumb question (assuming, of course, that you have read the RFP carefully). Nor do you need to worry about being unfair to competitors. That is the grantor's worry, and the competitors'!

If the information (or interpretation) you ask for is important, the grantors will probably give it to you and respect you for asking for it. They may also give it to your competitors in writing, in order to be fair. Or maybe they won't—in which case you will have an edge.

Only by understanding the project as completely as possible can you make the important decision of whether or not to apply.

Let Them Help You Write the Proposal

Once you decide to apply for a grant, program officers can be especially helpful. They can help you plan the project, review drafts of your proposal, and give you examples of successful proposals.

A university Spanish professor wanted to hold a conference that would bring together foreign-language experts from throughout the nation. The general theme of the meeting would be: What can we do to improve the American people's interest in and ability to speak languages other than English?

This was a timely topic, as the President's Commission on Foreign Languages had just issued a report on the problems caused by the American people's lack of capabilities in other languages (e.g., fewer business contracts abroad and a resulting deficit in the balance of trade). The commission had recommended that Congress introduce legislation to authorize and fund regional centers to improve the foreign-language-speaking interest and ability of the general public.

Going to his dean, the professor asked for $5,000 of "seed money" to hold the conference. He expected that then, if legislation were introduced to fund the regional centers, his university would be prepared to apply and would have an edge on the competition. Luckily, the dean did not have enough money. He promised $2,500 and suggested that the professor get the balance from outside sources.

The professor then went to his grant administrator, who invited a program officer from a state-funded public-policy council to come to the university and discuss the project with the professor. First, the professor described what he wanted to do and why. After listening carefully, the program officer spoke.

"It won't be necessary," he said, "for your university to contribute half the funds. My agency typically pays at least $7,000 to $10,000 for this sort of conference. We do require a contribution on your part. But it can be in-kind rather than the hard dollars you mentioned. For example, the costs of holding this meeting today can be counted—your time counts."

The program officer then went on to point out that some of the topics to be included in the conference were *not* important to his agency. Others—those that specifically related to public policy—were. He offered a step-by-step plan for developing the proposal: (1) review the legislation on foreign language; (2) identify the issues—what should be happening that isn't, what is happening that shouldn't be; (3) find public speakers on both sides of each issue; (4) back them up with academicians (historians, social scientists, philosophers) to defend their positions. He also suggested a way of tying the project in with the local educational television station, thereby attaining a wider audiencc.

Through further discussion, the program officer and the professor were able to identify a number of foreign language issues that were of mutual interest. The professor frankly pointed out that he still wanted the conference to include some topics that did not pertain directly to public policy.

An easy solution was reached. The program officer suggested that one day of the conference be scheduled for policy issues, the other for more general concerns. His agency should then be asked to fund the portion of special interest to it. This had been done successfully several times in the past.

Before leaving, the program officer had a final comment. "When you get your draft ready," he told the professor, "I'd be happy to review it and comment on it for you. Let's work together before you submit the formal proposal."

At the end of the meeting, the grant administrator thanked the program officer. "Would you be able to tell me," she asked, "about what the chances are for this proposal to be funded?"

"Excellent," he replied. "When our staff has the opportunity to discuss a project in advance, almost all the resulting proposals are funded. For those proposals that come to us without prior consultation, however, the rate is much lower; less than one of four is funded. You can see how important it is not to work in a vacuum."

Had the professor merely read the program guidelines and turned in his project as originally planned (an unscheduled mixture of public-policy and general-foreign-language issues), the proposal would almost certainly have been rejected. Instead, he had an excellent chance of success, help in designing and writing up the project, and a wider audience for his conference through television. He learned that he could reasonably ask for more money than he originally intended—and simultaneously save the $2,500 the dean had offered.

Naturally, the ability of grantors to provide this thorough kind of proposal development service varies. Few grantors, for example, will come to your organization to plan a project. (But never discount this as a possibility.) Almost all grantors will be available to meet with you at their agency and give you as many good ideas as possible, based on—of course—your original idea. Many grantors will review and critique a draft of your proposal, especially if you allow plenty of time before the formal proposal deadline. They will also tell you whether or not other projects similar to yours are being funded, who the project directors are, and how to contact them. If you ask, they will give you copies of successful proposals from prior years.

The key is—ASK. *Let* the grantors help you develop and package your idea so that it has the best chance to be funded. If the grantors are too busy, the worst that can happen is that they will say "no." They will still be glad that you thought enough of their expertise to talk to them. Usually, however, you will receive help and have a definite advantage over any of your competitors who relied on printed agency guidelines only.

Let Them Help You Ask for the Right Amount

The Spanish professor discovered that $2,500 was too little to ask for. Many times, however, would-be project directors want too much. They can't tell from the program guidelines how much money is available, so they plan a top-notch program that will cost far more than the sponsor can pay.

Before the project is developed, you should get some realistic range of funds that may be available. Usually, there are some printed clues. For example, you may be able to get a list of last year's awards, or the RFP or program announcement may refer to "man years" of effort. If there are no printed clues, the best approach is a direct one.

Call or visit the grantors. Ask approximately how much money they expect to award per grant (a high and a low range). They may not tell you, in which case you will not have really lost anything. Or they may—and then you will be ready to plan your project.

If they won't give you a dollar amount, talk to them about the project itself. What staff do they envision? Tell them what staff you are planning and ask for their reactions. Chances are you will learn what resources should be included in your budget, and then you can easily price them and ask for the right amount.

Let Them Advocate Your Proposal

Elliot Aronson, in his book *The Social Animal*, discusses many ways of persuading people to do what you want them to do. Based on results of social-psychological experiments, he advises, "If you want someone to form more positive attitudes toward an object, get him to commit himself to own that object."(7)

The implications are clear. If you can get program officers involved in the planning of your proposal, they can help you to get it funded. They can do this within their own agency. They can also take your proposal to other agencies.

"The easiest proposal I ever wrote," a grant administrator told the authors, "was a two-paragraph letter to one of the best-known private foundations in the country. Within two weeks, my college received a $25,000 award."

Why such a brief proposal? Here is the background. Several months earlier, the project director had submitted a proposal to a federal department. The proposal was for American economists to work with Mexican counterparts to collect and merge input-output commodities data at key U.S.-Mexico border locations. In addition to collecting the data, the project director wanted to hold binational seminars. A federal program officer had been invited to participate in the planning of this project, along with key representatives from Mexican organizations. A preproposal planning meeting had been held on the project director's campus, and the program officer was a key participant in the meeting. Once the proposal was submitted, the federal department provided over $200,000 for the data collection portion of the project. No funds were provided for the seminars.

To help out, the program officer (who was firmly committed to the entire project by this point) flew to New York and verbally obtained the $25,000 commitment for the binational seminars from the private foundation. All that was needed was an official letter asking for the money. Because the program officer had been involved early and believed in the project, she was willing to help get it funded by her own federal department and also to serve as an advocate to get support from another grantor.

Grantors can do this. They know who else is likely to be interested in your project. They can tell you about these possible sources of funding or give the extra effort to arrange for the funding themselves. Naturally, there must be a considerable amount of preliminary involvement before they are likely to do this. The case just described is rare, but it does happen. Never count on it—but always consider it a possibility that you can help make happen.

More commonly, program officers serve as advocates for your ideas within their own agencies. It is typically the program officer who selects the review panel for your proposal. If the right people are on this panel (those who will be most likely to favor your ideas), you will have a better chance of being funded.

Several years ago, an information systems professor submitted a proposal to study computer reports: How could they be formatted so that they would be best understood by different personalities? Some people, for example, might be most comfortable with columns of numbers; others might easily read graphs; and still others might prefer written words. The idea was that businesses and education can use the computer to provide information the way most compatible with employees' personalities. Naturally, there would have to be a cost benefit involved, so the study would also investigate the effectiveness of decisions based on various computer report formats.

The proposal was rejected.

Later, the grant administrator talked about the proposal with the program officer, who pinpointed the problem immediately.

"This was a well-written proposal," he said, "on an interesting idea. The study, however, involved elements of both 'hard' science (computer report formats) and 'soft' science (personality traits). The reviewers were hard scientists only."

"Please," he continued, "encourage Professor X to resubmit. I'll arrange for reviewers with both hard and soft science backgrounds to evaluate the next proposal."

It is especially important that research proposals be reviewed by persons with the appropriate scientific background. Program officers can make this happen.

Sometimes you may have better ideas about who is qualified to review your proposal than the program officer does. If so, recommend these potential reviewers, either in your proposal or in discussions with the program officer. You can even tell the program officer whom you *don't* want on your review panel. An NSF program officer, on being asked how grantees could use their contacts with her effectively, said "To seek useful information—when are review meetings held, who is involved, suggestions as to either appropriate or *inappropriate* reviewers."

In addition to using the right reviewers, the program officer can be an advocate for your proposal by giving you resources at his or her disposal. Although the complete funding of your project will usually depend on favorable review by others as well as the program officer, there may be an opportunity for partial support from the program officer alone.

Two young natural scientists proposed to study the origins of life by collecting samples from the Red Sea. Because neither had a track record of successful research, and because their idea was so novel, their proposal was rejected.

Fortunately, they were not discouraged. They didn't give up, as inexperienced researchers are likely to do. Instead, they telephoned the program officer, explained fully the implications of their research, and asked for any help available, even if it was less than they had asked for. The program officer, intrigued with their research idea and enthusiasm, managed to get them round-trip airplane tickets from the West Coast to Egypt and 30-day passage on an oceanographic research vessel in the Red Sea.

"Officially," their proposal had been turned down. "Unofficially," they were given the resources they needed to begin their study.

Let Them Give You Advance Information

By making calls at funding agencies, "You generally learn of impending procurements far in advance of the time you would have if you waited for the CBD [*Commerce Business Daily*] to advise you,"[8] according to Holtz.

Finding out what a particular funding agency will be doing next month or next year is just as important as finding out whether or not this agency is interested in what you want to do. By asking program officers what their plans are, you can find out about (1) new programs that will be advertised, including deadline dates and funding levels, and (2) end-of-year money that will be available for supplements to existing projects or small new projects.

If you know, for example, that the guidelines for the Department of Education Citizens' Education Program are scheduled to be printed in the *Federal Register* at the beginning of next month, that the deadline will be 30 days later, and that there are no changes from last year's program guidelines, you can start developing your project ahead of others.

Or if you learn that the Peace Corps will be advertising in the *CBD* for six training programs in Latin America next spring, and you get the details about each of these programs before the RFPs come out, you can make some intelligent decisions about which program(s) you can best compete for.

Grantors realize that solicitations in the *CBD* and regulations in the *Federal Register* are commonly published very close to the official deadline for proposal receipt. Since they want to receive the best proposals possible, they will usually give you advance information.

Let Them Create an RFP Based on Your Idea

If you discover that grantors *don't* have plans for future programs, or that the plans they do have are vague, here is an opportunity for you to help them by telling them about your ideas and showing how these fit into the general mission of their agency. You can also provide materials that will assist the program officer in preparing an RFP. If your idea is so specialized that you and your organization are probably the only ones capable of carrying it out, the RFP may be justified as a "sole source" procurement. Although there would be negotiation over cost, there would be no competition. You would receive the award.

Even if the RFP were advertised, who else would be as prepared as you to respond? Who would know the RFP was coming out?

The authors know of a $1.9-million "open" solicitation. As required, it was advertised in the *CBD.* Not unexpectedly, only one organization responded. The RFP was received in the successful bidder's offices at 4:00 P.M. on a Tuesday.

The proposal was due in the grantor agency by 3:00 P.M. on Thursday of that same week. Of course, the successful bidders knew that the RFP would be arriving and had already written their proposal. Other organizations could not have received the RFP any sooner. How could they possibly have submitted a competitive proposal?

That RFP might as well have been a sole source procurement. Because of the timing, only the grantee organization that had been in on the planning (and knew the solicitation was coming) could compete.

Let Them Solve Potential Problems before the Award

Sometimes potential problems occur after the proposal is submitted and before it is officially awarded. If you talk to grantor officials, these problems may, in many cases, be resolved. If you remain silent, waiting until after the award, it may be too late to solve the problems.

At a large teaching college, a young faculty member applied for funding to do an archaeological project in Yugoslavia. He was excited about the proposed project and seemed confident that he would receive an award. He applied in September, and throughout the year, as the college grant administrator saw him occasionally in the campus cafeteria, the faculty member would say that he was expecting to hear from the granting agency any day now. The grant administrator hadn't seen any award documents but shared her friend's enthusiasm.

Late in May, the award had not arrived. But the young professor came into the grant administrator's office one Friday and informed her that he had ordered the van that was budgeted in the proposal. He said that the van would be in on Tuesday, and that he would be putting the down payment on the van with his personal check. "You can pay me back as soon as the grant comes in," he told the administrator.

Well, you can imagine how quickly the grant administrator got on the phone to find out (1) whether there really was going to be an award and (2) how soon the effective date could be. Fortunately, there was going to be an award. Unfortunately, the starting date would be July 1.

When the grant administrator informed the grantor representative of the van problem, the grantor official agreed to change the effective date to the date the down payment was to be made on the van. Getting the earlier starting date negotiated was crucial to the success of this project. Since the faculty member needed to get the van to Yugoslavia by July 1 for use during the summer archaeological dig, the lead time for purchase of this equipment was necessary. The earlier start date was also crucial to the personal finances of the faculty member. Had he purchased the van before the effective date, he would have been out the money he planned to spend on it, since the funding-agency regulations would have prevented the grant administrator from reimbursing him for any purchases prior to the effective date of the award.

When the grant administrator contacted the grant officer before the award, the problem was easily eliminated. Had the grant administrator waited, the official award would have carried a July 1 starting date—and the project director would have lost $6,000!

Let Them Tell You Why You Didn't Win

When you consider the energy and money that go into writing proposals, it is amazing that all rejected proposal writers do not routinely follow up on their investment by finding out why they weren't funded. Yet it is the exception, rather than the rule, for unsuccessful proposal writers to ask for evaluations of their proposals.

You are entitled to do this under the Freedom of Information Act. You can also request copies of successful proposals and the evaluations of these as well as of your own proposal. The funding agency must make these available to you within 10 days.

After you have read the printed materials, it is especially helpful to request a debriefing from the grantor representative(s) who was involved in the review process. This can be done in a meeting (if you are located near the grantor or have a healthy travel budget) or by telephone. The importance of a debriefing is that often you will learn things informally that could not be included in the more official, printed proposal-review records.

In California, a first-time proposal submitter was rejected. He felt that his demonstration plan to help mentally retarded preschoolers was so important that he wasn't going to give up. He called the Bureau of Education for the Handicapped program officer in charge of his proposal review and asked why he had been turned down. He learned that the reviewers had liked his idea, but the proposal had not been written well enough.

The proposal submitter polished up the writing and submitted it the next year. Again, it was rejected. Disappointed but still determined, he checked back with the program officer. This time, the proposal had come very close to being funded. Only minor modifications were needed, and the program was fully funded for the next three years.

A rejected proposal, like a novel or an invention, is not necessarily a poor idea. It is an investment of time and money that should be carefully reviewed in every aspect before it is discarded. One or two rejections should never discourage anyone with an original project.

Let Them Help You Negotiate the Best Deal

"They want me to do my project this year for $25,000," a project director complained to the grant administrator. "That won't even cover my salary!" The project director had received what he thought was a take-it-or-leave-it offer to continue his regional dissemination of Teacher Corps materials.

"Have you talked to the program officer?" asked the grant administrator.

"No, but my colleagues who are doing this program in other parts of the country tell me that they are being held to last year's funding levels."

"Oh," said the grant administrator. "Well, then, how did you do it for $25,000 last year?"

"Last year I was on sabbatical," replied the project director. "We didn't put any charges for my salary in the grant because the university was paying me and I was free to spend all my time on the grant."

Armed with this information, the grant administrator called to enlist the grant officer's help. He explained why the program had been such a bargain last year and was able to negotiate a more reasonable take-it-or-leave-it offer of $40,000.

By contacting the grantors, the grantees were able to negotiate a better deal. It rarely hurts to ask for help, if you can give good reasons.

Let Them Help You Get More for Less

Spending money is basically a grantee responsibility. But sometimes grantors can help. In Chapter 6, there were numerous ideas for enlisting grantor assistance, for example how to get free supplies, find excess property, get access to federal telephone lines and GSA purchasing, and borrow equipment.

A grant administrator was finalizing a contract with an Agency for International Development (AID) grant officer for a 30-day program to train 50 visiting Brazilian educators in facilities planning. The Brazilians spoke Portuguese; the American trainers spoke English. There was money in the budget for an interpreter, but none for translation equipment.

"Don't you have any of this equipment at your university?" asked the grant officer.

"No," replied the grant administrator, "and we can't afford to buy it for this one program."

Once he knew about the problem, the AID grant officer was able to help. He contacted a U.S. State Department colleague and arranged for a temporary loan of some far more sophisticated equipment than the university could have managed to buy.

If the grantors know what you need, they may be able to help. But they will know only if you tell them.

Let Them Help You Avoid Under-, Over-, and Unallowable Expenditures

When asked, "How have you used contacts with sponsor program officers or grant officers to get and spend grant and contract dollars more effectively?" a grant administrator answered, "To free up pending extensions, renewals, and awards; to get approval for cost changes and increases; and to get support for rule interpretations favoring the objectives of my projects."

When asked "How could grantees use their contacts with you to get and spend grant and contract dollars more effectively?" a grant officer replied, "By checking things out ahead of time. It's better for them to ask a silly question than to go ahead and do something that can cause them extra expense or a disallowance."

Clearly, grantors want to be asked. Once they are, they can help you by (1) *moving* papers faster; (2) *approving* requests; and (3) *consulting* to prevent possible disallowances.

The "moving" may even involve physical effort. Several years ago, when the federal fiscal vear ended June 30. a grant administrator visited an Office of Education grants management office in early June. Her specific purpose was to find out whether a certain grant officer even existed. For a month, she had tried to contact him by phone. He was (reportedly) always "on the other line," but he never returned her calls.

Three months earlier she had requested approval to transfer funds from the equipment category of a Bureau of Education for the Handicapped (BEH) grant into the salary category. Because the grant period ended in two months, it was critical that she talk with him. Every week of delayed response meant that the opportunity to spend hundreds of salary dollars was lost.

On entering the Grants Management Office, the grant administrator knew exactly what had happened. Stacks of proposal files, approximately knee high, covered most of the floor in the long narrow room. She had to pick her way past 20 or so grant officers' desks before reaching the grant officer she had been trying to contact.

Sure enough, her grant officer *was* "on the other line." The massive onslaught of proposals to be awarded before the end of the fiscal year had clogged the whole grants management system. There were not nearly enough people, phone lines, file cabinets, or even floor space to handle the work load.

This particular grant administrator, however, came away successful. After finishing his phone negotiation, the real-live and actually friendly grant officer physically moved and sorted through nine stacks of proposals before coming to her file. Once he had "moved" the paperwork on, the final approval was simple. The man with signature authority was sitting on a stack of awards outside the door to his office. He couldn't get inside until the files were moved, so he was glad to sign off for her.

In this case, the papers would not have moved, nor the request been approved, without personal contact!

Another way that grantors can help is by consulting to prevent unallowable expenditures. If you are designing new systems or procedures that may affect the allowability of grant expenditures, it often makes good sense to discuss your plans with auditors or grantor officials before installing the systems or initiating the procedures. The alternative is to defend them afterwards, when you may or may not be able to prove that what you did was right. Either way, you lose, because you will have to spend valuable staff time and effort in preparing your defense.

Auditors, like doctors, should not be "after" people. They should not always have to diagnose your problem; far better that they tell you ahead of time what to do to prevent it.

If you are not sure whether a particular cost item is allowable, call your grant officer and ask. If you are not sure if a particular system of accounting for efforts on grants is acceptable, call your auditor and ask. If the paperwork isn't moving, call (or visit) the grantors to help it along. Contacts with grantor representatives are an excellent insurance against making over-, under-, and unallowable expenditures.

Let Them Help You with Cash Management

Grantors, like grantees, can accumulate paperwork overloads. When this happens, your invoices may be moving very slowly. If this becomes a recurrent problem, or if there is a great deal of money at stake, you should ask for help.

Probably, you won't know the grantor account clerk who processes your invoices. This clerk is usually working on a "first-in, first-out" basis, so your check won't be prepared until the clerk has taken care of those ahead of you.

If the delay is hurting your organization or the work on your grant, you should contact your grantor representatives. Usually, the grant officer will be able to help you unclog the paperwork. There may even be a way to simplify the accounting work to accomplish your main goal of getting paid sooner.

One grantee organization, for example, was experiencing six-month delays in receiving payment from the Department of Defense. When the organization enlisted the help of the grantor's grant officer, they discovered that the delays were caused by the way the invoices were being prepared. The grantee's clerk was presenting a great deal more detail on the invoices than necessary. Then, the clerk who received the invoices had to recalculate all the details to come up with some broader cost categories for payment purposes. Everyone was pleased and the invoices moved much more quickly once the grantee's clerk simplified the invoices.

The "Politics" of Contacts

So far we have talked about the many ways that grantors can help you when you contact them. This poses the question: Who contacts whom? When? And how?

"There are things you officially know, and things you officially don't know but know anyway," a project director with over 20 years of experience told us.

He was referring to the formal and informal lines of communication that are very much a part of the grant-spending game.

Formal Lines of Communication

Although the formal lines of communication seem simple enough, sometimes even experienced project directors ignore them. Basically, any official communication regarding grant spending should be handled as shown in Figure 37.

Usually, in the first three contacts, information is sought. For example, the project director asks the grant administrator (through the grant officer to the program officer) for approval to change some part of the work scope or to spend money in a different way than intended originally. In the last three contacts, the information is sent back: "Yes, you can do what you wanted to," or "No, you can't." The answer must go through the grant officer and the grant administrator to the project director.

Sometimes the opposite is true, with the information being sought by the program officer and given by the project director—again, through the intermediaries. For example, the program officer may want an interim report on the technical progress of the project. In this case, the numbering of the communications is reversed.

The important point is, *any communication regarding obtaining or spending grant funds must go through all these channels in order to be official.*

There are two drawbacks to formal communication. First, it is obviously time-consuming. Sometimes it takes several months for the project director to receive information from the program officer (or vice versa). This is especially true if letters, instead of phone calls or meetings, are used. Worse yet, the original communication is subject to misinterpretation at each stage. The message that the project director intends for the program officer may not be clear even when it finally arrives.

The project director of an AID technical assistance project had the opportunity to hire a nationally recognized educational facilities planner to help Brazilian secondary-school personnel design schools. A special advantage was that the planner spoke Portuguese. AID approval was required, and the project director dutifully went through formal channels. Three months after the nomination papers were submitted to AID (via the grant administrator, via the grant

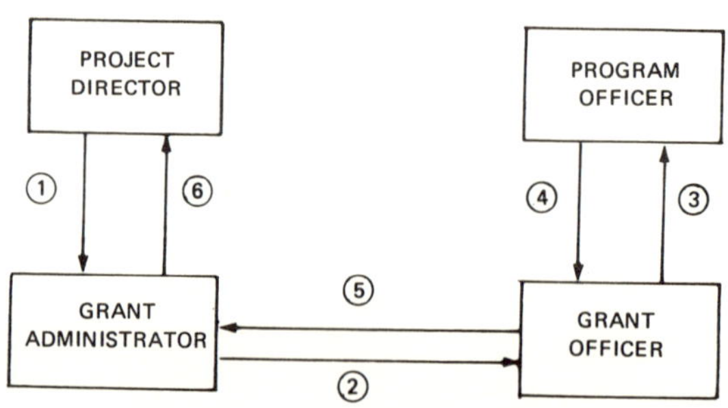

Figure 37. Formal communication.

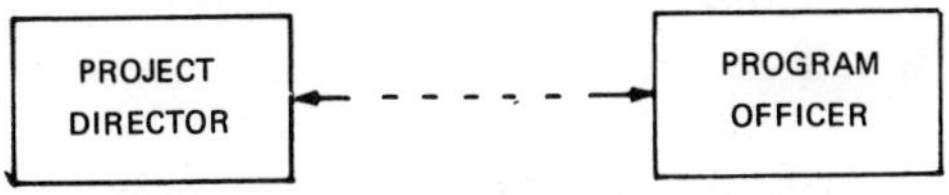

Figure 38. Informal communication.

officer, to the program officer), the appropriate approval came back (via the grant officer, via the grant administrator, to the project director).

By then, the nominee had tired of waiting and had found another job. The project had three months of unspent salaries and related costs that could not be carried over to the next grant period. The project director's original message ("This is a great guy; let's rush the paperwork to get him approved") might as well have been in Portuguese.

It is easy to see why informal communications are needed!

Informal Lines of Communication

Informal lines of communication are commonly used, especially by experienced project directors, and look like Figure 38.

There are several advantages to informal communications. Usually, they are verbal (through a phone call or a meeting), and thus, only one contact is needed. Also, there is far less opportunity for the project director to misunderstand the program officer's message, and vice versa. More exchange is possible.

There is a drawback, however. No matter what the program officer and the project director agree to do informally, if it involves the expenditure of grant funds (or a change of work scope) and is not officially approved, the grantees may lose money. Or the project's work scope may ultimately be affected.

For instance, an aerospace engineering faculty member got together with a vice-president of research (same as a program officer) at a local aerospace firm. The faculty member agreed to do weapons research at the firm's headquarters for 50% of his time during the fall semester. He started in September, without getting the usual institutional approvals. Two months later, a contract arrived on campus. The grant administrator could not accept it because it called for classified research to be done, and campus policy prohibited this. The university missed the opportunity to do joint research with local industry, the faculty member lost the equivalent of a month's pay, and the project was scuttled in mid-term.

In many cases, it is the program officer who unintentionally misleads the project director. The program officer may say that it is okay to spend money in another way than originally planned, or that supplemental funds will be coming so it's okay to spend at a higher rate, and so forth. This is all verbal, of course, and if the project director acts on this advice without getting official backup, problems can and often do occur. The program officer, like the project director, is mainly concerned with getting the research or service done, and not with the regulations. As a result, either the project director or the program officer may unwittingly agree on actions that may lead to unrecoverable or, later on, disallowed costs.

So how *should* contacts be made? Ideally, communications between grantors and grantees should contain a healthy mix of formal and informal contacts.

Recommended Lines of Communication

To speed the process along, and to ensure that program officers understand project directors' messages (and vice versa), normally the first line of communication is informal. The project director discusses a request or problem with the program officer. Once they agree on a course of action, if grant spending is involved, a formal request is initiated by the project director. The process is shown in Figure 39.

Had this mix of formal and informal communications been used to speed up the employment of the Portuguese-speaking educational facilities planner for the AID project, the outcome could have been considerably different. And the next time an employee was hired for that project, it was.

That time, before preparing the official nomination papers, the project director called his program officer at AID. "Here's the background of the person we want to hire," he said, reading off key qualifications from the résumé. "Will you approve this appointment?"

During the next two days, the program officer did some informal checking of her own, some of it with AID and Brazilian personnel in Rio de Janeiro. As a result, she called the project director back. "Your man is acceptable to the people he will be working with," she said, "and I will see that the paperwork gets processed expeditiously. Meanwhile, it's perfectly okay for you to hire him. You have my word that the appointment will be approved, and we want him to get started."

At this point, the project director went to his grant administrator and explained the verbal okay. The grant administrator, based on eight years of experience with this particular project and the grantor personnel, allowed the immediate employment and meanwhile started the formal paperwork. It was a calculated risk, of course, that somehow the approval might fall through. The alternative, however, was not a risk at all. If the appointment didn't take place immediately, the ability to spend some of the grant money (and collect the associated indirect funds) would have been lost.

Usually, the combination of informal followed by formal contacts as just described is sufficient. Sometimes, however, if problems need to be resolved immediately, or if they are especially complex, informal communication takes place between other parties than the program officer and the project director. The program officer and the grant officer may talk informally; the grant officer

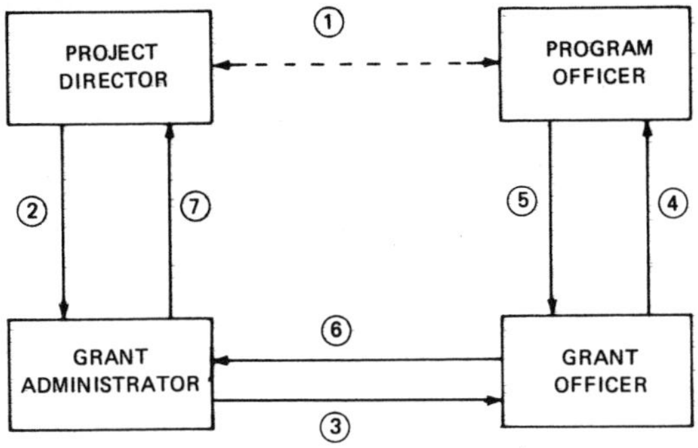

Figure 39. Recommended communication.

and the grant administrator may talk informally; and the grant administrator and the project director may do the same. For example, if the grant administrator had not had experience with the AID program and personnel, he might have informally called the AID grant officer and done some further checking before allowing the nominated employee to be hired. The formal contacts must still take place afterwards, but at least, all parties have as much information as possible to base decisions on.

Inappropriate Lines of Communication

You may have noticed that there were no diagonal lines of communication in the formal and informal networks just depicted. At an institute on federally sponsored grants, Perry Hendricks advised the participating grant administrators, "Generally, let them [faculty] handle the contacts with the program officer (project monitor, technical officer, etc.). . . . You handle the contracting officer, grant administrator, etc."(9)

Usually, diagonal communications, such as those depicted in Figure 40, are inappropriate. Project directors and grant officers don't communicate; grant administrators and program officers don't either.

When asked "How could project directors use their contacts with you to get and spend grant dollars more effectively?" a federal grant officer answered emphatically, "NOT me. They should work with their institutional sponsored research officer, business officer, or whatever."

Nor do program officers communicate with grant administrators. "I don't normally have contacts with grantee institutional officers," remarked a program officer from a large federal agency. "I deal with the project directors."

Typically, program officers and grant administrators don't do business together, nor do project directors and grant officers. Most of them prefer it that way.

Occasionally, however, there are appropriate exceptions. During a grant

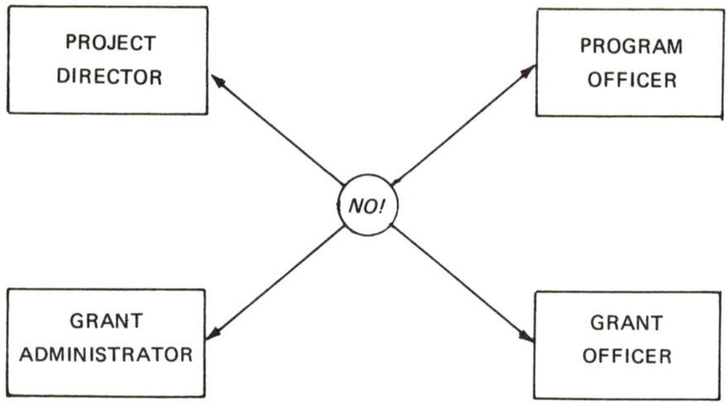

Figure 40. Inappropriate communication (usually).

negotiation, for example, usually all parties are present, and there is productive communication among them. During the project period, if there is a visit by the program officer, usually both the project director and the grant administrator are present, for at least part of the time. (This is for courtesy, rather than business reasons.) Also, if the grantee is located at a distance from the grantor, the grant administrator may make calls to the program officer, on behalf of the project director. This is usually done when the grant administrator is visiting a number of grantor agencies, to save travel funds.

Finally, those grant administrators who have responsibility for *developing* grants do legitimately communicate directly with program officers for business purposes. This is all, however, *before* a project starts. By making these contacts, the grant administrator is performing a service to potential project directors and to program officers—helping to get them together. Willner and Hendricks[10] emphasize the importance of the grant administrators' finding out from program officers what grantor funding priorities are—and then matching these priorities to the project directors' interests.

So these are the usual lines of communication. Now the question is "When do you use them?"

When to Make Contacts

As already noted, grantees should contact grantors when help is needed. Just as important, you should contact them when you *don't* need their help.

Do you thank them on receiving an award? Do you let them know when particularly interesting events or results occur during the project? Do you invite them to participate in special events? Do you send them copies of journal articles, newsclippings, or other publicity about your (and *their*) project? If you are in their city on business, do you stop by to give them a status report? Do you thank them after the project is over?

It is just as rewarding to contact grantors to provide them with information and appreciation as it is to let them know about problems.

Depending on the relationship you establish with the grantors, it may also be appropriate to contact them just to be sociable. If you have developed a friendship and enjoy talking about nongrant as well as grant matters, you may want to invite them to lunch or to play racquetball when you (or they) are in town.

You don't even have to be in the same city. One California-based university research administrator carries on a long-distance chess game with a program officer at a large Washington funding agency. They each keep a chess board set up in their 3,000-mile-distant offices and phone the moves back and forth from time to time. Of course, business can take place in the phone calls as well, but the communication lines are open and are probably used more frequently than if there were no chess moves to make.

A project director we know enjoys sailing, as does his program officer. Whenever the program officer comes to town, he stays at the project director's house, and they always spend at least one afternoon on a catamaran in the bay.

Whether your contacts take place when you need help, when you give information or thanks, or when you just want to enjoy each other's company, they will probably be more effective if you make them *early*. This is especially important if you are asking for help. Don't wait until the last minute, when the problem has grown out of proportion; it may be too late for the grantors to solve it.

A program officer was asked, "How can grantees use their contacts with you to help them?" He stressed the importance of timing, answering, "By bringing problems to my attention *early,* so that some arrangement can be made to deal with them—especially with respect to budget changes."

The PI of an international economics research project did just that. His grant's work scope required that data collected in the United States be merged with data collected in Mexico. Because of political problems in Mexico, the research there was suspended. Knowing that he would be unable to complete his study on schedule, the PI notified the program officer of the problem. The program officer was able to extend the time for performance of the grant and also to get a $37,000 supplement to cover the costs of the delay. There was no rush or pressure involved, since the PI told the program officer of the problem six months before the original termination date of the grant. There was ample time for both informal and formal communications in order to arrive at a solution of the problem.

Even if your contacts are made to express appreciation, to provide information, or just to be sociable, they are likely to be more effective if made early. For example, if someone thanks you spontaneously right after receiving a gift, it usually conveys more appreciation than a thank you note a month later. If someone gives you information at the time an event of interest to you is happening, or shortly thereafter, you feel more a part of the action than if the news is "warmed over" and perhaps gets to you after you've already heard it from other sources. And finally, if someone is arranging to have lunch or play tennis with you, you need to make room for it on your social calendar; the plans must be made ahead of time. We all react this way in day-to-day dealings with other people, and—as emphasized throughout this book—grantors are people (and busy people). They will appreciate being given the consideration you would want yourself.

The "when" of contacting grantors is really quite simple:

1. Contact grantors when you need help.
2. Contact grantors to give thanks and information.
3. Contact grantors to be sociable (as appropriate).
4. Contact them early.

When Not to Make Contacts

Before contacting grantors to get help, be sure that you really need it. Grantors have many demands on their time. They are usually happy to work with you when their assistance is required but prefer you to screen out problems that should be handled by your organization.

"We depend heavily on the university-sponsored research administrator and believe that the PI should deal through that person rather than coming to us with every little thing. It's sad, but true, that we just can't take the individualized interest in every project or every question. It's not that we're not interested; it's rather that we don't have the time with 1,200 staff to award 13,000 grants a year and monitor over 30,000 active awards and review over 25,000 proposals in one year," a grant officer said.

The grant administrator should be thoroughly familiar with the regulations governing various grants. Usually, these regulations allow some degree of latitude in resolving grant problems. For example, it may be possible for the grant administrator and the project director together to agree to a transfer of funds between cost categories, as long as this transfer does not exceed some regulated amount.

So Rule Number One is "Don't contact grantors to ask for help when you can handle the problem yourselves."

Neither should you contact grantors too frequently over the same problem. Once you have called it to their attention and asked for help, allow the grantors a reasonable amount of time to work on the problem, and don't keep bothering them about it. A grant officer told us that her biggest complaint about grantees was "Pushiness–lack of cooperation. They fail to send items in on time and then call to say 'Where's my grant approval?' when it's been on my desk one day."

Rule Number Two? If you do ask grantors for help, don't be pushy about getting it.

Sometimes, however, a problem is so urgent or unusual that heavy and frequent contact is necessary. You may have to ask the grantors to do special favors for you (bend the rules) in order to resolve the problem. Experienced grants professionals have probably done this at one time or another. The key is to know when *not* to do it. Save your requests for special favors for a few occasions of real importance.

A college grant administrator had to decide whether or not to ask for special favors for two project directors. Each of them had the same problem: they needed an award to be back-dated. The two awards were being granted by the same agency.

The circumstances surrounding these problems were different. In one case, an experienced project director had a history of submitting proposals too late to be funded as early as he wanted to start his projects. This project director had been informally assured by the program officer that his late proposal could be processed by March 1, but it wasn't. The project director started his project anyway, without telling the grant administrator. Then, at the end of the month, wanting to be paid, he notified the grant administrator of the delayed award and asked him to get the grantors to back-date it.

In the other case, an inexperienced faculty member applied for his grant early. He naively requested a starting date (July 1) that was when he wanted the actual work on his project to begin. He did not allow the month of planning time (hiring help, getting equipment purchased, and so forth) that would be necessary for the project to succeed. The project was to take place overseas, so this lead time was especially critical. Arrangements had been finalized with the U.S. embassy abroad for work to start July 1. During June, the faculty member made purchases with his own money, expecting to be repaid once the grant came in. Fortunately, he told the grant administrator what he had done before the official award was received.

The grant administrator decided to ask for a back-dated award for the inexperienced faculty member. He was confident the problem would not occur again, now that the faculty member understood the importance of the starting date. For the experienced faculty member, however, the grant administrator did not ask for a back-dated award. In this case, no harm would be done to the project by waiting. Also, he did not want to reinforce undesirable behavior on the part of the project director (submitting the proposals late, collaborating with the program officer without keeping the grant administrator informed, and starting the project on his own before the grant was received).

The special favor was granted for the international project. Had the grant administrator also tried to get a back-date on the other project, it probably would have been refused, since it was mainly for the convenience of the project director. It might have jeopardized the chances of the other request, since agency policy was to discourage frequent back-dating and to allow it only under specially justified circumstances.

Rule Number Three of when not to make contacts is this: Don't use contacts with grantors to ask for special favors or hurry-ups unless the problem is urgent and you can justify your request.

When your contact with grantors is to provide information or thanks, rather than to ask for help, there are still rules to follow. If you are meeting with grantors, don't come without something to say. Once you have said what you planned to, don't linger. Usually, a meeting should last between a half hour and an hour if it's for an information-sharing purpose. Sometimes 15 minutes is long enough.

Rule Number Four is very simple: Don't make contacts that waste grantors' time.

The last rule of when not to make contacts is this: Don't make contacts that may place grantors in an awkward position, either (1) by putting grantors in an apparent conflict-of-interest situation or (2) by asking them to do something illegal.

An apparent conflict of interest could occur because of social contacts. If you are too buddy-buddy with the grantors, if too many good projects come your way, and especially if you pay for all the wining and dining and so forth that you and the grantors do together, you may be creating the appearance, at least, of a conflict of interest. Most grantors are sensitive about this. Some will not even allow you to pay for a lunch! Others accept lunches graciously but would balk at a larger investment on your part. Grantor agency rules vary on this, so it is best to work with grantors to decide when it is and is not appropriate for you to pay. If you know them well enough, you can simply ask.

One grant administrator, for example, has worked out a comfortable arrangement with a grant officer. Whenever she is in Washington, she enjoys having lunch with him. It is mainly a friendship rather than a grant-talk lunch, although some business inevitably transpires. The arrangement they have agreed to is a rotating one: one time she pays, the next time he does.

Social contacts can be both enjoyable and productive. Whenever you make them, be considerate of the grantors and avoid allowing even the appearances of a conflict of interest.

Nor would you want to put grantors (or yourself) in an awkward position by asking them to do something illegal. For example, a key period in any contract solicitation is the time after the procurement is announced and before it is awarded. Grantors must be especially careful to treat all possible applicants fairly, and often the only contact permissible is through the grant officer. Yet, direct communication with the program officer would certainly be helpful. You need to be sensitive to the rules of the particular agency you are working with. Once you understand these rules, however, they may work to your advantage.

For example, a contract of close to a million dollars was being advertised. The project had been conducted by University X for over 10 years, but because the funding was so high, each year a solicitation had to be issued and competition encouraged.

The director of the ongoing project asked his secretary to arrange for a meeting with the program officer to discuss the *new procurement.* The request was huffily denied by the program officer, a military man who was especially sensitive to "the book." His agency allowed no contact between program people and prospective applicants during the procurement period.

Not to be discouraged, the project director decided to use "the book" to help him. The current project had some administrative problems: program officers were supposed to work with grantees to provide ongoing support; shouldn't he ask for a meeting with the program officer to discuss *ongoing project concerns?*

He did, and the program officer was quite willing to meet *on that basis.* Rather than asking the program officer to do something illegal (meet with a prospective applicant), the project director had now asked the program officer to do his job (help the director of an ongoing project). At the beginning of the meeting, the program officer carefully established its purpose. Once that was accomplished, he proceeded to help with the ongoing project by suggesting remedies for the current problems. Not surprisingly, these remedies were implemented immediately, and the results were described in the proposal for the next year's project. University X won the contract.

To sum up, you should be sensitive to the times it is *not* appropriate to make contacts with grantors. This will vary among agencies, but the basic ground rules have been given.

1. Don't contact grantors for help unnecessarily.
2. If you do ask for help, don't contact grantors too frequently about the same problem.
3. Don't contact grantors to ask for hurry-ups or special favors unless the problem is urgent. Limit your extraordinary requests.
4. Don't waste grantor's time by contacting them when you have nothing to say or by staying too long when you do.
5. Don't make contacts that may place grantors in an awkward position, either by putting grantors in an apparent conflict-of-interest situation or by asking them to do something that is illegal (or that might give the appearance of illegality).

How to Make Contacts

Throughout this chapter, there has been evidence of good things that happened because grantees contacted grantors. A university received a $1.9 million contract without any competition. Two young natural scientists did research on a scientific vessel in the Red Sea (even though their project had been officially turned down). An archaeologist was permitted to start his Yugoslavia project early and so was reimbursed for a $6,000 van he would have had to pay for himself. A Spanish professor discovered that he could get more money than he expected and have a great deal of help in writing his proposal. Economists were given an extra six months and $37,000 to merge their data with those of Mexican counterparts. And more!

If you have been in the grants business awhile, you will recall incidents like these. If you are new, you may be thinking, "Yes, but *how* does all this happen? You have to 'know someone' to get started. How do you get to the point where you're sailing and playing chess with the grantors? If you aren't, will grantors help you the way the authors of this book say they will? How can I possibly ask someone to lunch when I'm afraid to pick up the phone and call them?"

If you are thinking along those lines, you should be encouraged to know that some of the incidents just reported were "cold." The PIs who went to the Red Sea and the Spanish professor had never before contacted the helping grantors, or any other grantors, for that matter. These were their first experiences in seeking funds.

Another "cold" contact was worth $92,000 to a reading specialist. She had developed a program to teach basic skills to prisoners. When she heard that there might be some money available from the state department of adult education, she asked her grant administrator to arrange for a meeting in the capital city with the program officer. (Since she had never applied for a grant before, she asked the grant administrator to go with her.)

As it turned out, the man she needed to see was on location in her city. His secretary contacted him, and he agreed to meet with the reading specialist and the grant administrator at their office.

"I'm here," he said, as he entered the room, "but I don't know what you could possibly want from me."

The reading specialist nervously admitted that she wanted his money!

From that inauspicious beginning, the meeting grew specific. It turned out that the adult-education-program deadline had been the previous Friday. The reading specialist talked about her project anyway. Because the program officer became so interested in it, he mentioned that he had one set of application forms left in his car. If she would walk him to the parking lot, he would give her the forms and a one-week extension of the deadline.

Two months later, the reading specialist received a $92,000 grant, and the latest word is that the program officer called to ask her to apply for a $15,000 supplement.

As this example demonstrates, all grantees (experienced and inexperienced) can make effective contacts. You don't have to know someone. If you need help, you just have to ask. You can do this in meetings or in phone calls, or by writing and then following up with a meeting or a phone call. Contacts are that simple when you are asking for assistance.

When you are not asking for specific assistance, when you want to build relationships that lead to long-term networks of support and friendship, then the contacts are not so simple. You are not a phone call away. But there are many easy ways to get started. The list can be as lengthy as you are creative. Common ways that grants professionals have *established, maintained,* and *expanded* relationships with grantors follow.

Schedule a First Meeting at the Grantor's Office. "Federal funding agencies encourage consultations on applications either by telephone or by personal visits," writes Virginia White, in a section of her book entitled "How to Interact with the Funding Organization."[(11)]

Many granting agencies are located in Washington. Others are in your state capital or hometown. Even if you live far away from Washington, if your organization does (or hopes to do) business with the federal government, it's important for you to go there and meet personally with grantors. You can arrange your appointments so that you see six to eight people in one day. Usually one half hour is enough time for a first meeting—an hour at most.

How do you make the appointments? Usually it's best to send a letter, describing the nature of your business first. Then, you or your secretary can arrange for a meeting by phone. If your organization belongs to a professional group that supports an office in Washington (or your state capital), usually a staff member in that office will schedule your meetings.

For example, staff at the Office of Federal Programs (OFP) of the American Association of State Colleges and Universities will arrange appointments for OFP participants. Frequently, state university and college systems have Washington offices, as do many community college districts.

If you want to meet with a private or corporate foundation official, it will probably be more difficult. They are not noted, as are government officials, for an "open-door" policy. Instead, according to Koch, they seem to work on a " 'mushroom' theory: things grow best in the dark."(12) It's difficult to find out whom to see and what kinds of support may be available to grantees.

If you want to schedule meetings with private or corporate officials, try asking first. If you are refused, you may need to ask colleagues who already have established contacts to get you in.

For example, a director of nursing in the Los Angeles area wanted to get support from a national private foundation. (We'll call it White.) She tried in vain to meet appropriate White officials. Then a colleague at Hospital N told her that White was funding a program there. The colleague invited her to visit when White officials came to do their annual review of the Hospital N project. As a result, the director of nursing established contact with White officials and within a year had her own program funded for $110,000.

Serve on a Grantor Proposal-Review Panel. Most grantors establish proposal-review panels. They want experts from outside their agencies to read proposals and help make funding decisions. Sometimes, grantors pay people to do this; $100 per day is typical. At the very least, they will pay travel and per diem expenses when the review takes place away from your home. If you serve on a review panel, you will get to know and work with grantors. As a bonus, you will understand the proposal-review process better.

If you are well known in your academic field, you will probably be invited to serve on a review panel at some time or other during your career. In other cases, grantors put out a printed call for applications for review service. Anyone can apply. If you want to be on a panel, it's best not to wait for either an invitation or printed application forms. Instead, let program officers know that you are interested. Give them your résumé, along with a letter offering to help.

Be an Intern for the Grantor. It may be possible for you to get to know grantors by serving as an intern in their offices. You offer your services to them for some relatively short period of time, in exchange for some training.

A large university in the West hired an employee to administer about $3 million worth of new multicultural grants. Because the university wanted to get off to a good start in administering the funds, arrangements were made with the grantors for the new employee to be trained in their offices for two months. This worked well for the sponsor. There were practically no problems with the grants later on because of the specialized training provided. It was similarly helpful to the university.

In this case, a long-term support relationship developed between the grantees and the grantors. The university had been creative in arranging for the internship, as there was no official program of internships offered by the grantor. You can be creative in arranging internships also.

Be an IPA Employee for the Grantor. You can develop long-term cooperative relationships with federal grantors by working in their offices, actually doing their jobs, for one or two years. Title IV of the Intergovernmental Personnel Act of 1970 authorizes the "temporary exchange of personnel between federal executive agencies and states, local governments, institutions of higher education, and Indian tribal governments for work of mutual concern and benefit."(13) The mechanics of this exchange are fairly simple. You may either be detailed or accept a temporary assignment to work for grantors. If you are detailed, your employer continues to pay your salary. If you are on temporary assignment, the grantor pays.

Persons who return from IPA service frequently receive grants from the agencies they worked for shortly after the required waiting period. For example, an IPA returnee we know received two grants, totaling $80,000, as soon as he was eligible to do so. Besides getting more grants for themselves, IPA returnees can help others in their organizations, by telling them which grantors to see and arranging for introductions.

If you want an IPA position, or if you want someone else in your agency to get one, contact the IPA coordinator for the grantor agency of interest to you. If you want general information about the program as it relates to all federal agencies, contact the IPA Office in the Office of Personnel Management (formerly the Civil Service Commission).* This office is responsible for developing policy and regulations, providing information, and monitoring federal use of the program.

Ask a Grantor to Be an IPA Employee for You. Since the IPA program started, over 6,000 assignments have been made. Although the majority have been from nonfederal (grantee) to federal (grantor) positions, approximately 40% of the assignments have been for federal employees to work at nonfederal agencies.(14)

Although you can get to know grantors in their own offices, ideally it's bet-

*The Office of Personnel Management is located at 1900 E Street, N.W., Washington, DC 20415 (202-632-5373).

ter to get them to come to you. You can offer IPA assignments by contacting the offices mentioned in the preceding paragraphs. If federal employees work in your offices, they will have the opportunity to understand your organization and its programs better; they will be certain to remember you later when you need their help.

Join Professional Organizations. You can get to know grantors by joining professional groups and then attending meetings and participating in committee activities. For example, many grant administrators belong to the Society of Research Administrators (SRA)* or the National Council of University Research Administrators (NCURA).† Grantor officials (grant officers, generally) belong as well. Program officers and project directors who share similar academic backgrounds usually belong to the same professional groups also. An example is the American Psychological Association.

When grantees and grantors get to know each other at professional organization meetings, they can do so on an "equal" basis, with neither asking for favors. The communication can be relaxed and social interaction enjoyed. If you belong to a professional association, look over the membership roster and make a point of getting to know grantor officials with interests similar to yours. If you don't belong to any, find out what professional organizations your potential grantors are in and consider joining.

Attend Workshops and Seminars Where Grantors Will Be Speaking. Another neutral meeting ground is provided at workshops and seminars where grantors have been invited to speak about their agencies. Your meetings with grantors, in these cases, will not be on an equal basis, as you will be there primarily to learn from them. However, neither will you be asking for specific favors or help at this point. There will probably be some opportunity to relax and be sociable with some of the grantors.

The National Graduate University,†† for example, conducts grant-related institutes in Washington and at key locations around the country. Sometimes 30 (or more!) grantors speak during the three-day institutes. Many, although not all, of these grantors attend the opening-night reception, join the participants for meals, and are generally available for informal discussions before and after their presentations.

Invite Grantors to Speak at Your Organization. It is far easier than many

*Additional information about the Society of Research Administrators may be obtained by writing to SRA Executive Office, 1100 Glendon Avenue, Suite 2104, Los Angeles, CA 90024, or calling 213-825-4243.

†Additional information about the National Council of University Research Administrators may be obtained by writing to NCURA National Office, One Dupont Circle, Suite 540, Washington, DC 20036, or calling 202-466-3894.

††Additional information about the National Graduate University may be obtained by writing to Division of Special Studies, National Graduate University, 1101 North Highland Street, Arlington, VA 2201, or calling 803-527-4800.

people realize to get grantors to come to your agency and speak about their programs. Many grantors will gladly accept an invitation to participate in a one-day workshop or seminar. Most federal and state government officials have travel budgets. It is often part of their job to get out and review what is happening in the field. It is also their responsibility to represent the government and tell clients and taxpayers about their agency. If grantors belong to professional organizations, they also travel to attend annual meetings and on other organization business.

If you ask a governmental grantor to speak to the personnel of your agency, it won't cost you a cent for travel. Government employees could not accept travel funds if you offered them. If you plan your request for a grantor to visit you so that it coincides with the grantor's field visit or conference travel or public relations trip to nearby cities (or your city), the travel will cost the grantor little or nothing extra. What you will be asking for is only a day of the grantor's time. If you are inviting nongovernmental grantors to speak, it is appropriate to offer to pay travel expenses.

When you invite grantors to visit you, you should send a letter, formally requesting their participation and explaining the activities planned for their visit. Before you send the letter, it's a good idea to find out whether or not the grantors want to come and, if so, when would be the best time for them. This may be done either through a professional group you belong to, mutual friends, or a personal phone call from you directly to the grantors.

The kind of activities you plan for the day can vary. You may want to invite many grantors and have them talk to a large number of people, some from neighboring institutions. You may prefer to invite one grantor to speak to a small group of people from your organization only. Or you may decide on some combination of large-group–small-group meetings. However you plan the day, it's important that some time be reserved for the grantor(s) to get to know you and your organization, in addition to talking about their organization. Tell them about your agency, show them your facilities, and meet with them on a small-group or even a one-to-one basis.

It really is not difficult to arrange for federal and state representatives to come to you. The authors have organized many such meetings and never fail to be surprised at how simple and inexpensive they can be. We have also arranged for private foundation grantors to visit us, but this can be more difficult. In one case, when we tried to organize a workshop through preliminary calls and follow-up letters, it was not successful. All but one of the eight private-foundation officials who orginally agreed to participate sent their regrets a week before the event! However, in other cases, when the arrangements were made through colleagues who knew the private-foundation officials, we were successful.

Invite Grantors to Speak at Professional Conferences. If you will be attending a professional conference, consider inviting a grantor to give a presentation there. Grantors we know from the National Science Foundation, the National

Institutes of Health, the Department of Housing and Urban Development, and many other agencies have been delighted to accept such invitations. Their presentations have added a great deal to the worth of the conferences. Usually, the grantees who asked them to come got to know them well when acting as their hosts.

Schedule "Maintenance" Meetings at the Grantor's Offices. All the techniques we have suggested so far have concerned how to meet the grantors in the first place. You can initiate any of these activities *without ever having met the grantors.* Once you have *established* a relationship, however, it is important to *maintain* and *expand* it. So, keep up the contacts you have made by using any of the methods just discussed by scheduling periodic appointments with grantors at their offices. If you have no "problem," you can use these meetings to exchange information. Tell them what you are doing and ask about new developments at their agency that could be of interest to you. These meetings need not (and should not) be lengthy. However, they should occur.

"Remember, you are dealing with other human beings who are really interested in what is going on in the field," a grant administrator told the authors. "They have been cut off in some instances from active participation in their technical specialty. You can fill them in on the latest developments, as well as give them information that they can use to get support for their programs from Congressmen on the Hill."

Arrange for Unscheduled Meetings near the Grantor's Offices. You can also keep up your contacts through unscheduled meetings. One grant administrator we know visits with many federal grantors semisocially. Whenever he is in Washington, he makes a point of being at a Department of Education cafeteria when it opens at 7:00 A.M. By spending an hour or so table-hopping, he enjoys the informal company of his grantor friends, gets a good breakfast, and probably learns much more than he could have in the grantors' offices.

Invite Program Officers to Make Site Visits to Your Projects. After your program has been funded, the program officer may occasionally visit you and review its progress. If so, you will get to know her or him, and she or he will understand your project better. One way to increase the chance that you will receive a site visit is to ask the program officer to make one. Sometimes the program officer needs a formal request in order to justify the visit.

A project director we know told us that he sends a "bread-and-butter" letter to his program officer at least once per grant period. This letter is one that invites the program officer to visit the project and states specific matters to be discussed during the visit.

"I need this kind of letter, which I can use as a wedge to convince my administrator to let me go," said his program officer, who was present when the project director talked to us.

Offer the Grantor a Job at Your Organization. Earlier, we suggested asking grantors to serve on IPA assignments at your offices. This could be done without having met the person who would be assigned. Without using the IPA, once you get to know certain grantors, you may want to ask them to work for you. This can be either on a short-term consultant arrangement or on a longer-term (one-year, perhaps) appointment. Universities, for example, can offer a nine-month temporary academic position. Your agency would, of course, pay the salary during the longer-term appointment.

If you would like the services of a grantor on a consulting basis, it may or may not be necessary for you to pay. If grantors are able to consult on their salaried time, there will be no charge to you. This assumes that what you ask them to do for you relates closely to their full-time responsibilities for the granting agency. For example, if the government has introduced some regulations affecting the way you prepare your indirect-cost rate, you may be able to ask an auditor to spend a couple of days with you, helping you to set up a system to implement the new regulations. In this case, there would be no charge.

On the other hand, suppose you wanted this same auditor to spend a month with you, helping you reorganize your accounting system so that you will be less likely to incur disallowances on grants. In this case, the auditor would probably have to take vacation leave, and you would pay him. Rules on whether or not grantors can accept payment vary, so be sure to check these before offering a position and/or payment.

Ask a Grantor to Collaborate on Professional Activities. Another way you can maintain and expand your relationship with grantors is to ask them to collaborate on professional activities. For example, if you have an idea for a journal article, and the expertise of grantors will improve its chance of publication, it is appropriate to ask if they will write it with you jointly. You might consider doing the writing, based on interviews with them. The point is, you and the grantor(s) will have been working together on a project of benefit to both of you.

There are many ways to establish, maintain, and expand your relationships with grantors. Some, but certainly not all, of them are:

- Schedule a first meeting at the grantor's office.
- Serve on a grantor proposal-review panel.
- Be an intern for the grantor.
- Be an IPA employee for the grantor.
- Ask a grantor to be an IPA employee for you.
- Join professional organizations.
- Attend workshops and seminars where grantors will be speaking.
- Invite grantors to speak at your organization.
- Invite grantors to speak at professional conferences.
- Schedule "maintenance" meetings at the grantors' offices.
- Arrange for unscheduled meetings near the grantor's offices.
- Invite program officers to make site visits to your projects.
- Offer the grantor a job at your organization.
- Ask a grantor to collaborate on professional activities.

In this chapter, we discussed many aspects of contacts between grantors and grantees. What all the do's and don'ts of contacts add up to is simply this: remember that grantors are people, strive to develop real (not artificial) cooperative working relationships with them, and be considerate. Usually, you will not get something you shouldn't just because you know someone. But you will be much more likely to get all you are entitled to if you take the trouble to make contacts with people who can and will be glad to help you. You will also stretch your grant dollars while providing your grantors with the kind of projects they want most.

10

Gamesplaying
An Obstacle to Cost-Effective Grant Spending

A project director claims his daily emergency, "But this time I do need it right away! It's a rush!"

A grant administrator states peremptorily, "You can't do that. It's against regulations."

A program officer conspires with a project director: "Well, why don't you just tell your grant administrator that we can't give you all the money you asked for? Then she will have to give up some of the indirect."

According to Dorothy Jongeward, author of *Everybody Wins: Transactional Analysis Applied to Organizations,*

> People play psychological games with one another that are similar to games like Monopoly or checkers. Each has predictable moves and rules. Psychological games, however, are not played for fun . . . . [They] can be a powerful force in preventing people and organizations from becoming winners . . . . Games cost organizations money.[1]

So far in this book, we have emphasized the importance of working cooperatively with people, and we have said that making contacts will help you stretch grant funds. Ironically, sometimes you may *waste* grant dollars because of your contacts. As Jongeward points out, people in organizations play psychological games with each other. Grant spenders are such people. Sometimes they play games.

It is unrealistic to expect that grant spenders will always cooperate. Project directors, grant administrators, program officers, grant officers, and support staff each have varying responsibilities and resulting needs. In order to fill their *individual* needs, they occasionally forget that they are part of a team and act as if they are out to take care of themselves at all costs, never mind what happens to the others.

At best, gamesplaying by grant spenders will prevent you from saving money. At worst, you will end up spending too much. If you don't recognize and understand the nature of the various games, you may find yourself participating in them. If you do recognize and understand the games, you may be able to stop them—or at least control them better.

Because gamesplaying is an obstacle to cost-effective grant spending, a discussion of it has been included in this book. Some issues to be examined are: What are the conflicting needs of grants players that lead to adversary relationships? Who plays the games? What are some typical game scripts?

What Are the Conflicting Needs of Grant Players That Lead to Adversary Relationships?

"Indirect is an absolute rip-off," a program officer complained. "Grantees charge all they can get and then don't even bother to provide their PIs with typewriters and suitable laboratory space." This view of indirect costs is usually shared by the project director, who wants as much money available as possible for the *direct* costs of the project. The program officer's and the project director's desire to reduce indirect costs often conflicts with the grant administrator's needs. Usually, the grant administrator's salary is paid by indirect recovery, as are such basic items as the heat and light in his or her office. Opposing needs for *direct versus indirect costs* generate a great deal of gamesplaying both before and after a grant is awarded.

A second set of conflicting needs is for *speed versus delay.* For example, it is to the project director's advantage to have requests concerning her or his grant handled immediately (purchases, special approvals, personnel requisitions, and so forth). On the other hand, the grant administrator needs time to process these requests in an orderly manner, so that there is less risk to the grantee organization that actions will be improperly executed. Also, the grant administrator can do a better job, using less time per task, when she or he doesn't have to drop everything else to give special hurry-up treatment to one project director.

Research versus paperwork is another pair of opposing needs. Project directors and their staff members have a limited time to do the project's technical work scope. Even if they donate extra time, which many do, the day never exceeds 24 hours! Therefore, the more demands from grantors for documentation, the less time will be available for the project. Grant administrators, however, can not do all the paperwork for the project directors. At the very least, project directors' signatures are needed. Grant administrators can succeed in their jobs only if project directors will provide the necessary documentation.

A fourth set of conflicting needs that fathers and their 17-year-old sons will recognize are those for *independence versus institutional oversight*. The son (like the project director) is confident that he can accomplish what he sets out to do. He has made his plans and has the special abilities to carry them out. Why does old Dad have to keep track of him? Why does he have to say when he'll get home? Doesn't Dad trust him?

In most cases, Dad not only trusts him but is proud of him. Similarly, institutions (represented by grant administrators) trust their project directors and are proud of them. But institutional administrators and parents share a common need. They are legally responsible for the actions of the project directors and sons, respectively. Because of this responsibility, institutions, like parents, must provide oversight.

The project director's need for independence not only conflicts with his or her institution's need to know what he or she is doing. It is often in direct opposition to the grantor's need to monitor the way its money is spent. So another pair of counteractive needs is *independence versus compliance with grantor regulations*. Project directors usually want carte blanche to carry out their projects. Complying with grantor regulations is often cumbersome. Sometimes it even keeps them from working on their projects.

For example, some grantors require that all questionnaires be reviewed and approved by them before being sent out. The trouble is, this review has been known to take six months. Grantor program officers recognize the difficulties of complying with their own agency's regulations. Often the program officers' need to "get the job done" conflicts with the necessity of following the rules. In contrast, it is an important part of the grant administrators' and grant officers' jobs to ensure this compliance.

So some pairs of opposing needs that lead project directors, grant administrators, program officers, and grant officers into adversary positions are:

- Direct versus indirect costs
- Speed versus delay
- Research versus paperwork
- Independence versus institutional oversight
- Independence versus compliance with grantor regulations

There are other conflicting needs, but those just mentioned are responsible for most of the gamesplaying that wastes grant dollars.

Who Plays the Games?

As you might suspect from the preceding discussion, everyone involved with grants has reasons for gamesplaying. After maintaining that all grants spenders have reasons to engage in adversary tactics, we add that not everybody does. Most of those who do play believe that these games are for the overall good of the project and justify them on that basis.

Gamesplaying occurs between almost all combinations of grants spenders. Adversary tactics occur most frequently between grant administrators and project directors. The grant administrator succeeds best at his or her job with high indirect costs; adequate time to process requests; more project director effort on paperwork; institutional oversight; and compliance with grantor regulations. In contrast, the project director needs lower indirect costs to leave more money for direct costs; speed in processing requests; ideally, no paperwork, so that she or he can spend all her or his time on the project; and independence from both institutional oversight and compliance with grantor regulations. In every case, the project director's and the grant administrator's needs conflict!

Program officers sometimes get into the act. Because their needs are similar to the project directors', occasionally they side with the project directors and play games with the grant administrators. "There is a natural alliance between program officers and project directors. We don't see each other as competitors," a program officer admitted.

Program officers also play games with grant officers, in order to get the job done. Describing how he managed to get around some of his agency's cumbersome regulations, one program officer confessed, "In dealing with grant officers, I tell them the things they need to know to accomplish their jobs. I don't tell them other things. The philosophical basis for my playing games with a grant officer is that *I want to accomplish something*. The grant officer is the support person. Without me, she or he has no function to perform."

Although program officers and project directors usually support each other because of their similar needs, on rare occasions they play games with each other. The program officer, for example, needs to keep both direct and indirect costs low, in order to fund more projects. In contrast, the project director wants more direct costs. So the program officer may "use" the project director to push for lower indirect costs and then not increase the direct costs accordingly. Or the project director may try to get more money from the program officer than necessary to do the project.

Naturally, there is not much gamesplaying between project directors and grant officers. We have already seen that the formal and informal lines of communications generally preclude contacts between these parties. Their needs conflict only in one case: the project director wants independence, while the grant officer needs him or her to comply with regulations. However, the grant officer can hold the grant administrator responsible for filling this need. Therefore, there is neither the opportunity nor the necessity for project director–grant officer gamesplaying.

Surprisingly, there seems to be little gamesplaying between grant administrators and grant officers. There is certainly the opportunity: they are connected by both formal and informal channels of communication. Although they both

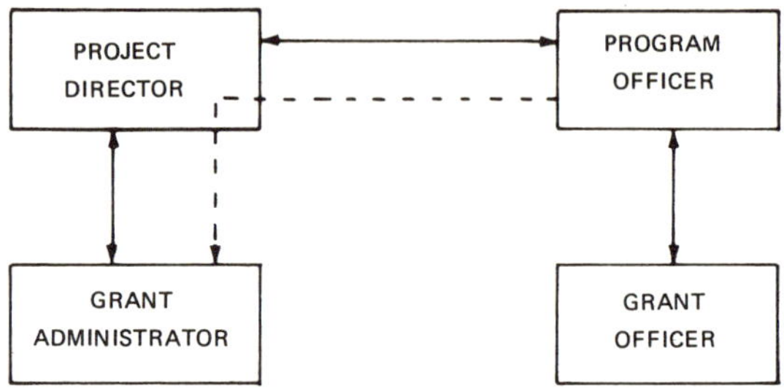

Figure 41. Typical gamesplaying patterns.

share the need to ensure compliance with grantor regulations, one would expect that sometimes the techniques for filling this need might vary. In general, not only do grant officers and grant administrators refrain from playing games with each other, but they also fail to initiate joint adversary tactics against project directors and/or program officers. The program officer quoted earlier, who told of the natural alliance between program officers and project directors, noted this, saying ". . . but there isn't one between grant officers and grant administrators."

Although there are undoubtedly individual gamesplaying and gang-up gamesplaying among all combinations of grants spenders, the most common patterns seem to be those shown in Figure 41.

What Are Some Typical Game Scripts?

Most of us have probably heard of and done some positive gamesplaying. For example, a grant administrator may make a carefully placed suggestion to a project director, one that could improve the project. Then, when the project director later follows up on the suggestion, genuinely believing it to be his or her own idea, the grant administrator refrains from taking credit.

While instances such as this one could be considered "gamesplaying," in this chapter they will not be. We will be examining only the *obstacles* to grant spending. Therefore, for our purposes, a "game" occurs when one (or several) of the players in the grant-stretching process puts his or her needs *above the mutual need of all players to spend grants cost-effectively*. Adversary tactics are used, instead of cooperative efforts. The persons initiating these tactics may or may not realize the impact of their behavior on the overall welfare of the others. The recipients of the adversary tactics may or may not realize that a game is being played.

Following are some games that are commonly played by grants spenders and that frequently end up costing both grantees and grantors money. Depending on your role in the grant-stretching process, you will probably recognize some or all of them. If you are relatively new to the grants business, you may not.

The "New" (Previously Funded and Completed) Research-Proposal Game

"We're aware that researchers will put in a grant to do an already-paid-for piece of research," a program officer said, when asked what kinds of gamesplaying he had encountered during his lengthy career.

When this happens, project directors are using adversary tactics against program officers. Fortunately, this type of game is rare, as it is dishonest. The game is unfair to the taxpayers or private donors, who end up paying twice for one project. It is unfair to the grantors, who think they are buying new research. It is unfair to the project director's institution, since—if the game is discovered—the institution's reputation will be tarnished. It is a complete waste of grant dollars.

The project directors who play it, however, may rationalize and believe that it is actually beneficial to others. Their need for recognition (a grant award) and paid time off to start new research (or to prepare a new proposal) may motivate them to use this strategy. "After all," they may reason, "if I get a grant, it looks good for my institution. And there is this very important research idea that I want to get into, but there just isn't time to write a proposal now. What's the harm?"

A variant of this game occurs when the project director gets two organizations to fund one project at the same time (at double the money necessary). (It is, of course, perfectly legal and desirable for two or more agencies to fund one project jointly when they all know about each other and share rather than duplicate the costs.)

How do you guard against duplicate funding? First, you must recognize it. Program officers have the best chance of doing this, by keeping current in their research fields. If work has been completed, it is possible that articles have been published as a result. Or if the PI has asked two organizations for funds simultaneously, the program officer has the opportunity to find out by talking with program officers at other granting agencies that support this type of research. To a large extent, however, the best defense against this game is to check thoroughly on project directors' reputations before funding them.

Because the game is so outright dishonest, it is probably the most difficult to recognize; it also wastes the most grant money.

The Bid-Low-but-Get-Lots-More-Later Game

Project directors and grant administrators play this game together against grantors and competitors. Before preparing the budget for a proposal, they try to find out whether the funding agency will be requiring changes after the project is awarded.

For example, suppose they are bidding on a project to train 50 Peace Corps volunteers to be able to take care of patients in El Salvador with tropical diseases. A doctor would be hired to teach the volunteers to recognize and treat the symptoms of the rare diseases. An instructor would be budgeted so that the volunteers could learn Spanish. And probably an official from the Ministry of Health in El Salvador would be paid to give the volunteers cross-cultural training so that when they arrived in El Salvador they would understand the local customs and would be accepted by the sick people there.

Now, suppose that all these employees plus the other costs of the project are realistically estimated at $200,000. The grant administrator and the project director may decide to bid low—to ask for only $175,000—*if* they are confident that the Peace Corps will have to make changes in the work scope after the project is awarded. What they are hoping (and counting on) is that the Peace Corps will end up needing 60 volunteers to be trained instead of the originally expected 50. Then, when the Peace Corps requests this change ("train another 10 volunteers, and give us the price"), the project director and the grant administrator will be able to ask for much more money, thus more than making up the loss they incurred in order to win the project. For example, the cost for the extra 10 trainees might be $75,000 or more. There would be little that the Peace Corps could do about the high prices at this point, since the project would probably be well under way, and it would make little sense for them to get another grantee to hire the doctor, instructor, and other staff just to train 10 people. The Peace Corps would be stuck accepting the high costs of the change.

In the bid-low-but-get-lots-more-later game, grantees try to determine the probability that changes will be required by the grantors once they receive the project award. If they are confident that there will be changes, they bid the project at break-even cost, *or less*—in order to win the award. Then, once the changes are requested, they jack the prices up unreasonably. There is no competition at this point!

This is "a dangerous game for amateurs," warns Holtz, in a section of his book that is entitled "Games Competitors Play."(2) Those initiating it will be hurt if they win the bid and then there are no changes. If there are changes, the grantors will be hurt. It will end up costing them more money than they might have spent if a supposedly higher-priced competitor had won.

Why does this game occur? Project directors have strong needs to get direct costs; grant administrators want the indirect costs. Their competitive juices are strong: Get the grant! Ironically, grantors who don't recognize the game for what it is believe that it suits *their* needs as well. They get what they originally want for less money and think (at least, until after the honeymoon is over) that they have stretched grant dollars.

In order to stretch grant dollars more effectively, grantors should not pay less than a fair price for the work to be done; grantees should not overcharge. Therefore, grantors—the victims of these adversary tactics—should recognize them when they occur. First, they can check the track record of prospective grantees. Is there a past history of bidding low and then hiking costs? If bids are unreasonably low, grantors should try to find out why. They should also consider whether changes will be needed in the work scope after the project is funded. If changes are likely, grantors should be especially cautious about awarding funds to unrealistically low bidders.

The Bid-low game is actually rather easy to spot and defend against. "It is played successfully only by experts," according to Holtz.(3) Even the experts must use it on new agencies, since once grantors have lost money on this ploy, they are unlikely to fall for it again—particularly with the same persons.

The Submit-the-Proposal-without-Institutional-Review Game

A grant administrator viewed a contract from the U.S. Forest Service with dismay. To begin with, there was no record in her office that the faculty member who was to do the project had ever submitted a proposal. To make matters worse, the numbers in the budget bore little resemblance to her institution's salary schedules or benefits rates. Only one weak connection could be made. The salaries appeared to be based on last year's rates, before the 15% cost-of-living increases were made. There were no indirect costs in it for her institution. However, cost sharing was budgeted. It seems that the faculty member who helped put this budget together (without any grant administrator's help) had promised all the indirect costs that the institution normally would have collected as a grantee contribution to the project!

In this case, the project director had played a game against the grant administrator. His strategy was set up along these lines: "If I go ahead and make the arrangements for this project on my own, the college will have to accept a contract once it comes in." The project director was a busy man. The Forest Service didn't require a grantee institutional sign-off when the proposal was submitted. So why should he bother with all that bureaucratic nonsense? His need for independence was placed above the institution's responsibility to oversee the proposal submission.

In one sense, this project director "won." He got away with cost-sharing all the indirect costs. It was too late for the grant administrator to negotiate more money, because all the U.S. Forest Service funds had been committed to other projects. The project director had successfully avoided the paperwork and review process when the proposal was submitted and had "proved" his independence. He was correct in his assumption that his college would not turn down the award.

In another sense, he lost. He had to reduce the time he and his students spent on the project. Because he hadn't checked with the grant administrator, he had budgeted salaries 15% too low. Since the college had to pay him at his current rate, they couldn't pay him for as much time as he originally planned to spend on the project. Not only was it too late for the grant administrator to negotiate indirect costs; it was also impossible for her to get additional direct costs (his salary) funded. The project director also ran into a problem with space. He had not considered where he would house the project. For obvious reasons, institutional officials hadn't had time to plan for the space. If the project director had worked with college representatives in the first place, instead of behind their backs, he could easily have got enough money for salaries, indirect costs for his institution, and space for the project.

The submit-the-proposal-without-institutional-review game is played with variations. Some project directors do not complete negotiations on their own; they just start them. For example, one grant administrator who was asked to describe gamesplaying that he had observed responded, "The game of getting a draft with budget and compromised costs sent to the sponsor before university approval has been secured—with protestations that the draft was clearly marked 'subject to approval,' but nonetheless hampering negotiations and reducing the amount of the award."

Usually, whatever variation of this game is played, there is only one winner: the grantors, who pay less for the project than its real costs. Sometimes even the grantors lose. If the project can not be successfully completed because of lack of institutional review and therefore inadequate planning, it doesn't matter that it has cost the grantor less. Some or all of the grant dollars may be wasted.

This game is recognizable, but often too late to correct some of the problems created. So the question is, How can it be avoided? Grantors can help by insisting that all proposals bear the signature of a grantee official. This will help but is no absolute guarantee. Unfortunately, in our experience, several project directors have unabashedly signed their own names on the dotted lines for institutional approval and have ended up receiving awards!

Grant administrators and other grantee officials can also help. They can simplify the review process for project directors, cutting bureaucratic red tape whenever possible. They can show how the project directors will benefit by using their services: by preparing budgets for them, getting copies of proposals made, interpreting grant guidelines, mailing proposals in time to meet grantor deadlines, and so forth. Besides offering incentives not to play the game, the grant administrators can administer disincentives after project directors have played it. (Particularly, if the project director is a repeat player.) These disincentives would include delay in processing the award, mandatory rebudgeting to be consistent with institutional policies and rates, or even, in extreme cases, refusal to accept an award that will be too costly to the institution.

The Let's-Cut-the-Indirect-Costs Game

Indirect costs are controversial. Each player regards them as "his" or "hers." Project directors notoriously object to their organization's taking indirect costs "off the top" of "my grant money." Grant administrators view grant fund ownership somewhat differently, conceding that the direct costs do belong to the project director but maintaining that the indirect costs (which are added after the project director computes all the project costs) are "institutional" money. Grant administrators recognize, of course, that this money is used to pay their own salaries. (Figure 42.)

A grant administrator jokingly mentioned the indirect-cost ownership conflict to a grant officer. "How about that?" she said. "Dr. X claims I'm taking too much of *his* money for indirect costs, when the indirect costs are really the university's."

"What do you mean, *the university's*?" the grant officer smiled. "I consider indirect funds *my* money."

So much for indirect costs. All parties identify closely with them, but their tactics vary.

"One of the things that project directors and program officers do very informally is push for the university to give up indirect costs. The project director will use the government as a wedge in dealing with the university structure," a federal program officer noted, adding, "I'm very willing to be that wedge."

Informal ways in which the program officer can push to get indirect costs

Figure 42. To grant administrators' dismay, some project directors are very creative and persistent in trying to reduce indirect costs.

reduced are by telling the project directors that only a certain amount of money is available or that their proposals won't be competitive if their institution's full indirect-cost rate is charged. The expectation is that the project director will relay these messages to the grant administrator, who, after all, wants to get an award.

Sometimes, the pressures are more formal. In one case we know of, the program officer telephoned the grant administrator directly. "Dr. Multicultural Project has told me the difficulties he is experiencing because your college insists on charging full indirect costs on his project," the program officer said. "We want you to reduce these costs in next year's proposal."

Dr. Multicultural Project coincidentally walked into the grant administrator's office just after the call had been completed. "I've done some preliminary estimates and I can't do my project next year if you don't do something about your indirect costs," he stated.

As it turned out, the grant administrator did not agree to lower the indirect costs, the program officer awarded the full amount requested, and the project director did do his project. The "game," in this case, failed.

Many times, however, the let's-cut-the-indirect-costs game succeeds. It succeeds because the program officer and the project director, working together (or the project director working alone), are able to generate enough pressure on the grant administrator to get her or him to play. Inexperienced grant administrators may not even realize what is happening. They genuinely believe they have only one choice: reduce the indirect or there will be no award. The grant officer, who has no personal stake in either reducing or increasing indirect costs, remains neutral. This leaves the grant administrator alone to face the pressures.

"If the game succeeds, so what?" you may be thinking. "Grant dollars *are* stretched." In the short run, and for the particular project involved, that is true. In the long run, however, grant dollars are wasted. A great deal of administrative time and energy are spent playing this game. Even if the project director is willing to donate her or his time, the efforts of grantee vice-presidents, deans, or other managers who must be involved in the decision to forgo indirect costs are expensive. These efforts are also charged to grants, because they are used in calculating the indirect-cost rate.

A vicious circle is started. Indirect costs are real. They must be recovered, or the organization will go out of the grant business. If one project director doesn't pay (or pays less), others must pay more. The rate itself will eventually go up, thus making it even more objectionable to project directors and program officers. It will look less and less competitive.

Also, auditors value consistency. If they discover that a grantee is indiscriminately using its full negotiated indirect rate on some projects and reducing it on others, they may rightfully question the validity of the rate. Disallowances may occur.

What can be done to discourage the game? First, grant administrators must recognize the game when it is started and refuse to play it. They can do this by (1) referring the project director (and the program officer, if necessary) to established institutional policies on indirect costs and (2) calling the grantor's grant officer to find out the grantor's official policy governing the payment of indirect costs.

If the grantee institution has no formalized indirect policy, the grant administrator should help to develop one. It is important to have this policy in writing, as it can be used to support the case for collecting full indirect costs. In addition, if the grant administrator finds out, on calling the grant officer, that the grantor's policy is to pay full indirect costs, then the grant administrator will have more ammunition to support his or her case for collecting full indirect costs.

Refusing to play the game, once it has started, is a remedial measure. Better yet, grant administrators should take a preventative stance, by helping project directors to understand what indirect costs are and why it is important that they be included in grant budgets. For example, few project directors realize that they are usually spending grant money *before* their institutions collect it from the grantors. If a project director has a $200,000 grant, with payments six months in arrears, the *interest* charges on $100,000 could easily be $8,000–$10,000—a *real* expense (directly related to that grant) that the institution must pay.

Besides explaining to project directors what indirect costs are used for, grant administrators should serve as advocates for project directors. They should try to ensure that project directors do receive generous institutional support for those items that are normally included in the indirect-cost-rate calculation and therefore cannot be charged directly to grants.

For example, if the indirect-cost rate includes office equipment, the grant administrator should be sure that the project secretary is provided with a good typewriter (not some broken-down older model that no one wants). Similarly, if computer services, laboratory and office space, and certain specialized research equipment are included in the indirect calculation, then the project director should have generous access to all of these. Too often, grants are received after all the institutional resources have been allocated to nongrant personnel. The grant folks sometimes end up with the leftovers, so it is understandable in these cases that they play the let's-cut-the-indirect-costs game.

The Creative-Budgeting Game

This variation of the let's-cut-the-indirect-costs game is played by experienced project directors. It is frequently targeted at the program officer instead of the grant administrator. The object, however, is the same: to get more money for the direct costs of the project. This game starts at the proposal stage; the heavy action takes place after a grant is received.

Here is how it works. A project director from an organization that has an indirect-cost rate based on salaries and wages prepares a federal grant budget. He asks for *more* salary money than he intends to use. He knows that indirect costs will be calculated on this salary, thus *raising the total grant*. He also knows that grantors can not unilaterally reduce the indirect-cost rate, so they will pay the higher amount.

Once the grant is awarded, the project director "discovers" that he really doesn't need all that salary money after all. He requests permission to transfer the salary (and the related indirect-cost) money into other budget categories, such as travel and supplies. Because he doesn't want to be too obvious, these discoveries are made periodically throughout the grant period. Requests for transfers, especially small ones, are usually approved routinely. They are not scrutinized nearly as closely as the original budget request because the grant funds have already been committed by the grantor.

Just to give you an example of the arithmetic involved in this game, suppose that project director Extra Smart really needs $10,000 in salary money and $2,000 for chemical supplies. Also, she will be presenting the results of her research at the American Chemical Society meeting, and this will cost another $500 for travel. Smart's research firm has an indirect-cost rate that is 50% of salaries and wages. This means that her actual budget is that shown in Figure 43.

Smart, however, would like a bit of a cushion in her budget because there's another conference in New Orleans that she would like to attend. If she showed this as a direct cost in her budget, the grantors might not approve. So she does some creative budgeting. The *direct costs* of her budget will remain the same ($12,500), but she will budget them a bit differently than she plans to spend them (see Figure 44). By taking $1,000 that she plans to spend for supplies and putting it in the salary category, Smart has generated an additional $500 in indirect costs. Once the grant comes in, she can transfer the $1,000 out of salaries back into supplies. *When funds are transferred out of the salary category, the associated funds ($500 in this case) must be transferred out of the indirect-cost category*. Director Smart will, of course, transfer the $500 from indirect costs to travel—to be used for the New Orleans trip.

A variation of the creative-budgeting game is played against the grant administrator instead of the program officer. At the proposal stage, the project director budgets *less* salary money than he or she intends to use, putting more money

Salaries	$10,000
Travel	500
Supplies	2,000
Total Direct Costs	$12,500
Indirect Costs (50% of $10,000)	5,000
Total Costs	$17,500

Figure 43. Director Smart's real budget.

Salaries	$11,000
Travel	500
Supplies	$1,000
Total Direct Costs	$12,500
Indirect Costs (50% of $11,000)	5,500
Total Costs	$18,000

Figure 44. Smart's creatively inflated budget.

into non-indirect-bearing costs such as student stipends and consultants and thus *lowering the total grant*.

Then, after the grant is awarded, the project director "discovers" that he or she really needs more salary money. There conveniently happens to be extra money in the consultant's category, but there isn't enough, by coincidence, to cover the indirect costs related to the increased salary category.

Suppose, for example, that after Director Smart submitted her budget, Jack Broke, her program officer, called.

"Look," he says, "we're really low on funds. Please send me a revised budget for your project. You can have *$17,000*. I don't care how you budget it, but that's all we have."

Smart, of course, still needs the same resources. She sends in the revised budget shown in Figure 45.

Once the grant is received, Smart asks to transfer $2,000 from supplies to salaries, where she really needs it. She has already taken care of her New Orleans trip in the travel budget, since Jack Broke told her that he didn't care how she sent her budget in (translated, "I'm not going to look too closely at the categories"). The problem is that when money is transferred into salaries, money should also be transferred into the indirect-cost category. And there is no money left to transfer in, since Smart will need everything for the direct costs of her project.

Once any grant has been awarded at an artifically lower amount, it is usually too late to get more money from the grantor. So what does the grant administrator do in this case? Frequently, the project director's ploy succeeds. The grant administrator agrees not to charge indirect fees on the money transferred into the salary category.

The creative-budgeting game—either variation—can be played even if your

Salaries	$8,000
Supplies	4,000
Travel	1,000
Total Direct Costs	$13,000
Indirect Costs (50% of $8,000)	4,000
Total Costs	$17,000

Figure 45. Smart's creatively deflated budget.

institution does not have an indirect-cost rate based on salaries and wages. The key is to identify which cost items are subject to indirect charges and which are not. Budget estimates can then be manipulated accordingly.

What's wrong with this game? It apparently serves the project director's purposes. It is frequently used successfully, and many grant administrators (or program officers, as the victims may be) never even realize that they have played it. There are several problems, however.

When the game is used to *increase* the total award, the grantor spends money that could have been more productively used on other projects. One reason that project directors put money into salaries is that they know that funds for an extra 5% (or some small portion) of their time is less likely to be refused than, say, funds for two conference trips or luxury equipment. For example, if the grantor who reviewed Extra Smart's first budget knew that she planned to transfer funds in order to spend $500 for a trip to New Orleans, the grantor might have cut her budget and given that $500 to another project director who had no travel funds.

When the game is used to *decrease* the total award, the grantee institution is unable to collect full indirect costs, and all the problems inherent in the let's-cut-the-indirect-costs game apply. Smart's institution, for example, would have lost $1,000 that other projects would have had to make up.

In either case, the game results in the spending of a great deal of unnecessary administrative time (with related costs) in processing all the requests for budget transfers. Project directors, grant administrators, grant officers, and program officers must all participate. Realistic budgeting at the proposal stage could make all the budget transfers unnecessary.

How can this game be stopped? First, it must be detected. This is especially difficult at the proposal stage. Even after a grant is awarded, it is hard to determine the difference between legitimate requests for budget transfers due to unexpected events and requests for budget transfers that were "preplanned." About the only way that either program officers or grant administrators can know that a game is being played is to look at the pattern of past behavior on the part of the project director.

If the project director has a history of transferring money out of indirect-bearing categories (like salaries) into other categories to which indirect fees are not applied, then the program officer can reduce the award to reflect more realistic spending patterns before the project is started. If the project director has a pattern of transferring money into indirect-bearing categories (and then asking his or her institution to forgo the indirect costs on these transfers), the grant administrator can simply refuse to forgo the indirect costs.

The It's-a-Rush! Game

In the old story, a little boy screams "Wolf!" so often that when a real wolf finally chases him, everybody ignores his cries for help. Some project directors "cry wolf" by making almost every purchase request an emergency, whether it is or not.

At one grantee agency, with a volume of over $10 million in grants per year, the manager checked on how frequently the emergency purchasing policy was being used. It turned out that over 75% of all purchases during the two-month period studied were made on an emergency basis. This cost the agency money for an extra purchasing clerk, hired because of all the nonroutine paper-processing. The indirect-cost rate of the agency subsequently went up 3%, and—although the clerk could not be blamed for all of the increase—her salary was responsible for some of it.

In this case, it was easy to understand why the project directors so frequently called requests a "rush." If they didn't, all the other so-called emergency requests would come first, and they might have to wait several weeks or longer before getting any action! In other cases, project directors may simply be putting their own needs above those of others. It's tempting to think, "Well, they (grant administrators and purchasing clerks) are getting all my indirect money. They ought to be able to give me same-day service."

The biggest problems with the It's-a-rush game are not, however, the increased indirect costs that may result or the inequities that may occur when some project directors' needs take precedence over others'. Instead, one major problem is the increased *direct* costs that may result. Usually, grantees must pay a premium price when they purchase items under rush conditions. They lose the opportunity to save grant dollars by getting competitive prices. Another major problem is that, like the boy who called wolf, the project director may be jeopardizing his or her credibility in a real emergency.

How can this game be stopped? First, it must be recognized. A quick look through a suspect project director's account file will spot the it's-a-rush gameplayer. Most of his or her purchase requests will be labeled with "Need by tomorrow" or "Emergency" or "Will pick up today." Once the game is recognized for what it is, the grant administrator can refuse to play. She or he should evaluate the request (to try to determine the presence of a real wolf). But once satisfied that the request is not an emergency, she or he should be firm about processing it routinely.

It's better, of course, to discourage project directors from initiating the game, instead of penalizing them once it has begun. As a first step, grant administrators should examine the nonemergency services they provide. Are they adequate? Could they be improved? If regular services are satisfactory, project directors will be less likely to demand special treatment. It is also important for grant administrators to make project directors aware of the inequities and extra costs that occur because of nonroutine purchases. Most project directors do not place their own needs above those of their colleagues, nor do they knowingly increase the costs of research projects.

The You-Can't-Do-That (and-Here's-Why-Not) Game

"I am so tired," a project director complained, "of my grant administrator's telling me *why I can't* do something. The reason I went to him in the first place was to find out *how I can*!"

The grant administrator's role is to support the project director, to help make the project a success. Yet, too frequently, when project directors run into a problem in which what they need to do conflicts with some grantor regulation, the grant administrator is no help at all. "No way," she or he says. "You can't do that. Look at paragraph 2 on page 1136 of regulations A-Z."

Why isn't the grant administrator more helpful? It's easy for her or him to quote chapter and verse of some regulation that *forbids* certain activities. Most of those regulations were delivered with the grant award document, or they are available in the institution's grant administration library. The grant administrator is busy and doesn't have time to do the creative searching necessary to justify what the project director wants to do. Also, the grant administrator may dislike risk. By staying with the commonly used regulations and saying "no," he or she avoids taking chances.

But in taking the policeman position, the grant administrator may be losing an opportunity to use grant dollars more effectively. If he or she investigated grantor regulations, justification might be found for the project director to do what needs to be done. It is in everyone's interest for the project to be successful, and when the project director has a legitimate request, she or he should be helped. When the grant administrator fails to provide this kind of service, any existing spirit of teamwork between him or her and the project director is jeopardized. In its place, the project director sees a bureaucrat who "doesn't understand me or my project."

What can be done to discourage grant administrators from playing the you-can't-do-that game? First, project directors must detect it. As with the other games, it is useful to determine whether there is a pattern of this sort of behavior. Then, if there is a history of a grant administrator's always saying "no," the project director can ask frankly why the grant administrator will not investigate the situation further. He or she can insist on reasonable answers. (Of course, once reasonable answers are given, they should be accepted!)

It's better, however, for the project director to help the grant administrator to understand why a particular request is so important to the success of the project. This is not always easy to do on paper alone. So it is useful to invite the grant administrator to visit project headquarters, to talk with other staff members (or clients or participants), or to view ongoing experiments. When the grant administrator is included in the project action, she or he is more likely to feel a real commitment to the technical (as well as the regulatory) grant activities. As a result, she or he will be less likely to play the you-can't-do-that game and may even throw herself or himself wholeheartedly into finding out how you *can*.

Although much of the action in the you-can't-do-that game is initiated by grant administrators, it should be noted that grant officers play it as well and for many of the same reasons. As official guardians of their agency's regulations, they can easily find ways to say "no" to requests made by either program officers within their agency or grant administrators (on behalf of project directors) at the grantee organization.

The Do-It-First-and-Ask-Later Game

The best defense against the you-can't-do-that game is for the project director to go ahead and do what he or she wants to do and then ask the grant administrator to justify this action.

For example, if a tape recorder is required, and the grant regulations forbid the purchase of this type of equipment, the project director might charge it on an open purchase order and then explain to the grant administrator later why the equipment was necessary. Or if the grant limits project activities to one county, the project director might give seminars at a local community college in the next county without telling the grant officer until later.

Project directors play the do-it-first game to fill their needs for independence from both institutional oversight and grantor regulations. They justify it on the grounds that this is in the best interest of their project; they have to get the job done. Also, they are afraid that if they ask first, it will take too long to get an answer, or the answer will be "no."

A star project director (we'll call him Mr. Free Lance) at a southwestern college played the game successfully for two years. Because he had brought in over $2 million in various grants, no one challenged him. Lance did as he pleased—others justified his actions later.

Then, Director Lance tried to rush through a $200,000 purchase for educational records and tapes. There was no line item in the grantor-approved budget to cover this expenditure; nor was there mention of the use of these materials in his proposals. Lance did not go to his grant administrator to ask for help in getting grantor approvals. Instead, he rushed to the desk of the purchasing clerk (who knew nothing about his grant but did know his "star" status) and demanded an open purchase order number, while he waited.

Fortunately, the clerk was more afraid of processing a $200,000 purchase order without proper authorization then she was awed by Lance's status. She refused to cooperate. As a result, Grant Administrator Cautious was called in. When Cautious called the grantors, the best he could get was permission to spend $20,000.

In this case, the do-it-first game failed. Many times, the game succeeds. The project director "wins." Because the actions have already been taken, the grant administrator *must* search creatively (or get special approvals from the grantor) to justify them. What else can she or he do?

The biggest problem is that usually the grantee institution loses money because grant expenditures are disallowed at a later date. In the disguised-but-real-life case just described, between $180,000 and $200,000 could have been disallowed later, depending on how successful the grant administrator was in getting approval for even a $20,000 expenditure after the fact.

It is about as hard for the grant administrator to prevent the project director from playing do-it-first as it is for the project director to keep the grant administrator from playing you-can't-do-that. The best the grant administrator can usually do is recognize the game when it occurs and confront the project director with it directly. The harm that is done should be pointed out to the project director and his or her future cooperation enlisted. In the long run, once disallowances have occurred, institutional officials at a higher level will be aware of the problem. They will probably make their displeasure known to the project director, which may discourage too much independent behavior.

The It's-Okay-to-Do-That Game

A grant administrator, when asked which gamesplaying caused him the most problems, said, "The program officer who *seems* to be unaware of the constraints of the regulations of the federal government (or other grantor agency), who conveys to the project director that the only important thing is to get the job done and that the paperwork is just a nuisance."

A project director, responding to the same question, said, "The program officer told me it was okay to go ahead and add personnel, but then the grant officer wouldn't approve them later."

When program officers tell project directors to take certain actions and spend money in certain ways, they may say, "Don't worry about approvals; we can get them later." But this is done through the informal communication channels, and never in writing. Problems occur when the grant officer fails to approve what has already been done, because these actions are against regulations.

In the short run, the project director and the program officer may "win." They conduct the project the way they, with their technical expertise, believe it should be done. In the long run, the grantee institution stands to lose money, for grant charges may be disallowed. Had the program officer consulted the grant officer before telling the project director to go ahead, perhaps another way (within the regulations) could have been found to conduct the project.

How can the game be prevented? Since it is the grantee institution that gets hurt, it is up to the grant administrator to discourage this sort of gamesplaying. While developing rapport with the project director and getting to understand the project better, she or he should point out the problems inherent in relying on a program officer's okays without getting formal approvals. It might be useful for her or him to give a few examples. The grant administrator can then offer to help the project director get the necessary approvals. All this, of course, must take place before the game is under way.

Why and How Should Gamesplaying Be Stopped?

These games scripts and others that grant spenders use may serve the needs of individuals, but they are counterproductive to everyone's goal of conducting successful projects at reasonable costs. There are many reasons for this.

The grantor may spend more money on a project than was needed. The grantee may receive less money than was necessary to get the job done. The grantee may incur disallowances after the grant is finished. The opportunity to save money on purchases may be lost. The grantee's indirect-cost rate may ultimately be increased. Project directors who don't play games are treated inequitably, since they pay more of the indirect costs and receive slower services. The opportunity to undertake special activities that would enhance the project is lost because grant administrators are unwilling to try to justify them.

Most important:

1. A great deal of time and energy is wasted, by everyone who participates (whether willingly or unwillingly) in the games.
2. Adversary tactics only damage any existing cooperative spirit between the grants spenders and replace it with antagonism.

Games reinforce the program officer's and the project director's attitudes that "We are outcome-oriented, but the fiscal types care only about process." They similarly validate the grant administrator's and the grant officer's suspicions that "Program types couldn't care less about the regulations. You have to watch them every minute."

With all these reasons for *not* playing games, why play them? Sometimes, it is the human but selfish urge to put one's own needs first—at any cost. More frequently, gamesplayers do not understand the impact of their actions. They genuinely believe that they are acting in the best interests of the project—which they figure is in the best interests of everyone else (grantees and grantors) involved.

Figure 46

So the best defense against counterproductive gamesplaying lies in *understanding* the needs and responsibilities of all the people concerned in any grant. Program people must try to involve fiscal people in the technical aspects of their projects; fiscal people must be sure that the program people understand the importance of regulatory and fiscal activities. Just as in sports, grants "players" must learn to work as a team. (Figure 46).

Other preventative measures lie in (1) training all parties to recognize when games are being played; (2) establishing institutional policies that discourage gamesplaying; and (3) improving institutional services for projects in order to satisfy the project director, who is, after all, the key figure in every grant.

An important rule for stretching grant dollars is this: Don't play counterproductive games. Be a team player. Save your energies for productive activities so that *everybody wins*!

11

Your Role
Organizing for the Grant $ S-T-R-E-T-C-H!

Knowing is not enough; we must apply.
Willing is not enough; we must do.
–Goethe

The Mushroom Research Agency went from an annual volume of $6 million to almost $10 million in grants in one year. As a result, many of its established grant-spending systems broke down. Even though new purchasing, payroll, and accounting support staff were hired, problems occurred.

Manual procedures and unwritten policies that had formerly worked so well were no longer effective. Project directors received notices of grant awards as late as six weeks after the projects should have started. Several award documents were lost. Purchases were held up for weeks at a time. Yet, large payments to some suppliers were made earlier than necessary.

Recognizing the need for new systems to accommodate Mushroom's growth, the executive director hired a team of management consultants.

"Tell me," he said, "what should we be doing to provide better services to our project directors and to ensure that we are filling our responsibility for fiscal administration of the grants? How can we save money while doing both?"

The consultants spent six months at the agency, interviewing staff and examining records. They produced a massive report, containing many excellent recommendations. For their services, they charged $150,000.

The report was read and filed; *the recommendations were never implemented.*

Although "The Mushroom Research Agency" is a fictitious name, this really happened–just as reported here.

Throughout this book, the authors have been your consultants (at less cost!). We have tried to suggest many ways in which you and others on your grant-spending team can stretch grant dollars. *Knowing* these techniques, however, is not enough. Nor is a cooperative attitude—even *willing* to help is not enough.

The key is *action.* As Goethe said, "We must do." So if you shelve this book without acting on any ideas you find in it, your investment of reading time and the price of the book will be wasted—as was the $150,000 spent by Mushroom.

Of course, one person can't singlehandedly take care of all the grant-stretching activities we have described. Nor should *you.* If you don't happen to be the president or executive director or a manager in your organization, you can't even tell other people what grant-stretching techniques they should be using. And even if you are, a great deal of firmness and tact will be needed to inspire your personnel to make effective changes in their customary activities.

Successful grant-stretching requires *organization* to ensure that all responsibilities will be assumed by someone. So let's think about the hospital or university or other agency you work for. How well is it organized and what can you, in your position, do to help?

Who in Your Organization Is Responsible for Each Grant-Optimizing Activity Mentioned in This Book?

A checklist (Figure 47) is provided on the following pages to help you answer this question. Filling in the blanks should spell out the strengths and weaknesses of your organization. If you are not sure which position handles a particular responsibility, you may want to get someone else from your organization to help you complete the checklist.

This checklist is obviously designed for *grantee* use. By *positions* we mean project directors, grant administrators, and purchasing, payroll, accounting, or other *grantee* staff. Since most of the actual spending on grants occurs in the grantee institution, plans for "organizing for the grant $ stretch" are directed toward its employees.

Grantor readers, however, please stay with us. Although the checklist is not applicable to you, the general discussion of organizing techniques in the rest of this chapter is.

As you review the blanks in the checklist, you will notice there is a space to show that "No one" is carrying out a specific activity. You should check this box as follows:

✗ when nobody at all is doing a certain task, or
✓ when some person(s) are doing a task but not all of the time.

The distinction is important because your agency is probably in better shape if you have a ✓ than if you have a ✗ !

Now, please turn to page 270 and complete the checklist before reading on.

Is There Someone in Your Organization Responsible for Each Activity?

Review your answers on the checklist. Are there any grant-stretching activities that no one is responsible for? How many? Have you any idea how much money could be *saved* if that activity were assigned to someone? How much would it *cost* you to pay someone to do it?

In determining your answers, consider the tasks that go along with each responsibility. Quantity buying, for example, can refer to many kinds of purchases. Even if your employees are generally using this technique, could they be missing some opportunities?

For example, at a university-connected research foundation (one that administers grants on behalf of nearby university faculty), no one was responsible for the bulk purchase of copying services. As a result, small to middle-sized Xeroxes and Kodaks and Savins proliferated among the centralized foundation offices and decentralized project offices. Almost everyone was paying 4¢ or 5¢ per copy.

The manager of this foundation assigned one of his staff members to study the situation and make recommendations. The time this staff member spent could not have cost more than $100, at most. As a result, a large copying machine was leased to service the centralized foundation offices plus many of the nearby project offices. The features of the machine and the quality of the copies produced were far superior to those of the former models. Yet the price per copy averaged less than 2¢. Thousands of dollars were saved, as a result of a $100 investment to fill this gap.

If your organization has gaps, you may be able to save more money than it would cost you—simply by hiring a new employee or giving unassigned responsibilities to existing staff.

If Several Persons Share Responsibilities, Are Their Activities Coordinated?

Look at your list again. In some instances, are two (or more) persons responsible for the same activity? If they are, there is a possibility that:

1. Each person assumes that the other is taking care of the job, so neither does it.
2. Both parties do the job, but either half-heartedly or sporadically.
3. Both parties do the job completely all the time.

None of these situations is desirable. They all waste money!

For instance, at the Mushroom Research Agency, a combination of all these situations occurred. There were no written policies concerning the responsibility for reviewing payroll cards. Physically, the cards went from the project director to one of four grant administrators, who then sent the cards to the payroll clerk.

FIGURE 47. A CHECKLIST OF WAYS TO STRETCH GRANT DOLLARS

Who, where you work now, carries out each of the activities listed? Place a check (√) in the appropriate box(es) to the right of each task listed. If more than one person is taking care of an activity, place a check in each box where it is appropriate.

Activities	Project director	Grant admin.	Purchsg. staff	Payroll staff	Acctg. staff	Top mgmt.	No one	Column ideal*
IN DECIDING TO APPLY FOR A GRANT Determine cost of applying								
Estimate chances of success								
Identify matching funds requirements								
Check on availability of staff, other resources								
Review project "fit" with organizational mission								
IN PREPARING THE BUDGET Find out grantor funds available								
Determine resources needed								
Explore alternative, less expensive resources								
Estimate direct costs								
Estimate indirect costs								
Estimate program income								
Estimate cost sharing								
Prepare budget justifications								
Approve any indirect costs to be forgone								
Approve other cost sharing								

IN NEGOTIATING THE AWARD

Preparation								
Serve as negotiation team leader								
Serve as negotiation team member								
Call a prenegotiation team meeting								
Read (or reread) the proposal								
If renewal project, estimate remaining funds								
Prepare optional budgets								
Develop strategy for reducing work scope								
Obtain additional justification for costs								
Obtain additional justification for tasks								
Attempt to determine what grantor has negotiated with others								
Agree on minimum funds and terms acceptable								
Gather informal information about grantors								
Gather and review grantor regulations, RFP, other printed materials								
Evaluate bargaining position								
Plan negotiation strategies								
During negotiation								
Reevaluate bargaining position								
Revise strategies accordingly								

Activities	Project director	Grant admin.	Purchsg. staff	Payroll staff	Acctg. staff	Top mgmt.	No one	Column ideal*
IN ESTABLISHING AND MAINTAINING GRANTS POLICIES AND PROCEDURES								
Monitor fiscal aspects of projects								
Monitor technical aspects of projects								
Establish and maintain grants policies concerning:								
Affirmative action								
Cash management								
Consultants								
Copyrights								
Cost sharing								
Equipment inventory								
Equipment sharing								
Fringe benefits								
Indirect costs								
Patents								
Payroll								
Personnel								
Purchasing								
Travel								

IN SPENDING THE GRANT								
Compare alternatives before purchase:								
Research designs								
Geographical considerations								
Scheduling activities								
Staffing patterns								
Donations								
Grantee contributions								
Loans								
Shared use								
Used versus new								
Remodel versus new								
Make versus buy								
Lower versus higher quality								
Rent or lease versus buy								
Risk versus no risk								
Alternatives within and between budget items								
New technology versus old technology								
Purchase for less:								
Donations								
Trades								

Activities	Project director	Grant admin.	Purchsg. staff	Payroll staff	Acctg. staff	Top mgmt.	No one	Column ideal*
Bids for competitive prices and terms								
Discounts (cash, quantity, trade, and special relationships with suppliers)								
Timing of purchases								
Negotiating								
Buying foreign								
Tax avoidance								
Detection of overcharges								
Save by using grantee buying power: Quantity institutional buying								
Quantity consortium buying								
Acquisition of surplus property								
Save by using grantor buying power: Federal excess property								
National Technical Information Service								
Data-processing and computer facilities								
Federal Telephone Service								
General Services Administration purchasing								
Other in-kind contributions and discounts								

IN AVOIDING OVER-, UNDER-, UNALLOWABLE EXPENDITURES							
Call a grant "kickoff" meeting, to plan grant spending							
Encumber grant funds as they are committed							
Review fiscal reports regularly							
Avoid overexpenditures: Transfers between line items							
Requests for supplemental funding							
Avoid underexpenditures: Expenditure projections during grant period							
Requests for carryover funding							
Requests for no-cost extensions							
Avoid unallowable expenditures: Knowledge of grantor regulations							
System for updating these regulations							
In-house training for project directors							
"Political pressure" reduction							
IN MANAGING CASH Collect grant funds as soon as possible: Advance payments							
Letters of credit							
Progress payments							
Timely computation of indirect charges							

Activities	Project director	Grant admin.	Purchsg. staff	Payroll staff	Acctg. staff	Top mgmt.	No one	Column ideal*
Timely billings to funding agency								
Systematized follow-up on late payments								
Pay out grant funds as slowly as possible: Credit from suppliers								
Favorable payment terms								
Invest idle funds favorably								
IN CONTACTING THE GRANTORS Get help to decide whether or not to apply for funds								
Get help to develop and/or write the proposal								
Get help to ask for the right amount								
Get grantors to advocate your proposal								
Get advance information on funding priorities								
Get help to solve potential problems before award								
Get information about why your proposal was rejected								
Get help to negotiate an apparent take-it-or-leave-it offer								
Get help to avoid under-, over-, and unallowable expenditures								
Get help with cash management								

*Ideally, who *should* be doing this task? Complete after reading through page 279.

Because the cards came to their desks, the grant administrators and the payroll clerk were assumed to be (and felt) responsible for the accuracy of the cards.

When the consultants started interviewing the Mushroom employees, they spoke to each of the five people with apparent pay card responsibility.

"On the pay card, do you total up the number of hours claimed, to ensure accuracy?"

"Do you check to see that the employee wrote in the correct pay rate?"

"How do you know that the project director's signature is authentic?"

"Do you find out whether there is money in the grant budget to cover the payment?"

"How would you know if an employee submitted two pay cards, totaling more than 100% effort?"

The answers to these, and many similar questions, showed that the activities of persons responsible for pay cards were not coordinated. No one was confirming the pay rate. Both the grant administrators and the payroll clerk sporadically authenticated the project director's signature, depending on how busy they were. Everyone was faithfully totaling up the hours. This was the easiest (but most time-consuming) thing to do.

The consultants recommended a solution to these difficulties. The grant administrators, they said, should approve a pay rate, an appointment period, and a level of effort as soon as an employee was hired. They should make sure that there was enough money in the project budget to pay that employee. This information should be given to the payroll clerk. From then on, no pay cards should go to the grant administrator at all; all should go directly to the payroll clerk, who would be responsible for verifying and checking all the information on the card.

If you find that responsibilities are being shared at your organization, that does not necessarily mean no effort, partial effort, or duplication of effort. It could be that your employees are coordinating their efforts, as the consultants recommended that the Mushroom staff do.

It is relatively easy to find out whether there is coordination. Consider what specific tasks are necessary to carry out a general responsibility. Then ask each employee who shares this responsibility: (1) Do you do this task? and (2) Do you do it all the time?

Do the Responsible Employees Have the Knowledge They Need to Get the Most out of Your Grant Dollars?

It's possible that your emmployees have all the grant-stretching responsibilities covered. Yet, they may not have the knowledge to carry these duties out most effectively.

Do your grant administrators, for example, know about government excess property and how to get it? Do your purchasing clerks know how to get tax exemptions? Does your accountant know about letters of credit?

At a minimum, each of the people you identified as being responsible for a particular grant-stretching activity should know all the techniques in this book that relate to his or her job. They should, of course, know much more.

No matter what responsibilities your employees have, they—and you—will benefit as their knowledge increases. Therefore, they should be given opportunities to talk with colleagues in the grant business and to update their skills through workshops and seminars.

One grant administrator ("Don") was able to save his university-connected research foundation thousands of dollars, just by talking with a colleague ("Jack") at a professional meeting.

"Don," Jack volunteered, "remember those disallowances your college and mine had to pay last year, because of faculty effort-reporting methods?"

"Don't remind me. I certainly do."

"Well, I have a tip for you. After we sent Uncle Sam the check for our disallowances, we decided to try a long shot, to get the money back from the state. Our reasoning was that the state college billed us for the services of its faculty and we paid the bills. Then the Feds told us we paid too much, and they collected the money from us. So, we figured, why shouldn't the state (which controls the budget for our college) reimburse us? And, by golly, they just did."

"Smart idea," said Don. "Wish I'd thought of that. Do you mind if I try it too?"

He did try it and saved his foundation $17,000, just by getting a good idea during a brief conversation with a colleague.

Is There a Better Way to Combine Tasks and Positions to Get the Most out of Your Grant Dollar?

Look at the checklist again. You filled in the responsibilities as they are now assigned to people at your organization.

Is there duplication of effort? *Are* there gaps, with responsibilities unassigned? Is an invisible employee named "No One" responsible for many of the grant-stretching tasks? Are higher-paid employees doing some routine tasks that could be easily accomplished by lower-paid help? Are some people doing too much or too little? Are people doing the jobs for which they are most qualified?

It's worthwhile to examine the *combination* of responsibilities for each employee position. Is this combination best for both your organization and the employee?

For example, does the person who prepares the budget have any responsibility for negotiating it? That would seem to be a good combination, since the budget preparer could probably explain and defend it better than someone else could;

also she or he would not have to spend as much time preparing for the negotiation as someone unfamiliar with the budget would.

Or does the person who prepares the fiscal reports also do the grant billings and collect the payments? If so, this would seem like too much responsibility for one person and too little internal control for your agency.

Neither combination, however, is "right" or "wrong." Decisions about combining responsibilities must be based on your organization: its size, the backgrounds and personalities of its employees, and many other local considerations.

So, knowing what you know about your organization and its people, how *should* responsibilities (ideally) be assigned? Read the checklist again, this time filling in the blanks in "Column ideal." Beside each responsibility listed, assign the employee position (or name of employee if your agency is small) that you believe to be optimal, based on everything you learned in this book and everything you know about your organization.

Please complete "Column ideal" on the checklist on page 270–276.

Are your ideal assignments approximately the same as those now existing in your organization? If so, you are probably working for a well-organized institution.

Do your assignments vary considerably from current practices? If so, your institution may be losing opportunities to stretch grant dollars. Possibly, some changes should be made.

What Can You Do?

If you are the top manager and have authority to do what you please, the answer is easy. If your organization is "ideal" now, stick with it. If improvements could be made, go ahead and "fill in the gaps," coordinate, and train employees. Reorganize as necessary to achieve your goals.

Top managers, of course, are a minority. If you don't have the power to reorganize and tell other people what to do officially, there are still many things you can do to help your agency stretch its grant dollars—and thus improve your own chances of getting to the top.

Look at the checklist again. Which responsibilities are yours? Are you currently accomplishing all the grant-stretching activities associated with your job? If yes, congratulations! If no, you can save your organization money by doing more.

You do have control of your own role. Can you streamline the responsibilities you currently have? How can you work less and accomplish more? How can you cut down on paperwork? How can you be more proactive and less reactive? If rush pressures can't be eliminated, can they be reduced?

You can also help others to do their jobs better. If you have learned something that others may not know about, you can share your knowledge with them (diplomatically, of course). For example, if you know that the purchasing clerk is not routinely requesting discounts, perhaps you could casually mention to her or him how much money so-and-so has saved by doing that.

But what can you do about those responsibilities that have not been assigned to anyone? Ironically, if there are unfilled gaps at your organization, you may know more about it than your boss does. Presumably, if your boss knew about them, she or he would have filled them!

So here is where your help can be most valuable. Let your manager know about the ways in which your organization could be stretching grant dollars, but isn't. You could discuss your ideas casually or present formal recommendations, depending on the working relationship you have established.

No matter what position you hold in your organization, or what role you play in the grant-stretching process, you can contribute a great deal: *your knowledge, your cooperation,* and *your action.*

A

Definition of Terms

Advance payments. A method of receiving funds from a federal sponsor. This method of payment can be used when the grantee does not have a continuing relationship with the grantor and/or the amount of money needed is less than $120,000 per year. Payment is made by Treasury check, not by letter of credit. (See **Letter of credit.**)

Best-and-final offer. When a funding agency gives the prospective contractor an opportunity to change any aspect of the original proposal. The prospective contractor is not required to make changes. A funding agency will ask for a "best-and-final offer" in competitive contract situations where it wants to obtain the best price and terms possible.

Carryover funding. In a multiyear project, carryover funding permits the grantee to use the current year's unexpended money during the following project period. Permission to carry unexpended monies into the next project period must be obtained from the sponsoring agency.

Code of Federal Regulations (CFR). The CFR is an annual codification of federal regulations, many of which pertain to the management of grants. The CFR is published as a set of more than 50 paperback books. All grantees should have access to a set of the CFR in order to administer awards properly. (See ***Federal Register.***)

***Commerce Business Daily* (*CBD*).** A newspaper published every business day by the Department of Commerce. It is the medium through which the federal government announces bidding opportunities for procurement of services, equipment, materials, or research through contracts. The *CBD* also announces contract awards, subcontracting leads, and foreign business opportunities. All firms and agencies interested in doing business with the federal government should read the *CBD*.

Contract. A legal instrument used by government agencies and other organizations to purchase or lease property or services. It may also be used by the federal government to acquire property or services intended for ultimate public use. The federal government announces bidding opportunities in the *Commerce Business Daily*. (See **Grant**; **Cooperative agreement**; ***Commerce Business Daily***.)

Cooperative agreement. A legal instrument used by the federal government that can be described as being a "cross" between a grant and a contract. It is used to transfer property, money, services, or anything of value to a recipient in order to accomplish a public purpose authorized by federal statute (and not the purchase or lease of property or services for the direct benefit of the federal government) whenever substantial involvement between the recipient and the federal government is anticipated in the performance of the contemplated activity. (See **Contract; Grant.**)

Cost-plus-fixed-fee contract. Provides for a fixed fee to the contractor in addition to reimbursement for costs incurred. The fee remains constant, but it can change if the scope of the contract is changed. (See **Fixed-price contract**; **Cost reimbursement contract.**)

Cost reimbursement contract. Provides for the reimbursement of allowable costs in the performance of the contract. It does not provide for a fee. Educational institutions and other nonprofit institutions are usually awarded cost reimbursement contracts. (See **Fixed-price contract; Cost-plus-fixed-fee contract.**)

Cost sharing. The contribution that a grantee must make to help fund the total cost of a project. Virtually all grants require some cost sharing by grantees, ranging from less than 1% to 50% or more, depending on the nature of the project. Cost sharing may be "in-kind," where services or materials are donated to the project. Some projects require a cash contribution, known as a *hard match*. Many grantee organizations have institutional cost-sharing agreements with the federal government.

Direct costs. Project costs that can be identified specifically with a particular sponsored project. Direct costs include such budget categories as salaries, fringe benefits, travel, supplies, equipment, consultants, communications, and publications.

Disallowances. When project funds have not been spent as they were intended, an auditor may "disallow" the expenditures. When this occurs, the grantee must refund the disallowed amounts to the granting agency. Disallowances can be prevented if care is taken to ensure that all expenditures are reasonable, allocable, and consistently treated and that they conform to limitations or exclusions in the sponsored agreement. (See **Unallowable expenditures.**)

Encumbrance. Funds on a project that have been committed for a specific purpose but that have not yet been recorded as spent. For example, equipment that has been ordered may not arrive and may not be paid for until a month or more has elapsed. The funds were committed (encumbered) when the equipment was ordered, but the funds are not yet recorded as having been spent.

Excess property. Excess property is property that is under the control of a federal agency and that is not required for the agency's needs. A report of the excess property is filed with the General Services Administration (GSA), which then tries to find another federal agency that can use it. Sometimes federal agencies give the property to grantees or contractors, who use it on federally sponsored projects. Excess property is usually in better condition than surplus property (see **Surplus property**). In most cases, the federal government retains title to excess property, although some agencies (NSF, Department of Interior) can transfer title to grantees and contractors.

Federal Management Circulars. Federal publications that contain certain basic, standard requirements that relate to federal assistance programs. Some circulars apply to all grantees; others are prepared for certain categories of grantees, such as hospitals and educational institutions. Cost sharing and indirect costs are the subjects of two Federal Management Circulars.

Federal Register. A daily newspaper, published Monday through Friday by the Government Printing Office. It is the medium for informing the public of the activities of the executive branch of the government. Legal documents, as well as rules and regulations for implementing federally funded grant programs, appear in the *Federal Register*. Agencies interested in seeking grants from the federal government should read the *Federal Register* daily. Regulations that appear in the *Federal Register* later appear in the Code of Federal Regulations.

Fixed-price contract. Used when the total cost of the work to be done or the goods to be supplied can be estimated fairly accurately. The contractor must complete the work for a firm, agreed-upon amount of money. (See **Cost reimbursement contract; Cost-plus-fixed-fee contract.**)

Fringe benefits. Persons employed on grants and contracts are eligible to be covered by fringe benefits. Some benefits, such as social security (FICA), unemployment insurance, workers' compensation, and others are required by law. Other benefits, such as health, life, and dental insurance, are not mandated by law but can be offered to employees. Fringe benefits are usually included as a direct-cost category in proposal budgets. Some institutions, however, include fringe-benefit charges in their indirect costs.

General Services Administration (GSA) purchasing. When equipment or supplies are purchased on some contracts, and title to the items purchased will remain with the federal government, it may be possible to buy through the GSA. The advantage of buying through the GSA is that large discounts may be obtained. Fewer agencies are now eligible for GSA purchasing than in the past.

Grant. The method of transferring property, money, services, or anything of value to a recipient in order to accomplish a public purpose authorized by statute when no substantial involvement of the federal agency is anticipated in the performance of the activity (see **Contract; Cooperative agreement**). Grantees are usually educational institutions, hospitals, and other nonprofit organizations.

Grant administrator. The individual at the grantee organization who helps the project director to plan the proposal budget, spend the money, and ensure that all grantor regulations are followed during the course of the project. The grant administrator may also be responsible for negotiating the award and for responding to audit questions after the project is completed.

Grant officer. The grant officer is employed by the granting agency and is responsible for monitoring expenditures and ensuring that grantor regulations are being followed. The grant officer negotiates the award for the grantor, approves any changes required by the grantee during the project, and may take action on audit findings after the project has been completed. The grant officer's principal responsibility is fiscal, not programmatic or technical. (See **Program officer.**)

Indirect costs. Costs that are incurred in carrying out a grant but that cannot be clearly identified and funded as a direct cost. Included in indirect costs are general administrative expenses; light, heat, and janitorial expenses; library expense; maintenance; space; and many other "hidden" costs. A grantee's indirect-cost rate is established through negotiation with the federal government. Proposal budgets should include a certain amount for indirect costs. Indirect costs are usually calculated as a percentage of either salaries and wages or modified total direct costs. Some grantees have an "on-site" indirect-cost rate and an "off-site" rate.

Letter of credit. An instrument that authorizes a grant recipient to draw funds needed for immediate disbursement. Grantees are eligible for letters of credit when (1) there is or will be a continuing relationship between the grantee and the federal funding agency for at least a year, and the total amount of advances to be received from the grantor is $120,000 or more per year; (2) the grantee maintains procedures that minimize the time elapsing between the transfer of funds from the Treasury and their disbursement by the grantee; and (3) the grantee's financial management system meets certain standards for fund control and accountability.

National Technical Information Service (NTIS). The NTIS collects and disseminates technical report information generated by government-funded research. The NTIS offers computer-generated custom bibliographic service of more than 250,000 abstracts of federally sponsored technical reports.

No-cost extension. A mechanism for extending the time period of a grant without additional funds being provided by the sponsor. It is used when the work of the grant has not been completed and there is money remaining in the budget. The funds that remain can be used during the extension period. Permission for a no-cost extension must be obtained in writing from the sponsoring agency.

OASC publications. Regulations issued by the Office of the Assistant Secretary, Comptroller (OASC), within the former Department of Health, Education, and Welfare. The publications were prepared to impose basic standards applicable to DHEW grant recipients.

Office of Management and Budget (OMB) Circulars. Similar to Federal Management Circulars in that they impose basic standards on federal grant recipients. (See **Federal Management Circulars.**)

Program officer. The individual at the grantor agency who has major responsibility for selecting projects to be funded and for ensuring that the projects are successfully completed. Although program officers may decide how much money each funded project will receive, their primary responsibility is programmatic or technical, not fiscal. (See **Grant officer.**)

Progress payments. A method of receiving funds from a federal sponsor when the grantee does not qualify for a letter of credit or for advance payments. Progress payments are reimbursements, and the grantee must bill the funding agency regularly. (See **Letter of credit; Advance payments.**)

Project director. The individual who initiates, plans, and carries out the project. The project director is employed by the grantee agency and is responsible for the successful conduct of the project. The project director is sometimes referred to as the principal investigator.

Prospectus. A short preliminary proposal. It is a written document that describes briefly what kind of project will be conducted, why funding is being requested, when the project will be done, how it will be done, who will do it, and how much it will cost. Usually, the prospectus is no more than five pages in length. Some funding agencies require a prospectus, or preproposal, prior to the submission of a formal proposal.

Request for proposal (RFP). RFPs are sent by funding agencies to organizations that respond to announcements of contracting opportunities. RFPs are documents that include a statement of the required work; the desired performance schedule; the criteria that will be used to evaluate proposals; legal provisions; deadline dates; and other information. Most federal RFPs are announced in the *Commerce Business Daily*.

Site visit. In some cases, where large sums of money or long-range support is involved, a grantor agency will want to visit a prospective grantee prior to making an award. Grantors may want to obtain fiscal information, inspect facilities and equipment, and meet with representatives of the institution. The potential grantee should be prepared to show its strengths and to demonstrate its commitment to the project.

Supplemental funds. Additional money awarded to a grantee agency for a project. Supplements may be made to allow a project to continue for an extended period of time, to expand the project's work scope, or to prevent unforeseen cost overruns. Grantees must request supplemental funds in writing as much as several months before the project is due to terminate.

Surplus property. Excess property that is offered by the GSA to all other federal agencies and that no agency wants. It can then be donated for authorized purposes, such as education and public health, or offered for sale to nonfederal organizations. Most surplus property is not in good condition or has a very specific use. The good items have already been snapped up as "excess property" by other federal agencies. (See **Excess property.**)

Many states provide access to state surplus property to state-funded agencies. The state may have warehouses where potential buyers can look over the merchandise. The cost is generally minimal. As with the federal government, state surplus property is made up of items that no other state agency wants.

Transfer between line items. It is sometimes necessary on a project to spend more money in one budget category than originally proposed while spending less than planned in another category. When a grantee finds that she or he is running short of funds in one category and has unused money in another, she or he can request a transfer of funds between line items, that is, ask the sponsoring agency for permission to "move" money from one category to another where it is needed. Failure to obtain permission for a transfer can result in an audit disallowance.

Unallowable expenditures. Project funds that have been spent for a purpose not permitted by the sponsor or not provided for in the budget. For example, purchase of first-class airplane tickets would be an unallowable expenditure. Purchase of *any* airplane tickets would be an unallowable expenditure on a grant that provided funds only for equipment. To be considered allowable, an expenditure must be reasonable, allocable, and consistently treated and must conform to limitations or exclusions in the sponsored agreement. (See **Disallowances.**)

B

Sample Purchasing Policy and Forms

(*Name of Institution*)
Purchasing Policies and Procedures

One of the most important services provided by the foundation in its support of university activities is the *procurement of supplies, equipment, and services* for campus and sponsored programs. The policies and procedures outlined in this document are designed to meet the following objectives:

1. To provide a well-defined, efficient purchasing system that will meet the needs of our clients for purchasing transactions.
2. To provide a flexible and practical system that recognizes and accommodates immediate-need situations as they arise.
3. To provide a system that meets the standards of governmental regulations and sound business practices, that is,
   a. A system that promotes maximum competition and thereby secures for the user the most favorable prices and terms.
   b. A system that provides for prior review of proposed purchases to ensure allowability (per foundation expenditure review guidelines).
   c. A system that provides the necessary documentation to meet audit standards.

Purchasing Policies

1. All purchases in excess of $50 must be reviewed and approved by the foundation prior to commitment. All such commitments must then be made by the foundation purchasing office.
2. For purchases of $500 or less, documentation of alternative bids need not be obtained or indicated on the purchase-order request form. However, it is the policy of the foundation to encourage project directors to seek the most advantageous terms on all purchases.

3. For purchases of over $500 and up to $2,000, *verbal* quotations must be obtained from three alternative vendors and recorded on the purchase-order request form.
4. For purchases greater than $2,000, *written* quotations must be obtained from three alternative vendors and attached to the purchase-order request form.
5. Written justification will be required in all cases where the lowest bidder is not selected to receive the order. The degree of justification needed depends on the difference between the lowest bid and the selected bid.
6. Written justification will be required for all "single-source" or "no-substitution" purchases.
7. Emergency purchasing procedures (set forth below) are intended for use only in genuine immediate-need situations. Since adequate project planning should minimize the need for emergency purchases, and since the processing of emergency orders is a costly proposition, frequent use of these procedures by a project director cannot be allowed.
8. Purchases of *services* in excess of $2,500 shall normally be made via a formal subcontracting process. Subcontracting procedures will be issued separately.
9. Purchase-order requests for airline tickets need not be accompanied by bid information, even if the amount is over $500.
10. These purchasing policies and procedures do not apply to reimbursements for travel (except airline tickets) and hosting expenses, consulting services, or honoraria. These items are covered by separate policies and procedures.

Purchasing Procedures

1. *Regular Purchasing Procedures*
   a. Project director (or designee) shall complete the purchase-order request form in accordance with the instructions on the reverse side of the form.
   b. The purchase-order request form should then be signed by an individual authorized to sign for the project (an individual with a signature card on file with the foundation) and sent to the foundation.
   c. After review in the grants and contracts administration department, the purchase-order request form will be forwarded to the purchasing office for issuance of the purchase order.
   d. If review results in disapproval of the purchase-order request, the form will be returned to the originator with a written explanation of the rejection and, if appropriate, suggestions as to what steps should be taken to complete the purchase successfully. Purchase orders will normally be issued within three working days after receipt of the purchase-order request at the foundation.
2. *Optional Procedure for Small Purchases*
   Any purchase, no matter how small, may be initiated and completed via the regular purchasing procedures outlined above. However, in the interest

of practicality and convenience to project directors, this optional procedure may be used for purchases of $50 or less. The $50 limit is a rigid one and includes sales tax and any deposits or other surcharges. Requests for reimbursement of more than $50 will result in the issuance of a check for $50. Also, the purchase must be allowable; that is, it must be reasonable and allocable to the account being charged, and sufficient funds must exist in the account and line item being charged. The procedure is as follows:

a. The project director (or designee) may purchase the item(s) using personal funds or a credit card.
b. Reimbursement may then be obtained by submitting a check request for the amount of the purchase accompanied by an itemized receipt. *Cash register receipts will normally not suffice.*
c. The foundation will issue a reimbursement check, usually within three or four days after receipt of the check request.

Note: Larger purchases may not be broken down into a series of smaller ones in order to use the above procedure.

3. *Emergency Purchasing Procedures*

There are occasions in the performance of research and educational projects when immediate needs arise that cannot be met through the normal procurement process. The following procedures are intended to meet these needs while maintaining the administrative control required by project sponsors. There are three alternative procedures outlined below.

a. *Telephone Orders*
   (1) Project director (or designee) shall deliver a properly completed purchase-order request form to the foundation (grants and contracts administration department). The purchase-order request should be clearly marked "Emergency" and should include justification for using the emergency procedure.
   (2) After approval by grants and contracts administration, the purchase-order request will be hand-carried to the foundation purchasing office.
   (3) Foundation purchasing personnel will initiate the purchase by telephone.
   (4) A written confirming purchase order will then be sent to the vendor by the foundation purchasing office.
b. *Hand-Carried Orders (Local Vendors)*
   (1) Purchase-order request form should be completed and delivered as in a (1).
   (2) The project director (or designee) shall then take the approved purchase-order request to the foundation purchasing office.
   (3) Foundation purchasing personnel will then type a purchase order to be hand-carried to the vendor by the project director (or designee).
c. *Emergencies at Times Other Than Foundation Business Hours*
   (1) Purchases of supplies, equipment, or services by the project

director during off hours may be reimbursed on submission of a check request, itemized receipts, and a complete written explanation of the emergency.

(2) Such requests shall not exceed $500 and *shall be honored only in dire emergencies that absolutely require immediate action.*

(3) The request for reimbursement and accompanying documents must be submitted to the foundation at the earliest possible time after making the purchase.

PURCHASE ORDER REQUEST

(NAME OF INSTITUTION)

DEPARTMENTS TO COMPLETE ALL INFORMATION

A copy of the Purchase Order, as mailed from this office will automatically be sent to you for your records. If you desire a copy of this request, please make a carbon.

SUGGESTED VENDOR: (Alternate Vendor see instructions on reverse side)
Name ....
Address ....
City .... State .... ZIP ....
Quoted By .... Date ....
Phone Number .... Quoted Price ....
F.O.B. .... Terms .... Delivery Date ....

Charge to ....
Code ....
Confirm P. O. No. ....
Date Material Required ....
Date ....
Expiration Date ....
☐ Reg. ☐ Pickup ☐ Prepaid ☐ Emergency

ALTERNATE VENDOR (See instructions on reverse side)
Name ....
Address ....
City .... State .... Zip ....
Quoted By ....
Phone Number .... Quoted Price ....
F.O.B. .... Terms .... Delivery Date ....

ALTERNATE VENDOR (See instructions on reverse side)
Name ....
Address ....
City .... State .... Zip ....
Quoted By .... Date ....
Phone Number .... Quoted Price ....
F.O.B. .... Terms .... Delivery Date ....

QUANTITY	DESCRIPTION — COMPLETE ENOUGH TO ALLOW COMPETITIVE BIDDING	UNIT PRICE	TOTAL

DELIVERY LOCATION: Attention ....
....
.... Bldg. .... Rm. No. ....

CHECK ONE: Equipment ☐ Supplies ☐
Equipment Component ☐ Other ☐
☐ Please notify if suggested vendor is not used

....
Signature of Foundation Representative Date

....
Signature of Project Director

Figure B-1a

INSTRUCTIONS

1. NO ALTERNATE VENDOR IS NEEDED FOR ANY PURCHASES UP TO $500.00 — OR FOR THE PURCHASE OF AIRLINE TICKETS FROM A TRAVEL AGENCY.

2. **TELEPHONE QUOTATIONS** — Purchases over $500.00 and up to $2000.00.

   Three alternate vendors must be contacted by the Project Director — for firm prices, terms, and availability. When vendors have been contacted, this information should be indicated on the Purchase Order Request. **List three or more vendors** including **address, telephone number, name of individual who quoted price** and the **date.** Furnish sufficient specifications to solicit competitive bids even though item proposed is a "Single Source" item. **Include model number, description, size, color,** and any other applicable specifications that might be necessary to assure purchase of the correct item. Descriptive literature or brochures should be attached if available.

   If three bids are not obtained by the Project Director, the order will **not** be processed until Foundation Purchasing obtains the required bids. Purchasing will place the order with the lowest bidder, if identical product. Prior approval from the Project Director is not needed to place the order with the lowest bidder. When three sources are provided, Purchasing will call alternate vendors, on test basis, to confirm quoted prices and to assure maximum discounts are obtained. (See note below)

3. **WRITTEN QUOTATIONS** — Purchases over $2000.00.

   The Project Director must obtain three written quotations, either by mailing Foundation "Request for Quotation" forms or contacting vendors and requesting written quotations. Written quotations must be attached to the Purchase Order Request, as supporting documents, as well as descriptive literature if available. Sufficient specifications to solicit competitive bids, even though proposed item is "Single Source," must be furnished. **Include model number, description, size, color,** and any other applicable specifications that might be necessary to assure purchase of correct item.

   If three bids are not obtained by the Project Director, the order will not be processed. Foundation Purchasing will obtain the required bids. If vendor has not responded by "Quotation Due Date," Purchasing will follow-up as to the reason and document the Purchase Order Request. (See note below)

NOTE:

Purchase will be made from the Vendor with the most advantageous prices and terms regardless of personal preference of the Project Director.

WE MUST BE COMPETITIVE — "Single Source" or "No Substitutions" is not enough information. Justification for "Single Source" should include:

a. Unique performance factors of the product specified.
b. Why these specific factors are required.
c. What other products have been examined and why rejected.
d Indicate if item is "Equipment Component."

ALTERNATE VENDOR JUSTIFICATION:

....

....

....

....

....

....

....

....

....

Figure B-1b

(NAME OF INSTITUTION)

REQUEST FOR QUOTATION

DATE: .... QUOTATION DUE DATE: ....

QUOTATION REQUESTED FROM: ....

RETURN QUOTATION TO: ....

ATTENTION: ....

ATTENTION: ....

TELEPHONE NO: ....

NOTE: Any deviation from the specifications must be clearly identified and fully described. No charges for any other purpose will be allowed over and above the prices quoted on this sheet. The right is reserved to accept or reject quotations on each item separately, or as a whole. If unable to quote, please return this form so marked.

QUANTITY	DESCRIPTION	UNIT PRICE	EXTENSION

F.O.B. POINT: .... DELIVERY DATE: ....

TERMS: .... CASH DISCOUNT: ....

THIS QUOTATION EXPIRES: ....

DISTRIBUTION:
- **WHITE — Return to Sender**
- **YELLOW — Foundation File Copy**
- **PINK — Vendor Copy**

BY ....

TITLE ....

Figure B-2

PURCHASE ORDER **P.O.**

NAME OF INSTITUTION
ADDRESS
TELEPHONE NUMBER

ALL CORRESPONDENCE, INVOICES, SHIPPING MEMOS, PACKAGES, DELIVERY SLIPS, ETC., **MUST** SHOW THIS NUMBER. IF FACTORY SHIPMENT, ADVISE THE FACTORY TO COMPLY.

SEND INVOICES AND BILLINGS IN TRIPLICATE TO ABOVE ADDRESS	VENDOR CODE:
TO:	C/G CONTROL:
▪	CHARGE TO:
▪	DATE:
▪	P.O. EXPIRES: Do not ship after this date/or advise

☐ **SHIP TO:**	☐ **SHIP TO:**

SHIP BY:	F.O.B. POINT:	TERMS:	DELIVERY REQUIRED:

QUANTITY	**DESCRIPTION**	**UNIT PRICE**	**TOTAL**
	Subject to the terms and conditions shown here and on reverse side		

EDUCATIONAL DISCOUNT REQUESTED

By:

NOTE: IF PRICES HAVE NOT BEEN CONFIRMED AND THE UNIT COST OF ANY ITEM EXCEEDS THE AMOUNT SHOWN BY 10%, **DO NOT SHIP.** CONTACT

AN EQUAL OPPORTUNITY EMPLOYER

Figure B-3

C

Sample Travel Policy and Forms

(Name of Institution)
Travel Policies and Procedures

Intent to Travel Procedure

A purchase order must be obtained from the foundation prior to making any travel reservations with a travel agency. (See form example attached.)

First Class Travel Is Not an Allowable Expense

Purchase the *least expensive* round-trip or special-rate ticket available. Air travel must be "economy class." If "first class" is requested, the foundation will be responsible only for the economy-class rate.

Travel by Private Automobile versus Air Travel

Should the traveler choose to use a private automobile for personal convenience, the reimbursement will be 17¢ per mile without certification, or the equivalent of a round-trip air fare ticket, whichever is less. Justification for the use of a privately owned automobile must be included with the travel reimbursement claim. Also, travel time may necessitate adjustment in subsistence per diem allowance.
EXAMPLE: Air Travel Time–1 hour; driving time–8 hours.

Commercial Automobile Rental

If a rental car is needed, a purchase-order request may be submitted to the foundation along with justification of why a rental car is needed. A purchase order will be issued with a discount slip. These must be hand-carried by the traveler and submitted to the car rental agency to ensure a discount. (See form examples attached.)

Use discretion when renting an automobile. Car rentals are not always necessary and may not be an allowable expenditure. Automobiles of the compact or medium class should be rented, without extra charge items such as convertible bodystyle, expensive or luxury items.

Insurance: Collision and Medical Insurance on a Car Rental

1. Collision insurance, called *collision damage waiver, is an allowable expenditure.*
2. Medical insurance, called *personal accident insurance, is not an allowable expenditure.*

Bus–Shuttle Service

Information regarding shuttle–bus service is available from the travel agency or hotel. This service should be utilized whenever possible to and from the airport.

Travel Advance

1. If a travel advance is needed, a check request for travel advance should be submitted for 80% of the estimated out-of-pocket expense. Include method of calculation. (See form example attached.) Minimum advance limit is $25.00. No travel advance will normally be issued to persons having travel advances outstanding in excess of 30 days.
2. If travel arrangements are canceled, the advance check must be returned or reimbursement made to the foundation travel coordinator. TRAVELER IS ACCOUNTABLE FOR ADVANCE UNTIL CLEARED THROUGH THE FOUNDATION.

In-State Travel: 24-Hour Period

Per Diem of $46.00, itemized as follows:
$25.00 per day for lodging–maximum
$17.50 per day for meals (breakfast $3, lunch $5.50, dinner $9)
$3.50 per day–incidental expense

Exception to In-State

When supporting documents are received, such as a copy of conference announcement, registration application, registration fee form, or meeting notice–information, REASONABLE additional hotel charges will not be questioned.

Less than 24-Hour Travel

The traveler on travel status for less than 24 hours and at least 25 miles from work headquarters may claim subsistence expenses incurred before or after the regularly scheduled work day. There is no lunch allowance. See schedule below:

	Breakfast	*Lunch*	*Dinner*
Leave $1\frac{1}{2}$ hours before 8:00 A.M.	Yes		
		No	
Return $1\frac{1}{2}$ hours after 4:30 P.M.			Yes
Leave $1\frac{1}{2}$ hours before 8:00 A.M.	Yes		
		No	
Return before $1\frac{1}{2}$ hours after 4:30 P.M.			No
Not leave $1\frac{1}{2}$ hours before 8:00 A.M.	No		
		No	
Return $1\frac{1}{2}$ hours after 4:30 P.M.			Yes
Not leave $1\frac{1}{2}$ hours before 8:00 A.M.	No		
		No	
Return $1\frac{1}{2}$ hours before 6:00 P.M.			No

Note: Time limits also apply to 24-hour travel.

Out-of-State Travel

For out-of-state travel, claimant may be authorized lodging expenses as indicated below, supported by a voucher.

$35.00 per day for lodging (approximate)
$17.50 per day for meals (breakfast $3, lunch $5.50, dinner $9)
$ 3.50 per day–incidental expense (24-hour period)

Vouchers

Vouchers and supporting documents must be submitted with all claims for reimbursement. *EXAMPLE:* Hotel bills, auto rental, parking fees–toll charges, taxi receipts, airline tickets, conference fees, etc. IF NOT ATTACHED, claim will be adjusted and deductions made (until receipts are presented). Receipts for meals and $3.50 incidental expense are not required.

Unallowable Expenses

Dinner meetings, laundry, liquor–bar bills, valet service, tips, etc., are not allowable expenditures. Additionally, the foundation will not be responsible for fines, traffic tickets, or insurance charges incurred by the traveler. Lastly, no reimbursement will be allowed for transportation by a motorcycle or a motor-driven cycle.

Hotel Reservations

1. Each person is responsible for his/her own hotel reservation as well as PAYMENT for accommodations.
2. If reservations are made at a hotel where conferences or meetings are to be held, REQUEST SPECIAL RATES.

3. Rooms for DOUBLE OCCUPANCY or SUITES for one (1) person are not allowable expenditures.
4. FOOD–BEVERAGES–MISCELLANEOUS charges included on hotel bills are not allowable and will be deducted from the travel claim. These items are covered under per diem allowance.
5. Telephone charges may be allowable, provided they are stated on the claim as business charges and documented as follows:
   a. Name and number of party called (include area code)
   b. City and state
   c. Reason for call
   d. Time and date

NOTE: Your travel agency may provide the service of making hotel reservations; however, *they are not responsible for paying the hotel bill* or justification of any charges in excess of the allowable rate.

Claims for Reimbursement

To obtain reimbursement for travel expense, a travel-expense claim form should be completed. This claim should itemize travel expenditures, with receipts attached. All expense claims should be attached to a check request that has been approved and signed (by the project director). Completed travel claims should be sent to the travel coordinator at the foundation for review and processing. (See form examples attached.)

Incorrect claims will be handled in one of two ways:

1. The claim will be adjusted and a check issued for the allowable portion of the claim.
2. The claim will be returned and no payment will be made.

In either of the above cases, the claimant will have the opportunity to correct the claim or secure the needed documentation and resubmit the claim for full payment.

Local Mileage Reimbursement

1. Where a privately owned automobile is used, the claimant will be allowed 17¢ per mile without certification. MILEAGE CLAIMS MUST BE FILED MONTHLY.
2. The local mileage form is to be used only when no per diem is requested. If mileage plus per diem is to be claimed, file a State STD 262 form. (See form example attached.)

Insurance on Privately Owned Automobiles

1. Each employee who plans to drive his/her own vehicle should be aware that the insurance policy maintained by the foundation is applicable only to the liability of the employee that is over and above the liability insurance maintained by the employee.
2. The normal practice of insurance carriers is to allow the occasional use of

privately owned automobiles on business trips without an increase in premium rates. If the privately owned automobile is used consistently on foundation business, an employee should contact his/her insurance carrier, who may change the premium class with a corresponding increase in premium rate.

Long-Term Travel: More than 31 Consecutive Days

Employees who are required to be in one location for extended periods are usually able to arrange for accommodations at a lower rate than is charged for day-to-day occupancy. Employees who are in one location for *31 or more consecutive days* may claim $29 per day. This amount includes the $3.50 incidental allowance.

Continuous Indeterminate Field-Assignment Allowance

1. An employee on field assignment away from his/her headquarters who *does not maintain a permanent residence* away from the job site will be authorized an allowance of $29.00 per day. Reimbursements for 12 hours or less will be calculated as $14.50 (one half the long-term allowance).
2. An employee on field assignment away from his/her headquarters *who maintains a permanent residence elsewhere* while living at the job site will be authorized an allowance of $29 per day provided one of the following conditions exists:
   a. Permanent residence is occupied by employee's dependents.
   b. Permanent residence is being maintained and held vacant by the employee at an expense to him/her in excess of $200 per month. For the purposes of this rule, maintenance costs are not limited to rent or basic mortgage payment.

To qualify for this per diem allowance, an employee must submit whatever evidence the agency may require substantiating the existence of either (a) or (b).

Foreign Travel

Claimant will be reimbursed actual *reasonable* daily expenses, three meals per day plus lodging.

Receipts and vouchers must be submitted for all expenses incurred. *EXAMPLE:* Hotel bills, food, auto rental, cab fare, parking fees–toll charges, airline tickets, train tickets, conference fees, etc. IF NOT ATTACHED, claim will be adjusted and deductions made (until receipts are presented).

PURCHASE ORDER REQUEST

(NAME OF INSTITUTION)

DEPARTMENTS TO COMPLETE ALL INFORMATION

A copy of the Purchase Order, as mailed from this office will automatically be sent to you for your records. If you desire a copy of this request, please make a carbon.

SUGGESTED VENDOR: (Alternate Vendor see instructions on reverse side)
Name Name of travel agency
Address ✓
City .... State .... ZIP ....
Quoted By Name of person contacted Date ....
Phone Number ✓ Quoted Price ....
F.O.B. .... Terms .... Delivery Date ....

✓Charge to ....
Code ....
Confirm P. O. No. ....
Date Material Required ....
✓Date ....
Expiration Date ....
☐ Reg. ☐ Pickup ☐ Prepaid ☐ Emergency

ALTERNATE VENDOR (See instructions on reverse side)
Name ....
Address ....
City .... State .... Zip ....
Quoted By ....
Phone Number .... Quoted Price ....
F.O.B. .... Terms .... Delivery Date ....

ALTERNATE VENDOR (See instructions on reverse side)
Name ....
Address ....
City .... State .... Zip ....
Quoted By .... Date ....
Phone Number .... Quoted Price ....
F.O.B. .... Terms .... Delivery Date ....

QUANTITY	DESCRIPTION — COMPLETE ENOUGH TO ALLOW COMPETITIVE BIDDING	UNIT PRICE	TOTAL
1	Round-Trip Airfare Ticket: Economy-Class Only For: (Name) Place: (Destination) (to-from) Date: (Month, Day, Year) Purpose of Travel Contact Person: Phone #		80.00

DELIVERY LOCATION: Attention If tickets are to be delivered by the travel agency, please indicate.
.... Bldg. .... Rm. No. ....

CHECK ONE: Equipment ☐ Supplies ☐
Equipment Component ☐ Other ☑
☐ Please notify if suggested vendor is not used

.... Signature of Foundation Representative Date

.... Signature of Project Director

Figure C-1

PURCHASE ORDER REQUEST

(NAME OF INSTITUTION)

DEPARTMENTS TO COMPLETE ALL INFORMATION

A copy of the Purchase Order, as mailed from this office will automatically be sent to you for your records. If you desire a copy of this request, please make a carbon.

SUGGESTED VENDOR: (Alternate Vendor see instructions on reverse side)
Name .... Hertz Car Rental
Address .... Destination (Airport)
City .... State .... ZIP ....
Quoted By .... Date ....
Phone Number .... Quoted Price ....
F.O.B. .... Terms .... Delivery Date ....

✓Charge to ....
Code ....
Confirm P. O. No. ....
Date Material Required ....
✓Date ....
Expiration Date ....
☐ Reg. ☐ Pickup ☐ Prepaid ☐ Emergency

ALTERNATE VENDOR (See instructions on reverse side)
Name ....
Address ....
City .... State .... Zip ....
Quoted By ....
Phone Number .... Quoted Price ....
F.O.B. .... Terms .... Delivery Date ....

ALTERNATE VENDOR (See instructions on reverse side)
Name ....
Address ....
City .... State .... Zip ....
Quoted By .... Date ....
Phone Number .... Quoted Price ....
F.O.B. .... Terms .... Delivery Date ....

QUANTITY	DESCRIPTION — COMPLETE ENOUGH TO ALLOW COMPETITIVE BIDDING	UNIT PRICE	TOTAL
1	Automobile Rental: Intermediate/Standard For: (Name of Traveler) Date: (Dates of Travel) Place: (Destination) (to-from) Estimated Number of Miles: Justification:		

DELIVERY LOCATION: Attention .... N/A
....
.... Bldg. .... Rm. No. ....

CHECK ONE: Equipment ☐ Supplies ☐
Equipment Component ☐ Other ☑
☐ Please notify if suggested vendor is not used

....
Signature of Foundation Representative Date   Signature of Project Director

Figure C-2

FORWARD TO FOUNDATION OFFICE OF GRANTS AND CONTRACTS

(NAME OF INSTITUTION)

CHECK REQUEST

PRINT IN INK OR USE TYPEWRITER ONLY, PLEASE

All spaces below must be completed. Sample signatures of authorized approving representatives must be on file in the Foundation office and must agree with signatures on this request.

Amount of check requested: $151.00 Date of Request: ✓

Payee John Doe
Name (30 Spaces)

Payee's Address ✓
Address (30 Spaces)

City, State, Zip Code (22 Spaces)

CHECK DISTRIBUTION

☐ Mail to Payee's Address.
☐ Aztec Center Ticket Agency
To be picked up by: ______
☐ Foundation Code: ______

Account Number and Subcode ✓

Nature of Expense ✓ Travel Advance, Dates of Travel, Purpose of Travel

Explanation for Instruction Only:

Total Exp. of Travel	$345.00
Less Airfare (to be billed by travel agency)	156.00
Balance	$189.00
80% of 189.00	$151.00

✓
PROJECT SIGNATURE ______ DATE ______ FOUNDATION SIGNATURE ______ DATE ______

FOR ACCOUNTING USE ONLY

☐ MISC. ADVANCE ☐ MISC. REIMB. ☐ TRAVEL ADVANCE ☐ TRAVEL REIMB.
☐ MILEAGE ☐ SALARY ADVANCE ☐ REFUND ______ ☐ OTHER ______

PAYMENT AUTHORIZATION

FOR FOUNDATION USE ONLY		P.O. NUMBER	INVOICE
VENDOR NUMBER	VOUCHER NUMBER		

TC	ACCOUNT NUMBER/SUBCODE	INVOICE DATE	DUE DATE	AMOUNT	P/F	
						CHECK NUMBER
						DATE
		CHECK TOTAL				

Figure C-3

TRAVEL EXPENSE CLAIM

(OUT OF STATE TRAVEL)

CLAIMANT'S NAME	DEPARTMENT	
John Doe		
POSITION	DIVISION OR BUREAU	PHONE
Asst. Director		
RESIDENCE ADDRESS	HDQRS ADDRESS	
4455 5th Avenue		
CITY ZIP CODE	CITY ZIP CODE	

(1) MONTH/YEAR 5/79 (2) DATE	TIME	(3) LOCATION WHERE EXPENSES WERE INCURRED	(4) SUBSISTENCE	(5) TRANSPORTATION (A) COST OF TRANS.	(B) TYPE USED	(C) BETWEEN WHAT POINTS (NOTE—"AND RETURN" IF ROUND TRIP)	(D) CARFARE, TOLLS, PARKING	(E) PRIVATE CAR USE MILES	AMOUNT	(6) BUSINESS EXPENSE	TOTAL EXPENSES FOR DAY
10/5	6:00 am	San Diego	17 50	156 00	A	Denver Colo	3 00	15	2 55	21 00	200 05
6			21 00							21 00	42 00
7			21 00							21 00	42 00
8			21 00							21 00	42 00
9	5:00 pm	Denver Colo	12 00			San Diego	3 00	15	2 55		17 55

6:00 am on 5th thru 5:00 pm 9th, is (4) 24 hr periods, so claimant is entitled to misc. exp. of 3.50 per 24 hr period (this amount is figured in the total above).

NOTE Claimant had airfare ticket prepaid on P.O., and also had an advance of $150.00 from foundation (these amounts will be deducted from bottom of claim).

(7) REMARKS OR DETAILS (ATTACH VOUCHERS WHEN REQUIRED)

D- Taxi/Limo from Airport/Hotel, Hotel Airport (receipts req)	343 60
E- Mileage, to Airport/Home, Home/Airport	
6- Hotel Expenses (receipts required) Less Airfare/prepaid	156 00
Less Travel Advance	151 00
For mileage reimbursement rates which exceed 17 cents per mile, I certify that the actual cost of operating the vehicle was equal to or greater than the rate claimed. CLAIMANT'S SIGNATURE ▶ must be filled in	36 60
(8) Conference or convention attendance under B/C Rule 708 approved. Signature of dept. head, principal deputy or chief admin. officer. ▶ (9) PRIVATE CAR LICENSE NUMBER must be filled in AGENCY ACCOUNTING OFFICE USE ONLY Paid by Revolving Fund Check Number	CLAIM TOTAL

I HEREBY CERTIFY That the above is a true statement of the travel expenses incurred by me in accordance with Board of Control Rules in the service of the State of California and that all items shown were for the official business of the State of California, and if a privately-owned vehicle was used, I have met the requirements as prescribed by S.A.M. Section 0754.

Signature of Officer approving payment	Signature of claimant	Date
▶ project director sig. (must have)	▶ claimant sig. (must have)	

Figure C-4

TRAVEL EXPENSE CLAIM IN-STATE TRAVEL (less than 24 hrs)

CLAIMANT'S NAME: John Doe	DEPARTMENT
POSITION: Asst. Director	DIVISION OR BUREAU — PHONE: 6009
RESIDENCE ADDRESS: 4455 5th Street	HDQRS ADDRESS
CITY: San Diego, CA — ZIP CODE: 92120	CITY — ZIP CODE

(1) MONTH/YEAR 4/78 (2) DATE	TIME	(3) LOCATION WHERE EXPENSES WERE INCURRED	(4) SUB-SIST-ENCE	(5) TRANSPORTATION (A) COST OF TRANS.	(B) TYPE USED	(C) BETWEEN WHAT POINTS (NOTE—"AND RETURN" IF ROUND TRIP)	(D) CARFARE, TOLLS, PARKING	(E) PRIVATE CAR USE MILES	AMOUNT	(6) BUSINESS EXPENSE	TOTAL EXPENSES FOR DAY
4/7	8:00 am	San Diego		24 60	A	Los Angeles	2 00	14	2 38		28 98
4/7	7:00 pm	Los Angeles	9 00			San Diego	2 00	14	2 38		13 38

*EXPLANATION ON SUBSISTENCE: Claimant did not leave prior to 6:30 am, therefore not entitled to breakfast allow. Claimant returned after 6:00 pm, therefore he is entitled to dinner allow.

When travel is less than 24 hrs, there is no lunch allowance.

These rates are based on leave time being 1-1/2 hrs prior to 8:00 am and/or returning 1-1/2 hrs after work time.

(7) REMARKS OR DETAILS (ATTACH VOUCHERS WHEN REQUIRED)

D- Limo/Taxi, Airport/Hotel, Hotel/Airport (receipts req) TOTAL 42 36

E- PC Mileage, to/from Home/Airport

Less Airfare/prepaid (if prepaid on P.O. by Foundation) 24 60

For mileage reimbursement rates which exceed 17 cents per mile, I certify that the actual cost of operating the vehicle was equal to or greater than the rate claimed.

CLAIMANT'S SIGNATURE: must be filled in

(8) Conference or convention attendance under B/C Rule 708 approved. Signature of dept. head, principal deputy or chief admin. officer.

(9) PRIVATE CAR LICENSE NUMBER: must be filled in

AGENCY ACCOUNTING OFFICE USE ONLY — Paid by Revolving Fund Check Number

CLAIM TOTAL: 17.76

I HEREBY CERTIFY That the above is a true statement of the travel expenses incurred by me in accordance with Board of Control Rules in the service of the State of California and that all items shown were for the official business of the State of California, and if a privately-owned vehicle was used, I have met the requirements as prescribed by S.A.M. Section 0754.

Signature of Officer approving payment	Signature of claimant	Date
project director sig. (must have)	claimant sig. (must have)	

Figure C-5

FORWARD TO FOUNDATION OFFICE OF GRANTS AND CONTRACTS

(NAME OF INSTITUTION)

LOCAL MILEAGE REIMBURSEMENT CLAIM

PRINT IN INK OR USE TYPEWRITER ONLY, PLEASE

EXPLANATION: This form should be filed monthly and pertains only to private vehicle mileage. This form should NOT be used when per diem is requested. If per diem is requested, mileage and all other expenses should be itemized on a State of California "Travel Expense Claim" form (STD 262).

CHECK DISTRIBUTION

☐ Mail to Payee's Address.

☐ Aztec Center Ticket Agency
To be picked up by: ______

☐ Foundation Code: ______

Amount of Check Requested $ ______ Date of Request ______

Payee ______
Name (30 Spaces)

Payee's Address ______
Address (30 Spaces)

______
City, State, Zip Code (22 Spaces)

ACCOUNT NUMBER AND SUBCODE

MONTH DAY YEAR	DEPARTURE LOCATION	DESTINATION	ODOMETER READING START	ODOMETER READING ENDING	NUMBER OF MILES	PARKING/ TOLL CHARGES	PURPOSE OF TRIP
TOTALS Front and Back (Form continues on reverse)							TOTAL CLAIM $

I HEREBY CERTIFY THAT THE ABOVE IS A TRUE STATEMENT OF THE OFFICIAL TRAVEL PERFORMED BY ME:

LICENSE NUMBER OF VEHICLE USED ______ SIGNATURE OF CLAIMANT ______

PAYMENT AUTHORIZATION

FOR FOUNDATION USE ONLY				DESCRIPTION
VENDOR NUMBER	VOUCHER NUMBER			
				MILEAGE REIMB.

TC	ACCOUNT NUMBER AND SUBCODE	INVOICE DATE	DUE DATE	AMOUNT	
					PROJECT SIGNATURE DATE
					FOUNDATION SIGNATURE DATE
					CHECK NUMBER
CHECK TOTAL					DATE

Figure C-6

D

Sample Consultant/Independent Contractor Forms

(NAME OF INSTITUTION)

AGREEMENT FOR THE PERFORMANCE OF INDEPENDENT CONTRACTOR AND PAYMENT AUTHORIZATION

(All areas of this form must be completed prior to commitment)

DATE	ACCOUNT NUMBER AND SUBCODE

CHECK DISTRIBUTION

☐ Mail check to Payee's address.
☐ Aztec Center Ticket Agency. To be picked up by: ____
☐ Foundation Code ____

CONTRACTOR COMPLETES

1.a. Name: (First, Middle Initial, Last — PLEASE PRINT) b. Social Security Number

c. Street Number and Name | City | State | Zip | Country

d. Dates services are to be performed: ....

e. Detail description of services to be performed: ....

f. REGULAR EMPLOYMENT status of person rendering service: Title, Home Institution, Special Credentials, etc. (In addition please attach a vita. If this is for a workshop, also attach a brochure or flyer). ....

g. Fee is calculated at $.... per .... = TOTAL FEE $

h. Payment will be made upon receipt of invoice:
☐ At the completion of all services.
☐ At the following designated intervals: ....

i. AGREEMENT of Independent Contractor: I agree to perform the services described above at the rate indicated. I have read and agreed to all of the covenants, conditions, and stipulations on both sides of this form. I understand that I am not an employee of San Diego State University Foundation because I follow an independent trade or profession, and will not be subject to control and direction as to the details and means for accomplishing the anticipated result of my service.

DATE ____ CONTRACTOR SIGNATURE ____

PROJECT DIRECTOR COMPLETES

2. CERTIFICATION AND JUSTIFICATION REGARDING THE NEED FOR THESE SERVICES:
I hereby authorize the obligation of funds (indicated in item 1.g above) and certify to the following conditions which I understand the requested performance agreement must meet.

a. Outside services are essential because: ....

b. The objective selection process for the below named contractor included the following steps: ....

c. The fee is justified because it is calculated at the rate:
....paid the contractor in his/her home institution;
....customarily paid this contractor by federal and/or non-federal contracting agencies;
....other (explain) ....

DATE ____ PROJECT SIGNATURE ____

PAYMENT AUTHORIZATION

FOR FOUNDATION USE ONLY: VENDOR NUMBER	VOUCHER NUMBER	P.O. NUMBER	DESCRIPTION
			INDEP. CONTRACTOR

TC	ACCOUNT NUMBER AND SUBCODE	INVOICE DATE	DUE DATE	AMOUNT	P/F	
						G/C DIRECTOR SIGNATURE — DATE
						FOUNDATION SIGNATURE — DATE
G/C Initials:			CHECK TOTAL			CHECK NUMBER — DATE

Figure D-1a

STANDARD CONSULTING AGREEMENT

1. CONSULTANT SHALL SUBMIT AN INVOICE CONTAINING A CERTIFICATION OF THE TIME DEVOTED TO THE CONSULTANCY, AND A STATEMENT THAT ALL REQUIRED WORK HAS BEEN COMPLETED AS WELL AS A WRITTEN REPORT ON THE RESULTS OF THE CONSULTATION.
2. The Consultant agrees to indemnify, defend and save harmless Foundation, its officers and employees from any and all claims and losses accruing or resulting to any and all contractors, subcontractors, materialmen, laborers and any other person, firm or corporation furnishing or supplying work, services, materials or supplies in connection with the performance of this agreement and from any and all claims and losses accruing or resulting to any person, firm or corporation who may be injured or damaged by the Consultant in the performance of this agreement.
3. The Consultant and the agents and employees of the Consultant, in the performance of this agreement, shall act in an independent capacity and not as employees or agents of Foundation.
4. Without the written consent of Foundation, this agreement is not assignable by the Consultant either in whole or in part.
5. Time is the essence of this agreement.
6. No alteration or variation of the terms of this agrement shall be valid unless made in writing and signed by the parties hereto, and no oral understanding or agreement not incorporated herein, shall be binding on any of the parties hereto.
7. The consideration to be paid Consultant, as provided herein, shall be in compensation for all of Consultant's expenses incurred in the performance hereof, including travel and per diem, unless otherwise expressly so provided.

The Consultant shall not utilize any information, not a matter of public record, which is received by him by reason of this agreement, for pecuniary gain not contemplated by the terms of this agreement, regardless of whether the Consultant is or is not under contract at the time such gain is realized. The report survey or other product developed by the contract pursuant to this agreement is the property of the Foundation, and shall not be used in any manner by the Consultant unless authorized by the Foundation. Breach of this provision will make the contract voidable at the Foundation's option, and the Consultant shall be liable for any other damages incurred by Foundation as the result of such breach.

In signing this agreement, Consultant certifies that he is not an employee of the Federal Government or an employee of any other project sponsored by a Federal Agency, therefore not receiving dual compensation for the services provided herein.

The Foundation reserves the right to terminate this agreement upon written notice to the Consultant. All satisfactory work performed up to the time of such termination shall be paid in full by the Foundation upon submission of an invoice.

In witness whereof, the parties have caused this agreement to be duly executed as witnessed by their signatures on the reverse side of this form.

Figure D-1b

Important: See Reverse Side **First**

FORWARD TO
FOUNDATION OFFICE OF
GRANTS AND CONTRACTS

PRINT IN INK OR
USE TYPEWRITER
ONLY, PLEASE

HONORARIUM AND ONE-TIME PAYMENT REQUEST

All spaces below must be completed. Sample signatures of authorized approving representatives must be on file in the Foundation office and must agree with signatures on this request.

Amount of check requested: ______________ Date of Request: ______________

Payee ______________
Name (30 Spaces)

Payee's Address ______________
Address (30 Spaces)

____
City, State, Zip Code (22 Spaces)

CHECK DISTRIBUTION

☐ Mail to Payee's Address.

☐ Aztec Center Ticket Agency
To be picked up by: ______________

☐ Foundation Code: ______________

SOCIAL SECURITY NUMBER ______________

Account Number and Subcode ______________

SERVICE PERFORMED ______________
DATE TOTAL HOURS RATE

SERVICE PROVIDED FOR (Names of Project Staff or Seminar Group) ______________

DESCRIPTION OF SERVICE (If this is for a workshop, also attach a brochure of flyer)

REGULAR EMPLOYMENT STATUS OF PERSON RENDERING SERVICE — Title, Home Institution, Special Credentials, etc.:
(In addition please attach a vita) ______________

PROJECT SIGNATURE DATE FOUNDATION SIGNATURE DATE

PAYMENT AUTHORIZATION

FOR FOUNDATION USE ONLY		P.O. NUMBER	DESCRIPTION
VENDOR NUMBER	VOUCHER NUMBER		

TC	ACCOUNT NUMBER/SUBCODE	INVOICE DATE	DUE DATE	AMOUNT	P/F	
						CHECK NUMBER
						DATE
		CHECK TOTAL				

Figure D-2a

SAN DIEGO STATE UNIVERSITY FOUNDATION

HONORARIUM AND ONE-TIME PAYMENT

READ THIS BEFORE COMPLETING REVERSE SIDE

This form is to be used **only** to pay honorariums, short-term guest lecturers and small one-time payments to independent contractors.

An honorarium is defined as "a payment or award, usually in recognition of professional services or achievement, where custom, propriety, or agreement precludes the payment of a standard business rate of compensation." All honorariums may be paid through completion of this form regardless of the fee.

A guest lecturer is defined as "a recognized expert in a particular discipline, engaged to lecture a group, generally to supplement the lectures of the regular instructor." Lecturers rendering service for more than five days are usually paid through the regular payoll. Lecturers may be paid through completion of this form regardless of fee.

Small one-time payments may be made through this form to independent contractors, not State or Foundation employees, who will not be paid by the Foundation a total of more than $100 a month or $600 a calendar year.

Figure D-2b

E

Federal Excess Property Program Regional Offices

Federal Excess Property Program Regional Offices

REGION I
Chief, Utilization Branch
General Services Administration
Post Office and Court House
Boston, MA 02109
617-223-2686

REGION II
Chief, Utilization Branch
General Services Administration
26 Federal Plaza
New York, NY 10007
212-264-2623

REGION III
Chief, Utilization Branch
General Services Administration
7th and D Streets, S.W.
Rm. 6409
Washington, D.C. 20407
202-472-1277

REGION IV
Chief, Utilization Branch
General Services Administration
1776 Peachtree Street, N.W.
Atlanta, GA 30309
404-285-5521

REGION V
Chief, Utilization Branch
General Services Administration
230 South Dearborn Street
Chicago, IL 60604
312-353-6062

REGION VI
Chief, Utilization Branch
General Services Administration
1500 East Bannister Road
Kansas City, MO 64131
816-926-7585

REGION VII
Chief, Utilization Branch
General Services Administration
819 Taylor Street
Fort Worth, TX 76102
817-334-2341

REGION VIII
Chief, Utilization Branch

General Services Administration
Building 41
Denver Federal Center
Denver, CO 80225
303-234-3945

REGION IX
Chief, Utilization Branch
General Services Administration
525 Market Street
Mail Station 26
San Francisco, CA 94105
415-556-5845

REGION X
Chief, Utilization Branch
General Services Administration Center
Auburn, WA 98002
206-396-5481

F

Acquisition of Excess Government Personal Property by National Science Foundation Grantees

NATIONAL SCIENCE FOUNDATION
Office of the Director
Washington, D.C. 20550

Notice No. 58 February 17, 1978

IMPORTANT NOTICE TO PRESIDENTS OF UNIVERSITIES AND COLLEGES AND DIRECTORS OF NONPROFIT ORGANIZATIONS

Subject: **Acquisition of Excess Government Personal Property by National Science Foundation Grantees**

1. **Purpose.** This Notice restates the Foundation's policy and conditions on the acquisition and utilization of Excess Government Personal Property by National Science Foundation grantees to incorporate certain amendments to Chapter 101 of the Federal Property Management Regulations, (41 CFR), announced on Oct. 20, 1977, in the *Federal Register*.

2. **Policy.** As a means of expanding the ability of grantees to accomplish National Science Foundation objectives while conserving supply and equipment funds, the Foundation will continue to sponsor the transfer of excess Government personal property to Foundation grantees.

> Excess Government personal property includes all types of personal equipment and materials (except consumable items such as drugs, paint, etc.) used, or new, owned by the Federal Government and no longer needed by the holding agency, but having additional useful life. Under regulations established by the General Services Administration, the agency charged with operating this program, excess Government personal property may be reported to, or requested from GSA by other Federal agencies, including the National Science Foundation

The Foundation will sponsor the transfer of excess Government personal property to eligible organizations under one of the following conditions:

a. The use of the property significantly furthers a Foundation grant supported activity.

b. The property is such that it would have been procured under the grant for which property is being requested if additional grant funds had been available.

c. The property is used as part of the grant activity and subsequently for scientific research or science education purposes.

d. The property is classified by GSA as scientific equipment and has a unit acquisition cost of $1,000 or more (see Paragraph 7., Restrictions).

3. **Eligibility.** Eligible organizations are Foundation project grantees (see paragraph 7., below), which are public or private institutions of higher education, or nonprofit organizations whose primary purpose is the conduct of scientific research or science education activities. (State and municipal governments, public health units, hospitals, profit-making firms and individual principal investigators or project directors are not eligible for excess Government personal property under Foundation sponsorship.)

4. **Procedures.**

a. To receive information concerning the availability of property, an eligible grantee must make a request in writing to the Property Section, Post Award Projects Branch, Division of Grants and Contracts. Following such written request, the Foundation will arrange to place the grantee on GSA's mailing lists for information on the availability of property. A copy of the Foundation's request to GSA will serve as the acknowledgment to the grantee regarding placement on the GSA mailing list. It usually takes 6-8 weeks before catalogs are received.

b. When GSA information on available

Figure F-1a

excess Government personal property is received, the grantee should ascertain whether there are included any items which are necessary to accomplish the supported project.

c. Materials and equipment so selected should be inspected whenever possible (see paragraph 5., below), or the holding Federal agency should be contacted by the grantee to verify the condition of the items, because interpretation of condition codes varies among agencies.

d. If the condition of the item is acceptable, the grantee should "freeze" (reserve) items by calling the GSA office identified in the catalog. The verbal reservation should then be followed up by a letter. Items are usually allocated on a "first come, first served" basis. Since GSA may have several "freezes" on a piece of equipment, "first come, first served" is interpreted as the first approved written request received by the GSA office. However, preference will be given by GSA to agencies which do not grant title to equipment.

e. The grantee should next prepare and submit to the Property Section, NSF, a property request in 6 copies. A property request consists of Standard Form 122, "Transfer Order Excess Personal Property," and a *separate written justification statement*. The justification will explain why the property is needed to reduce the cost or enhance the performance under the specific grant for which the property is requested.

f. The SF-122 should be signed by both the principal investigator or project director, and an administrative official who is authorized to commit the organization in matters of business and financial affairs. The following information should also be provided on each SF-122:

(1) Name of Grantee Institution
(2) Grant Number
(3) Expiration Date
(4) "The above equipment is requested for use by a project grantee in support of scientific research or science education as outlined in the grant."
(5) Transfer is in accordance with the provisions of 41-CFR-101.43.

The transfer order should also identify the automatic release date (from the GSA catalog) to preclude loss of property before the transaction is processed.

g. The written justification should detail the scientific need for the equipment as it relates to the particular grant project under which the equipment is to be used, and should cite the conditions of this Important Notice as being binding upon the grantee, should the property be acquired.

h. Upon receipt by the Foundation, the property request will be reviewed. As confirmation of approval, the grantee will receive carbon copies of the SF-122 from the Foundation, and subsequently, from the General Services Administration. If the request is disapproved, it will be returned to the grantee with an appropriate explanation.

i. Upon receipt of the requested property, the grantee should immediately return a copy of the SF-122 to NSF as evidence of delivery. Cancellations by GSA, or nonreceipt within a reasonable period of time should also be reported to NSF, after follow-up inquiries have been made to GSA.

5. **Visiting Holding Agency Facilities.** Under current GSA regulations all non-Federal grantee representatives wishing to visit holding agency facilities to screen/freeze Government excess personal property must receive prior certification from GSA. (This certification is not required for those grantees who do their selecting from GSA Catalogs, and freeze property only via telephone requests.)

Normally, certification will be on a regional basis, however, NSF will, under certain circumstances, sponsor grantee representatives who need to make interregional visits in order to secure equipment not readily available within their region. Each person who plans to physically visit holding agency facilities must submit to the Foundation a completed GSA Form 2946 "Authorization Certificate to Select/Freeze Excess Personal Property." This form may be obtained from the Property Section, NSF, upon request. The GSA Regional Office in which the grantee organization is located will authorize all regional certifications and serve as principal coordinator on interregional requests. The authorization will be forwarded to the grantee via the Foundation.

6. **Dollar Limitation.** To insure equitable distribution of excess Government personal property, grantees may be authorized to acquire property under each NSF project grant up to a total acquisition cost equal to the dollar value of

Figure F-1b

that particular grant. Any request for excess property which causes the total to exceed the value of the grant will require additional justification beyond that requested in Section 4.e. above. A higher percentage of excess property requested under a particular grant by a grantee must be approved by an administrative level in the Foundation which is higher than the program manager who normally administers the grant. The Foundation will give full consideration to all factors in determining whether to approve transfers of excess property above the dollar value of a given grant. Grantees are therefore urged to be selective in their requests for excess Government personal property, to limit quantities of each item where possible, and to avoid stockpiling items for future use.

7. **Restrictions.** The Foundation will sponsor the transfer of excess Government personal equipment to eligible organizations only under "project grants." As defined in the GSA regulations, project grants refer to grants made for specific purposes with established termination dates; e.g. grants made to specific institutions to perform specific tasks within set time frames and costs. No excess property may be acquired on behalf of conference grants; publicaton-support grants; or travel grants. In addition, on "summer-type training" grants, no property may be acquired after the training period has terminated. Further, grantees should exercise careful judgment on the appropriateness of requesting excess personal property when only a short period of time exists between the date of the property request and the completion or successful accomplishment of the NSF-supported project activity. GSA will consider items of personal property as scientific equipment for transfer without reimbursement to the National Science Foundation for use by a project grantee when the property requested has a unit acquisition cost of $1,000 or more and is within Federal Supply Classification Groups 14 (Guided Missiles), 43 (Pumps and Compressors), 48 (Valves), 58 (Communication, Detection, and Coherent Radiation Equipment), 59 (Electrical and Electronic Equipment Components), 66 (Instruments and Laboratory Equipment), 67 (Photographic Equipment), 70 (General Purpose Automatic Data Processing Equipment, Software, Supplies, and Support Equipment), or 74 (Office Machines and Visible Record Equipment). Automatic data processing equipment, as defined in § 101-32.301, must be acquired under the provisions of Subpart 101-32.3 and § 101-32.4702. GSA will give consideration to the transfer without reimbursement of items of excess property in other Federal supply classification groups, and items with a unit acquisition cost of less than $1,000, when the National Science Foundation certifies that the item requested is a component part of or related to a piece of scientific equipment or is an otherwise difficult to acquire item needed for scientific research. Items of property determined by GSA to be common-use or general purpose property, regardless of classification or unit acquisition cost, shall not be tranferred to the National Science Foundation for use by a project grantee without reimbursement. Excess personal property may be transferred to a project grantee for the purpose of cannibalization: *Provided,* The granting Federal agency accompanies the transfer request with a supporting statement which clearly indicates that disassembly of the requested item for secondary use of its component parts, or for repair and maintenance of a similar item, has greater potential benefit than utilization of the item in its existing form and that a clear cost savings to the Government will result, subject to final determination by GSA.

8. **Costs.** Excess Government personal property is usually secured without cost. However, the recipient grantee should specify the method of shipment (see sample Form) and must pay all costs of packing, transportation, and subsequent installation, rehabilitation, and/or maintenance if required. Grant funds may be used to pay such costs.

9. **Title.** Title to excess Government personal property obtained by academic and other nonprofit grantees through Foundation sponsorship remains with the Government until the property is delivered to the grantee organization. Upon delivery, the grantee should forward to the Foundation a receipted SF-122 which clearly lists the items of property actually obtained by the grantee. Unless the Foundation informs the grantee to the contrary, when this SF-122 is received at the Foundation, title to all property acquired will automatically pass to and be vested in the grantee organization, subject to the understanding that such property will be used for scientific research or for science education purposes as long as it has a useful life.

Figure F-1c

At such time as the property is no longer useful for such purposes, it may be disposed of in accordance with institutional practices, but any proceeds therefrom shall be used by the grantee solely for scientific research or science education purposes. Under certain conditions, such as when highly specialized equipment is involved, NSF may retain title to excess property. When such a condition exists, NSF will inform the grantee. Excess Government personal property may not be transferred to a foreign country without the express written approval of the Foundation's Division of Grants and Contracts.

10. **Accountability and Recordkeeping.** While no particular type of classification of accounts or inventory system is required, the Foundation expects that the responsible officials of the grantee organization will exercise careful stewardship of excess Government personal property acquired in support of projects undertaken with the Foundation's financial assistance. In accordance with paragraph 5., above, relating to the dollar limitation on the amount of excess Government personal property provided by the Foundation, grantees should maintain appropriate inventory procedures which will enable them to identify those requests which require more extensive adminstrative and scientific justification. In those cases where title to excess Government personal property remains with the Government, the grantee must maintain suitable records to identify its locations, description, utilization and value. The use of excess Government personal property under an NSF grant is subject to inspection and audit by representatives of the Foundation at all reasonable times during the life of the grant under which the property was acquired.

Cancellation

This Notice supercedes Important Notice No. 58 on the same subject, dated October 10, 1974.

Additional Information

Further details may be obtained from the Property Section, Post Award Projects Branch, Division of Grants and Contracts, Room 201-A, National Science Foundation, 1800 G Street, N.W., Washington, D.C. 20550. The telephone number for the Property Section is (202) 634-7383.

Richard C. Atkinson
Director

Figure F-1d

References

Preface

1. "Grant Makers Meet to Form Strategy in the Wake of Proposition 13," *Foundation News*, September–October 1978, pp. 6–7.
2. "Newsgram," *U.S. News and World Report*, April 23, 1979, p. 21.
3. "Consumer Price Index for Urban Wage Earners and Clerical Workers," *Monthly Labor Review*, U.S. Department of Labor, Bureau of Labor Statistics, June 1980, p. 85.

Chapter 1

1. "Scientists Warn of Funding Lag," *Higher Education and National Affairs 28*(16), April 20, 1979, p. 3.
2. "FY 1980 Budget Figures for Education/Health Down from Last Year–Many Programs Eliminated," *Federal Notes 9*(12), February 2, 1979, p. 1.
3. "Devastating Cut for Nurses," *The Chronicle of Higher Education 17*(21), February 5, 1979, p. 4.
4. "Research Libraries' Collections Hit Hard by Inflation," *The Chronicle of Higher Education 17*(19), January 22, 1979, p. 1.
5. "Universities Charged with Widespread Misuse of Federal Research Funds," *Federal Research Report 14*(4), January 27, 1978, p. 21.
6. "Office of Education Gets 'Golden Fleece' Award," *The Chronicle of Higher Education 17*(17), January 8, 1979, p. 19.
7. "Grant Makers Meet to Form Strategy in the Wake of Proposition 13," *Foundation News*, September–October 1978, pp. 6–7.
8. W. Willner and P. B. Hendricks, Jr., "The Role of a Grants Administrator," in *Grants Administration*, National Graduate University, Washington, D.C. (1972), pp. 111–127.
9. "Timely Contract and Contract Closeouts Needed, GAO Reports," *College and University Reports 697*, October 3, 1978, pp. 6–7.
10. "Budget Chief to Crack Down on Unused Grant Money," *Federal Research Reports 14*(36), September 8, 1978, p. 229.

Chapter 2

1. "Federal Grantsmanship: The High Cost of Giving," *Foundation News*, July–August, 1979, p. 4.
2. F. E. Sladek, "Is Personal Contact Helpful?," *Foundation News*, September–October 1977, pp. 36–37.
3. H. Wile, "Warning: This Grant May Be Hazardous to Your Health," *NCURA Newsletter 10*(1), January 1979, pp. 2–5.
4. H. Wile, "Warning: This Grant May be Hazardous to Your Health," *NCURA Newsletter 10*(1), January 1979, pp. 2–5.

Chapter 3

1. "Cost Principles for Educational Institutions," Circular A-21, Office of Management and Budget, *Federal Register*, March 6, 1979, Part III, p. 12376.
2. "Cost Principles for Educational Institutions," Circular A-21, Office of Management and Budget, *Federal Register*, March 6, 1979, Part III, p. 12374.
3. "Cost Principles for Educational Institutions," Circular A-21, Office of Management and Budget, *Federal Register*, March 6, 1979, Part III, p. 12374.
4. W. F. McBurney and D. H. Merritt, "Requesting Support for Science Programs: An Exercise in Thoughtful Persuasion," *Journal of College Science Teaching 6*(2), November 1976, p. 87.
5. "Cost Sharing on Federal Research," Federal Management Circular 73-3, General Services Administration, Office of Federal Management Policy, December 4, 1973.
6. G. M. Larocque, *Consumerism, Federal Grants and You*, Exposition Press, Jericho, New York (1974), p. 140.
7. V. P. White, *Grants: How to Find Out About Them and What to Do Next*, Plenum Press, New York (1975), pp. 243–264.
8. H. R. Holtz, *Government Contracts: Proposalmanship and Winning Strategies*, Plenum Press, New York (1979), pp. 145–179.
9. V. A. Decker and L. E. Decker, *The Funding Process: Grantsmanship and Proposal Development,* Community Collaborators, Charlottesville, Virginia (1978), pp. 66–74.
10. T. A. Adamson, *Inside Grant and Project Writing*, Pam Publishers, Salinas, California (1979), pp. 25–39.
11. H. R. Holtz, *Government Contracts: Proposalmanship and Winning Strategies*, Plenum Press, New York (1979), p. 179.

Chapter 4

1. G. I. Nierenberg, *The Art of Negotiating*, Hawthorn Books, Inc., New York (1969), p. 3.
2. G. I. Nierenberg, *The Art of Negotiating*, Hawthorn Books, Inc., New York (1969), pp. 73–78.
3. G. I. Nierenberg, *The Art of Negotiating*, Hawthorn Books, Inc., New York (1969), pp. 80–81.
4. N. W. Beckmann, *Negotiations: Principles and Techniques*, D. C. Heath, Lexington, Massachusetts (1977), p. 27.
5. G. I. Nierenberg, *The Art of Negotiating,* Hawthorn Books, Inc., New York (1969), pp. 81–82.
6. W. Willner and P. B. Hendricks, Jr., *Grants Administration*, National Graduate University, Washington, D.C. (1972), p. 171.

7. H. R. Holtz, *Government Contracts: Proposalmanship and Winning Strategies*, Plenum Press, New York (1979).
8. "The Negotiation of Federal Grants and Contracts," *Special Report: Highlights of the Fall 1979 Liaison Officers' Meeting*, Office of Federal Programs, American Association of State Colleges and Universities, Washington, D.C., October 18, 1979, pp. 33–35.
9. T. A. Adamson, *Inside Grant and Project Writing*, Pam Publishers, Salinas, California (1979), p. 97.
10. "Procurement by Negotiation," Armed Services Procurement Regulations, in *Code of Federal Regulations (32 National Defense)*, Parts 1–39, pp. 325–363 (July 1, 1976).

Chapter 5

1. "Cost Sharing on Federal Research," FMC 73-3, General Services Administration, Office of Federal Management Policy, December 4, 1973, p. 4.
2. "Cost Sharing on Federal Research," FMC 73-3, General Services Administration, Office of Federal Management Policy, December 4, 1973, p. 4.
3. *NSF Grant Policy Manual*, National Science Foundation, Washington, D.C. (1977), Section 643.3, p. 50.
4. National Association of College and University Business Officers, Washington, D.C. (1978), pp. 51–64.
5. "Uniform Administrative Requirements, Grants and Agreements with Institutions of Higher Education, Hospitals, and Other Nonprofit Organizations," Circular A-110, Office of Management and Budget, *Federal Register*, July 30, 1976, Part II, p. 32035.

Chapter 6

1. F. Koch, "Fifteen Ways to Provide Valuable Support without Making a Cash Contribution," in *The New Corporate Philanthropy: How Society and Business Can Profit*, Plenum Press, New York (1979), pp. 58–67.
2. "Cost Principles for Educational Institutions," Circular A-21, Office of Management and Budget, *Federal Register*, March 6, 1979, Part III, p. 12376.
3. "Cost Principles for Educational Institutions," Circular A-21, Office of Management and Budget, *Federal Register*, March 6, 1979, Part III, p. 12379.
4. "SPC 7 Program Proposal Solicitation," Public Broadcasting Service, August 3, 1979, p. 9.

Chapter 7

1. "Addendum to Public Health Service Grants Policy Statement," U.S. Department of Health, Education, and Welfare, Public Health Service (DHEW Publication No. 77-50,000), October 1, 1977, p. 6.
2. "Grants for Scientific Research," National Science Foundation (NSF 78-41), August 1978, pp. 16–17.
3. "Cost Principles for Educational Institutions," Circular A-21, Office of Management and Budget, *Federal Register*, March 6, 1979, Part III, p. 12371.
4. "Cost Principles for Educational Institutions," Circular A-21, Office of Management and Budget, *Federal Register*, March 6, 1979, Part III, p. 12371.
5. "Cost Principles for Educational Institutions," Circular A-21, Office of Management and Budget, *Federal Register*, March 6, 1979, Part III, p. 12371.

6. "Grants Policy Statement," Public Health Service, DHEW Publication No. (OS) 77-50,000 (Rev.), October 1, 1976, pp. 14–29.
7. "Agenda, Meeting of the Committee on Governmental Relations," National Association of College and University Business Officers, October 3, 1979, pp. 3–4. (Mimeographed.)

Chapter 8

1. L. H. Haag, *Cash Management and Short-Term Investments for Colleges and Universities*, National Association of College and University Business Officers, Washington, D.C. (1977), p. 1.
2. L. H. Haag, *Cash Management and Short-Term Investments for Colleges and Universities*, National Association of College and University Business Officers, Washington, D.C. (1977), p. 25.
3. "Implementation of OMB Circular No. A-110; Uniform Policies," *Federal Register*, August 2, 1978, Part V, p. 34090.
4. "Implementation of OMB Circular No. A-110; Uniform Policies," *Federal Register*, August 2, 1978, Part V, p. 34090.
5. L. H. Haag, *Cash Management and Short-Term Investments for Colleges and Universities*, National Association of College and University Business Officers, Washington, D.C. (1977), p. 31.
6. J. F. Lordan, *The Banking Side of Corporate Cash Management*, Financial Publishing Company, Boston (1973), p. 32.
7. L. H. Haag, *Cash Management and Short-Term Investments for Colleges and Universities*, National Association of College and University Business Officers, Washington, D.C. (1977), pp. 32–33.
8. D. I. Fisher, *Cash Management in the Moderate-Sized Company*, The Conference Board, Inc., Report No. 559, New York (1972), p. 4.
9. D. I. Fisher, *Cash Management in the Moderate-Sized Company*, The Conference Board, Inc., Report No. 559, New York (1972), p. 10.
10. D. I. Fisher, *Cash Management*, The Conference Board, Inc., Report No. 580, New York (1973), p. 56.
11. J. A. Jones and S. K. Howard, *Investment of Idle Funds by Local Governments: A Primer*, Municipal Finance Officers Association of the United States and Canada, Chicago (1973), p. 7.

Chapter 9

1. R. Woodrow, "Five Things a Research Administrator Ought to Know," *NCURA News* *9*(5), May 1978, pp. 1–2.
2. R. Woodrow, "Five Things a Research Administrator Ought to Know," *NCURA News* *9*(5), May 1978, pp. 1–2.
3. Suffolk University Management Education Center, Boston (1978), p. 6.
4. L. A. Urgo, *Models for Money: Obtaining Government and Foundation Grants and Assistance*, Suffolk University Management Education Center, Boston (1978), p. 68.
5. Plenum Press, New York (1979), p. 49.
6. H. R. Holtz, *Government Contracts: Proposalmanship and Winning Strategies*, Plenum Press, New York (1979), pp. 119–120.
7. W. H. Freeman and Company, San Francisco (1976), p. 104.
8. H. R. Holtz, *Government Contracts: Proposalmanship and Winning Strategies*, Plenum Press, New York (1979), p. 50.

9. W. Willner and P. B. Hendricks, Jr., *Grants Administration*, National Graduate University, Washington, D.C. (1972), p. 127.
10. W. Willner and P. B. Hendricks, Jr., *Grants Administration*, National Graduate University, Washington, D.C. (1972), p. 126.
11. V. P. White, *Grants: How to Find Out about Them and What to Do Next*, Plenum Press, New York (1975), p. 220.
12. F. Koch, *The New Corporate Philanthropy: How Society and Business Can Profit*, Plenum Press, New York (1979), p. 24.
13. "How the Intergovernmental Personnel Act Can Assist Your Institution," *Special Report: Highlights of the Fall 1979 Liaison Officers' Meeting*, Office of Federal Programs, American Association of State Colleges and Universities, Washington, D.C., October 18, 1979, p. 35.
14. "How the Intergovernmental Personnel Act Can Assist Your Institution," *Special Report: Highlights of the Fall 1979 Liaison Officers' Meeting,* Office of Federal Programs, American Association of State Colleges and Universities, Washington D.C., October 18, 1979, pp. 35–36.

Chapter 10

1. D. Jongeward, *Everybody Wins: Transactional Analysis Applied to Organizations*, Addison-Wesley Publishing Company, Reading, Massachusetts (1976), pp. 6 and 23.
2. H. R. Holtz, *Government Contracts: Proposalmanship and Winning Strategies*, Plenum Press, New York (1979), p. 168.
3. H. R. Holtz, *Government Contracts: Proposalmanship and Winning Strategies*, Plenum Press, New York (1979), p. 168.

Index